D1615754

End-to-End DSL Architectures

Wayne C. Vermillion

Cisco Press

Cisco Press
201 West 103rd Street
Indianapolis, IN 46290 USA

End-to-End DSL Architectures

Wayne C. Vermillion

Copyright© 2003 Cisco Systems, Inc.

Published by:
Cisco Press
201 West 103rd Street
Indianapolis, IN 46290 USA

Printed in the United States of America 1 2 3 4 5 6 7 8 9 0

First Printing April 2003

Library of Congress Cataloging-in-Publication Number: 2002100659

ISBN: 1-58705-087-0

Warning and Disclaimer

This book is designed to provide information about building Cisco DSL networks. Every effort has been made to make this book as complete and accurate as possible, but no warranty or fitness is implied.

The information is provided on an "as is" basis. The author, Cisco Press, and Cisco Systems, Inc., shall have neither liability nor responsibility to any person or entity with respect to any loss or damages arising from the information contained in this book or from the use of the discs or programs that may accompany it.

The opinions expressed in this book belong to the author and are not necessarily those of Cisco Systems, Inc.

Feedback Information

At Cisco Press, our goal is to create in-depth technical books of the highest quality and value. Each book is crafted with care and precision, undergoing rigorous development that involves the unique expertise of members of the professional technical community.

Reader feedback is a natural continuation of this process. If you have any comments regarding how we could improve the quality of this book, or otherwise alter it to better suit your needs, you can contact us through e-mail at feedback@ciscopress.com. Please be sure to include the book title and ISBN in your message.

We greatly appreciate your assistance.

Publisher	John Wait
Editor-in-Chief	John Kane
Executive Editor	Brett Bartow
Cisco Representative	Anthony Wolfenden
Cisco Press Program Manager	Sonia Torres Chavez
Manager, Marketing Communications, Cisco Systems	Scott Miller
Cisco Marketing Program Manager	Edie Quiroz
Managing Editor	Patrick Kanouse
Acquisitions Editor	Michelle Grandin
Development Editor	Ginny Bess Munroe
Project Editor	Marc Fowler
Copy Editor	Gayle Johnson
Technical Editors	Steve M. Dussault
	Patrick Lao
	Peter Macaulay
	Rodney Thomson
	Rafael Vergara
Team Coordinator	Tammi Ross
Book Designer	Gina Rexrode
Cover Designer	Louisa Adair
Production Team	Mark Shirar
	Octal Publishing
Indexer	Tim Wright

CISCO SYSTEMS

Corporate Headquarters
Cisco Systems, Inc.
170 West Tasman Drive
San Jose, CA 95134-1706
USA
http://www.cisco.com
Tel: 408 526-4000
     800 553-NETS (6387)
Fax: 408 526-4100

European Headquarters
Cisco Systems Europe
11 Rue Camille Desmoulins
92782 Issy-les-Moulineaux
Cedex 9
France
http://www-europe.cisco.com
Tel: 33 1 58 04 60 00
Fax: 33 1 58 04 61 00

Americas Headquarters
Cisco Systems, Inc.
170 West Tasman Drive
San Jose, CA 95134-1706
USA
http://www.cisco.com
Tel: 408 526-7660
Fax: 408 527-0883

Asia Pacific Headquarters
Cisco Systems Australia,
Pty., Ltd
Level 17, 99 Walker Street
North Sydney
NSW 2059 Australia
http://www.cisco.com
Tel: +61 2 8448 7100
Fax: +61 2 9957 4350

Cisco Systems has more than 200 offices in the following countries. Addresses, phone numbers, and fax numbers are listed on the Cisco Web site at www.cisco.com/go/offices

Argentina • Australia • Austria • Belgium • Brazil • Bulgaria • Canada • Chile • China • Colombia • Costa Rica • Croatia • Czech Republic • Denmark • Dubai, UAE • Finland • France • Germany • Greece • Hong Kong Hungary • India • Indonesia • Ireland • Israel • Italy • Japan • Korea • Luxembourg • Malaysia • Mexico The Netherlands • New Zealand • Norway • Peru • Philippines • Poland • Portugal • Puerto Rico • Romania Russia • Saudi Arabia • Scotland • Singapore • Slovakia • Slovenia • South Africa • Spain • Sweden Switzerland • Taiwan • Thailand • Turkey • Ukraine • United Kingdom • United States • Venezuela • Vietnam Zimbabwe

Trademark Acknowledgments

All terms mentioned in this book that are known to be trademarks or service marks have been appropriately capitalized. Cisco Press or Cisco Systems, Inc., cannot attest to the accuracy of this information. Use of a term in this book should not be regarded as affecting the validity of any trademark or service mark.

The definition of AAA in Chapter 3, "TCP/IP over ATM," is taken from Webopedia by Internet.com, sponsored by the IEEE and is reprinted with permission from www.internet.com. Copyright, 2002, INT Media Group, Inc. All rights reserved.

About the Author

Wayne Vermillion was the senior instructor and course developer for all the DSL training within Cisco Systems, Inc. until August 2001, traveling around the world to present Cisco courses. His constant research and publication formed the basis of the Cisco Certified Internet Provider (CCIP) course, Building Cisco DSL Networks, for which he was also the editor and pilot instructor. At all levels of the Cisco certification program, he provided guidance for DSL testing. While with Cisco, Vermillion was solely responsible for analyzing and designing customized DSL and other telecom service provider training for all sizes of service providers, as well as specialized Cisco groups. He designed and implemented audience and task analysis tools, including pretesting and self-study, for the world's largest operator of telephone companies. That instructional design addressed tens of thousands of users for multiple technologies, including the world's then-biggest contract for DSL equipment.

Vermillion's previous publications include two editions of the guidebook *Multimedia is an Adjective* in 1993 and 1994. His academic background includes a master's degree in computer education and cognitive systems.

About the Technical Reviewers

Steve M. Dussault, CCIE No. 3073, is a senior consulting engineer for Networked Information Systems, a Cisco Systems Gold Partner. He also holds Cisco CCDP certification, CSS1 and Voice Access specializations, and Sun Microsystems certification. He designs and implements enterprise network solutions for Cisco customers worldwide. In his spare time he teaches entry-level and advanced scuba diving and enjoys the outdoors. He can be reached by e-mail at steve@awuwi.com.

Patrick Lao, CCIE No. 4952, has been a technical education consultant with Internet Learning Solutions Group (ILSG) since March 1998. He received a B.S. in electrical engineering technology from Cal Poly Pomona University and an M.S. in telecommunications management from Golden Gate University. He has been a CCSI since 1998. His certifications include CCIP, CCNP, and CCDP. He has more than 17 years of industry experience in technical training and course development.

Peter Macaulay, CTP, is a principal consultant with East by North, Inc., providing network design consulting, training, and keynote presentations on emerging technologies, including DSL, VoIP, and IP PBX systems. He is a certified trainer for the Convergence Technologies Professional (CTP) designation of the Telecommunications Industry Association (TIA).

Rodney Thomson, CCIE No. 10143, has a bachelor's degree in engineering (first class honours) in electronics and communications and a post-graduate diploma in digital communications. He has worked in the communications industry for ten years and at Cisco Systems in Proof of Concept Labs for three years. He lives in Melbourne, Australia with his beautiful wife. His passion is surfing (in wwwater, not on the wwweb).

Rafael Vergara is the founding CEO of IPISYSTEM, a Venezuelan company that sells, installs, and provides training for Cisco equipment. He was the second Certified Cisco Systems Instructor (CCSI) in Venezuela, and he is one of the very few Cisco DSL-certified instructors in Latin America. He is an external consultant for Cisco Systems in Venezuela. He has CCNA and CCDA certifications. He likes to read, walk, and play tennis.

Dedication

This book is dedicated to that nice lady in the white car who let me pull into traffic ahead of her this morning. If you practice random acts of kindness, especially when combined with common sense, you might find a book dedicated to you, too. Even if you aren't recognized in a book, know that you will be recognized in someone's heart and mind.

Acknowledgments

The DSL knowledge in this book would not have been possible without the initial tutelage of and continuing free support and help from Charles Ford, the godfather of Cisco DSL training. The book itself was propelled into existence by Kendall V. Scott, my authoring buddy. Thanks very much to Cisco Press acquisitions editor Michelle Grandin, who patiently and informatively coached me throughout the creation of this book.

Contents at a Glance

Contents

Introduction

Intended Audience

This book best meets the needs of these audiences:

- Telecommunications and Internet services provider personnel

- Telecommunications and information technology (IT) consultants

- Cisco Systems employees and Cisco Partners

- Anyone needing a reference source for the DSL portion of the CCIE Communications and Services exam

- Anyone who would appreciate a thorough yet accessible guide to DSL, both Cisco-centric and generic

Prerequisite Knowledge

Even if you know only enough about DSL to spell it, you can still benefit from the instruction in this book. However, this book is not intended for internetworking novices. You should have experience with IP protocols, routing, and switching, especially in Cisco style and terminology, to appreciate this book. This book presumes an existing knowledge equivalent to the Cisco course Interconnecting Cisco Network Devices (ICND).

If you don't have knowledge equivalent to the ICND course, knowledge of the Cisco IOS Software is strongly recommended, although it is not indispensable if you are familiar with other routing and switching technologies. An ATM background is quite helpful. Although Appendix B, "ATM Overview," is devoted to ATM, that material should serve as a review of your existing ATM knowledge. It covers the minimum ATM knowledge required for DSL rather than providing an entire lesson in ATM.

This Book's Intent

This book informs you thoroughly, from general industry concepts to specific Cisco software configuration commands, in planning, implementing, configuring, and managing DSL, in addition to using Cisco equipment. This book is also appropriate if you are preparing for the DSL portion of the CCIE Communications and Services exam.

This Book's Contents

This book is organized into seven chapters and four appendixes. Each chapter begins with an introduction of topics and ends with multiple-choice review questions that test your understanding of the chapter's contents and help prepare you for the Cisco certification examinations.

This book covers these topics:

- Chapter 1, "DSL Primer," introduces DSL and generic DSL equipment.

- Chapter 2, "DSL Impairments and Their Remedies," explains what technical and business dangers negatively affect DSL and how to compensate for these impairments.

- Chapter 3, "TCP/IP Over ATM," details the protocol layers, design and implementation considerations, and usages of the six common DSL architectures.

- Chapter 4, "Cisco DSL Products," describes the details of these devices:

  The Cisco 820 series of DSL routers

  The Cisco 6000 series of IP DSL Switches (see the following section, "Book Terminology and Conventions," to understand the use of the term IP DSL Switch instead of the more-general DSLAM)

The Cisco 6400 Universal Access Concentrator

- Chapter 5, "Security: AAA/SSG/RADIUS," reviews basic network concepts such as authentication, authorization, and accounting (AAA), before describing RADIUS in the DSL network and a DSL-specific suite of functionality, the Service Selection Gateway (SSG). This chapter concludes with an overview of DSL user security through Virtual Private Networks (VPNs).
- Chapter 6, "Cisco IOS Configurations," spells out the individual command lines and their meanings, as well as the resulting whole configurations for the devices described in Chapter 4.
- Chapter 7, "Cisco DSL Manager (CDM)," is the *only* publicly-available book or instructional source that presents this graphical user interface (GUI) software, from concepts and protocols down to the data field level.
- Appendix A, "Answers to Review Questions," gives the end-of-chapter review question answers, providing not only the answers but also explanations.
- Appendix B, "ATM Overview," is just a review and provides the minimum details for your existing knowledge.
- Appendix C, "Long-Reach Ethernet (LRE)," offers information about this increasingly popular technological family member of DSL as a bonus for you.
- Appendix D, "Glossary of Terms," is an enlightening and appropriately focused listing of the meanings of important terms and acronyms used in this book.

Book Terminology and Conventions

You might be puzzled by the use of the term IP DSL Switch to designate the Cisco 6000 series of DSL network elements rather than the generic DSL Access Multiplexer or the acronym DSLAM. The author has chosen to use the more-specific term, except where the more-generic term is referenced specifically in software, to emphasize the fast-developing nature of the sophisticated Cisco devices and their functionality.

All acronyms in this book are defined at least once, at their initial usage. The most important terms are defined in Appendix D.

Command Syntax Conventions

Command syntax in this book conforms to the following conventions:

- Commands, keywords, and actual values for arguments are **bold**. Bold is also used to indicate user input in the examples.
- Arguments (which need to be supplied with an actual value) are *italic*.
- Optional keywords and arguments are in brackets ([ ]).
- A choice of mandatory keywords and arguments is in braces ({ }).

CHAPTER 1

DSL Primer

This chapter introduces the basic technologies associated with the Digital Subscriber Line (DSL) system. There are several types of DSL, such as asymmetric DSL (ADSL) and symmetric DSL (SDSL). You will see the term xDSL used in this book and throughout the industry to stand for these different types. This chapter also provides an overview of xDSL equipment. For you to best understand xDSL architectures and the specific commands to configure those architectures, you should have a basic understanding of Asynchronous Transfer Mode (ATM). ATM is discussed sufficiently for xDSL in Appendix B, "ATM Overview," which you might want to review before going into the details later in this book, starting with references in this chapter.

After completing this chapter, you will be able to do the following:

- Define xDSL's place in the telco environment, including the broadband marketplace and the DSL solutions available to meet current needs.

- Define the family of xDSL technologies and describe both asymmetric and symmetric DSL variations in terms of their modulation, speed, and reach.

- Define generic customer premises equipment (CPE) and central office (CO) equipment, including the plain old telephone service (POTS) splitter, DSL access multiplexing (DSLAM), and aggregation equipment needed at the CO to support DSL service.

Introduction to DSL

An increasing use of rich multimedia applications and network servers for data storage and application support is dramatically increasing the demand for broadband services to desktop devices such as PCs.

Streaming video and storage area networks demand broadband networks for adequate performance. The addition of real-time synchronous video for training and conferencing, audio for entertainment, and voice over IP further increases this demand for bandwidth. In addition, LAN technology has developed faster than WAN technology. LAN users have options for 10/100/1000 Mbps Ethernet. These higher local speeds generate demand for higher speed on the WAN.

This bandwidth need is being pushed from corporate networks into the residential market as workers telecommute. PC activities such as web browsing, which now includes audio, video, and 3D simulation environments, require broadband connections. This bandwidth demand is also growing in homes and especially in the small office/home office (SOHO) business environment, also called the small/medium enterprise (SME) environment. Broadband services are most constrained in the local transmission environment, called the *last mile* or *local loop,* and this is the location of the DSL. The local loop or the last mile is the line between the customer and the telephone company's central office. Local loops use copper-based telephone wire.

LAN technology has developed faster than WAN technology. LAN users have options for 10/100/1000 Mbps Ethernet. These higher local speeds generate demand for higher speed on the WAN.

The density and original designs of metropolitan networks, local loops in densely populated areas, result in plentiful bandwidth to serve the corporate customer. Corporate offices are served by fiber, microwave, and copper. Bandwidth services with speeds into the gigabits per second are available to corporate customers, whose providers must allow for the highest-bandwidth and most-critical demands. In small business and residential networks, service of constant-rate data at high bandwidth is not needed for all applications. A technology that can integrate data types (voice, data, and video) with varying traffic quality contracts is required to meet future demands.

Local Loop Limitations

The challenge placed on carriers in the future is to provide high-speed data services in the local loop to residential customers. These customers are traditionally served with voice (analog) service only. Their local loops are not designed to support high-speed data services. Another part of the challenge is to provide high-speed services at a low cost, so the real challenge is low-cost, high-speed services.

The primary network that feeds homes is unshielded twisted-pair (UTP) copper. Little or no fiber exists for direct access to homes. Some small businesses are served by high-speed optical facilities, but the geographic distribution and lack of concentration of small businesses make it difficult for service providers to plan for distribution of traditional broadband services such as North America's Synchronous Optical Network (SONET) and European-defined, internationally-used Synchronous Digital Hierarchy (SDH).

Residential bandwidth until very recently has been delivered with dialup modems or ISDN Basic Rate Interface (BRI). The maximum rate of dialup connectivity is 56 kbps, and the maximum rate for ISDN BRI is 128 kbps, far below what is adequate for content-rich multi-media applications.

Meeting the demands of high-speed communications presents an incredible challenge for the telephone companies with their existing copper local loop infrastructure. Copper cabling cannot easily support the higher bandwidths. One solution is to replace the existing copper with a massive rollout of fiber-optic technology, but the cost is very high, and the time to accomplish the rollout would be unacceptable due to the immediate demand.

Hybrid Fiber Coaxial (HFC), a shared access medium well-suited to analog and digital broadcast, is not yet accepted around the world as adequate for simultaneous transmission of voice telephony, interactive video, and high-speed data communications.

Fiber to the Home (FTTH) is still prohibitively expensive. One alternative that is not yet commercially practical is a combination of fiber cables feeding neighborhood Optical Network Units (ONUs) and last-mile connections by existing or new copper. This topology, called Fiber to the Neighborhood (FTTN), encompasses Fiber to the Curb (FTTC), which has short final extensions from the metro cable to the customer premises, and Fiber to the Basement (FTTB), serving tall buildings with vertical drops.

DSL Transmission Services

DSL technology introduces a new family of transmission services that can provide high-speed data service over the existing copper infrastructure.

DSL is a transmission technology that uses existing twisted-pair telephone lines to transport high-bandwidth data to service subscribers. DSL, although considered an end-to-end solution, really occurs only in the local loop between the CPE and the central office's DSL device. Like analog modems, cable modems, wireless, and T1 lines, DSL by itself is a transmission technology, not a complete end-to-end solution. End users don't buy DSL. They buy services such as high-speed Internet access, an intranet, a leased line, voice over DSL, a virtual private network (VPN), and video on demand (VoD).

The term xDSL covers a number of DSL types. Overall, *xDSL services* are dedicated, point-to-point, and public network access over twisted-pair copper wire on the local loop (the last mile). In the OSI reference model, DSL is strictly Layer 1 (the physical layer). DSL can be implemented between a network access provider's (NAP's) central office and the customer site, or on local loops created either intrabuilding or intracampus.

The DSL Layer 1 connection consists of a pair of DSL modems on either end of a copper wire pair—at the subscriber end and at a central office or other point of presence (POP).

Most homes are served by four wires (two pairs) of copper UTP. This can support two phone lines, one of which is for dedicated data services such as DSL, ISDN, or a dialup modem connection.

One of the efficiencies of ADSL over other local loop data communication technologies is that ADSL can be transported over the same wire pair with existing POTS service without affecting ADSL's bit rate potential. Therefore, using one pair of copper wires, both POTS and ADSL data service can be supported.

Our century-old telephone network is designed specifically around the audible frequency range of 0 to 4 kHz. Voice band (analog) modems use tones in the audible spectrum and communicate via standard voice circuits (you can hear modems and fax machines "talking" to one another).

DSL uses inaudible high-frequency signaling to achieve megabit transmission speeds. DSL converts ordinary phone lines into high-speed data conduits by using frequencies of up to, and slightly above, 1 MHz. DSL connections are typically offered as a continual connection. This allows DSL customers to surf the web any time without dialing up. You'll learn in Chapter 3, "TCP/IP Over ATM," that several different TCP/IP architectures used in DSL networks, such as Point-to-Point Protocol over Ethernet (PPPoE), offer varying levels of security, including session logon with passwords.

DSL data rates range from 144 kbps to 52 Mbps depending on the xDSL variety, local loop condition, distance to the central office, and electromagnetic interference. Therefore, rate-adaptive DSL (RADSL) services vary in throughput depending on local loop conditions.

DSL's Competitors: Pros and Cons

The three main technologies presently in competition with DSL are analog modems, ISDN service, and cable modems. There are also business-oriented options such as T1/E1 service and fractional T1/E1 services, but these have drawbacks for universal implementation. In responding to residential broadband data needs, these and other technologies all fall short of surpassing the capability, readiness, and cost of DSL's availability without inserting new cable, especially when DSL is integrated with existing POTS service.

Private lines, such as 56 kbps Digital Data Service (DDS) and T1, require four wires for operation. SONET and SDH require fiber. These services tend to require special construction and thus result in very high costs per month and long installation intervals.

Analog Modems

In regard to performance, the traditional modem syncs at speeds much slower than ADSL (less than 56 kbps). This ceiling of 56 kbps is not guaranteed, and even lesser throughput (such as the realistic maximum of about 53 kbps) is subject to constant variation. Because access is dialup, it is subject to contention and call congestion. This means that when you dial a connection, you are contending with other users for the same bandwidth, leading to call congestion over the POTS network as well as at the provider's site.

Although ADSL can be implemented over the same twisted pair as the existing POTS service, DSL is an always-on connection that doesn't affect the voice service.

ISDN

Integrated Services Digital Network (ISDN) is a standardized and mature technology that never became popular and mainstream. ISDN and ADSL can support both voice and data over the same two-wire local copper telephone line. The basic rate interface (BRI) type of ISDN, the most common, consists of two 64 Kbps standard bearer channels and one 16 Kbps data channel. ISDN supports both telephone and computer connectivity and can carry both voice and data on the two bearer channels, one channel for each service. The data channel is for signaling overhead.

ISDN requires special telephones to combine data service with voice service. In the event of power loss, both voice and data services are unavailable. ADSL has no requirement for special telephones to be combined with voice service (POTS) on the same line. In a power failure, the ADSL modem dies, but telephone service is unaffected.

As most commonly implemented today by mainstream service providers, an ISDN subscriber speaking over the telephone effectively utilizes 50 percent of the available bandwidth. This half must be permanently reserved for voice service if voice is accommodated at all. ADSL bandwidth is unaffected by the use of telephone service.

ISDN (BRI) speeds are limited to a maximum of 128 Kbps, and nondiscounted installation costs are higher than the costs of DSL. From the service provider's point of view, ISDN is not easily implemented for the SOHO market. This is because connection space on the voice-switching equipment is quite valuable, so most providers prefer not to occupy this critical connection space with the routine data transmissions used in ISDN. After all, major service providers have depended on voice service for the vast majority of their business, whereas data transmission is a relatively new and lesser business offering. Scarcity of switching options on the voice network equipment frequently results in set monthly charges for ISDN in addition to usage charges. For installed ISDN networks, which are much more common in Germany and other parts of Europe than in the U.S., a specific variety of xDSL can be implemented that rides the existing ISDN lines. This ensures the financial viability of the existing ISDN investments by service providers and major customers.

In comparison with ADSL, ISDN is typically tariffed (billed) as a usage-based service, whereas ADSL is typically marketed at a flat rate. In terms of value, the 512 Kbps ADSL service is about three times the speed of basic-rate ISDN, but the cost is about equal in the U.S.

Cable Modems

Cable modems are theoretically much faster than DSL, but their speed is affected by the number of users on the cable bus network. Also, cable modem connections are not inherently secure. Subscribers on the same bus segment who initialize file and print sharing can expose their data to other users on the bus. Users' e-mail can also be broadcast to other users over cable modems. Unlike cable modems, ADSL utilizes an individual pair of conductors that are not shared with other subscribers, making it more secure. Lack of security on cable modem systems is a major consideration, especially because any security features such as firewalls must be installed by individual users.

The foundation of a cable modem system is the cable TV coaxial cable that extends in a bus topology through (mainly) residential areas. Subscribers attach to this common cable that terminates at a headend, where attached subscribers typically are linked to a fiber-optic transport system. Cable modems' shared-bus topology results in congestion and slower user response as more users attach to a particular cable segment simultaneously.

Both cable modems and private-line service are affected by the availability of cable service facilities in a residential location. The cost to create this infrastructure requires more than a single user's commitment. Thus, geographic availability might be limited, because the cable network has not been extended to sparsely-populated areas.

Aside from the security and simultaneous-usage detriments, cable modem offers impressive speed (30 Mbps downstream and 1 Mbps upstream). Due to signal repeatability, it has no prohibitive distance limitation within the cable provider's territory. In comparing cable modem service to ADSL, maximum distance and pricing are competitive, and throughput can be higher for cable modems.

T1/E1 Service for Businesses

T1/E1 service is usually too expensive for ordinary home or small-business usage. Fractional T1/E1 service might be appropriate for some small enterprises. Generally, T1/E1 service is for large businesses or institutions (such as schools). A T1 transports data at 1.544 Mbps, in the lower end of DSL's capabilities, and fractional T1 service starts around 384 Kbps. A T1 line requires all four wires of a traditional U.S. home or small-business installation. This results in a high initial installation cost, because more wire pairs almost always have to be installed to maintain regular voice service. In the U.S., a business or power user requesting T1 service receives T1 throughput speed (1.544 Mbps) using one of two DSL technologies—HDSL (four wires) or HDSL2 (standardized on two wires). This difference in implementation is important only to the service provider, who prefers not to use all four wires in the typical home or small-business infrastructure to deliver the throughput and access desired by the customer.

Wireless Networking

Wireless networking, although certainly the omnipresent wave of the future for first consumers and then businesses, is neither mature nor universally available yet. Its main drawback is its lack of range beyond line of sight. Accepted standards have yet to be defined. As soon as wireless is a mature and globally-accepted technology, its very nature will mean much more flexibility than any wired service such as DSL.

DSL Equipment

Equipment is usually diagrammed with a strict division between the central office/exchange side and the customer premises equipment (CPE), sometimes called customer-provided equipment. This section describes the basic CO/exchange equipment and the basic CPE equipment.

Customer Premises Equipment

CPE consists of the PC or another Internet Access Device (IAD) and a CPE modem—either an Asymmetric Transceiver Unit-Remote (ATU-R) or a Symmetric Transceiver Unit-Remote (STU-R). Because SDSL cannot be integrated with POTS service on the same wire pair, ADSL presents a more complex configuration when combined with voice traffic. In the Cisco world, the DSL modem is incorporated into a router and is represented by a small router symbol, as shown in Figure 1-1.

Figure 1-1   *The DSL Modem Symbol Looks Like a Cisco Router Symbol*

At the customer premises, the user's computer or IAD is connected to the ATU-R over a 10/100BASE-T Ethernet connection.

With ADSL, data traffic is carried using high frequencies above the POTS frequencies, as shown in Figure 1-2.

Figure 1-2   *Analog Voice Signals Occupy Only the Lowest Part of the Overall POTS Wire Frequencies*

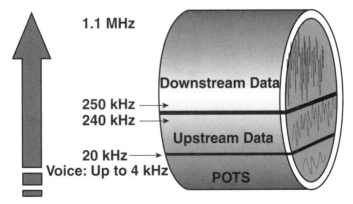

If voice traffic is present on the same copper pair as ADSL, the ATU-R can be connected to an external splitter device used to separate the voice and ADSL frequency. More commonly, a microfilter is used instead of an external splitter. The microfilter can be self-installed by the customer. Separating voice and data traffic provides fail-safe 911 services for POTS operation. The microfilter may be integrated into the ATU-R or attached to the analog telephone(s) in the home. Microfilters on the user's analog telephone equipment prevent off-hook interference between analog voice signal and ADSL signal. If the twisted wire pairs have been physically isolated at the splitter, which requires a provider technician service call, the loop is wired to a Network Interface Device (NID). Dispatching a technician to perform this work is called a *truck roll* in the telecom industry. If the customer can install equipment directly, the truck roll is avoided, and labor costs are saved. The NID serves as the point of demarcation (demarc) into the customer premises.

The user's computer can be a PC, Macintosh, or UNIX/Linux workstation. The computer must possess an IEEE 802.3/Ethernet network interface card (NIC) for connection to the ATU-R. This card allows the PC to generate Ethernet frames that are either bridged or routed into the DSL data network by the ATU-R. The ATU-R converts the Ethernet frame to ATM cells. These Ethernet frames ultimately are reconstructed from ATM cells by an aggregation router in the central office/exchange.

Central Office DSL

DSL subscribers are connected directly to the DSLAM equipment—specifically, the DSL modem cards in the DSLAM. These DSL modem cards have varying numbers of ports. One subscriber is directly connected to each port, which is the extent of the OSI Layer 1 DSL connectivity. The latest generation of DSLAMs have Layer 3 intelligence for IP switching, as well as Layer 1 multiplexing. They are called IP/DSL switches because of their IP functionality. In the Cisco world, the symbols for DSLAMs and IP/DSL switches differ only slightly. The DSLAM and IP DSL switch symbol is shown in Figure 1-3.

Figure 1-3   *Cisco DSLAM Symbol*

IP/DSL switches can be programmed for differential queuing based on the service level agreement and type of traffic. They include other software-enabled IP capabilities beyond the simpler multiplexer's functions. Differential queuing in the DSL world starts with the ATM classes of service (explained in Appendix B) and is further defined by DSL-specific parameters in DSL service level profiles. You'll learn about DSL profiles in Chapter 6, "Cisco IOS Configurations."

The DSLAM multiplexes DSL traffic from hundreds of DSL subscribers onto a high-speed ATM backbone network interface to the *Universal Access Concentrator (UAC)*, also called an *aggregator*. Its Cisco symbol is shown in Figure 1-4.

Figure 1-4   *Cisco Universal Access Concentrator Symbol*

The UAC may also concentrate other types of traffic besides DSL traffic.

The UAC selects the network service provider (NSP) to which the data should be forwarded and routes or switches the data accordingly across high-speed data trunks to the NSP.

When voice service (POTS) is combined with data on the same copper loop, voice and data traffic is split by frequency in the POTS splitter chassis (PSC) located in the central office/exchange. Rack-mounted and matched by design to the DSLAM (IP/DSL switch) capability and footprint, the PSC splits off voice traffic and routes it to the voice network. This preserves emergency calling, known as 911 calling in the U.S., by keeping voice traffic off the DSLAM and entirely on the robust voice network equipment, such as the Class 5 switch. POTS splitters are passive devices, which means that even with a loss of power or some other malfunction of the DSLAM (IP/DSL switch), voice traffic is preserved to the voice network. Figure 1-5 shows the overall DSL network with voice integration.

Figure 1-5   *DSL with Analog Voice*

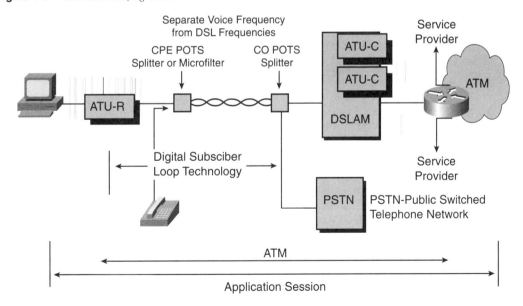

Whether split at the PSC or wired directly to the DSLAM-IP/DSL switch, data traffic is sent to the DSL modem cards on the DSLAM. There are varying types of DSL modem cards, each of which has a different number of DSL ports. Each port represents a single, dedicated DSL connection. An example is the eight-port ATU-C DMT card on the Cisco 6000 series of IP/DSL switches. From the DSLAM-IP/DSL switch, the data traffic is switched to the UAC over an ATM network. The data traffic is then processed by the UAC for onward routing.

xDSL Varieties

There are two broad divisions of xDSL—asymmetric (ADSL) and symmetric (SDSL). Current and future types are summarized in Table 1-1.

Table 1-1   *Summary of xDSL Types and Standards*

Asymmetric DSL	Symmetric DSL (Multiple Varieties of Symmetric DSL Are Marketed as "SDSL")
CAP—No standard	SDSL—No standard
G.DMT—(Worldwide) ITU G.992.1	HDSL—No standard
ADSL/ISDN (ADSL over ISDN)—No standard	HDSL2—(North America) ANSI T1.418
DMT2-(North America) ANSI T1.413.2 "G.Lite" or "half-rate DMT"—(Worldwide) ITU G.992.2	IDSL—ISDN over DSL
G.dmt.bis (ADSL2)—(Worldwide) G.992.3	SHDSL—(Worldwide) ITU G.991.2
G.lite.bis (half-rate ADSL2)—(Worldwide) G.992.4	
VDSL—No standard	

The difference between asymmetric and symmetric service is simple: Either the bit rate is the same for both upstream and downstream, or the throughput rate is higher for downstream than upstream. (*Upstream* refers to the traffic flow from the subscriber to the provider, and *downstream* refers to the traffic flow from the provider to the subscriber.) The ADSL line delivers more bandwidth downstream (from the central office to the customer site) than upstream. This imbalance arises from two factors: typical Internet usage habits, and a technical hindrance at the central office.

The first factor is seen in every online session, when residential and small business end users download bursts of rich graphics and multimedia content, and then they upload e-mail or text queries during a web-surfing session. The second factor is noticed at the CO when a specific kind of spectral interference called *crosstalk* prevents equally high upstream rates from the user to the network. This is because of conflicts among the different spectra generated by different types of modulations when different types of signals (such as ISDN and T1/E1) are bundled closely in groups of wires. These groups of wires are called *binder groups,* so the spectral interference phenomenon is called *binder group interference.*

Asymmetric DSL

With all varieties of ADSL, implementation is defined by this basic principle: Access speed varies with loop distance. There are two main varieties of asymmetric DSL—the so-called consumer ADSL and very high data rate DSL (VDSL). ADSL is fast enough for routine web surfing and electronic correspondence, including large file attachments. VDSL is designed to be fast enough for streaming video, such as on-demand movies. In general, the ADSL aggregate signal is a combination of several frequencies above the POTS frequency range. In the 0 to 4 kHz range is the POTS traffic. This means that unless there are regulatory restrictions or other man-made prohibitions, asymmetric DSL coexists safely by design with analog voice traffic on the same pair of twisted wires. For each analog telephone set on the same twisted wire pair as the ADSL modem, the subscriber installs a convenient, small microfilter, as discussed previously.

A guard band (neutral space) separates the POTS frequencies from ADSL data frequencies. Frequencies between 20 and 240 kHz contain the ADSL upstream data traffic. Frequencies above 250 kHz contain ADSL downstream data traffic.

Both consumer ADSL and VDSL are discussed in the following sections.

Consumer-Grade ADSL

As of the end of 2002, consumer-grade ADSL's maximum throughput is up to about 8 Mbps downstream, and upstream bandwidth ranges from 16 to 864 kbps. This ADSL type works at distances up to 18,000 feet (about 5488 meters) over an existing POTS line. ADSL's reach is variable for two reasons. First, most service providers are conservative in promising DSL service to customers located at the far end of the 18,000 foot boundary for voice telephony. This lowered estimate comes about because of transmission delays and other quality problems experienced by this farthest subset of users. On the other hand, companies such as ADTRAN, Inc., now offer ADSL repeaters to extend the reach to 30,000 feet (9144 meters).

VDSL: A Cable TV Killer?

VDSL delivers 13 to 52 Mbps downstream and 1.5 to 2.3 Mbps upstream over a single twisted copper pair at short distances. VDSL's operating range is presently limited to between 1000 feet and a maximum of 4500 feet (304.8 to 1382 meters). Service is variable in nature, and throughput decreases drastically over distance. Industry research is underway to expand this range, which is itself useful for campus or dense residential settings. VDSL has been rather optimistically nicknamed "the cable killer" because of its potential to deliver multiple, distinct video transmissions to multitenant units (MTUs) and multidwelling units (MDUs) such as dormitories and adjacent residences. However, VDSL has not yet achieved an accepted modulation standard. Long-Reach Ethernet (LRE), which is described in Appendix B, uses VDSL to provide a high-speed connection between the LRE CPE and the LRE switch over phone wires.

Symmetric DSL

As noted in Table 1-1, there are five basic types of symmetric DSL:

- Legacy SDSL
- HDSL (high data rate DSL)
- HDSL2 (high data rate DSL, second generation)
- IDSL (ISDN over DSL)
- SHDSL (single-pair high-rate DSL)

Each of these is discussed in the following sections.

Legacy SDSL

SDSL has several proprietary types. SDSL is best considered a generic description, because the several proprietary types are being subsumed by a single, worldwide standard for symmetric service. ITU formalized this standard as G.991.2, known as SHDSL.

HDSL

HDSL delivers 1.544 Mbps of bandwidth, equivalent to T1 speed, each way over two pairs of twisted copper wires. Because HDSL provides T1 speed, telephone companies have been using it to provision local access to T1 services whenever possible. HDSL's operating range is limited to 3658.5 meters (about 12,000 feet), so signal repeaters are installed to extend the service. HDSL requires two twisted pairs, so it is deployed primarily for PBX network connections, digital loop carrier systems, interexchange POPs, Internet servers, and private data networks. Service is consistent, meaning that speed does not change due to local line conditions.

HDSL2

HDSL2 was developed by the ANSI T1E1.4 committee specifically for T1 service transport (1.544 Mbps) and was designated T1.418. This North American standard uses a single pair of wires, unlike the nonstandardized HDSL, which uses two pairs of wires.

IDSL

This hybrid technology is attractive for providers who have extensive investments in ISDN infrastructure and user acceptance but who are integrating DSL in their provider network.

IDSL delivers up to 144 Kbps of symmetric bandwidth. It uses ISDN (2B1Q, or two binary, one quarternary bit) modulation. The speed is derived from BRI ISDN, using two bearer channels and one data channel (2B + D = 144, where B = 64 Kbps and D = 16 Kbps). IDSL is an always-on connection, so the data channel can be used for subscriber traffic rather than for signaling, as with regular ISDN BRI. IDSL terminates Frame Relay or High-Level Data Link Control (HDLC) or PPP over 2B1Q. IDSL's operating range is 18,000 feet (5488 meters), so signal repeaters are installed to extend the service. A single DSL access multiplexer or IP/DSL switch can accommodate both ADSL and IDSL with the appropriate ADSL and IDSL modem cards. IDSL was characterized as an interim solution as long ago as 1999's summer DSL Forum meeting.

SHDSL

SHDSL is the internationally accepted, spectrally friendly, repeatable symmetric service. SHDSL supports bit rates from 192 kbps to 2.312 kbps. SHDSL's ambitious goal is to replace all existing symmetric DSL technologies (HDSL, HDSL2, SDSL, and IDSL), as well as present high-speed wire transmissions (T1 and E1). Not only is SHDSL approved worldwide by ITU members, it also can be used with repeaters to extend its reach, and it is spectrally friendlier than the older versions of SDSL, ISDN, and T1/E1. SHDSL uses Trellis Coded Pulse Amplitude Modulation (TC-PAM) line code.

It is important to bear in mind that no type of symmetric service allows the use of analog phones on the same lines. As with all other types of symmetric DSL, SHDSL occupies all available frequencies on the copper wire, meaning that analog voice cannot be transported simultaneously with SHDSL on the same pair of wires.

The previous sections presented the descriptions and standards, where defined, for both ADSL and symmetric DSL. The next section presents a deeper view of the sound wave modulations that differentiate the various types of DSL.

ADSL Modulations

There are three basic types of modulations for transmission of sound over a digital medium:

- Amplitude modulation (AM)
- Frequency modulation (FM)
- Phase modulation (PM)

Amplitude modulation uses a voltage change to increase or decrease the size of peaks and valleys. For example, AM radio stations broadcast their programs using amplitude modulation.

Frequency modulation changes frequencies to cause increases and decreases in the space between waves. For example, FM radio stations broadcast their programs using frequency modulation.

Phase modulation shifts the point at which a wave begins by delaying the moment at which a wave begins transmission. Modern analog modems use a constellation of phase and amplitude combinations to represent various bit patterns.

How accurately an analog signal can be sampled (for both phase and amplitude) is the most important factor in determining modem speed. The more accurate the sampling, the more tightly packed the points within the amplitude and phase bit grouping can be, and therefore the higher the speed.

NOTE   This book uses the term *bit grouping* for simplicity instead of the more precise term *constellation*. Additionally, the university-level electrical engineering topic of constellations is not discussed in detail, because this is not necessary for you to master the Cisco DSL certification exams or apply your knowledge of Cisco DSL technology in the real world.

The previous overview of modulations is sufficient to enable you to compare the modulation schemes of the various types of xDSL, contrasting them for efficiency, spectral friendliness, and interoperability. Most types of xDSL, such as the proprietary CAP or the standardized DMT varieties, use combinations of these modulations. The next section describes the xDSL modulations.

CAP: The Early Days

The first widespread DSL modulation technique was Carrierless Amplitude Phase (CAP) modulation. Until the present century and its worldwide standardizations in DSL technology, CAP was the most popular form of ADSL. Globespan Semiconductor Inc. dominated CAP technology with its definitions.

NOTE   The term *CAP* can be misleading, because there is indeed a single carrier. Perhaps a better term would have been *Subcarrierless Amplitude Phase modulation*. The technology itself has been made obsolete by the worldwide standards of the more efficient discrete multitone (DMT) types, and Cisco dropped support of CAP a few years ago. There are still pockets of CAP implementations around the world in DSL networks, but these are being upgraded.

Discrete Multitone: The Modern Standard

A more sophisticated ADSL technology called DMT has at least four standards either deployed or under development. The most prevalent version of DMT is a worldwide standard called G.DMT (ITU standard G.992.1). The DMT family of standards are presently becoming the worldwide choice because they are standardized, and they have become standardized by the ITU because of their efficiency. DMT's multiple tones, or subcarriers, can counter multiple different sources of interference better than CAP's "all together" approach.

To illustrate, suppose that CAP is a single-file line of hikers, each with a backpack; these are the data bits moving sequentially. The lead CAP hiker (data bit group) encounters an obstacle, such as a boulder in the way, which forces him to slow down and detour. All the following hikers must similarly maneuver around the same boulder, slowing them all down. In the DSL world, this boulder might be a burst of electronic noise, temporary environmental conditions on the copper line, and so on.

Now suppose that DMT is represented by a line of hikers moving abreast, in a spread line, each with a backpack; these are the individual tones or subcarriers of data bits. Consider how this spread line of hikers, representing the discrete multiple tones of DMT, reacts to an obstacle. Only the single hiker faced with the boulder must slow down; the others proceed at the same pace, meaning that the vast majority of the data streams are unaffected by the obstacle or hindrance. Multiple interference obstacles must be faced by all the single-file CAP hikers in turn, whereas different DMT hikers cope individually with different hindrances without affecting the others. DMT even can shift the data load from one tone to another in a technique called bit swapping. To complete the hiking metaphor, this could be represented by a single, injured hiker asking another hiker to take part or all of his load. Only the adjacent hiker is slightly burdened. The vast majority of the others don't even slow down in their own transport of data bits.

In summary, DMT2 tends to be more robust in an environment of multiple impairments.

The industry migration from CAP to DMT has not been critical because CAP does offer lower-cost chipsets and requires less power, and CAP components have been readily available. Both DMT and CAP can automatically adjust their rates based on line impairments. DMT backs off or adjusts its rate in 32-Kbps decrements, a more granular and sensitive approach than CAP's 320-Kbps decrements.

DMT2

The North American version of full-rate DMT, DMT2, is also called Issue 2 because the heart of its technical definitions were specified by ANSI in a second issue (ANSI T1.413.2) of ANSI's original DMT standards. The first edition of standards, which came out a few years before DMT2, failed to achieve industry acceptance. Cisco DMT2 products are generally backward-compatible for DMT Issue 1 products, although Issue 1 products from other companies might present interoperability problems. The worldwide ITU standard, G.DMT (ITU G.992.1), differs only slightly from the ANSI second issue.

DMT2 consists of 256 4.3125 kHz channels, each containing a single Quadrature Amplitude Modulation (QAM) signal. These channels are also called bins or carriers, and each behaves as a single modem signal. DMT's bins are shown in Figure 1-6.

Figure 1-6   *DMT Combines Carrier Frequencies*

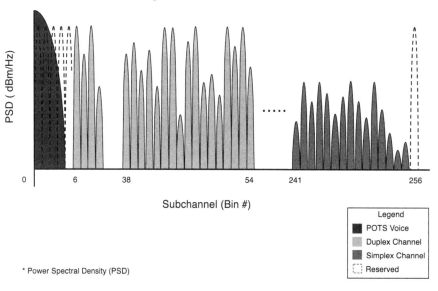

Thirty-two upstream carriers use bins 6 to 38 (approximately 25 to 163 kHz). These are duplex bins used for both upstream and downstream carriers. Two hundred forty-nine downstream carriers can use bins 6 to 255 (approximately 25 kHz to 1.1 MHz). Bins 39 to 255 are simplex bins used only for downstream carriers.

Bin 1 starts at 0 frequency (0 to 4.3 kHz). Bin 256 is reserved and ends at about 1.104 MHz. Bit capacity (called *symbol loading* in electrical engineering) in higher-numbered bins is limited by noise thresholds.

To compensate for noise on a given bin, DMT automatically adjusts the amount of data encoded on that bin. When an impaired carrier frequency is forced to reduce the throughput of bits, those bits are queued into an adjacent bin. As mentioned in the CAP/DMT hiking metaphor, this shifting of bits is called bit swapping, and it is handled automatically by DMT chipset technology.

Using multiple bins, DMT can compensate for combinations of impairments, such as attenuation, phase error, crosstalk, narrowband interference, and bridge taps, as shown in Figure 1-7.

Figure 1-7   *DMT Copes Well with Multiple Interference Sources*

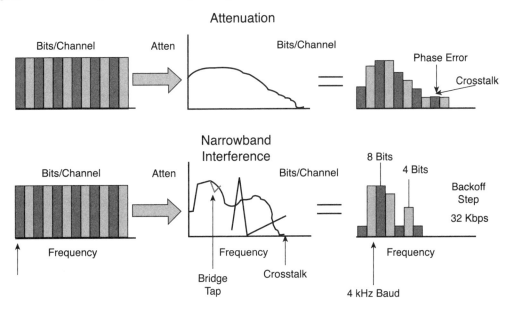

DMT decreases the bits per band until the carrier is nonfunctional. Each DMT carrier operates at 4000 baud and at a rate of up to 8 bits per symbol, or 32 Kbps per carrier.

The initialization (training) process takes about 24,000 symbols, or 6 to 20 seconds, as follows:

1 **Activation and acknowledgment (384 symbols)**—ATU-C and ATU-R detect each other and exchange information about timing and pilot tone options.

2 **Transceiver training (7808 symbols)**—Automatic gain adjustment, echo canceller, and channel equalizer training are performed.

3 **Channel analysis (18,186 symbols)**—Rate options are indicated, and subchannel Signal-to-Noise Ratio (SNR) analysis is performed.

4 **Exchange (about 200 symbols)**—Exchange of information about loop attenuation, performance margin, and number of bits supported takes place. Bit-loading selections are confirmed.

G.Lite

The ITU standard for a less complex and less powerful version of G.DMT is designated as G.992.2. It is frequently called G.Lite or half-rate DMT because it uses only 128 carriers rather than 256. Fewer bins are used to obtain a longer reach, but at slower speeds. The half-rate designation can be misleading, because the supported throughput is 64 kbps to 1.536 Mbps downstream and 32 kbps to 512 kbps upstream, which is obviously much less than half the maximum downstream rate of 256-carrier DMT. Like its faster counterpart, G.992.2 adapts its rate downward in response to impairments in decrements of 32 kbps. An appealing benefit is lower-cost chipsets, with less power requirements and less generated heat.

G.992.2 is also called *splitterless* because, unlike early versions of ADSL, a separate data line need not be split at the customer premises' NID. G.992.2 was the first ADSL variety designed specifically to be used with a microfilter on each telephone in the home. This early advantage has been incorporated into modern full-rate DMT, so half-rate DMT's main current advantage is its lower-cost and lower-demand chipsets.

G.992.2 interoperates with full-rate DMT using a handshake protocol designated by the ITU as G.994.1. This handshake mechanism allows DSL transceivers to exchange capabilities and to select a common mode of operation. This handshake protocol quickly analyzes whether the incoming signal uses 256 bins or 128 bins and sets the appropriate profile for the chipset. G.994.1 is currently an integral part of the startup procedure for ITU standards G.991.2, G.992.1, and G.992.2 (SHDSL, DMT, and half-rate DMT, respectively). Future ITU DSL standards will also be able to make use of this handshake protocol. Provisions are also included for exchanging nonstandard information.

ADSL2

The following definitions of ADSL2 and ADSL2+ are from Aware, Inc.

ADSL2 is a new standard recently completed and approved by the International Telecommunications Union (ITU) in 2002 that will supersede existing ADSL standards. Work being done under the headings of G.dmt.bis and G.lite.bis is nearing completion to designate G.992.3 and G.992.4 for full-rate ADSL and splitterless ADSL, respectively. Aware, Inc., an ADSL technology developer, is ensuring that chipsets using its ADSL2 technology will be interoperable with existing ADSL deployments, performing in both ADSL and ADSL2 modes of operation.

Much has been learned over the past three years of ADSL deployments, including areas where improvements in the technology would be particularly valuable. A wide variety of improvements are included in ADSL2, each with very different implications; some make the transceivers operate more efficiently, some make them more affordable, and some add functionality. ADSL2 innovations are summarized in the following list:

- **Interoperability improvements**—Clarifications and additions to the initialization and training algorithms improve interoperability between chipset suppliers.

- **Better performance on long lines**—Simplified bit groupings and an improved framing structure increase data rates over longer loops.

- **Better performance with bridged taps and interference**—A receiver-allocated pilot tone and the enabling of interference cancellation techniques provides better performance.

- **Diagnostic tools**—ADSL2 transceivers have extensive diagnostic capabilities, including a double-ended line-testing mode for trouble resolution that provides precise measurements of line noise, attenuation, and noise at both ends of the line.

- **Fast startup**—ADSL2 reduces initialization time from more than 10 seconds (as is required for ADSL) to fewer than 3 seconds.

- **Channelization capability**—ADSL2 transceivers can channelize its bandwidth, allocating different link characteristics to different applications. For example, a voice application might have low latency but a higher error rate, and a data application might have high latency but a lower error rate.

- **Power management**—ADSL2 includes low-power modes that provide statistical power savings and standby/sleep modes that reduce the overall transceiver power consumption. This is particularly important for remote DSL equipment, where heat is a challenging engineering problem.

- **All-digital mode**—ADSL2 enables an optional mode that allows for transmission of data in the voice bandwidth, adding 256 kbps of upstream data rate.

- **Bonding**—ADSL2 supports bonding of multiple phone lines using Inverse Multiplexing over ATM (IMA) and Ethernet. You will learn more about IMA in Chapter 4, "Cisco DSL Products."

ADSL2+

ADSL2+ is an extension of the new ADSL2 standard planned for consent at the ITU in early 2003. ADSL2+ allows for the doubling of the ADSL2 bandwidth from 1.1 MHz to 2.2 MHz, effectively doubling the maximum downstream data rate to more than 20 Mbps. The data rate increase is effective only on loops shorter than 8000 feet. This extension to ADSL2 has often been called ADSL+ in technical circles working on its development, but ADSL2+ will likely be the most common term used to clarify that it is in fact an extension of ADSL2 and not the first ADSL standard.

Table 1-2 summarizes the common xDSL technologies.

Table 1-2   *xDSL Overview Table*

	Modulation Scheme	Standard?	Maximum Downstream Bit Rate	Maximum Upstream Bit Rate	Maximum Reach	Repeatable?	Analog Voice Support?
ISDN	2B1Q	Yes	64, 128 Kbps	64, 128 Kbps	18,000 feet	Yes	If dedicated channel
IDSL	2B1Q	Yes	56, 64, 128, 144 Kbps	56, 64, 128, 144 Kbps	18,000 feet	No	No
HDSL	2B1Q	No	2 Mbps	2 Mbps	12,000 feet	Yes	No
HDSL2	2B1Q	Yes	2 Mbps	2 Mbps	12,000 feet	Yes	No

continues

Table 1-2 *xDSL Overview Table (Continued)*

	Modulation Scheme	Standard?	Maximum Downstream Bit Rate	Maximum Upstream Bit Rate	Maximum Reach	Repeatable?	Analog Voice Support?
SDSL	2B1Q (and others)	No	1.168 Mbps, varies	1.168 Mbps, varies	18,000 feet	No (theoretically possible, no marketed equipment)	No
SHDSL	TC-PAM	Yes	2.320 Mbps	2.320 Mbps	18,000 feet	Yes	No
ADSL	DMT2/992.1	Yes	8 Mbps (in theory; rounded down to 6.1 Mbps in reality)	640 Kbps	18,000 feet	Yes	Yes
	Modulation Scheme	Standard?	Maximum Downstream Bit Rate	Maximum Upstream Bit Rate	Maximum Reach	Repeatable?	Analog Voice Support?
ADSL	G.Lite/992.2	Yes	1.5 Mbps	512 Kbps	18,000 feet	Yes	Yes, designed for easy access
VDSL	TBD; presently both QAM and DMT	No	56 Mbps	TBD; at least 13 Mbps	4500 feet	Planned	TBD; not currently

DSL Quality of Service

Before starting this section, you must have a basic understanding of ATM classes of service, such as unspecified bit rate (UBR). You might want to read Appendix B, with its explanation of ATM basics, standards, and usage, before beginning the following material. This section describes the DSL-specific parameters that constitute the DSL quality of service (QoS). Although QoS is used synonymously in the ATM world with class of service (CoS), in a DSL context, quality of service has specific meaning. It includes parameters specific to the xDSL variety and service level agreement with the user.

You can configure numerous DSL QoS parameters as part of a fully-differentiated marketing and provisioning plan. A single ATM CoS (such as UBR) can have multiple DSL QoS levels. Conversely, a single DSL QoS can be associated with multiple ATM CoS levels (such as UBR and VBR). Every DSL subscriber could theoretically have a unique DSL QoS, although this would be too detailed by far. Conversely, all DSL subscribers might have the same DSL QoS, although this approach would not serve to differentiate market offerings. A robust business plan that implements all current xDSL varieties would probably need no more than about ten DSL QoSs.

The most obvious of the DSL QoS parameters is bit rate, both downstream and upstream in the case of ADSL, and also bit rate for symmetric DSL. Several QoS parameters are dictated not by a marketing plan but by technical considerations such as the variety of types of CPE modems in the network.

Following are several of the more common parameters that a provider may offer or consider for a robust DSL network:

- **Bit rate (downstream/upstream)**
- **Fast path or interleave path**—There are two latency paths for different traffic types. The choice between these paths depends on the tolerance of the traffic type to delay, of which latency is a measure, and the need for error correction, which causes delay.

  First, modern networks can ultimately depend on the TCP/IP layers of the OSI reference model to request and retransmit so-called traditional data packets. Therefore, these standard types of data traffic need not be delayed unnecessarily for intermediate error correction.

  Second, some types of video traffic cannot be separated into logical segments that are easily retransmitted without losing context. This motion video traffic, such as teleconferencing, must be corrected as much as possible en route.

  These two concepts gave rise to ADSL's two latency paths—the fast data path and the interleaved data path. The fast path provides minimal delay through the DSL chipset at the expense of retransmissions from end to end. A minimum interleave delay (or the fast path itself) should be used when carrying digitized voice traffic. The interleaved data path requires more overhead, reducing original traffic throughput, and more computing processing activity, and adds delay. The benefit of the interleaved data path is efficiently minimized retransmissions or end-result error in displayed data.

  On fast-path circuits, bit swapping helps improve line quality. As described earlier, bit swapping is a mechanism that allows DSL transceivers to reallocate bits between multiple carriers or subfrequencies. Bit swapping can optimize error reaction by attempting to maintain an acceptable margin for each bin. The margins are equalized across all bins through bit reallocation. The affected bin queues a certain number of bits per clock cycle in the adjacent bin, behind that bin's own load.

  The interleaved data path offers higher data integrity at the cost of increased latency.

  If an interleaved path is the option, what is the bit interleaving delay? What are latency considerations versus the need for retransmission of uncorrectable errors? If the DSL data uses the fast path, it reduces forward error correction (FEC) capabilities. The advantage is that reduced latency (delay) while using the interleaved path increases FEC capabilities, but the disadvantage is an increase in latency.

- **Operating mode (DMT or G.Lite)**
- **Training mode (quick or standard)**

- **SNR margin**—How much SNR do you specify?

- **Error-correction parameters**

- **Symbols per code word used for error correction**

- **Overhead framing**—The default overhead framing structure value is 3, signifying reduced-overhead fast framing. The following structure definitions and values can be used to configure overhead framing:

  — Framing mode 0 is full overhead framing with asynchronous bit-to-modem timing (enabled synchronization control mechanism).

  — Framing mode 1 is full synchronous overhead framing with synchronous bit-to-modem timing (disabled synchronization control mechanism).

  — Framing mode 2 is reduced synchronous fast framing, with reduced overhead, combining separate fast and sync bytes in the fast and interleaved latency buffers, respectively (64 kbps framing overhead).

  — Framing mode 3 is reduced merged fast framing, with reduced overhead, merging fast and sync bytes, using either the fast or interleaved latency buffer (32 kbps framing overhead). This is the default framing mode.

- **Bit swapping**—This option will be on or off. This might be necessary for interoperability among different manufacturers' equipment, or even different types of interfaces.

- **Power boost**—Although power boost is rarely specified for DMT, it might need to be defined for other modulations.

- **Bit rate alarm threshold**—Your company or division might have specified levels of service so that if traffic drops below that level, you receive an alarm.

- **Precise DMT standard**—Is G.994.1 enabled? (G.HS, the handshake protocol, performs autorecognition and autoconfiguration between full-rate and half-rate DMT, but some equipment might be limited to one or the other.)

- **Microcode**—As the DSL industry works toward transparent interoperability, you might be faced with the need to specify a particular microcode type in either the central office device (DSLAM-IP/DSL switch) or the CPE modem.

- **Echo cancellation**—If echo cancellation is used, it might require specification. Echo cancellation sometimes costs more in performance than it provides in error correction.

- **Coding gain**—DSL equipment such as newer Cisco gear can be set to auto, meaning that the system can adjust itself for optimal coding gain, or this might be configurable. (*Coding gain* is the capability to use digital techniques and redundancy to reproduce the bit sequence without requiring much absolute power. Generally speaking, when more coding gain is specified, less absolute power is needed to get the signal through.)

These specifications are the components of DSL QoS. You can see that these might require some detailed knowledge of different equipment types and their individual parameters.

Summary

In this first chapter, you learned about the market position of and uses for DSL. You have a well-rounded knowledge of the types of xDSL, along with their strengths and weaknesses. You also learned about the standards to which manufacturers should adhere. You learned enough about modulations to consider intermixing xDSL types and other telecommunications types within wiring bundles and on the DSL devices themselves. This chapter concluded with a listing of the various parameters that can be applied to DSL service levels. Later in this book, you'll see how to configure those parameters.

If it seems that DSL is a great solution for high-speed bandwidth over existing telephonic infrastructure, you're right! So why has DSL had birthing pains around the world? Why aren't we enjoying its benefits? The next chapter describes the bad news that must be balanced with the good news of DSL's flexibility in terms of type and theoretical availability of service. Specifically, the bad news concerns impairments or hindrances to DSL implementation, which you'll find out can be overcome.

Review Questions

The following review questions give you a chance to assess how well you've mastered the topics in this chapter. The answers to these questions can be found in Appendix A.

1 Of the following, which xDSL types are most closely related?

   A CAP and SDSL

   B Lite and HDSL

   C ANSI T1.413 and G.992.1

   D HDSL and G.SHDSL

2 How is analog voice traffic integrated with SDSL?

   A Signals are split by frequency

   B A microfilter is used

   C One wire of the pair carries voice, and the other one carries data

   D The analog voice traffic may not be integrated with SDSL

3 DSL is considered to exist in which OSI reference model layer?

   A Layer 2 or 3, depending on the modulation

   B DSL is not represented in the OSI reference model

   C Layer 1

   D Layer 2

4 Which of the following best describes the relationship of voice, video, and data applications?

   A   Voice, video, and data require the same QoS.

   B   Voice and video require the same QoS.

   C   Data and video require the same QoS.

   D   Data and voice require the same QoS.

5 Which parameter is not part of the DSL QoS?

   A   Maximum burst size

   B   Bit rate

   C   Coding gain

   D   Framing mode

CHAPTER 2

DSL Impairments and Their Remedies

Several factors of the existing voice telephony (POTS) infrastructure can slow down or prevent the implementation of DSL. These factors range from the inconvenience and delay of line sharing among incumbent and competitive providers (this is mainly a business and regulatory consideration) to the DSL-preventing use of load coils. Other factors include normal attenuation and the types and locations of differing modulation technologies, such as T1/E1, both within the wire plant and in the central office itself.

Even after a successful startup of DSL service, both intermittent and permanent factors can impair DSL traffic. These impairments include copper impedance mismatches in the wire infrastructure and bridged taps that add distance to the cable run and thereby impair DSL service.

This chapter explains these factors and impairments and provides some of the most common remedies you can use to overcome them. This chapter covers the following topics:

- Standard telephony problems
- DSL-specific technical impairments
- Investigating and overcoming impairments

DSL and Standard Telephony Problems

As with all wire-based transmissions, DSL copper wire impairments start with normal *attenuation*—the simple loss of signal strength over distance. Attenuation generally refers to any reduction in the strength of any type of signal, whether digital or analog. More precisely in the case of DSL, attenuation is the normal loss of signal strength over distance. Attenuation specifically is a logarithmic function of the power setting. As power increases, attenuation increases logarithmically. Also called simply *loss,* attenuation is a natural consequence of signal transmission over long distances. The extent of attenuation is usually expressed in units called *decibels (dB)*. In magnetic (metallic) and fiber-optic cables, attenuation is specified in terms of the number of decibels per unit of distance, whether per foot, meter, 1000 feet, kilometer, or mile. Less attenuation per unit of distance means more efficient cable transmission.

Crosstalk is a disturbance caused by the electric or magnetic fields of one telecommunication signal that affects a signal in an adjacent circuit. In a telephone circuit, crosstalk can result in your hearing part of a voice conversation from another circuit. The phenomenon that causes crosstalk is called *electromagnetic interference (EMI)*. In DSL, EMI also occurs when DSL-bearing cables with certain combinations of different modulation schemes, such as IDSL and ADSL, are adjacent to each other.

The telephone line has an impedance composed of distributed resistance, capacitance, and inductance:

- *Resistance* is the opposition that copper wiring (or any other substance) presents to the flow of electric current. The standard unit of resistance is the ohm.

- *Capacitance* is the ability of an object or surface to store an electrical charge. It is simply a measure of the capacity of the object's electrical storage capability. Capacitance is analogous to a jar's ability to hold a fluid. Just as some jars have more capacity than others, some objects have more charge-holding ability than others. Like the jar, this ability is related in part to physical size.

- *Inductance* is a property of an electric circuit by which a changing magnetic field creates an electromotive force, or voltage, in that circuit or in a nearby circuit. Inductance is also defined as the property of an electric circuit that opposes any change in current, so the behavior of inductance is the resistance of a coil of wire to any change of electric current through the coil.

The impedance varies according to the length of the loop, the wire's type of insulation, and whether the wire is aerial cable, buried cable, or bare parallel wires strung on telephone poles. For calculation and specification purposes, the impedance is normally assumed to be 600 to 900 ohms. If the instrument attached to the telephone line is of the wrong impedance, you would get a mismatch, or what telephone company personnel refer to as *return loss*. A mismatch on telephone lines results in echo and whistling, which the telephone company refers to as *singing*. All these factors must be programmed into the construction of DSL devices.

Telephone cables usually come in rolls of 500 feet (152 meters). Because most telephone lines are many thousands of feet from the central office (CO) or exchange, several cable splices are required. Each line splice attenuates the signal. The amount of line splice signal attenuation depends on the type of splice (solder, twist, or pegs) and the amount of corrosion inside the splice. Because the average distance of a local access line is more than 10,000 feet (3000 meters), the average local access loop has more than 20 splices. Each of these splices offers the potential for corrosion and increased resistance.

When it is necessary to transmit signals over longer distances via cable, one or more repeaters can be inserted along the length of the cable. The repeaters boost the signal to overcome attenuation. This greatly increases the maximum attainable range of communication. Only recently have repeaters become available for DSL, both for asymmetric and symmetric varieties.

Higher frequencies, such as ADSL's frequency range (25 kHz to 1.1 MHz), are especially vulnerable to signal loss. The existing POTS copper wire infrastructure, pairs of single-core copper wires twisted around each other, was not designed to carry broadband data access services. Bell transmission equipment was originally designed for the specified distance dictated by the Revised Resistance Design (RRD) rule, based on the resistance of copper itself. That distance was defined as a radius of 18,000 feet (5486 meters). The original copper infrastructure measured with the RRD rule was 24 AWG (American Wire Gauge), or .5 mm in diameter.

CSA Remote Terminals

Carrier Serving Area (CSA) design introduced unmanned remote terminals instead of central offices. This development came about as a technical response (smaller and automated equipment) to a market need. People wanted telephone service wherever they might be, not just in large cities served by central offices. CSA guidelines provide for loops of 12,000 feet (3658 meters) with unmanned remote terminals. These remote terminals are also called Digital Loop Carrier (DLC) systems, pedestals, huts, and other names, including the longtime AT&T standard Subscriber Loop Carrier (SLC). Central office connectivity to these remote terminals is provided by copper, or increasingly fiber, using a standard signaling interface defined in such protocols as GR-57 and GR-303.

NOTE   Telcordia Technologies Generic Requirements (GRs) are widely utilized and referenced. They are based on open industry collaboration to promote interoperability and interconnection technical specifications for new and existing technologies or services. These requirements address such areas as interface specifications, equipment capabilities, performance characteristics, and quality and reliability.

The specific Generic Requirements GR-57 and GR-303 address the following areas:

GR-57 applies to DLC systems. Selected transmission and signaling criteria from GR-57 can also be applied to DSL products. Specifically, GR-57 provides common values for the following:

- Characterization of loop current feed output

- Characterization of ringing output

- Detection of loop closure/loop open, including ring trip and flash

- Measurement of return loss and longitudinal balance

- Characterization of transmission path (such as loss, noise, and frequency response)

- Measurement of line-to-line interference such as crosstalk and impulse noise

The Telcordia GR-303 family of requirements specifies next-generation DLC criteria that support multiple distribution technologies and architectures (such as DSL, HFC, and fiber-to-the-curb) and a wide range of services (narrowband and broadband) on a single access platform.

In the past, these remote terminals were attached by multiple T1s (E1s) back to the CO, leading to an extensive, entrenched T1/E1 infrastructure that must be accommodated for DSL service.

For telephony, DLC systems offer the capability to rapidly add, delete, or change customer services without having to dispatch an installation technician. These later-generation CSA deployments typically used smaller wire than the older infrastructure, such as 26 AWG (.4 mm). Figure 2-1 shows CSA innovations, demonstrating that the introduction of remote terminals created a larger CSA. This resulted in complications for DSL because of the need for regulated sharing of the remote terminals and the need for smaller and hardier DSL equipment in the remote terminals.

Figure 2-1   *The Introduction of Remote Terminals Created a Larger CSA But Caused Complications for DSL*

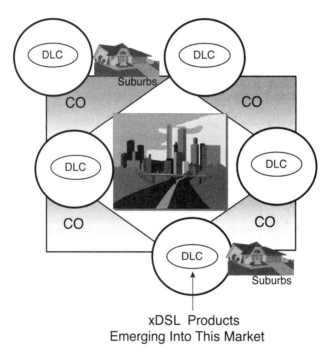

CSA Line Sharing

The CSA use of remote terminals creates impairments to DSL service that are increasingly due to business issues and the regulatory environment rather than technical considerations. To address size and power limitations in remote terminals because of the high concentration of T1 connections, DSL central office equipment manufacturers have steadily made more compact and efficient DSL equipment. This also addresses the market of multitenant units (MTUs) and multidwelling units (MDUs), such as office buildings, dormitories, and apartment buildings. Because most remote terminals (RTs) are not temperature- or humidity-controlled, the newer, smaller DSL equipment is environmentally hardened, such as the Cisco 6015. To avoid disruption to the existing T1-E1 services in remote terminals, equipment manufacturers have provided connections for T1s and E1s, including inverse multiplexing, which splits traffic from a single, large connection into two or more T1s/E1s. However, even with IMA, a remote DLC served with T1/E1 over copper does not have the bandwidth required to feed the DSL subscribers if there are many DSL subscriptions (called a *take rate*) at the DLC. These DLCs would need to be upgraded to fiber. The question then arises of how to upgrade with minimal disruption to existing service and how to divide upgrade costs between the original DLC owner and the DSL service provider. In spite of smaller DSL equipment, IMA, and other technical advances, government regulatory agencies and incumbent telephone service providers around the world are wrestling with how and where to allow access (colocation) to competitive DSL providers. This debate will continue globally for many years.

In the U.S., the Telecommunications Act of 1996 sought to bring about competition across various telecommunications markets. According to this Act, incumbent local service providers must now open, or unbundle, their facilities to competitors. To achieve that goal, Congress authorized the FCC to take deregulatory, pro-competitive steps to encourage new entrants into the telecommunications marketplace. Since passage of the 1996 Act, regulatory efforts, economic and market conditions, and technical innovations have helped begin to bring competition to markets nationwide, but the Act has been contested and argued in courts all over the country.

NOTE   Inverse Multiplexing over ATM (IMA) is described in more depth in Chapter 4, "Cisco DSL Products." Specific commands to enable IMA are defined in Chapter 6, "Cisco IOS Configurations."

DSL-Specific Technical Impairments

DSL has specific impairments beyond the normal metallic media considerations of attenuation and sharing of the voice telephony infrastructure. Specifically, DSL impairments include the following four topics:

- Load coils
- Bridged taps
- Crosstalk and frequency interference
- Copper impedance mismatches

These topics are illustrated in Figure 2-2 and are discussed in the following sections.

Figure 2-2   *Summary of DSL Media Challenges*

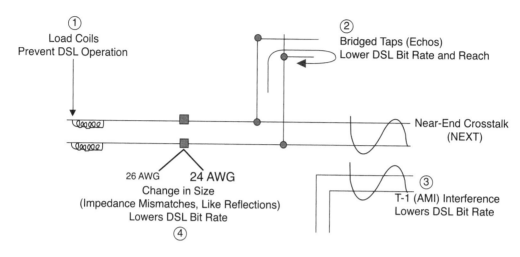

Load Coils

Early in the evolution of mass telephony, long loops had to be conditioned to maintain clear voice signals toward the end of the loops. Many telephone service subscribers, especially in rural areas, were more than 15,000 feet (4572 meters) from the central office. The telephone company reached most of these subscribers by adding extra inductance to the unshielded twisted-pair (UTP) wires. The process of extending the analog local loop with inductance is called *loading*. This compensates for wire capacitance and boosts the frequencies carrying the voice information. The electrical components used to produce these loaded local loops are known as *loading coils*. Loading coils, which look like coil springs, are wrapped around each wire pair of the UTP loop at specific intervals to extend the loop distance. This creates a low-frequency band pass filter with sharp cutoffs at the edge of the band pass. This blocking of frequencies above the voice range prevents the line from supporting DSL. Load coils are typically spaced every 6000 feet (1.8 km) along a long local loop, as shown in Figure 2-3. Only about 15% of all loops have loading coils, but finding out which loops have them is a challenge.

Load coils are not required for long-reach voice service in the modern era due to the extension of central office equipment to remote sites. Removing load coils is costly in terms of labor and time. There is no way to disable or neutralize load coils except removal. Because of the cost to remove them, some telcos decide not to remove all the load coils at the same time, or not until it is absolutely necessary for DSL service. Many DSL providers use a conservative distance in offering service and do not offer DSL services longer than 15,000 feet (4572 meters) from the central office.

Figure 2-3 *Load Coils Block DSL Service*

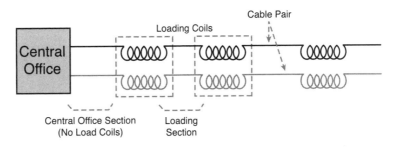

Bridged Taps

Bridged taps are branches from a main line. They are also called *half-taps* or *stubs*. The two main reasons for bridged taps are for residential service flexibility and to detour around areas of heavy construction. The main line is not cut to establish the bridge, just extended for the new portion. These stubs cause echoes and other forms of interference.

The first reason for bridged taps is for residential service flexibility. Unshielded twisted-pair copper is frequently tapped to service homes closer than the end of the wire, either to support old party line arrangements or just because it is easier. If 100 pairs of UTP are run down a block and a new phone is installed, it is generally easier to tap into a pair than to run new wire. This tapping for new service is illustrated in Figure 2-4. The copper pairs in the distribution cable that runs down the street are not cut to connect to a given customer's premises. Instead, the drop wire pairs are spliced into the distribution cable. This allows the same distribution pairs to be reused for another customer when a particular user's service is disconnected.

Another reason for bridged taps is to bridge around an area of dense construction so that telephone service is not disrupted by a cable cut. The tapped-in section has to follow easements (roadsides, railroad tracks, power line routes) to go around the construction area and then rejoins the main cable at another available access point. When the first tap is connected to a cable, hundreds or even thousands of cable pairs are half-tapped. After construction is complete, both the original lines and the bridged lines are frequently left in place, partly because of the expense of rerouting again and partly to allow for future expansion of service.

Bridged taps are acceptable for voice transmissions, but they severely limit the speed of digital information flow on the link and thus hinder DSL implementation. CSA guidelines specify the maximum allowable length of bridged taps:

- No more than 2500 feet (762 meters) total for all bridged taps combined.

- No single bridged tap longer than 2000 feet (609.6 meters) is allowed.

- Bridged taps less than 1000 feet (304.8 meters) are not recommended.

Figure 2-4 *Bridged Taps Frequently Are Created for New Service*

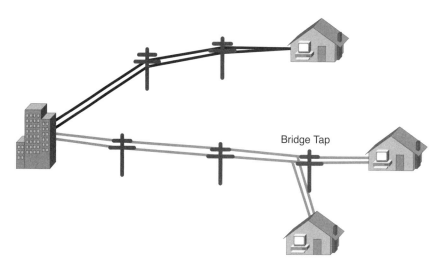

Some telephone companies neglect to thoroughly document that bridged taps are in place. The resulting wire pairs have those undocumented half-taps from previous repairs. In the telephone loop network, abandoned or undocumented extensions of wiring cause problems, especially for competitive new DSL providers. An incumbent local exchange carrier's (ILEC's) cable routes can change without the knowledge of a Competitive Local Exchange Carrier (CLEC) or ISP (Internet service provider), such as in the case of new construction in the area that requires loop rerouting. These *ghost* connections add unforeseen distance to DSL transmissions, causing mysterious signal loss in the incumbent network. In Figure 2-5, the would-be DSL subscriber farthest from the CO might have sporadic or unpredictable-service issues.

Figure 2-5 *Bridged Taps Create Varying Effects on ADSL*

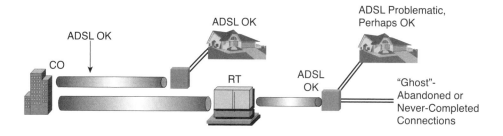

Extra phone wiring within a house is a combination of short bridged taps. In a home or small business, bridged taps might also be unterminated phone extensions where a phone is not presently in place, whether there used to be or will be a phone in that location. The unterminated tap can cause noise and radiate power that reduces signal strength. As you will learn in the "Overcoming Impairments" section of this chapter, a POTS splitter isolates the house wiring and provides a direct path for the DSL signal to pass unimpaired to the ADSL modem.

Crosstalk and Frequency Interference

Crosstalk is interference between two wires in the same bundle, caused by electrical energy. Also called *signal leakage*, crosstalk is defined more precisely as the undesired capacitive or inductive coupling of a signal from one communications channel to another channel, as shown in Figure 2-6. In other words, crosstalk occurs when some of the transmission signal energy leaks from the cable. This leakage is also called *signal egress* (emission from the line).

Figure 2-6   *Crosstalk Is Signal Leakage*

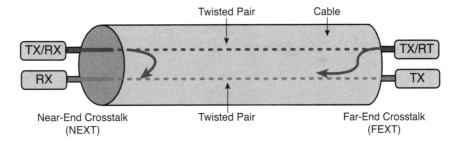

Generically, crosstalk results when energy transmitted on one wire pair is received on another pair. Crosstalk can be divided into two categories:

- Near-end crosstalk (NEXT)
- Far-end crosstalk (FEXT)

NEXT results when some of the energy that is transmitted in one direction is transmitted via one (or more) adjacent communication lines in the opposite direction. FEXT occurs when some of the digital signal energy leaks from one twisted pair to adjacent communication line(s) transferring a different signal in the same direction.

Metallic noise, a form of crosstalk, is a common occurrence that interferes with DSL service. Metallic noise originates from adjacent wire bundles or other sources. Crosstalk incompatibilities also exist between different types of DSL services themselves. In general, some signal bleed occurs between different services and the severity of metallic noise increases as a function of higher frequency. Accepted rules of DSL deployment limit ten DSL pairs in one wiring bundle, or sheath of cables. These groupings of cables are also called cable bundles.

Near-end crosstalk is especially prevalent in the central office, home of the largest concentrations of wires, as shown in Figure 2-7. NEXT is especially troublesome with T1/E1 cables. CO near-end crosstalk prevents equal transmission upstream and downstream in the ranges above the POTS frequencies—that is, above 4 kHz. This creates the opportunity for asymmetric DSL. (Fortunately, this coincides with the usage patterns of the typical Internet user, who receives much more data down from the network than he sends up from his site.) Because symmetric DSL uses all available frequencies, even those from 0 to 4 kHz that would otherwise be used for voice signaling, there is no inequality between upstream and downstream signal rates.

Figure 2-7 *Crosstalk Occurs in the Central Office*

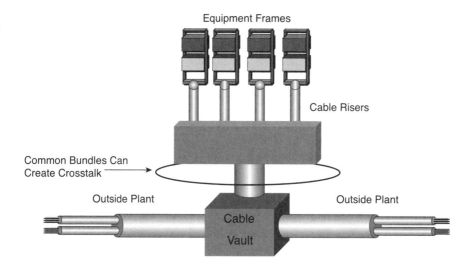

Consider the downstream traffic, from the CO (provider network) to the customer premises, in which the provider sends a high-frequency signal supporting a high bit rate. That signal radiates a strong electromagnetic field, which can be absorbed by other pairs, and the effect gets worse over distance. In the downstream direction, the number of cables gets smaller and smaller in a binder group, because they contain fewer and fewer pairs. Assuming that the cable plant is entirely UTP-based, the cables start off as large cables of 250 pairs or more, split into cables of 50 pairs or so, then perhaps into cables of 25 pairs, and, ultimately, drop to five pairs. At the customer premises, there are probably no more than one or two pairs. So crosstalk near the end user can be an issue, but a relatively minor one, because there are fewer and fewer pairs with which the signal can interfere as the distance grows longer and longer, and the pair count in the cable gets smaller and smaller.

Now consider the same signal in the upstream direction, from the end user to the network. The cables contain more pairs as the distance grows longer as the signal gets closer to the network edge, so the problem of crosstalk grows worse and worse. Therefore, it is technically much easier to send a relatively high-frequency signal downstream than it is back upstream.

A critical subset of near-end crosstalk is the spectral interference generated by T1/E1 cables in the same or an adjacent binder group, or sheath of wiring in the CO. T1 lines use Alternate Mark

Inversion (AMI) coding, which impairs the higher frequencies of ADSL when T1 cables are adjacent to DSL cables in the wiring plant. To counteract this impairment, ADSL and T1 lines must be physically separated into different binder groups or sheaths. If the T1 line is in the same bundle, crosstalk interference occurs. If the T1 line is in an adjacent (neighboring) bundle, crosstalk interference might or might not occur. When in a remote bundle, T1 lines do not cause interference.

Another source of spectral interference that impairs DSL service is the 2B1Q (two binary, one quarternary bit) modulation of ISDN and legacy symmetric DSL (SDSL) types. (In some parts of the world, this might be 3B1Q, but the same principle applies.) All can be countered with adequate separation of wire pairs within the cable bundles. How much separation is required? The optimal solution is not to combine ISDN/IDSL/legacy SDSL wire pairs with ADSL wire pairs in the same cable bundle.

Copper Impedance Mismatches

DSL is affected by impedance mismatches caused by changes in the size of telephone wiring in the circuit. *Impedance* is the total opposition that a device or circuit offers to the flow of a signal, measured in ohms. It comprises resistance, conductance, and inductive and capacitive reactance. The copper cable's resistance (impedance) depends on the cable's size (diameter). The resistance of the copper wire increases as the diameter decreases (as the AWG number increases). Typically, older plant wiring is 24 AWG (.5 mm), and newer plant wiring is 26 AWG (.4 mm).

When line resistance is higher, more signal energy is dissipated through the line, and less energy is transferred to the receiving device. Any impedance mismatch in the local loop causes echo. There can be many impedance mismatches in the local loop, resulting in many echoes. When the signal energy encounters a mismatch, not all of the energy is allowed to go through. Some of the energy goes through the mismatch, but some of that energy bounces off the mismatch and returns to its starting point and bounces again, just like an echo or a reflection, as shown in Figure 2-8.

Figure 2-8   *Impedance Mismatches Create an Echo Effect*

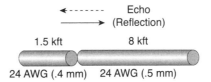

To maintain signal integrity in high-frequency applications such as DSL, it is necessary to maintain closely matched impedance within the circuit. Wire splices or simple corrosion can also cause copper impedance mismatches. Even natural temperature and humidity changes cause impedance mismatches as the copper shrinks and expands.

Impedance mismatches can also occur when a telephone is connected to the local loop over which DSL is operating or when a second telephone is added to a circuit.

The DSL problem arises when the digital receiver gets both signals. There is a cacophony of pulses, and the receiver sees them as noise. Although the DSL provider cannot remedy wire size differences in the local loop, line splitters or microfilters counteract the impedance caused by ordinary telephones on the DSL circuit. Without these controls over the use of telephones, the momentary spike of noise caused by the telephone ringing can disrupt the DSL connection, requiring resynchronization.

NOTE   Copper wiring size changes can occur as users add phone extensions in their homes. One year they might use 28 AWG to add a telephone to a bedroom, and later they might use 24 AWG to add another bridged tap extension in the living room. Mixing the wire gauge in the home is a common source of impedance mismatches. This might cause DSL interference, but it is very hard to identify.

Overcoming Impairments

This section covers common techniques used to overcome impairments or at least compensate for them:

- Automatic rate adaptation
- Two latency paths for different traffic types
- SNR (Signal-to-Noise Ratio) margin
- Loop testing

Automatic Rate Adaptation

A rate-adaptive digital subscriber line (RADSL) varies the achieved bit rate according to line quality and distance. This mass deployment technology preserves reach as the rate adjusts to local loop conditions if possible. The term RADSL was first applied to CAP modulation when it was discovered that with a bit of engineering, CAP would retrain (resynchronize) its bit rate systematically downward from the provisioned speed in response to impairments until it achieved a bit rate at which it could stay synchronized. In the Cisco DSL world, when the connection is synchronized and stable, it is said to be *trained* or *trained up*.

Rate adaptation has been designed into modern discrete multitone (DMT) DSL modulation. Each of the 256 (or 128) DMT subcarriers automatically adapts its bit rate in response to impairments. This adaptation is self-adjusting. That is, an ADSL DMT modem tests the line at startup and adapts its operating speed to the fastest the line can handle on a continuing basis, as shown in Figure 2-9. This downward rate adjustment may occur over and over as transient impairments affect the line quality, but only in a downward direction. In other words, after the rate is adjusted downward, it does not automatically return to the provisioned, higher rate, even when the impairments are removed. Adjusting the rate upward requires a manual retrain, such as rebooting the ADSL modem. RADSL also works well for almost all modern types of line code modulation.

Figure 2-9   *Rate Adaptation Yields Different Results*

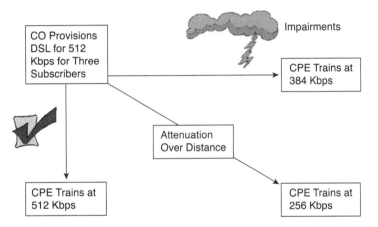

Two Latency Paths for Different Traffic Types

One basic remedy for impairments is to allow some latency for error correction. *Latency* is a measure of delay. There are two distinct latency paths for data transfer over the ADSL local loop. These two paths arose from two concepts of accommodating different types of traffic.

First, modern networks can ultimately depend on the transport or application layers of the OSI reference model to request and retransmit data packets when there are errors. Therefore, data traffic need not be delayed unnecessarily for intermediate error correction.

Second, some types of video traffic cannot be separated into logical segments that are easily retransmitted without losing context. This motion video traffic, such as teleconferencing, must be corrected as much as possible en route.

These two concepts gave rise to ADSL's two latency paths—the fast data path and the interleaved data path. The fast path provides minimal delay through the DSL chipset at the expense of retransmissions from end to end when there are errors. A minimum interleave delay (or the fast path itself) should be used when carrying packetized voice traffic, because packetized voice traffic must not have a total end-to-end delay of less than 150 ms, or voice quality is affected unacceptably.

The interleaved data path offers higher data integrity at the cost of increased latency. The interleaved data path requires more overhead, reducing original traffic throughput, and more computing processing activity, and adds delay. However, the interleaved data path efficiently minimizes retransmissions or end-result errors in received data.

On interleaved circuits, bit swapping helps improve line quality. *Bit swapping* is a mechanism that allows DSL transceivers to reallocate bits between multiple carriers or subfrequencies. Bit swapping can optimize error reaction by attempting to maintain an acceptable margin for each bin. The margins are equalized across all bins through bit reallocation. Think of a line of soldiers advancing abreast, each with a backpack of equal weight. If one soldier stumbles (if one carrier or bin encounters noise), he can pass on part of his load to the next soldier. In other words, the affected bin queues a certain number of bits per clock cycle in the adjacent bin in addition to that bin's own load.

Interleaving is critical to forward error correction (FEC). FEC optimally lets a receiver detect and fix errors associated with a data packet without requiring the sender to retransmit any data. FEC has three primary components in ADSL:

- Interleaving
- Reed-Solomon Encoding
- Trellis Coding

Interleaving, which by itself does not correct any errors, makes it easier for Trellis Coding (TC) (also called Trellis Coded Modulation [TCM]) and Reed-Solomon (RS) Encoding to correct errors. Trellis Coding and Reed-Solomon are two FEC algorithms. To function properly, they must be used in the interleaved data path.

Error-correction algorithms are similar to standard software file-transfer protocols to ensure data integrity. In the case of error-correction algorithms, the procedure takes place in both ends in the modem hardware. Both Reed-Solomon Encoding and Trellis Coding reduce throughput in the data path, because both schemes add data bits to the path.

Interleaving is the process by which bits are reordered so that errors due to impulse noise (bursts of errors) are spread over time. If noise corrupts a set of packets, fewer consecutive pieces of data are lost. Imagine that you are watching a movie, but you know you will be called away to accept telephone calls (you know that transmission errors are inevitable). It is much easier to reconstruct what you missed of the movie if you are absent for more but shorter intervals (the inevitable errors are spread over time) rather than missing fewer but longer segments of the movie (missing many consecutive bits in transmission). This has the effect of spreading the error throughout the bit stream and reducing its effect on consecutive bits, as shown in Figure 2-10. Error-correction algorithms such as Reed-Solomon Encoding and Trellis Coding can therefore more precisely predict the contents of the corrupted data packets. The fast path bypasses the interleaver to provide minimal delay through the DSL chipset while reducing FEC effectiveness.

Figure 2-10 *Bit Interleaving Minimizes Consecutive Errors*

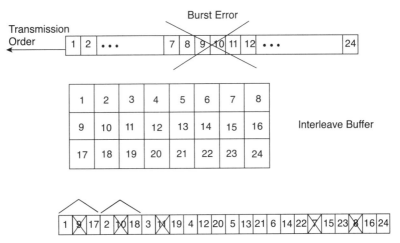

Of course, the same algorithm used to interleave or scramble the bits at one end of the DSL connection must be applied at the other end to deinterleave or unscramble the bits into their original order. This algorithm takes time and processor cycles to execute. There must also be some checking mechanism to ensure that the bits were reassembled into the correct sequence. This verification is accomplished by sending along samples of the deinterleaved, or unscrambled, data bytes. These data bytes are the same information as the interleaved bits and therefore are redundant data, so they decrease the bandwidth available for original data. These redundant bytes are also called *check bytes* or *FEC bytes* because of their use. More check bytes mean more thorough validation of the interleaving process and more precise correction by error-correction algorithms such as Reed-Solomon Encoding and Trellis Coding, but at the cost of diminished bandwidth.

Reed-Solomon Encoding and Trellis Coding, the FEC algorithms, are similar to standard software file-transfer protocols to ensure data integrity. The details of both Reed-Solomon Encoding and Trellis Coding, as well as data integrity algorithms in general, are beyond the scope of this book and general DSL courses, although a general summary is provided here.

In the case of error-correction algorithms, the procedure takes place in both ends in the DSL modem hardware. The sending modem performs a complex mathematical computation on the data content. The result of this calculation is attached to the data packet as an error-control value before it is transmitted. The receiving modem repeats the error-control calculation on the received data packet. If the result of the calculation by the receiving modem is equal to the error-control value contained in the packet, the packet is accepted as containing correct data.

Reed-Solomon Encoding uses generated code words through a complex arithmetic process to anticipate the next string of bits, thereby verifying and correcting errors. This process can achieve error correction at the rate of 16 bit errors per 1000 bits transmitted. Reed-Solomon Encoding is particularly effective on burst errors.

The redundant data (FEC check bytes) required for FEC are included in the data field of the DMT frame, thus reducing the number of bytes used to encode the original data. The frame is divided into several parts called code words. Each code word includes the data to be protected (variable length: L) and the redundant information. The redundancy is always 4 bytes for each code word in the common standards. The redundancy ratio is $4 / (L + 4)$. This amounts to about 10% maximum redundancy (if L is 36 bytes), or a 10% reduction in the bandwidth available for the original traffic.

4 redundancy bytes in a code word allows correction of up to 2 false bytes anywhere in each code word. 1 bit wrong or all bits wrong within a byte are equally corrected. If N code words are interleaved in the DMT frame, the correction capability is 2N bytes.

Trellis Coding allows modems to check for transmission errors with a redundancy bit. Modems can tolerate twice the noise in the channel as usual. Trellis Coding is true error correction because for small errors, it does not force a retransmission but actually fixes the errors. Trellis Coding is particularly valuable for "dribbling" (small but continuous) bit errors.

NOTE   Trellis Coding is mandatory on the updated ADSL standard (G.dmt.bis). Here are other components of the ITU standard G.dmt.bis:

- Additional 96 to 192 kbps greater downstream for most loops

- Reduced framing overhead

- 1-bit signal constellation

- Adaptable pilot tone location

- Mandatory Trellis Coding and R=15 RS Encoding

- Explicit rate negotiation

- Tone reordering for RFI robustness

- Additional ~256 kbps upstream and downstream speed for "all-digital mode" (get rid of POTS option)

- New, advanced line diagnostics

- Precision measurement of line noise, loss, and SNR is built into modems at both ends of the line

- Standard messages to convey measured results to the other end of the line while in service

- Reduces the need to dispatch technicians to the field to diagnose trouble from RFI, crosstalk, and bridged taps

- Reduced power consumption while idle permits greater equipment density with a better power backoff algorithm

- Seamless rate adaptation improves the ability for performance to track line conditions

- Ability to disable tones to aid spectral compatibility

- Improvements to aid multivendor interoperability

- Extended training intervals

- Explicit rate negotiation

In addition to FEC, xDSL also uses standard Cyclic Redundancy Check (CRC) bytes to detect errors. CRC does not provide error correction. CRC bytes are allocated per DMT frame. More check bytes per DMT frame means that the transmitted data can be verified more closely, but more check bytes means that more overhead is used at the expense of original data bandwidth.

SNR Margin

Another remedy for impairments is the automated separation and ongoing measurement between the desired signal and the undesired noise. The *SNR (Signal-to-Noise Ratio) margin* (also called noise margin) measures the separation between the desired signal level and the noise level in decibels (dB). More formally, signal-to-noise is the ratio of the amplitude of the desired signal to the amplitude of noise signals at a given point in time. During the initialization of ADSL modems, the SNR is measured to determine how much data bandwidth can be supported by a particular loop while supporting a standard bit error rate (BER). All modern DSL equipment automatically measures the margin and provides this figure to the technician in a simple measure of dBs. On a continuing basis, the SNR margin determines how much SNR overhead is available in case the loop changes due to transient impairments such as temperature changes or crosstalk. A higher SNR margin provides more protection against data corruption, but it lowers the data rate to be trained up. In the DSL world, the universally accepted bit error rate is a standard minimum for modern data traffic, 1 errored bit per 10,000,000 (10E-7). In general, the higher the SNR margin, the more data rate a channel can handle while maintaining the standard BER. For multiple carrier modulations such as DMT, the SNR margin is calculated for each individual subfrequency.

The Cisco default SNR margin, which is generally accepted throughout the DSL industry, is 6 dB. On a clean POTS line, the DSL connection might achieve a much higher SNR margin than this, and it will vary according to local impairments, but 6 dB is the accepted minimum for reliable DSL service. If the margin automatically rises above the default, it provides more tolerance for transient impairments. On the other hand, if the POTS line is so impaired that the minimum SNR margin cannot be achieved, the DSL connection is terminated and then resynchronized using a lower bit rate in an effort to achieve the minimum margin. This rate adaptation process is repeated until the minimum SNR margin is met, at the expense of the bit rate.

Loop Testing

Loop testing refers to testing the transmission path between a service provider's central office and a subscriber's premises. Testing the local loop is as vital a step as configuring the DSL equipment or provisioning the circuits.

Loop testing has two different functions: electrical loop characterization and Centralized Repair Service Bureau. In the first function, the subscriber loop's electrical characteristics are measured to verify that the loop is operational and to isolate and identify the fault when repair is required. In the case of a Centralized Repair Service Bureau, information is generated to enable informed inquiries about the subscriber end point status (the drop) and to let technicians be dispatched efficiently and effectively in response to a subscriber complaint or trouble report generated by mechanized test equipment.

Both these functional areas integrate three basic elements—parametric testing, transmission testing, and digital I/O testing. *Parametric testing* ensures modem interoperability at the physical level, including separating voice and data and minimizing signal interference and distortion. *Transmission testing* involves checking bit-error rate go/no-go tests that ensure that the modem works within specifications, with or without wire-line impairments. *Digital I/O testing* focuses on digital interfaces for subscriber/network connections. The idea is to verify correct functionality of the control and transfer of data through complex backplanes and digital interfaces.

Conventional outside plant designs might be many kilometers in length and traverse many facilities. Therefore, loop testing has traditionally required labor-intensive manual processes, such as making physical connections. Establishing a new xDSL service involves testing many lines—perhaps millions—as part of prequalification, which can add significant expense. Born of the need to reduce these costs, accelerate prequalification, and advance technology, mechanized loop testing (MLT) is increasingly common. MLT can reduce labor expenses, increase on-time service provisioning, and reduce outage times by automating test functions. MLT allows the provider to manage network-wide testing under a single, cost-effective central point of control. Personnel other than skilled technicians can run and interpret MLT tests.

ILEC Loop Management

ILECs initially relied on existing tools deployed to support POTS in the copper loop to support DSL deployment. Because the ILECs could use a line that was already in service for voice, some of the uncertainty about the loops being able to work properly for carrying DSL data traffic was eliminated. Even now, most incumbents are still installing and are just beginning to use DSL-specific remote test equipment. Instead, the incumbents have relied on engineering inventories bolstered by low-frequency testing done out of the Class 5 switch. ILEC testing verifies loop length, and its design inventory indicates whether any impediments such as load coils or bridged taps are on the line. However, TeleChoice research has found that these inventories are accurate only between 60 and 80 percent of the time. When the line doesn't support service even after it looked like it could, the ILEC's procedures revert to the costly and time-intensive procedure of sending out a technician with handheld test equipment to identify and try to correct the problem.

CLEC Loop Management

CLECs have integrated DSL-specific remote test equipment into their networks. Although DSL test equipment cannot see through most splitters, this was not a concern, because the CLECs were deploying services on dedicated loops and therefore did not require splitters. They could colocate test equipment in front of their DSLAMs and gain an accurate picture of the capabilities and condition of the loops that were being handed over to them. Existing DSL test equipment cannot see through splitters in a DSL-over-POTS environment. Splitters create a need for additional wiring in the CO. With additional wiring, cross-connections are often mishandled, and when this occurs, providers have no direct way of knowing what the problem is. A few providers, including at least one incumbent, are now placing DSL test equipment in front of the splitter. For competitive providers, this is a solution only if there is sufficient room to colocate a splitter in their cage.

Specifically for DSL, loop testing should take into account all the impairments and allow for reasonable remediation. The overall objectives of DSL cable qualification are to determine the classes and qualities of service that may be offered and to locate impairments that might degrade or prevent service so that they may be cleared.

The following sections describe the basic procedures and types of tests used in loop qualification.

Starting with the Existing Records

Initial loop qualification consists of a records check. Qualification testing of the line consists of sending a technician to the customer's demarcation point and connecting an Asynchronous Transceiver Unit-Remote (ATU-R) test set for ADSL or connecting a 200 KHz or 400 KHz transmission impairment measurement set (TIMS) tester for SDSL.

The ILEC performs the records check, the first step in verifying readiness for basic service. A typical check determines the distance of the demarcation point from the CO. Other items might include checking the records for the presence and location of load coils and/or bridged taps.

Several parameters are used to qualify the local loop:

- Frequency response
- Time domain reflectometry
- Noise metrics
- Discrete multitone testing
- Load coil detection
- Service tests
- Test equipment

Frequency Response

A measurement of frequency response indicates the line's available bandwidth. DSL services can carry more digital information per second than dial-up modems because they utilize higher frequencies to carry the information. One of the most limiting factors for xDSL implementation is the local loop's inability to carry the high frequencies required for DSL. For example, as discussed earlier, loading coils on a local loop cut off the high frequencies, thereby preventing ADSL operations.

Time Domain Reflectometry

Time domain reflectometry (TDR) is a cable-testing technique that was originally developed to detect faults on power transmission lines. It has been used in analog telephony for many years. Only recently have TDR measurements become required for DSL deployments. With this test, a pulse of energy is injected into a line. When the energy pulse encounters the end of the cable or any other change in impedance (a short circuit, load coil, or bridged tap), part or all of the energy is reflected toward the TDR equipment. The signal reflection is measured to determine the distance to the fault.

Noise Metrics

Noise and impulse noise measurements let the service provider identify undesired intermittent or steady state disturbances that could affect data transmission between the provider's serving office and the subscriber. Electrical disturbances can come from man-made or natural sources, such as the crosstalk energy from T1 or E1 lines. Impulse noise can intensify if water enters a cable sheath and acts as a partial conductor.

Discrete Multitone Testing

256-tone DMT loss tests measure the signal loss of each tone (every 4.3 kHz) and the noise in each band. The number of bits that can be carried per tone can be calculated. Conventional testing of communications channel quality uses Bit Error Rate Testing (BERT), the measure of the ratio of defective bits passed to total bits, representing the network's quality.

ADSL presents two problems for BERT testing. First, the analog sources of defective ADSL bins are masked during training, making BERT a measure of the effective error rate. Second, BERT uses a trained data pipe consisting of two modems and a physical link. As a result, BERT is not a measure of the specific modem being tested. Finally, with DMT ADSL's many bins, BERT is unable to resolve bit error to a specific bin. Consequently, conventional testing via BERT is inadequate to detect subtle operational errors for DMT ADSL unless the errors are sufficient to substantially affect the basic data rate.

DSL providers can verify maximum data rates using SNR measurements with the missing-tone test technique. A missing-tone test, which can be implemented as a hardware/software solution, ensures correlation of a rapid functional test result with industry BERT test specifications. The missing-tone test is based on the measurement of noise in a missing tone (one of the tones in the DMT spectrum is turned off while all the others remain on) relative to the signal levels of the tones that are present. This causes the missing tone to expose residual noise.

Load Coil Detection

Most telephone companies have introduced practices for the systematic removal of loading coils from lines. Typically, only lines that are greater than 18,000 feet (5486 meters) contain load coils. Most test devices, both rack-mounted and portable types, can detect load coils by sending particular tones over the circuit and then measuring the results. Bear in mind that load coils absolutely prevent xDSL operation, because they block frequencies above the normal voice range. There is no way to counteract load coils other than complete removal, which is a time-consuming and labor-intensive task.

Service Tests

Specialized test sets can emulate the DSL modem. These service confirmation tests normally use the same chips and technologies that are used in modems. If a connection can be made, this type of test set can indicate the presence and service level (upstream and downstream connection rates) of the line under test. Even though an LEC might not offer the higher rate at the time of testing, it might want the technician to log the maximum rate for future reference. If the maximum achievable rate is low compared to the expected rate, line maintenance might be in order before higher rates can be offered. If a line fault exists, however, only a cable qualifier can be used to determine the true source of the problem. Testing the line requires the provider to send a synchronization bit to the customer premises equipment. The SYNC signal is then sent back to validate service availability. Synchronization bits that are sent from the transmitter to the receiver and then back again are used to synchronize the clocks on both ends.

Test Equipment

The equipment used to qualify local loops covers a wide range of technologies. Rack-based IP multiplexer (MUX) devices can be used to test the local loop. As shown in Figure 2-11, handheld devices can weigh as little as a pound, and they might be equipped with an internal speaker and a 2.5 mm headset connection. Noise-canceling headsets are available for placing calls and for use while testing in high-noise environments.

Figure 2-11 *Handheld Testing Devices Are Increasingly DSL-Specific*

Some manufacturers have a complete software solution for testing the local loop. Technicians in the field run tests from handheld devices and communicate with a central office responder rack-based unit to run and report line tests. The office responder unit is the computer-based brain behind running automated local loop testing software. It stores all the test templates and determines which tests should be initiated. The responder unit then compares all test results to the individual templates for optimal service. The result is a pass/fail indication sent to the handheld device in the field.

Summary

In general, most potential DSL subscribers must be within 5486 meters (18,000 feet) of the central office equipment, whether in a traditional CO or in a remote terminal. This distance represents the traditional Carrier Serving Area (CSA) defined by remote terminals that extend voice service from the central office, and it has been accepted over decades for voice service. The relatively recent use of DSL repeaters is extending this reach. DSL equipment can be installed in a remote terminal, but the equipment must be made compact and environmentally hardened. Even before the equipment is accepted, regulatory issues must be addressed to define colocation and line sharing between the incumbent provider and the competitive DSL provider.

More than a century of copper telephony infrastructure must be evaluated before DSL technologies can be implemented over the existing POTS network. Legacy voice technology might present impairments that prevent DSL service entirely or at least inhibit optimal DSL service. In some cases, the cost to remove impairments might be so great that providers opt not to offer DSL in certain areas or might limit advertised bit rates. These impairments include the following:

- Load coils (prevent DSL operation)

- Bridged taps (can lower the DSL bit rate and must be calculated to offer DSL service guarantees)

- Crosstalk and frequency interference (countered by careful separation of cables with different modulations)
- Copper impedance mismatches (must be documented and calculated for their effect throughout the copper plant)

Countering impairments starts with modern DSL's own automatic rate adaptation. Protection from unwanted noise is measured by the SNR margin. Although sophisticated error-correction algorithms are available (such as Reed-Solomon Encoding and Trellis Coding), these error-correction algorithms depend on the use of bit interleaving to spread out the error bits for maximum efficiency. Together, bit interleaving, with its redundant check bytes, and error-correction algorithm(s) create en route delay and processor loads that are unnecessary for certain types of traffic, such as standard IP data traffic, which can be retransmitted from end to end without taxing the processors and adding delay. This traffic rides in the fast path. Other types of traffic, such as streaming video, cannot be efficiently retransmitted in the case of received errors and must be corrected as much as possible en route. This traffic rides in the second of two paths, the interleaved path.

Review Questions

The following review questions give you a chance to assess how well you've mastered the topics in this chapter. The answers to these questions can be found in Appendix A.

1 Which of the following impairments always prevents ADSL implementation?

   A AM radio interference

   B Impedance mismatch

   C Load coils

   D Bridged taps

2 Which of the following is *not* one of the three primary methods of forward error correction in ADSL?

   A Trellis Coding

   B DMT

   C Interleaving

   D Reed-Solomon Encoding

3 Reed-Solomon Encoding divides the data frame into several parts that are called what?

   A Cells

   B Code words

   C Tins

   D Codes

4 What does Trellis Coding do with small data errors?

   A   It retransmits them to the sender.

   B   It adds correcting cells and retransmits to the sender.

   C   It fixes the errors without resending them.

   D   Trellis Coding cannot handle small data errors.

5 Which of the following describes the interleaving process?

   A   It reorders bits so that errors due to impulse noise are spread over time.

   B   It reorders frames so that errors due to impulse noise are spread over time.

   C   It reorders cells so that errors due to impulse noise are spread over time.

   D   It corrects burst errors through mathematical reconstruction.

6 The SNR margin represents which of the following?

   A   Error correction

   B   Separation between the desired signal and the noise signal

   C   Overcoming distance attenuation

   D   The precedence of signal purity over signal bit rate

7 True or false: Bridged taps prevent DSL operation.

8 Reed-Solomon Encoding is most effective on what type of errors?

   A   Large gaps in sequential bits

   B   Bursty errors

   C   T1 binder group interference

   D   Impedance mismatches

9 What makes it much easier for Trellis Coding and Reed-Solomon Encoding to correct errors?

   A   FEC

   B   SNR

   C   Interleaving

   D   Crosstalk

10 What is one way to compensate for the amount of attenuation in a signal path?

   A   Add a repeater to the cable to boost signal strength.

   B   Boost signal strength by adding loading coils.

   C   Change the cable pair to unshielded twisted-pair to increase signal strength.

   D   Nothing can reduce the amount of attenuation in a line.

11 What form of crosstalk occurs when a signal is affected by leaking digital signal energy moving in the opposite direction?

   A   FEXT

   B   NEXT

   C   Front-end

   D   FEXT and NEXT

12 Which of the following factors inhibits DSL service at the remote terminals?

   A   Access

   B   Environmental factors

   C   Space

   D   All of the above

13 What is the primary function of digital loop carriers?

   A   To bundle multiple ISDN lines in a service area

   B   To terminate subscribers' ISDN lines from the central office

   C   To overcome the limitations of the central office coverage area

   D   To add, move, and delete subscribers in a central office

14 Why must load coils be removed?

   A   They limit frequency response to below DSL frequency range.

   B   They create crosstalk.

   C   They add attenuation.

   D   They need not be removed completely for DSL service at lower bit rates.

15 Which of the following is *not* an objective of DSL cable qualification?

A Locate faults that cause bad, poor, or no service so that they may be cleared.

B Confirm the functionality of the physical line between the subscriber and the serving central office.

C Determine which service levels can be offered to the customer.

D Determine the number of devices required for service.

16 Which test works by injecting a pulse of energy into a line and timing the return of any reflections caused by cable abnormalities?

A Service

B TDR

C 256-tone DMT loss test

D Frequency response

17 Which test indicates the line's available bandwidth?

A TDR

B Load coil detection

C Frequency response

D Noise and impulse noise

18 Initial qualification consists of a what?

A Record check

B TIMS test

C 256-tone DMT loss test

D TDR test

19 Which test's measurements let the service provider identify disturbances that could affect the transmission of data between the provider and the subscriber?

A Noise and impulse noise

B Load coil detection

C Frequency response

D Service tests

CHAPTER 3

TCP/IP Over ATM

This chapter compares the main architectures for an end-to-end DSL architecture. Because DSL depends on ATM for switching beyond the DSL network itself (that is, through the local loop and into the network cloud), and because the predominant routing protocol in today's internetworking is TCP/IP, this chapter is most properly titled "TCP/IP Over ATM." This chapter starts with an overview of useful functionalities for DSL networks, such as security, and the protocols that enable those functionalities, such as authentication, authorization, and accounting (AAA). The chapter continues with sections for each of the six major architectures, including the most commonly deployed architecture, Point-to-Point Protocol over Ethernet. The last two topics, L2TP and MPLS VPN, are not strictly used in DSL networks. They have much significance beyond the local access network. While reading about these six architectures, you should bear in mind that no DSL network would ever use all six methods simultaneously, or even more than three types on an ongoing basis. Even the technical evolution of a long-time DSL network would include no more than two or three of these access methods in reaching its current network state.

This chapter's six DSL architectures are as follows:

- Integrated Routing and Bridging (IRB) (RFC 2684, which made obsolete RFC 1483)
- Routed Bridge Encapsulation (RBE) (RFC 2684)
- Point-to-Point Protocol over Ethernet (PPPoE) (RFC 2516)
- Point-to-Point Protocol over ATM (PPPoA) (RFC 2364)
- Beyond DSL: Layer 2 Tunneling Protocol (L2TP) (RFC 2661)
- Beyond DSL: Multiprotocol Label Switching (MPLS) tunneling (most specifically defined by RFC 2917, although at least six related RFCs address MPLS)

We include IRB and discuss it first among the architecture-specific sections, although it is the simplest, oldest, and least-robust of all the architectures, for a couple of reasons. First, there are still quite a few IRB-based DSL networks around the world. Second, because IRB is the simplest architecture of all, it provides a very good baseline for comparison among all the architectures.

Beyond the details of each of the architectures, this chapter provides a bonus—an explanation of Easy IP. Easy IP is detailed in the section "PPP/IPCP (RFC 1332) and Cisco IOS Easy IP." Briefly stated, Easy IP uses a combination of Dynamic Host Configuration

Protocol (DHCP) and Internet Protocol Control Protocol (IPCP) so that the user's DSL router can obtain its IP address automatically when the router is powered on.

Upon completing this chapter, you will be able to do the following:

- Compare the six described architectures' features relating to

  — Complexity of equipment

  — Simplicity of configuration

  — Security

  — Scalability

  — Post-deployment support

- Describe the operation of Network Address Translation/Port Address Translation (NAT/PAT) in the DSL environment and list its availability by type of access architecture being used.

- Describe the implementation of the most commonly used security protocol in DSL networks and identify the other security protocol option, TACACS+.

- Describe L2TP tunneling, used to implement a DSL Access VPN solution.

- Describe MPLS and MPLS VPN, as well as how MPLS VPN can be deployed on DSL networks.

The first section previews features that are common to some or all of the different access architectures; it defines NAT, PAT, and security protocols. This introductory section also discusses the format in which each architecture is defined—each architecture's protocol involvement, IP addressing possibilities, and difficulties; security; and other considerations for implementation.

Architectures Overview

As you can see in Figure 3-1, security and scalability drive up cost and complexity. Although security and low cost are what informed users want in their DSL service, scalability with low complexity is desired by service providers.

Scalability is a bilevel consideration that includes

- The service provider's own growth as DSL sales increase the number of DSL users

- The growth of the DSL users' own networks, from adding computers in the home to business expansion

Figure 3-1   *Positioning of DSL Access Architectures*

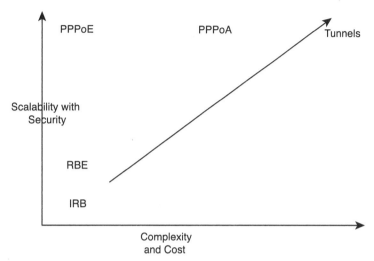

The earliest versions of DSL modems were bridges between a 10BASE-T Ethernet on the host side and RFC 1483 (now RFC 2684) encapsulated bridge frames on the WAN DSL side. Because bridging is very simple to understand and implement, and because it made use of low-cost CPE, it remained the most common DSL access architecture until now. Bridging, especially IRB, is not easily scalable, and it offers no security. Upgrading the architecture and software to achieve better scalability and security while preserving the installed base of modems is an argument for either RBE, which at least plugs the holes in IRB security, or PPPoE, which offers reliable authentication. Both of these more-modern successors to IRB can use an existing, bridged modem deployment while offering scalability and security.

Security and Other Protocols in DSL Architectures

This section is an overview of the different protocols that may be available with the various TCP/IP architectures. The architectures themselves, such as PPPoE, are described in detail in their own sections after the overview of the related protocols. To help you sort the architectures by complexity as you read through the various architecture sections, consider each one's capability for various functionalities, such as security, primarily AAA. As shown in Figure 3-2, AAA represents a desired set of functions. AAA is a system in IP-based networks that controls user access to network resources and keeps track of the activity of users over the network.

Figure 3-2 *AAA: Function, Protocol, Product*

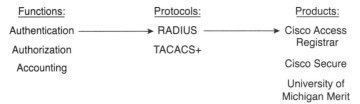

The excellent online Webopedia by Internet.com, sponsored by the IEEE, defines AAA more precisely as follows:

- *Authentication* is the process of identifying an individual, usually based on a username and password. For our Cisco DSL network purposes, an AAA server (such as a RADIUS server) can be used to authenticate DSL users when you're using an access architecture such as PPPoE or PPPoA. For Point-to-Point Protocol (PPP), either PAP or CHAP can be used as the authentication protocol.

- *Authorization* is the process of granting or denying a user access to network resources after the user has been authenticated through the username and password. The amount of information and the number of services the user has access to depend on the user's authorization level.

- *Accounting* is the process of keeping track of a user's activity while accessing the network resources, including the amount of time spent in the network, the services accessed while there, and the amount of data transferred during the session. Accounting data is used for trend analysis, capacity planning, billing, auditing, and cost allocation.

Remote Authentication Dial-In User Service (RADIUS) is the more common of the two primary security protocols that provide AAA service. AAA services usually depend on a dedicated RADIUS server that exchanges data with a Layer 3 DSL aggregation router such as the Cisco 6400 Universal Access Concentrator (UAC). As an example, with outside DSL, when you dial in to the ISP from your PC using an analog modem, you must enter your username and password. This information is passed to a RADIUS server, which checks that the information is correct and then authorizes access to the ISP system.

RADIUS is one of two primary security protocols that enable AAA functionality. AAA itself is available in robust DSL network architectures such as PPPoE and PPPoA. AAA services are not available with simpler DSL access architectures such as IRB and RBE.

RADIUS was developed in the mid-1990s by Livingston Enterprises (which has since been acquired by Lucent).

NOTE   Although it isn't an official standard, the RADIUS specification is maintained by a working group of the Internet Engineering Task Force (IETF). You can learn more about RADIUS at the IETF link at ietf.org/ids.by.wg/radius.html.

RADIUS is more common than the more powerful and more complex protocol Terminal Access Controller Access Control System (TACACS). TACACS, originally described in RFC 1492, has been reengineered over the years by Cisco. The current version is called TACACS+, which reflects the many enhancements made to the original TACACS protocol. Although TACACS+ is a powerful security tool used elsewhere in internetworking, it is rarely found in DSL networks, so this book does not discuss it.

With the more-advanced Layer 3 (L3) DSL access architectures, such as PPPoE and PPPoA, you can configure RADIUS for either of two authentication protocols to manage the first A in AAA. You should remember the concepts of PAP (Password Authentication Protocol) and CHAP (Challenge Handshake Authentication Protocol) from earlier studies of Cisco technology.

Authentication with PAP

The simpler PAP provides a method for a remote node to establish its identity using a two-way handshake. This is done only upon initial link establishment. After the PPP link establishment phase is complete, a username/password pair is repeatedly sent by the remote node across the link until authentication is acknowledged or the connection is terminated. PAP is not an encrypted authentication protocol. Passwords are sent across the link in clear text, and there is no protection from playback or trial-and-error attacks. The remote node is in control of the frequency and timing of the login attempts.

Authentication with CHAP

The more secure of the two authentication protocols provided through RADIUS as part of PPPoE and PPPoA is CHAP. It is invoked initially and periodically during the session to verify the remote node's identity using a three-way handshake. After the PPP link establishment phase is complete, the host sends a challenge message to the remote node. The remote node responds with a value calculated using a one-way hash function (typically message-digest algorithm MD5). The host checks the response against its own calculation of the expected hash value. If the values match, the authentication is acknowledged. Otherwise, the connection is terminated. CHAP provides protection against playback attack through the use of a variable challenge value that is unique and unpredictable. The use of repeated challenges is intended to limit the time of exposure to any single attack. The host (or a third-party authentication server, such as a RADIUS server) controls the frequency and timing of the challenges.

PPP, over both Ethernet (PPPoE) and ATM (PPPoA), includes two vital protocols as well as the user traffic. As with security authentication, neither IRB nor RBE supports the more-advanced capabilities of Link Control Protocol (LCP) and Network Control Protocol (NCP), which are key benefits of PPP. These two protocols are explained in their own sections.

General Data Flow

Starting from the user's point of view, the PC transmits an Ethernet frame that carries an IP packet. In the case of asymmetric DSL (ADSL), the IP packet is received by an Asymmetric Transceiver Unit-Remote (ATU-R), the DSL modem/router at the customer premises. (For IRB, RBE, and PPPoE, the ATU-R uses bridging; for PPPoA, the DSL device uses routing. Both of these techniques are explained in detail later for each architecture.)

This original Protocol Data Unit (PDU) is then sent to the ATU-R's ATM Adaptation Layer (AAL), where a trailer is attached, indicating the end of the original IP packet. As you can see in Appendix B, "ATM Overview," there are different AALs. The most commonly used AAL in today's DSL networks is ATM Adaptation Layer 5 (AAL5). The resulting data unit is segmented into 48-byte cells by the AAL5 layer. It is then passed to the ATM layer, where the 5-byte ATM header is added to each cell. The ATU-R forms the ATM cells into discrete multitone (DMT) frames (the prevailing DSL modulation). The DMT frames are forwarded via DSL to the DSL access multiplexer (DSLAM) or IP DSL Switch, depending on the architecture and its implementation at the network edge. The DSLAM is a Layer 2 DSL Access Multiplexer; the IP DSL Switch is a DSLAM that is enabled for Layer 3 routing as well as multiplexing and switching. The ATU-R uses a specific framing method, as shown in Figure 3-3. The main frame, called a superframe, comprises 68 ADSL data frames. Each data frame fills the payload from the two ADSL paths, or buffers (interleaved buffer and fast buffer). Depending on the architecture, the ATU-R either routes or bridges the data to the central office. In the case of DSL bridged access, such as with IRB, RBE, and PPPoE, the contents are bridged Ethernet frames.

Figure 3-3   *DMT Frame*

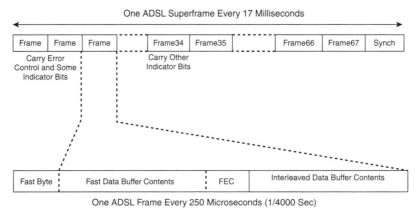

The central office DSL device receives the DSL frame and unpacks the ATM cells. If this device is a Layer 2 DSLAM, it forwards the ATM cells to the Layer 3-enabled aggregation router. If the receiving CO device is an IP DSL Switch, Layer 3 capabilities are onboard, and the following step is carried out inside the IP DSL Switch itself.

The Layer 3 device reassembles the ATM cells into the AAL5 PDU format in the SAR (segmentation and reassembly) process. The device then verifies and removes the AAL5 trailer, followed by verifying and removing the PPP header. Now that the data is back in IP packet form, the Layer 3 device (IP DSL Switch or aggregator) routes the IP packet to its destination. In some cases, this might mean reconverting the IP packet to ATM cells for transmission over an ATM network, which is carried out through the same device's SAR process again. (For more details about this process, see Appendix B.)

IP Addressing

IP addressing is perhaps the single most important issue when designing a DSL network. IP addressing can dictate security, post-deployment maintenance of remote modems, and scalability.

If both the PC and the ATU-R require IP addresses, this is a further reason to consider address allocation. This is necessary for post-deployment troubleshooting of remote installed modems. It might be that the service provider's model furnishes ATU-Rs to users at little or no cost to the end user, such as in an initial marketing campaign. In this case, the provider's modem service model probably provides for quick replacement of the customer unit after limited remote troubleshooting by provider personnel. This reduced service can also apply to service providers acquiring older networks with entrenched early-generation modems.

You can see that IP addressing options depend less on the capabilities of the particular ATU-R model and software and more on the provider's business model. In any event, IP addresses for either the PC or the ATU-R or both can be applied statically or supplied dynamically.

Static addressing for the user's PC requires a truck roll by the service provider, or the ISP must enable and direct the subscriber to configure a unique IP address on the PC.

Virtual Templates

The RFC 2684-based architectures IRB and RBE, as well as the RFC 2516-based PPPoE, make use of a virtual template on the Layer 3 termination device, such as the router module on the Cisco 6400 UAC. A *virtual template* is a virtual interface with all the interface characteristics of a physical interface. It is assigned a unique network IP address. IP addresses may be conserved by sharing a recognized address with a physical interface using an unnumbered interface. The IP address pool is identified that will be used to hand out an IP address to the PCs and ATU-Rs as needed during session startup for bridging and PPPoE.

Dynamic IP Addressing

Dynamic addressing references a pool of IP addresses from which the IP address is assigned upon authentication or another initiating event. Addresses can be assigned using DHCP. For bridging and PPPoE architectures, DHCP can be applied through the use of virtual templates on the Layer 3 device, such as the Cisco 6400 UAC.

If PPPoA or PPPoE is implemented in the DSL network, you can also use IPCP or even a combination of DHCP and IPCP when using PPPoA or PPPoE (as explained later in this chapter and in Chapter 6's configuration explanations). Defined in RFC 2131, this protocol lets you dynamically and transparently assign reusable IP addresses to clients. Cisco IOS Easy IP Phase 2 includes the Cisco IOS DHCP Server, an RFC 2131-compliant DHCP server implementation on selected routing platforms.

Wherever it is configured, the DHCP address pool can contain registered addresses from the service provider, or the pool can use private addresses. If private addresses are to be used, NAT or PAT must be configured on the ATU-R or on the central office/exchange equipment. It's interesting to note that DHCP not only delivers addresses but also provides the subnet mask, the default gateway address, static routes, the domain name server address, and the domain name itself.

As an alternative to DHCP, the RADIUS server at the central office could assign the IP address.

One common service provider business model is the bundling of IP addresses, such as categories for a single IP address, two to five addresses, and six to ten addresses, all at different fees. Again, the business model dictates the IP address allocation and the overall choice of the DSL access architecture. If the service provider needs strict control over the number of users, you can choose a more-restrictive IP allocation scheme that forces users to purchase extra service for extra host devices. Strict control over numbers of hosts allows for more-tailored service revenues, but it also facilitates long-haul transmission backbone traffic planning when the total number of users is known, so the decision is not completely monetary.

On the other hand, a restrictive IP allocation scheme might not be competitively enticing to power users and small businesses that want the freedom to expand their LANs. In this case, PPPoA (especially when combined with NAT or PAT) renders the numbers of hosts invisible when behind the NAT/PAT router at the client edge.

NAT and PAT (RFC 1631)

As shown in Figure 3-4, NAT converts outside public addresses to inside private addresses, which is useful for configurations that have multiple host devices behind the unit that share the DSL connection. NAT is unavailable when you're running basic bridging (RFC 2684 bridging using IRB or RBE). This function is used in conjunction with DHCP to provide dynamic private IP address assignment and translation in the PPPoA and PPPoE configurations. NAT renders the DSL user's LAN IP addresses invisible to the Internet, making the remote LAN more secure.

Figure 3-4   *NAT*

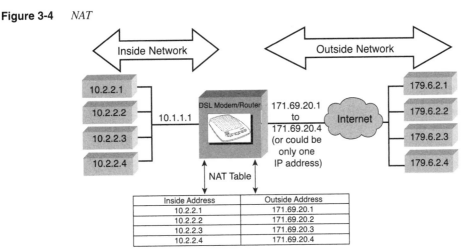

In NAT generally and in Cisco IOS Easy IP in particular, the LAN is designated as *inside* and uses addresses that are converted into one or more registered addresses in the registered network (designated as *outside* or WAN).

For translating from one external address to multiple internal addresses, known as *overloaded NAT,* Cisco devices can use PAT, a subset of NAT. This integrates the IP port numbers with the address.

PAT uses unique source port numbers on the inside IP address to distinguish between translations. Because the port number is encoded in 16 bits, the total number could theoretically be as high as 65,536 port numbers per IP address. PAT attempts to preserve the original source port; if this source port is already allocated, PAT attempts to find the first available port number, starting from the beginning of the appropriate port group—0 to 511, 512 to 1023, or 1024 to 65535. If there is still no port available from the appropriate group, and more than one IP address is configured, PAT moves to the next IP address and tries to allocate the original source port again. This continues until PAT runs out of available ports and IP addresses.

PPP/IPCP (RFC 1332) and Cisco IOS Easy IP

The PPP/IPCP combination lets users configure dynamic IP addresses over PPP when using a router, such as the Cisco 827 DSL modem. A Cisco IOS Easy IP router uses PPP/IPCP to dynamically negotiate its own WAN interface address from the aggregation router. Although the individual components of Easy IP are not unique, having been defined in the various RFCs, it's the particular combination of DHCP, PPP, and IPCP by Cisco IOS Easy IP that minimizes the router's configuration.

Cisco IOS Easy IP contains a full DHCP server that supports many DHCP options, as defined in RFC 2132, "DHCP Options and BOOTP Vendor Extensions."

Implementation Considerations for IP Address Allocation

Now that you have seen many of the possibilities for allocating and managing IP addresses in the DSL network, this section summarizes the questions to be answered when designing an IP address allocation:

- How many DSL subscriber connections will be serviced currently and in the future?

- Related to the number of subscribers, will the accounting be per-subscriber or per-virtual circuit (VC)? (Bear in mind that a single ATM VC's bandwidth can be shared among multiple users.)

- If more than one user shares the same DSL connection, do all users need to reach the same final destination or service, or different service destinations? What is the service support model for post-deployment troubleshooting? Does this include service for any preconfigured legacy DSL modems?

- Will the business model allow for unrestricted IP address allocation so that users can expand their own networks, or will there be strict licensing of IP addresses?

- Where does the subscriber's connection terminate? That is, does the circuit responsibility end at the service provider's aggregation router, or is the connection forwarded to other corporate gateways or Internet service providers (ISPs)?

- Do either or both the PC and the subscriber's DSL modem/router need an IP address?

- Does the service provider or the final service destination provide the IP address to the subscriber's CPE?

- Are the provided IP addresses public (registered) or private?

- Does the service provider provide any value-added services such as voice or video? Does the service provider require all subscribers to pass through a particular network before reaching a final destination?

- How does the service provider bill subscribers—flat rate, per session usage, or by services used?

You must answer the preceding questions before settling on a particular IP address allocation scheme. Those answers in turn determine the use of particular protocols, AAA functionality, and IP address allocation and management schemes. Together, all this information helps determine the choice of architectures. In the next section, each currently implemented architecture is described individually, along with the various business and technical considerations that depend on the information you've just considered.

DSL Architectures

Architecture choices are driven by business considerations as much as (or more than) by optimal topology. Higher scalability and security means more cost and complexity. Automated IP address allocation techniques simplify DSL network addressing but require more capable (and therefore more expensive) devices. On the other hand, restrictive licensing of users enables a simpler business and support plan. These are just some of the business and technical aspects of architecture selection that you must consider as you read through the following discussions.

Integrated Routing and Bridging (IRB)

This section describes the protocol stack, connectivity, IP addressing considerations, and advantages and disadvantages of an end-to-end ADSL architecture using IRB based on RFC 2684 bridging. Early ADSL deployments used bridging, and some older networks still use it, although more-sophisticated architecture designs are quickly replacing IRB.

IRB Overview

RFC 2684 IRB permits subscriber-to-subscriber communication, but broadcasts must be (and almost always are) limited. This configuration step prevents either inadvertent or intentional flooding of a bridged network with bandwidth-consuming networking traffic such as unnecessary Address Resolution Protocol (ARP) requests for IP addresses. However, certain legitimate broadcasts still require communication with all subscriber devices. Therefore, unless the broadcast limits are configured precisely, such relatively simple problems such as a host device's "flapping" into and out of service, with its attendant ARP and other requests, can cause problems on the IRB-based network.

A simple, low-cost CPE device can be used for IRB, either an internal or external ATU-R requiring minimal configuration. However, post-delivery CPE management is very limited without extra configuration, which is optional. On the other hand, this might be the desired business model: providing low-cost CPE devices and replacing rather than repairing them in the event of problems. MAC-layer encapsulation in AAL5 is the most common IRB technique.

RFC 2684 bridging has no security validation, meaning that there is no inherent login with password verification, and certainly no encryption. That is, bridging in its original form is either on or off.

IRB Protocol Stack

As shown in Figure 3-5, bridge protocol data units (BPDUs) are sent to the ATU-R's AAL5 layer, where an AAL5 SNAP header and a trailer are attached. The trailer indicates the end of the original IP packet. The resulting data unit is segmented into 48-byte cells by the AAL5 layer and is passed to the ATM layer, where the 5-byte ATM header is added to each cell. As you read in the introductory section of this chapter, the ATM cells are formed into DMT frames (the prevailing DSL modulation) by the ATU-R and are forwarded via DSL to the DSLAM or IP/DSL Switch.

Figure 3-5   *RFC 2684 Bridging Protocol Stack, Used in IRB and RBE*

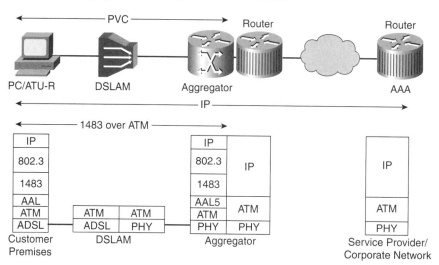

The central office DSL device receives the DSL frame and unpacks the ATM cells. If this device is a Layer 2 multiplexer, a DSLAM, it forwards the ATM cells to the L3-enabled aggregator. If the receiving CO device is an IP DSL Switch, Layer 3 capabilities are onboard, and the following step can be carried out inside the IP DSL Switch itself. The bridged PDUs are terminated, and the IP packet is then routed from the L3-enabled aggregation to the destination.

The maximum transmission unit (MTU) and maximum receive unit (MRU) sizes cannot exceed 1492 bytes, unlike the 1500+-byte size that is acceptable for routing solutions such as PPPoA.

IRB Connectivity

IRB is configured on the aggregator, which uses a Bridged Virtual Interface (BVI). This is a routable interface to a bridge group of multiple Ethernets in the DSL network. The BVI receives the bridged packets and determines whether to bridge to other ports in the same bridge group or to route to other destinations. IRB can reference up to 255 bridge groups. Spanning tree is enabled on all bridged interfaces to avoid loops.

IP Addressing in IRB

In IRB, the ATU-R acts as a bridge. The ATU-R does not require an IP address, so IP addressing options depend mainly on the provider's business model. If post-deployment ATU-R management is desired for troubleshooting, the CPE must be assigned an IP address. This is seldom the case, though, because the main benefit of IRB is low-cost modems that may be deployed at or below cost as part of the original network rollout and that are designed to just be replaced in the case of failure.

If IP addressing is used, addresses can be either supplied dynamically through DHCP or RADIUS or applied statically. In either case, the addresses may be either registered or private addresses. The DHCP server must be somewhere else besides the ATU-R. DHCP services can be on the L3 concentrator or on any router or DHCP server in the service provider network. Static addressing for the user's PC requires either a truck roll by the service provider or enabling and directing the subscriber to configure a unique IP address on the PC. This solution is another contradiction to the IRB advantage of *deploy-and-dispose* modems.

Advantages and Disadvantages of IRB

IRB advantages include the following:

- The main advantage of IRB is that it works with all existing DSL modems and may be applied with very simple modems.

- IRB may be easily migrated to PPPoE, which is a much more scalable and secure architecture, with the same, simple, bridged modems.

- IRB allows multiple RBE sessions per VC, meaning that multiple PCs can share a single DSL line.

Disadvantages of IRB are as follows:

- All hosts on point-to-multipoint interfaces receive broadcast and multicast traffic.

- IRB overhead traffic decreases the availability of route processing on some Layer 3 aggregator devices.

- There is no inherent accounting, so another technology must be used for accounting. (You will learn about one such technology, called Service Selection Gateway [SSG], in Chapter 5, "Security: AAA/SSG/RADIUS.")

- To support virtual private networks (VPNs), the service provider can have a dedicated bridge group per VPN. The service provider must ensure that routing is restricted between VPNs, either by access lists or policy routing.

- IRB, based on RFC 2684, is susceptible to broadcast storms and possible denial of service (DoS) attacks.

- The ATU-R modem is in bridging mode, so DHCP cannot be run locally.

- There is no remote management of ATU-R, because no IP address is present, absent advanced configuration, which contradicts IRB's inherent simplicity and its low-cost equipment needs.

IRB Implementation Considerations

In the future, IRB will be found only in legacy networks, where lower-cost modems are desired, or where lower-cost modems are already in place without resources to upgrade the installed user base. Provider network scalability is limited, as is user network scalability. No user authentication is possible. Scalability and security are the main drivers for migration from IRB to a more capable architecture, such as PPPoE.

IRB Summary

IRB is the simplest, least-scalable, least-secure, and lowest-cost DSL architecture. Its limits mean that IRB is found only in older networks. But the understanding of those limits informs the selection of upgraded architecture.

Routed Bridge Encapsulation (RBE)

This section describes the end-to-end ADSL architecture using RBE. This RFC 2684-based technique preserves the simplicity and lowest cost of IRB, including the existing legacy remote modem deployment. It adds the benefits of Layer 3 functionality. Although RBE has its own disadvantages, it is still preferable to IRB.

Service providers are opting for RFC 2684 bridging using RBE or are moving toward PPPoA or PPPoE, which are highly scalable and very secure, although more complex and difficult to implement. RBE can use the existing IRB CPE that would otherwise be too expensive and time-consuming to replace, and migration from IRB is transparent to the end user, requiring no changes to the ATU-R configurations. Even on the aggregator, RBE uses almost identical Cisco IOS configuration of AAL5 SNAP as RFC 2684 bridging. Figure 3-6 shows the general topology of a sample DSL network with RBE. IRB runs each packet through the bridging forwarding path and, when appropriate, the routing forwarding path. In other words, it requires a Layer 2 and a Layer 3 lookup. In contrast, RBE assumes that the packet is to be routed and runs the packet through the routing path only. This eliminates the need for BVIs and bridge groups, even though the subscriber side is bridged, because the router assumes that each interface is routed. Without bridge groups in an RBE network, there are no bridge-group scalability limits. Additionally, no spanning-tree algorithm is necessary because of Layer 3 control.

Another performance advantage of RBE is support for Cisco Express Forwarding (CEF), introduced in Cisco IOS Software Release 12.1(5)T.

Figure 3-6   *RBE Topology*

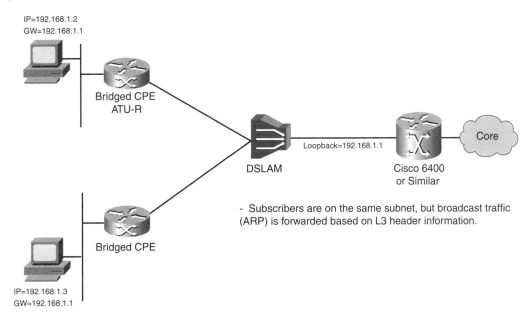

RBE overcomes the broadcast issues of IRB partially by using point-to-point ATM inter-faces. The ATM point-to-point subinterfaces can be numbered interfaces or unnumbered to other interfaces. The number of supported interfaces is based on VC limits for hardware and software on the aggregator. Numbered interfaces mean one subnet per interface, which consumes IP addresses. This can be remedied with unnumbered interfaces. Unnumbered interfaces allow multiple CPEs using the same (unnumbered) interface to be on the same subnet. DHCP is presently supported on unnumbered interfaces.

Without DHCP (which is fully available for use by RBE), each customer must have a static route. DHCP does permit some extra, configurable security for RBE: With identification of the preaggregation permanent virtual circuit (PVC) by the DSL aggregators, you can use that to give an IP address (or not!). This address can still be a static address, because it is just distributed over DHCP.

Knowledge of the PVC lends itself to another localized security aid. Each incoming ATM VC (each client) could have an access control list assigned to it, which makes sure that only the IP address coming from that ATM VC is permitted to route out the gateway VC.

A further answer to IRB's broadcast issues is configuring proxy ARP on the aggregation device to limit where broadcasts are directed. Proxy ARP is a variation of ARP, the Internet protocol that handles requests for connectivity information in an IRB-based setup. ARP maps a Layer 3 IP address to a Layer 2 MAC address.

When using proxy ARP, the aggregation device in the POP sends an ARP response on behalf of an end device (the DSL CPE) to the requesting host. Rather than making all customer devices receive a request for connectivity information, proxy ARP acts on the end device's behalf and looks up the connectivity information in its local ARP table.

Connectivity information is no longer broadcast throughout an entire bridge group. Instead, each ARP request and response is transmitted only between the CPE and the POP across a virtual circuit.

The elimination of broadcasts also reduces bandwidth use on the access links and extra resource consumption in the headend router. From a network security standpoint, address information is no longer transmitted to other DSL users, so they do not have access to, and thus cannot imitate, outside IP addresses.

RBE Protocol Stack

RBE makes use of the same protocols in the same order as IRB, because both use RFC 2684 protocol mapping. The subscriber side contains an Ethernet-WAN bridge, and RBE is used to terminate the RFC 2684 bridged connection at the aggregation router.

The user packets are first placed inside a Logical Link Control/Subnetwork Access Protocol (LLC/SNAP) frame. The LLC/SNAP layer adds a frame header to identify the type of packet carried (bridged Ethernet, IP, IPX, and so on).

After the LLC/SNAP frame has been assembled, the PDU moves down to AAL5 to gain a trailer, and the ATM cells are eventually transmitted via DSL, as you learned in the previous IRB section.

The central office DSL device receives the DSL frame and unpacks the ATM cells. If this device is a Layer 2 multiplexer, a DSLAM, it forwards the ATM cells to the L3-enabled aggregator. If the receiving CO device is an IP DSL Switch, Layer 3 capabilities are onboard, and the next (and last) two stages are carried out inside the IP DSL Switch itself.

The aggregation router then reassembles the ATM cells into the bridged frame. Last, the Cisco 6400 or a similar device routes the bridged traffic to the appropriate destinations.

NOTE   Connectivity for RBE is exactly the same as for IRB, so that information is not repeated here.

IP Addressing in RBE

IP addressing for the user PC in RBE is exactly the same as for IRB. It may use either static address assignments or DHCP. DHCP may be implemented through virtual templates on the L3 device, although this is not the only way to implement DHCP, nor are virtual templates required for RBE. As discussed in this chapter's introduction to IP addressing, virtual templates are software definitions that are applied to multiple ATM connections. They contain such options as the range of IP addresses to be handed out to RBE-connected DSL devices, as well as in IRB and PPPoE.

In RBE, a single virtual circuit is allocated a route, a set of routes, or a subnet. The trusted environment is reduced to only the single customer premises represented by either the IP addresses in the set of routes or the addresses in the subnet. The ISP also controls the addresses assigned to the user. This is done by configuring a subnet on the subinterface to that user. Therefore, if a user misconfigures equipment with an IP address outside the allocated address range (possibly causing ARP packets to flow up to the router), the router generates a *wrong cable* error and refuses to enter the erroneous IP-to-MAC address mapping into its ARP table. Otherwise, SP/ISPs that provide a full subnet for more than one subscriber should know that one user can assign the wrong address to a PC or Ethernet-attached device, such as a printer, and cause connection problems for another user.

Some service providers/ISPs provide private IP addresses to their subscribers. They must then perform NAT at the service destination router.

It is possible for an SP/ISP to restrict the number of PCs that can access the service at one time. Configuring the maximum users on the Ethernet interface restricts the number of PCs that can access the service.

However, this method has a flaw. If three PCs are configured to use the service, and one of the subscribers adds a network printer (which has its own MAC address) during a time when one of the PCs is idle, the PC's MAC address disappears from the CPE's ARP entry.

If the printer becomes active while a PC is idle, the printer's MAC address is entered into the ARP entry. When a user decides to use this PC to access the Internet, it is unavailable, because the CPE already has allowed three MAC entries. The strategy of limiting users on the CPE can be used, but care should be taken in fixing the numbers.

Advantages and Disadvantages of RBE

RBE is an especially good solution for integrating one or more legacy bridging networks with less-complex DSL CPE. In these cases, it offers an interim standardization before growing to PPPoE or PPPoA.

As end users become more educated and more concerned with security issues, and as security threats become more widespread, the service provider can avoid IP hijacking, ARP spoofing, and broadcast storms with RBE.

Other advantages of RBE include the following:

- It supports existing (legacy) bridged ATU-R devices and works with all existing DSL modems. RBE offers advanced services such as SSG, which you will read about in Chapter 5. Advanced services mean that network access providers/network service providers (NAPs/NSPs) can provide secure access to corporate gateways without managing end-to-end PVCs using Layer 3 routing or Layer 2 Forwarding/Layer 2 Tunneling Protocol (L2F/L2TP) tunnels. In other words, RBE is available for use with L2TP, as are PPPoA and PPPoE. Hence, service providers can scale their business models for selling wholesale services.

- RBE allows multiple RBE sessions per VC, meaning that multiple PCs can share a single DSL line.

The primary disadvantage of RBE is that the ATU-R does not issue a DHCP or IPCP request for an IP address when it is configured in bridging mode. This means that there will never be remote management of ATU-R, because the ATU-R has no IP address. On the other hand, as discussed previously for IRB, perhaps the provider's business model does not call for remote management and troubleshooting of the deployed modem, so this RBE limitation might not be a disadvantage.

RBE Summary

As with PPPoE, RBE's availability for legacy or low-cost bridging modems is its biggest advantage. RBE does not offer PPPoE's subscriber security, but RBE certainly closes some IRB security holes. Unlike PPPoE, RBE does not require any host CPE software (PPPoE client software) such as that required by PPPoE.

Point-to-Point Protocol Over Ethernet (PPPoE)

This section describes implementing an end-to-end ADSL architecture using PPPoE. PPPoE has gained popularity around the world because it offers intelligent capabilities comparable in some aspects to Layer 3 functionality, such as security, while providing an easy migration from simple bridging, even using the same simple DSL modems in many cases.

It's important that you can identify the protocols used for PPPoE. As in the other sections of this chapter, you will see the advantages and disadvantages of PPPoE.

PPPoE Overview

PPPoE is its own protocol, not just PPP encapsulated in an Ethernet frame. In general, PPPoE has a few of PPPoA's attributes, such as security authentication, but it is much more like bridging. For instance, PPPoE uses almost identical Cisco IOS configuration of AAL5 SNAP as RFC 2684 bridging.

PPPoE requires either PPPoE client software on the user PC or inherent PPPoE client capability at the ATU-R. The PPPoE software client must comply with RFC 2516 (the PPPoE RFC). In the case of simple bridging CPE, this software must be installed on each PC on the subscriber side. More-robust ATU-R devices such as the Cisco 827 can be configured directly as the PPPoE client, meaning that the host device (PC) is not configured with the PPPoE client software.

For the PC (or other host computers, such as a Macintosh or UNIX/Linux workstation), PPP client software is available to match the host, such as Windows PPPoE Client Software Application (WINPoET) or Enternet.

When client software is used, PPPoE allows a PPP session encapsulated in an Ethernet frame from the user PC PPPoE client software to be bridged through a simple bridging device such as a low-cost ATU-R. The ATU-R acts as an Ethernet-to-WAN bridge. The PPP session from the user PC is transported over Ethernet to the ATU-R and then from the ATU-R over the ADSL connection as ATM cells. The PPP session can be terminated at either a local exchange carrier central office or an ISP point of presence. The termination device is an aggregator such as the Cisco 6400 UAC, or it can be a Layer 3 IP-enabled IP DSL Switch, as shown in Figure 3-7.

Figure 3-7   *PPPoE Session*

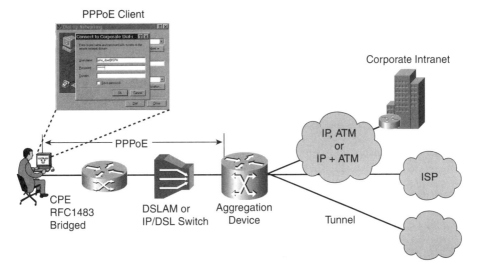

PPPoE Protocol Stack

The PPP packet includes the LCP as well as the user traffic. LCP negotiates link parameters such as packet size and type of authentication. Overall, the LCP establishes, configures, tests, maintains, and terminates the data-link connection to ensure that the line quality is suitable for the transmission of Layer 3 routed protocols, such as Internet Protocol (IP) and Internetwork Packet Exchange (IPX).

One vital function of the LCP is authentication. If specified by the configuration, authentication must take place before the network-layer protocol phase.

LCP procedures include loopback detection to ensure that the interface is indeed communicating with an interface other than itself. Loopback detection makes use of onboard clock-generated random numbers called *magic numbers*. These 32-bit numbers always match when there is only one endpoint. There is a slight chance that these randomly-generated numbers might be matched from two different endpoints. To lessen this chance, several magic numbers may be sent in one block, and/or the request acknowledgment from the endpoint can be sent specifying a different magic number value. If the two magic numbers are the same, LCP brings the link down and up again to renegotiate the magic numbers.

Another function of LCP is to negotiate the MRU. This size depends on the architecture, especially RFC 2684-based IRB and RBE and RFC 2516-based PPPoE. For PPPoE, the MTU and MRU sizes cannot exceed 1492 bytes, unlike the 1500+-byte size that is acceptable for routing solutions such as PPPoA. The PPPoE header is six octets, and the PPP PID is two octets. If neither peer changes the default, this option is not negotiated. This configuration option may be sent to inform the peer that the implementation can receive larger packets or to request that the peer send smaller packets. The peer is not required to take advantage of the limit. For example, when a negotiated MRU is indicated as 2048 octets, the peer is not required to send any packet with 2048 octets.

PPPoE Connectivity

PPPoE connectivity is similar to PPP in dial mode. Because PPPoE is based on the dial model, it requires the subscriber to enter a username and password every time for service connection to the L3 device. This is done via the PPPoE client software installed on the host or through the PPPoE configuration on the Cisco 827.

The opening connections for PPPoE connectivity are shown in Figure 3-8.

Figure 3-8   *PPPoE Connectivity*

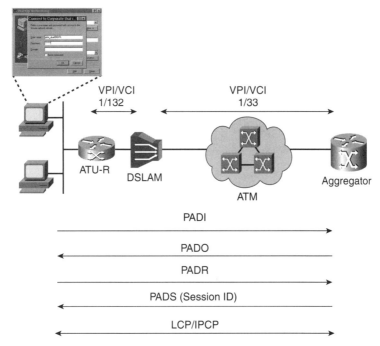

RFC 2516 defines four steps in the PPPoE discovery stage. When discovery is complete, both peers know the PPPoE session ID and the peer's Ethernet address, which together uniquely define the PPPoE session. The steps are as follows:

Step 1   The host broadcasts an initiation packet. The host sends the PPPoE Active Discovery Initiation (PADI) packet with the destination_MAC address set to the broadcast address. The PADI consists of one tag indicating what service type it is requesting.

Step 2   When one or more access concentrators or routers receives a PADI it can serve, it replies by sending a PPPoE Active Discovery Offer (PADO) packet. The destination_MAC address is the unicast address of the host that sent the PADI. If the access concentrator cannot serve the PADI, it must not respond with a PADO. Because the PADI was broadcast, the host may receive more than one PADO.

Step 3   The host sends a unicast session request packet (PADR). The host looks through the PADO packets it receives and chooses one. The choice can be based on the services offered by each access concentrator. The host then sends one PPPoE Active Discovery Request (PADR) packet to the access concentrator it has chosen. The destination_MAC address field is set to the unicast Ethernet address of the access concentrator or the router that sent the PADO.

Step 4   The selected access concentrator or router sends a confirmation packet (PADS). When the access concentrator receives a PADR packet, it prepares to begin a PPP session. It generates a unique session ID for the PPPoE session and replies to the host with a PPPoE Active Discovery Session confirmation (PADS) packet. The destination_MAC address field is the unicast Ethernet address of the host that sent the PADR.

As soon as the PPPoE session begins, PPP data is sent as in any other ATM encapsulation. All Ethernet packets are unicast.

A PPPoE Active Discovery Terminate (PADT) packet may be sent by either the host or the access concentrator any time after a session is established to indicate that a PPPoE session has been terminated.

Multiple PPPoE sessions can run on a single virtual channel because each PPPoE session carries its own session ID. The maximum number of sessions supported per VC might be in the tens of thousands, depending on the L3 aggregator device, although manufacturers and service providers generally decrease the maximum due to memory and software degradation and security concerns. For instance, in the Cisco world, the default number is only 100 sessions per VC to avoid DoS attacks, when the network could be overwhelmed by an ungoverned number of sessions attempted. Even this number is usually adjusted downward significantly.

Host routes pointing back to the PPPoE client on the user PC are installed during PPP negotiation on the aggregator, and it is over these host routes that the packets are forwarded to the user PC from the aggregator. The aggregation router could be an IP DSL Switch or a universal concentrator if Layer 2 DSLAMs are used instead of IP DSL Switches.

NOTE   Subinterfaces on the aggregator are configured for PPPoE and must be bound to a virtual template interface. As noted earlier, a *virtual template* is a virtual interface with all the interface characteristics of a physical interface. It is assigned a unique network IP address. IP addresses may be conserved by sharing a recognized address with a physical interface using an unnumbered interface. The IP address pool is identified that will be used to hand out an IP address to the PCs during PPP startup. You will learn to configure virtual templates in Chapter 6, "Cisco IOS Configurations."

The entire data unit is then sent to the ATU-R's AAL5 layer, where a trailer is attached, indicating the end of the original IP packet. The AAL5 layer segments the resulting data unit into 48-byte cells, and then it is passed to the ATM layer, where the 5-byte ATM header is added to each cell. The ATU-R forms the ATM cells into DMT frames (the prevailing DSL modulation) and forwards them via DSL to the DSLAM or IP/DSL Switch.

The central office DSL device receives the DSL frame and unpacks the ATM cells. If this device is a Layer 2 multiplexer, a DSLAM, it forwards the ATM cells to the L3-enabled aggregator. If the receiving CO device is an IP DSL Switch, Layer 3 capabilities are onboard, and the following step is carried out inside the IP DSL Switch itself.

The Layer 3 device, whether IP/DSL Switch or aggregator, typically refers to a RADIUS server to authenticate and authorize the user, although this can be done within the L3 device itself.

IP Addressing in PPPoE

One of the major configuration issues when setting up a PPPoE connection is IP addressing. The user's PC requires an IP address regardless of whether PPPoE client software is installed. If client software is not installed, and the Cisco 827 DSL router is used as the PPPoE termination for DSL, the PC and the 827 both need IP addresses. As with other DSL architectures, addresses may be either private or registered IP addresses. The IP addresses can be either supplied dynamically through IPCP or DHCP or applied statically. DHCP can be implemented on the Cisco 827 to allocate IP addresses to the client devices, such as multiple PCs on the user LAN.

If the subscriber has only Internet access from the NSP, the NSP terminates those PPP sessions from the subscriber and assigns an IP address. This is usually accomplished by referencing a named pool with dynamic addresses, such as on the virtual template, from which the IP address is assigned. In any case, the Ethernet NIC on the PC does not need an IP address to start the PPPoE session.

The PPP sessions can also be tunneled (using L2TP) from the aggregator to the final destination or home gateway router, which eventually terminates the PPP sessions, at which point dynamic address allocation is possible. Static addresses are also possible in tunneling as long as the final destination has allocated those IP addresses and has a route to them.

Advantages and Disadvantages of PPPoE

In general, PPPoE does not suffer from the added costs and increased deployment complexity inherent in PPPoA. Specifically, PPPoE needs only minimal configuration on the ATU-R. For a dedicated ATU-R, no extra configuration might be required.

The most negative issue going against PPPoE as the sole architecture for broadband services is the use of lower-cost, less-robust CPE, but PPPoE requires third-party client software on the host PC.

On the other hand, this can also be one of PPPoE's strengths, because it allows ISPs and competitive local exchange carriers (CLECs) to brand and control their service in a way that otherwise would not be possible, starting with strict accounting of connections and IP addresses. Because they do not own the infrastructure or control the CPE, the only way these companies can deliver consistent services is through the software they control and provide to customers.

In addition, well-designed third-party PPPoE client software can provide operational benefits to both the subscriber and the service provider. Among these benefits are network management and diagnostic capabilities that can identify operational problems and automatically offer resolutions. This data, available to help-desk staff, can also dramatically reduce the time it takes to resolve the problems of customers who call for assistance.

Other advantages of PPPoE include the following:

- It supports existing (legacy) bridged ATU-R devices and works with all existing DSL modems while offering advanced services such as SSG or tunneling. Advanced services mean that NAPs/NSPs can provide secure access to corporate gateways without managing end-to-end PVCs, using Layer 3 routing or L2F/L2TP tunnels. Hence, service providers can scale their business models for selling wholesale services.

- PPPoE allows multiple PPPoE sessions per VC, meaning that multiple PCs can share a single DSL.

- PPP enables per-session AAA. Per-session accounting allows the service provider to charge the subscriber based on session time for various services offered. Per-session authentication is based on PAP or CHAP. Authentication overcomes the security limitation in a bridging architecture. One outcome of per-session authentication is individualized troubleshooting. The NSP can easily identify which subscribers are on or off based on active PPP sessions rather than troubleshooting entire groups, as is the case with bridging architecture.

- Last but not least among PPPoE's advantages, the NSP can oversubscribe by deploying idle and session timeouts using an industry-standard RADIUS server for each subscriber.

Disadvantages of PPPoE include the following:

- The service provider must maintain a database of usernames and passwords for all subscribers, because currently there is no support for authentication based on the ATM connection itself (VPI/VCI).

NOTE   If tunnels or proxy services are used, the authentication can be done on the basis of the domain name, and the user authentication is done at the corporate gateway. (This reduces the size of the database that the service provider has to maintain.) You will learn more about tunnels later in this chapter and in Chapter 6's configuration instructions.

- For low-cost, simple DSL modems that cannot be configured as the PPPoE client, PPPoE client software must be installed on all hosts (PCs) connected to the Ethernet segment. This means that the access provider must bear at least partial responsibility for the ATU-R and/or the client software on the PC. Partial responsibility can include delivery and installation, or at least testing and specification of the client software, as well as providing adequate information to the end user to maintain the host software.

- Because PPPoE implementation uses RFC 2684 bridging, it is susceptible to broadcast storms and possible DoS attacks.

- The ATU-R modem is in bridging mode, so DHCP cannot be run locally.

- There is no remote management of ATU-R, because no IP address is present.

- The last disadvantage of PPPoE is relatively minor for modern, highly efficient aggregators: Point-to-point subinterfaces require more router CPU resources (cycles).

To conclude the advantages and disadvantages of PPPoE, you should consider the use of NAT and PAT, which are available in PPPoE. On the one hand, NAT/PAT offer almost infinite expansion of user LANs without support and additional configuration by the provider. This same user LAN growth is invisible to the provider, meaning that licensing of additional users is not supported and the provider cannot accurately calculate bandwidth needs. Therefore, NAT/PAT must be considered as part of the overall business model before their use can be judged an advantage or disadvantage.

PPPoE Implementation Considerations

PPPoE is a good solution in the following scenarios:

- When multiple PPP sessions per PVC are desired, especially if per-user authentication is needed

- When dynamic L2 service selection is desired

- When a lower-cost modem is desired or is already in place without resources to upgrade the installed user base and/or authentication and accounting are desired

There are not any realistically prohibitive scenarios for PPPoE, which is why it is the world's most commonly deployed DSL architecture.

PPPoE Summary

PPPoE is the architecture of choice for many service providers because it is highly scalable for both the provider and the end users, and it provides user authentication.

Point-to-Point Protocol Over ATM (PPPoA)

This section describes the encapsulations, data flow, IP addressing considerations, and design considerations required for implementing an end-to-end ADSL architecture using PPPoA. PPPoA has created high interest and is gaining service provider popularity. It will form a larger portion of future ADSL deployments.

PPPoA Overview

PPP is defined in RFCs 1331 and 1661 as a standard method of encapsulating different types of higher-layer protocol datagrams across point-to-point connections. It extends the high-level data link control (HDLC) packet structure with a 16-bit protocol identifier that contains information about the packet's contents.

PPP is defined for use specifically with AAL5 in RFC 2364. PPPoA operates in either of two modes—LLC/SNAP or Virtual Circuit-multiplexing (VC-mux).

In the PPPoA model, as shown in Figure 3-9, the ATU-R encapsulates user data (PDUs) of various types in PPP frames. With PPPoA, the PPP session is between the ATU-R and the aggregation router; the PPP link is terminated at the provider's aggregation router.

Figure 3-9   *PPPoA at a Glance*

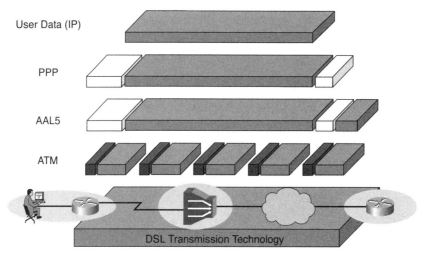

This Layer 3 aggregation router typically refers to a RADIUS server used to authenticate and authorize the user, although this can be done within the L3 device itself. Host routes are installed during PPP negotiation on both the ATU-R and the aggregator, and it is over these routes that the packets are forwarded. The aggregation router can be an IP DSL Switch or a universal concentrator if Layer 2 DSLAMs are used instead of IP DSL

Switches. Subinterfaces on the aggregator are configured for PPP and must be bound to a virtual template interface.

Depending on the capabilities of the particular ATU-R model and software, the ATU-R can receive its IP address from the aggregation router via IPCP. It can be configured as the DHCP server for the subscriber PCs, and it can be configured to perform NAT/PAT if private addressing is used for the subscriber PC.

PPPoA Protocols

The PPP packet includes two vital protocols as well as the user traffic—LCP and one of several types of NCPs. The LCP establishes, configures, tests, maintains, and terminates the data-link connection to ensure that the line quality is suitable for transmitting L3 protocols. A second protocol used by PPP is one of several types of NCPs. This comes into use after the data link is established by the LCP. NCP establishes and configures the applicable network-layer protocols, because PPP is designed to allow the simultaneous use of multiple network layer protocols. The NCP contains information about the higher-layer protocols, including IP and IPX. For example, the PPP NCP for IP is IPCP.

PPPoA Protocol Stack

The general PPPoA protocol stack is shown in Figure 3-10.

Figure 3-10 *PPPoA Protocol Stack*

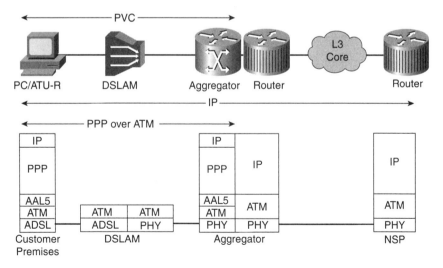

Starting from the user's point of view, the PC transmits an Ethernet frame that carries an IP packet. The ATU-R receives the Ethernet frame, removes the Ethernet header and trailer, and adds a PPP header. In addition to the user data, the ATU-R includes specific PPP information, such as security parameters for transport across the ADSL loop and the DSLAM.

If the CO DSL termination point is a Layer 2 multiplexer, a DSLAM, it forwards the ATM cells to the L3-enabled aggregator. If the receiving CO device is an IP DSL Switch, Layer 3 capabilities are onboard, and the following step is carried out inside the IP DSL Switch itself.

The L3 device reassembles the ATM cells into the AAL5 PDU format in the SAR process. The device then verifies and removes the AAL5 trailer, followed by verifying and removing the PPP header. Now that the data is back in IP packet form, the L3 device (IP DSL Switch or aggregator) routes the IP packet to its destination. In some cases, this might mean reconverting the IP packet to ATM cells for transmission over an ATM network, which is carried out through the same device's SAR process again.

IP Addressing in PPPoA

The user's PC and the ATU-R both require IP addresses. These addresses can be either supplied dynamically through DHCP and IPCP or applied statically.

In the PPPoA architecture, IP address allocation for the subscriber DSL modem uses IPCP negotiation, the same principle of PPP in dial mode. IP addresses are allocated depending on the type of service a subscriber uses. If the subscriber has only Internet access from the NSP, the NSP terminates those PPP sessions from the subscriber and assigns an IP address. The options for the user's PC IP address include dynamic and static addressing. IP addresses may be dynamically allocated either from a locally defined DHCP pool on the ATU-R or from the RADIUS server in the central office/exchange.

For static addressing, the service provider might provide a set of static IP addresses to the subscriber (and ATU-R) and might not assign IP addresses dynamically when the subscriber initiates the PPP session. In this scenario, the service provider uses the RADIUS function only to authenticate the user.

The PPP sessions can also be tunneled (using L2TP) from the aggregator to the final destination or home gateway router, which eventually terminates the PPP sessions. The final destination or home gateway router negotiates IPCP and can provide an IP address dynamically to the ATU-R. Static addresses are also possible in tunneling as long as the final destination has allocated those IP addresses and has a route to them.

The PC may obtain an address through DHCP from the ATU-R. This requires a DHCP address pool configured on the ATU-R. Also, the ATU-R must be configured either for DHCP relay as an intermediary between the PC and the service provider's DHCP server or as a DHCP server of its own. Either DHCP designation can be combined with NAT/PAT on the ATU-R for the subscriber PC with PPPoA.

When the ATU-R is configured for AAL5SNAP, as in bridging and PPPoE, one PVC can be used to carry multiple protocols, such as combining IP and IPX. If the AAL5MUX configuration is used, as in PPPoA, each PVC is dedicated to a single protocol, such as only IP or IPX.

Advantages and Disadvantages of PPPoA

The advantages of PPPoA are as follows:

- The architecture inherits most of the advantages of PPP used in the dial model.

- A PPPoA implementation involves configuring the ATU-R with PPP authentication information (login and password). This is a major advantage of PPPoA over simpler bridging implementations such as IRB and RBE, which have no security. That is, PPP enables per-session AAA. Per-session AAA allows the service provider to charge the subscriber based on session time for various services offered.

- IP address conservation at the DSL modem allows the service provider to assign only one IP address per subscription. When the ATU-R is configured for NAT, all users behind that ATU-R can use a single IP address to reach different destinations. IP management overhead for the NAP/NSP for each individual user is reduced while conserving IP addresses.

- NAPs/NSPs provide secure access to corporate gateways without managing end-to-end PVCs, using Layer 3 routing or L2F/L2TP tunnels. Hence, service providers can scale their business models for selling wholesale services.

- Troubleshooting individual subscribers is another advantage of PPPoA. The NSP can easily identify which subscribers are on or off based on active PPP sessions rather than troubleshooting entire groups, as is the case with bridging architecture.

- The NSP can oversubscribe by deploying idle and session timeouts using the industry-standard RADIUS function for each subscriber.

Disadvantages of PPPoA include the following:

- The relative complexity of the routing configuration on the more-capable ATU-R for PPPoA increases both labor and hardware costs.

- PPPoA has only a single session per VC. Because the username and password are configured on the ATU-R, all users behind the DSL modem for that particular VC can use only one set of services. Users cannot randomly select different sets of services, but you can use multiple VCs and establish different PPP sessions on different VCs. Of course, using multiple VCs increases configuration complexity, further increasing labor costs and the need to train service provider support personnel.

- The service provider must maintain a database of usernames and passwords for all subscribers. If tunnels or proxy services are used, the authentication can be done on the basis of the domain name, and the user authentication is done at the corporate gateway. This reduces the size of the database that the service provider has to maintain.

- If a single IP address is provided to the CPE and NAT/PAT is implemented, certain applications, such as IPTV or others that embed IP information in the payload, will not work.

- One other disadvantage of PPPoA is relatively minor for modern, highly efficient processors: Point-to-point subinterfaces require more router CPU resources (cycles).

PPPoA Implementation Considerations

In general, PPPoA is indicated by the following factors:

- Host-based software is not desired or is impossible
- Authentication and accounting are desired
- Intelligent DSL modems are to be used
- IP address conservation is important
- End-user scalability must be allowed

Labor costs, including training, deployment, and configurations of modems and central office equipment, must be factored into the costs of any PPPoA implementation.

PPPoA Summary

PPPoA (RFC 2364) uses AAL5 as the framed protocol and supports all ATM mapping options.

PPPoA is the architecture of choice for many service providers because it is highly scalable, for both the provider and the end users, and it enables L3 functionality, including security.

Considerations for deploying PPPoA include added costs of the higher functionality.

L2TP Tunneling

Layer 2 Tunneling Protocol (L2TP) is an emerging IETF standard that combines the best features of two existing tunneling protocols: Cisco's L2F and Microsoft's Point-to-Point Tunneling Protocol (PPTP). L2TP supports multiple protocols, as well as private IP addresses, over the Internet. This section describes the components of an L2TP tunnel, identifies the encapsulations supported over an L2TP tunnel, and describes L2TP connectivity.

Using L2TP, an ISP or other access service can create a virtual tunnel to link the customer's remote sites or remote users with corporate home networks. Think of a field employee who must dial in from different remote sites and who needs direct access to her company's intranet. This employee's corporate notebook computer or other device can be configured to open a secure, transparent virtual tunnel with a minimum of login requirements. This quick, secure connection is called a *virtual private network (VPN)*.

NOTE   A VPN is a way to use a public telecommunication infrastructure, such as the Internet, to provide remote offices or individual users with secure access to their organization's network. A VPN can be contrasted with an expensive system of owned or leased lines that can be used by only one organization. A VPN works by using the shared public infrastructure while maintaining privacy through security procedures and *tunneling protocols* such as L2TP. By encrypting data at the sending end and decrypting it at the receiving end, the protocols in effect send the data through a tunnel that cannot be entered by data that is not properly encrypted. An additional level of security involves encrypting not only the data, but also the originating and receiving network addresses.

Virtual Private Dialup Networking (VPDN) is very similar to VPN. It uses the same technology used in VPNs to let remote users connect to a corporate office at a significantly reduced cost. Typically, a remote user uses a phone line to connect to a corporate office. Long distance charges accrue if the required phone call is not a local one. This expense can be avoided through the use of a VPDN. The user makes a local call to an ISP. The user's data is then encrypted and tunneled to the VPDN router at the corporate office. Special software and/or hardware is used to make this happen on the user's computer.

Traditional dialup networking services are not standardized for field employees and present their own headaches. Moreover, dialup services support only registered IP addresses, which limits the types of applications that are implemented over VPNs. L2TP supports unregistered and privately administered IP addresses over the Internet, as well as multiple routed protocols. This enables the use of the existing access infrastructure, such as modems, access servers, and ISDN terminal adapters. It also allows enterprise customers to outsource dialout support, thus reducing overhead for hardware maintenance costs and 800-number fees. It also allows them to concentrate corporate gateway resources.

VPNs provide the appearance, functionality, and usefulness of a dedicated private network within the public infrastructure. VPNs are cost-effective because users can connect to the Internet locally and tunnel back to connect to corporate resources.

As you will read elsewhere in this book, the VPN feature for MPLS allows a Cisco IOS network to deploy scalable Layer 3 VPN backbone service with private addressing, controlled access, and service-level guarantees between sites.

The ATU-R can be configured for bridging (PPPoE) or routing (PPPoA). The hosts must be configured with the tunnel destination IP address and may be configured with L2TP client software drivers, such as Microsoft's L2TP product.

L2TP Elements

L2TP is made up of the following components, which are also shown in Figure 3-11:

- **L2TP access concentrator (LAC)**—The user PC or the ATU-R connects to the LAC, which resides between the home (corporate) network and the remote user. The LAC's job is to tunnel PPP frames through the Internet to the local L2TP network server (LNS). This includes any protocol carried within PPP. From the last mile, the DSL network viewpoint, the LAC initiates incoming calls (from the remote Internet service) and receives outgoing calls (from the DSL CPE to the remote Internet service). The LAC and its counterpart, the LNS, may be the same type of device, such as a Cisco 6400 or another capable router.

- **L2TP network server (LNS)**—The LNS is the termination point for the L2TP tunnel where the home LAN is located. From the point of view of the DSL CPE, the LNS is the LAN access point where PPP frames are processed and passed to higher-layer protocols. An LNS can operate on any platform capable of PPP termination. The LNS handles the server side of the L2TP protocol, although it can initiate the outgoing call to create a tunnel. The LNS and its counterpart, the LAC, may be the same type of device, such as a Cisco 6400 or another capable router.

- **Tunnel**—A virtual pipe between the LAC and the LNS that carries multiple PPP sessions. It consists of user traffic and header information necessary to support the tunnel. The tunnel profile can be in the local router configuration or on a remote RADIUS server.

- **Session**—A single, tunneled PPP session. Also referred to as a *call*.

- **AAA**—The authentication, authorization, and accounting server used to store domain and user information. These industry-standard functions verify the user's account, validate the user's permissions, and track the actions taken and selections made, such as extended services, for each user. At the LAC, the AAA server stores domain information necessary to identify and establish the tunnel to the remote LNS. The LAC may authenticate the tunnel using either a RADIUS server or a locally defined database of usernames and passwords. At the LNS, the AAA server stores user information needed to authenticate the user to the remote LAC. In the case of PPPoE, the user logs in as user1@isp.com. For PPPoA, the ATU-R is preconfigured with this username.

Figure 3-11 *L2TP Components*

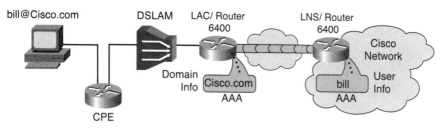

L2TP Protocol Stack and Encapsulation

The L2TP protocol stack, shown in Figure 3-12, is an extension to PPP, which is an important component of VPNs. L2TP can support either PPPoA or PPPoE encapsulation on the PVC coming from the CPE. The LAC accepts this PPP session and establishes the L2TP tunnel to the LNS. After LCP has been negotiated, the LAC partially authenticates the end user with CHAP or PAP but does not process PPP packets. User authentication is done on the LNS, where the call terminates. At the provider's site, such as the corporate home, information necessary to identify the remote LNS can be stored in the AAA server or can be entered directly into the LNS configuration.

Figure 3-12 *L2TP Protocol Stack*

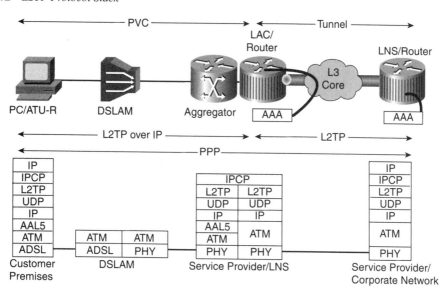

L2TP uses the User Data Protocol (UDP) as the transport layer protocol.

L2TP Connectivity

The tunnel endpoints, the LAC and the LNS, authenticate each other before any sessions are attempted within a tunnel (see Figure 3-13). Alternatively, the LNS can accept tunnel creation without any tunnel authentication by the LAC. As soon as the tunnel exists, an L2TP session is created for the end user.

Figure 3-13 *L2TP Connections*

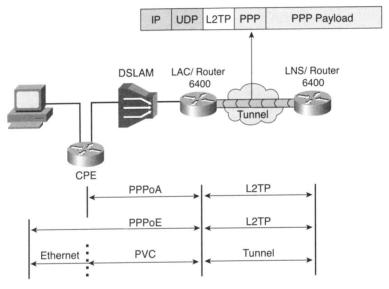

The PPP session can be terminated on a Cisco 6400 or tunneled to another L2TP network server. If the L2TP session is terminated on the Cisco 6400, you can use another form of tunnel to transport traffic to the service provider. (MPLS, which is described later, is an important form of tunnel.)

L2TP uses two types of messages—control and data. Control messages are used to establish, maintain, and clear a tunnel and to set up and clear sessions. Data messages are used to encapsulate PPP frames being carried over the tunnel.

L2TP guarantees the delivery of control messages through a control channel. Messages in the control channel have sequence numbers used to detect loss or out-of-order delivery. Lost control messages are retransmitted. Data messages may also use sequence numbers to reorder packets and detect lost packets.

Suppose that the scenario requires a VPDN, meaning that the tunnel is established through the public switched telephone network (PSTN). The VPDN connection between a remote user and the LNS using L2TP is accomplished as follows:

Step 1 The remote user initiates a PPP connection to the ISP, using the analog telephone system, such as a field employee who dials the local modem bank, or ISDN.

Step 2 The ISP network LAC accepts the connection at the service provider's Point Of Presence (POP), and the PPP link is established.

Step 3 After the subscriber-end host and the LNS negotiate LCP, the LAC partially authenticates the end user with CHAP or PAP. In DSL's implementation of VPDN, the username or domain name is used to determine whether the user is a VPDN client.

Step 4 The LAC propagates the LCP-negotiated options and the partially authenticated CHAP/PAP information to the virtual template interface on the LNS. If the options configured on the virtual template interface do not match the negotiated options with the LAC, the connection fails, and a disconnect is sent to the LAC.

Step 5 If everything is configured properly, the *username@domain*** name is used to verify that the user is a VPDN client and to provide a mapping to a specific endpoint LNS. The tunnel endpoints (LAC and LNS) authenticate each other, and the tunnel opens.

L2TP tunnels are described by identifiers that have only local significance at each end of the tunnel. The LAC and LNS ends of the tunnel have different tunnel IDs. The tunnel ID sent in each message is that of the recipient's end of the tunnel, not the sender. Tunnel IDs are selected and exchanged during the tunnel setup process. The LAC uses the tunnel ID declared by the LNS, and the LNS uses the ID declared by the LAC.

As soon as the tunnel exists, an L2TP session is created for the end user. L2TP defines that multiple PPP connections can share the same tunnel using independent sessions. L2TP sessions exist within the tunnel and also have session identifiers defined during the session setup process. Like the tunnel IDs, these session IDs also have only local significance. The session ID sent in a message is that of the recipient's side, not that of the sender's side.

The end result is that the exchange process appears to be between the dialup client and the remote LNS exclusively, as if no intermediary device (the LAC) were involved. PPP frames from remote users are accepted by the ISP's POP, encapsulated in L2TP, and forwarded over the appropriate tunnel. The customer's home gateway accepts these L2TP frames, strips the L2TP encapsulation, and processes the incoming frames.

L2TP IP Addressing

NCP negotiates what Layer 3 protocol to use. For IP you can use IPCP. During IPCP the Cisco 6400 or a similar device can dynamically assign IP addresses over PPP.

IPCP, a function of PPP, is a means by which a remote host (computer) gains an IP address when connected to the IP-based Internet. This address is used to route data to that host while the host is communicating across the Internet.

PPP/IPCP and DHCP are different methods of assigning addresses. The former method is valid only for PPPoA and PPPoE, and the latter address assignment method is valid for all DSL network architectures, including bridging. For the DHCP method, the gateway router or RADIUS server allocates the IP address to the xTU-R. The xTU-R acts as a DHCP server for the PC connected to the LAN interface.

For the host PPP session, you can use local pools, RADIUS, or Proxy RADIUS. If you are using L2TP multihop, the host gets a new IP address from the service provider during L2TP tunnel negotiations. These addresses are not routable within the service provider core.

Advantages and Disadvantages of L2TP

Advantages and disadvantages of L2TP include the following:

- L2TP is a good solution for roaming customers and combinations of remote sites. It can also be used with simple, legacy DSL CPE.

- L2TP requires one tunnel (or more) per service provider per POP. Each router, such as each node route processor on the Cisco 6400, establishes one tunnel with the service provider's LNS. This might demand more hardware. The available number of tunnels and sessions per tunnel might limit very large deployments.

- L2TP requires an IP path between the hosts and the aggregator, which adds some complexity to the initial configuration.

L2TP Summary

Tunneling provides the security and standardization of a private network, transparent to the user within the public network. The components of L2TP tunneling are the L2TP access concentrator and the L2TP network server. A tunnel is a virtual pipe between the LAC and the LNS. The tunnel and the interim sessions have identification numbers of local significance only. An AAA server can be used to store both tunnel and user attributes. L2TP can support either PPPoA or PPPoE encapsulation on the PVC coming from the CPE.

Multiprotocol Label Switching (MPLS)

VPNs provide the appearance, functionality, and usefulness of a dedicated private network. The VPN feature for MPLS allows a Cisco IOS network to deploy scalable Layer 3 VPN backbone service with private addressing, controlled access, and service-level guarantees between sites. The MPLS standard, published by the IETF, evolved from Cisco developments.

This section describes the basic premise of MPLS, identifies the elements of an MPLS-VPN network, and relates those elements to each other in terms of connectivity.

MPLS itself is a high-performance method of forwarding packets (frames) through a network. It lets routers at the edge of a network apply simple labels to packets (frames). ATM switches or existing routers in the network core can switch packets according to the labels with minimal lookup overhead. This is called *label switching*. Figure 3-14 shows generic MPLS operation.

Figure 3-14   *MPLS Operation Example*

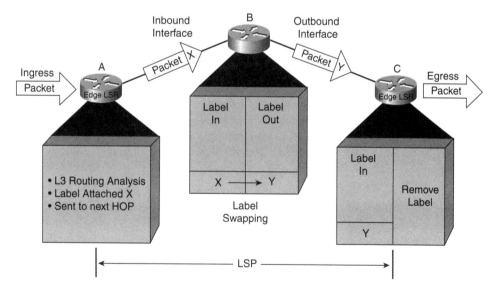

LSR = Label Switch Router
LDP = Label Distribution Protocol
LSP = Label Switch Path

To help you understand basic MPLS functionality, keep in mind the three drawbacks of traditional IP forwarding:

- Routing protocols are used on all devices to distribute the routing information.

- Regardless of the routing protocol, routers always forward packets based on the destination address only. The only exception is policy-based routing (PBR) that bypasses the destination-based routing lookup.

- Routing lookups are performed on every router. Each router in the network makes an independent decision when forwarding packets.

MPLS helps reduce the number of routing lookups, because the analysis of the Layer 3 header is done only once.

In label switching, the Layer 3 header is then mapped to a fixed-length value called a *label*. The inclusion of this label on each packet is the main feature of MPLS. The label is a 32-bit field added between the Layer 2 and Layer 3 header in the packet environment or in the VPI/VCI field in the ATM environment. At subsequent hops through each MPLS router in the network, labels are swapped and forwarding decisions are made by means of MPLS forwarding table lookup for the label carried in the packet header. Hence, the packet header does not need to be reevaluated during packet transit through the network. Because the label is of fixed length, the MPLS forwarding table lookup process is both straightforward and fast.

The label summarizes essential information about routing the packet, including its destination, VPN membership, quality of service (QoS), and traffic engineering (TE) route.

With label switching, the complete analysis of the Layer 3 header is performed only once: at the edge label switch router (LSR), which is located at each edge of the network. At the ingress LSR, the Layer 3 header is mapped to a fixed-length label. This label is removed by the egress LSR before it is passed to non-MPLS devices.

TE is enabled by MPLS. Traffic engineering allows service providers to predictably control traffic throughout the network. TE also lets the network quickly and automatically reroute traffic when failure or congestion conditions are detected. In addition, traffic engineering ensures that all available network resources are optimally used during times of failure or traffic rerouting. The result is a network that maximizes its resources and capacity during normal operation by avoiding network hot spots and areas of hyperaggregation.

Traffic engineering is also important because links between any two points in a network are relatively fixed and quantifiable, and, in many cases, the cost to increase that capacity is high. Effective traffic engineering and higher utilization of available links can provide both long- and short-term cost savings. Some service providers claim that after implementing TE mechanisms, their usable network capacity increased by as much as 40 percent. But until their networks are connection-oriented from core to edge, a capability that MPLS can provide, service providers are missing out on the full advantages that traffic engineering can offer.

Constraint-based routing and congestion-aware routing (CR) are terms used to describe networks that are fully aware of their current utilization, existing capacity, and provisioned services at all times. Traditional IP routing protocols, including Open Shortest Path First (OSPF), Intermediate System-to-Intermediate System (IS-IS), and Border Gateway Protocol (BGP), are not inherently congestion-aware and have to be modified to enable such awareness.

MPLS modifies traditional IP routing protocols to become constraint-based. This is important, because as soon as connections have been configured (either by dynamic signaling or by static provisioning), the Layer 2 and Layer 3 network becomes fully aware of the amount of bandwidth being consumed, as well as the parts of the network being used to route the connections. This information can then be propagated to the accompanying IP routing protocols that are exchanged by all IP routers, creating a truly congestion-aware view of the network and its current topology. Then, all future network requests can be directed to their destination by not only the "shortest path first" (as defined by OSPF) but also by a path that guarantees the bandwidth requirements of the IP application or service.

At each router across the network, only the label needs to be examined in the incoming cell or packet to send the cell or packet on its way across the network. The inbound interface and label indicate the matching outbound interface and outbound label. The MPLS device can then substitute the outbound label for the incoming (this is called label swapping) and forward the frame. At the other end of the network, a corresponding edge device swaps the label for the appropriate header data linked to that label.

A key result of this technology is that forwarding can be based on a single table lookup from a fixed-length label. The labels have only local significance between adjacent MPLS nodes. The adjacent label tables on each device combine to form a path through the MPLS network called a Label Switch Path (LSP). LSPs are a sequence of labels at each node along the path from the source to the destination.

MPLS Elements

The components that make up an MPLS VPN network are shown in Figure 3-15. At the edges of the network are customer edge (CE) routers. CE routers are part of the customer network and are not VPN-aware. Provider edge (PE) routers are where most VPN-specific configuration and processing occurs. PE routers receive routes from CE routers and transport them to other PE routers across a service provider MPLS backbone. In the middle of the network are provider (P) routers, or LSRs, which implement a pure Layer 3 MPLS transport service. Note that P routers in the backbone are not VPN-aware and therefore provide much more scalability. Hence, P routers do not have to carry customer routes, preventing routing tables in P routers from becoming unmanageable. VPN information is required only at PE routers, and it can be partitioned between PE routers. PE routers need to know VPN routing information only for VPNs that have direct connections.

Figure 3-15 *MPLS Components*

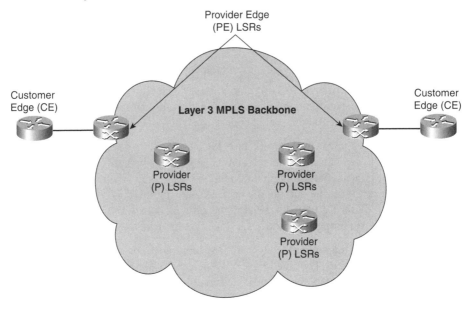

An *edge node* is an LSR connected to a non-LSR. A packet enters the MPLS network through an *ingress LSR* and leaves the network through an *egress LSR*.

The PE router connects to the CE router. A Cisco IP DSL Switch can be configured to function as a PE router in an MPLS-VPN network, and the ATU-R is the CE. PE routers exchange routing information with CE routers using static routing, Routing Information Protocol version 2 (RIPv2), OSPF, or Enhanced Interior Gateway Routing Protocol (EIGRP). Although a PE router maintains VPN routing information, it is required to maintain VPN routes for only VPNs to which it is directly attached. This design eliminates the need for PE routers to maintain all the service provider's VPN routes.

MPLS Protocols

The success of MPLS is due largely to the label distribution protocol (LDP). This protocol communicates labels and their meaning among LSRs. It assigns labels in edge and core devices to establish LSPs in conjunction with routing protocols such as OSPF, IS-IS, RIP, EIGRP, and BGP. The MPLS framework embodies a set of features enabled by the Connection-Oriented Link Layer (COLL) to maintain the predictability required for next-generation IP services.

In MPLS-VPN, a label stack is used to forward VPN data traffic. A label stack consists of two labels. The first label identifies the egress PE router, and the second label is used by the egress PE router to select which VPN/CE to forward the packet to.

An IGP routing protocol or static routing can be used to propagate routing information between the CE router and the PE router.

MPLS-VPN uses MP-BGP (multiprotocol BGP) among PE routers to facilitate customer routes (VPN routes). This is facilitated through extensions to BGP to carry addresses other than IPv4 addresses. In particular, a new address family of VPN-IPv4 address is used.

MPLS Connectivity

Each VPN is associated with one or more VPN routing/forwarding instances (VRFs). A VRF defines the VPN membership of a customer site attached to a PE router. A VRF consists of an IP routing table, a derived CEF table, a set of interfaces that use the forwarding table, and a set of rules and routing protocol parameters that control the information that is included in the routing table.

Packet forwarding information is stored in the IP routing table and the CEF table for each VRF. A separate set of routing and CEF tables is maintained for each VRF. These tables prevent information from being forwarded outside a VPN and also prevent packets that are outside a VPN from being forwarded to a router within the VPN.

During operation, the PE router exchanges routing updates with the CE router, translates the CE routing information into VPN-IPv4 routes, carries them via MP-BGP, and exchanges VPN-IPv4 routes dynamically with other MP-BGP peers (other PE routers). The accumulating and changing data is kept in a VPN routing/forwarding table. This is the set of routing information that defines a customer VPN site that is attached to a single PE router. Each PE router maintains a VRF for each of its directly connected sites. Multiple interfaces on a PE router can be associated with a single VRF if these sites all participate in the same VPN. Each VPN is mapped to a specific VRF.

MPLS Advantages and Disadvantages

Although this particular topic is beyond the scope of this DSL book, we can say that MPLS advantages such as security and interoperability outweigh the disadvantages of internetworking sophistication and personnel training costs.

MPLS Summary

MPLS optimizes VPNs, which create a private network environment within a public infrastructure. MPLS lets routers at the edge of a network apply simple labels to frames that allow routers in the network core to easily switch these frames. The label summarizes essential information about routing the packet to its destination. In MPLS, the packet header is analyzed only once at the ingress LSR.

The components of an MPLS-VPN are

- PE routers
- CE routers
- P routers

Summary

This chapter started with a discussion of common, available functionality such as security and IP addressing options. These capabilities are implemented in different ways with different protocols in the more-sophisticated architectures (or are not implemented at all in simple bridging). Building on the functionality overview, the enabling protocols were identified, and then, where present, were located in the protocol stacks and described in the connectivity discussions for each architecture. Each DSL network architecture also presented guidelines for consideration of implementation. Finally, outside the local loop DSL environment itself, virtual private networking and MPLS were described.

The following review questions allow you to test your knowledge of these architectures and their usages in the DSL world.

Review Questions

1   How is the number of required PPPoE servers determined?

   A   By determining the number of connections needed

   B   By determining how many DSLAMs are required

   C   Through the assignment of IP addresses

   D   By determining the number of subscribers supported

2   The characteristics of PPPoE most closely match the characteristics of what?

   A   Dial mode

   B   Server mode

   C   PPP mode

   D   None of the above

3   Determining whether the service provider or the final service destination is providing the IP address to the subscriber's PC is an example of what?

   A   PPPoE advantage

   B   PPPoE implementation consideration

   C   PPPoE disadvantage

   D   PPPoE application

4 Which of the following PPPoE processes is *not* the same as for PPPoA?

  A Accounting

  B Authorization

  C Authentication

  D Client configuration

5 What is an advantage of using PPPoE over IRB?

  A It provides scalability.

  B It provides security.

  C It can use simple, already-deployed DSL modems.

  D All of the above

6 PPPoE is based on which protocol?

  A SSG

  B AAL5

  C OSPF

  D None of the above

7 Which of the following is *not* part of PPP's LCP functions?

  A Link establishment and configuration

  B Link termination

  C Transmission layer protocol negotiation and configuration

  D Link layer quality consideration

8 What is a disadvantage of using RFC 2684 bridged?

  A When the CPE is in bridging mode, it is not concerned with which upper-layer protocol is being encapsulated.

  B It has no user authentication.

  C Minimal configuration of the CPE is required.

  D It has multiprotocol support for the subscriber.

9 Where could the user PC using DHCP get its IP address with RFC 2684 bridged configurations? (Select all that apply.)

   A Aggregator

   B NSP DHCP server

   C DSLAM

   D ATU-R

   E E.IP/DSL Switch

10 With RBE configured on a Cisco 6400, the interface automatically _____ data traffic.

   A Bridges

   B Routes

11 With RFC 2684 bridged, the ATM cells carry what?

   A IP packets only

   B LLC/SNAP frames

   C Ethernet frames

   D IPX packets only

12 Which of the following is an advantage of using RBE?

   A It provides QoS.

   B It has less security vulnerability than IRB.

   C Its CPE software provides traceability.

   D It provides authentication.

13 Which of the following statements about RBE is not true?

   A Spanning tree is enabled on all bridged interfaces to avoid loops.

   B The ATU-R does not require an IP address. If management is desired, the CPE must be assigned an IP address.

   C IP addresses can be provided by a DHCP server, which can be on the 6400 or any router or DHCP server in the service provider network.

   D The number of supported interfaces is based on VC limits.

14 What is the function of the CPE DSL modem in the RFC 2684 bridged architecture?

A RIP v1

B RIP v2

C Static routing

D Transparent bridge

15 Using PPPoE, what is the default setting on a virtual circuit in the Cisco world to limit DoS attacks?

A 50 sessions per VC

B 100 sessions per VC

C 500 sessions per VC

D 250 sessions per VC

16 What is an advantage of using PPPoE?

A It provides QoS

B It provides security

C None of the above

D A and B

17 Attributes that are used to authenticate the tunnel user are kept at which location in the L2TP environment?

A The LAC

B The AAA server at the LAC

C The LNS

D The AAA server at the LNS

18 What must be created on the LAC to allow it to accept an incoming tunnel request?

A Local authentication database

B VPDN group

C LNS AAA server address

D PPP login

19 Which of the following statements are true of L2TP?

   A   L2TP tunnel identifiers have network-wide significance.

   B   The LAC and LNS sides of the tunnel have different IDs.

   C   Tunnel IDs are selected and exchanged during tunnel setup.

   D   The session ID is set equal to the tunnel ID.

20 Which L2TP component usually initiates the L2TP tunnel?

   A   LNS

   B   AAA server

   C   CPE

   D   LAC

21 Which of the following statements is false?

   A   The LAC partially authenticates the end user with CHAP or PAP.

   B   The end user is authenticated on the LNS.

   C   The user's IP address is used to verify that the user is a VPDN client.

   D   End user traffic is carried in a tunnel session.

22 Which PPP protocol contains information about higher-layer protocols, including IP and IPX and their control protocols (IPCP for IP)?

   A   NCP

   B   LLC

   C   PCP

   D   NLP

23 Where are user PDUs encapsulated in PPP frames for PPPoA?

   A   At the central office

   B   At the DSLAM

   C   At the ATU-R device

   D   None of the above

24 The Ethernet frame header and trailer are transmitted from the PC to the what?

  A ATU-R

  B DSLAM

  C NSP's aggregator

  D NSP's IP DSL Switch

  E Central office

25 What is the greatest advantage of using PPPoA?

  A It has a single session per CPE on one VC.

  B It makes optimal use of Layer 3 features.

  C Using multiple VCs increases configuration complexity.

  D Authentication overcomes the lack of security present in a bridging architecture.

26 The IP address of the subscriber's PC can be provided by what? (Select all that apply.)

  A Static configuration

  B DHCP server on the ATU-R

  C DHCP server on the aggregation router

  D DHCP server on the RADIUS device

27 Determining whether the service provider or the final service destination is providing the IP address to the subscriber's CPE is an example of what?

  A PPPoA advantage

  B PPPoA implementation consideration

  C PPPoA disadvantage

  D PPPoA application

28 Which of the following is *not* one of PPP's LCP functions?

  A Link establishment and configuration

  B Link termination

  C Transmission layer protocol negotiation and configuration

  D Network layer quality consideration

29 Which of the following is a PPP NCP function?

   A Verification of magic numbers

   B Encapsulation into the PPP frame

   C Authentication

   D Identification of user data protocol

30 In MPLS, where is the analysis of the Layer 3 header performed?

   A At each node

   B At the CPE

   C At the ingress edge LSR

   D At the egress router

31 A label can be inserted where? (Select all that apply.)

   A Between the Layer 2 and Layer 3 header

   B In the AAL5 trailer

   C In the VPI/VCI field

   D In the SNAP header

32 An IP/DSL Switch can be configured as what?

   A CE

   B LSR

   C LDP

   D PE

CHAPTER 4

Cisco DSL Products

This chapter describes the various Cisco devices that can make up an end-to-end DSL network. It starts with Cisco's customer premises equipment (CPE) in the small office/home office (SOHO) market, also called small/medium enterprise (SME). The chapter continues through the central office (CO)/exchange equipment, featuring the Cisco 6000 series of DSL access multiplexers (DSLAMs)/IP-DSL switches, and includes the Cisco 6400 Universal Access Concentrator (UAC). CO-type equipment includes the compact Cisco 6015 IP-DSL switch that provides Inverse Multiplexing over ATM (IMA) for copper-connected T1/E1-intensive remote terminals as well as small COs/exchanges. Connectivity and capability "feeds and speeds" are described for each device, as well as caveats and best-use recommendations.

Upon completing this chapter, you should be able to

- Identify Cisco xDSL CPE hardware models by capability
- Identify the components of the Cisco 6000 family of IOS-based DSLAMs/IP-DSL switches
- Describe those components' functions within the xDSL system
- Interpret all Cisco 6000 series devices' status and alarm indicators
- Identify the components of the Cisco 6400 UAC
- Describe the UAC components' functions and physical connectivity

Customer Premises Equipment

Cisco CPE includes the SOHO series of DSL routers and the 820 series of business-class routers.

Cisco SOHO 70 Series (SOHO Series)

The Cisco SOHO series of DSL routers is also called the 70 series. Although you should always consult the current Cisco documentation to verify each model's characteristics, the SOHO series generally includes these parameters:

- Alcatel discrete multitone (DMT) chipset for industry interoperability
- Web-based installation
- xDSL loop analysis, providing remotely-gathered information to analyze the following:
  - Line quality and data transfer rates
  - Train speeds for upstream and downstream
  - Bit error rate
  - Margin
  - Chipset status
  - Bits per frequency bin
- Centralized administration and management:
  - Simple Network Management Protocol (SNMP)
  - Telnet
  - Local management through the router console port

The Cisco 70 series of DSL routers also provides a graphical user interface tool, the Cisco Router Web Setup (CRWS) tool, that even nontechnical users can use to set up the router. Users simply connect a PC to the router, point a web browser to the router, and then follow the simple, diagrammed instructions on the screen. For experienced network managers, the CRWS tool lets network managers enter router configuration items such as username and password, configure NAT, and turn on a stateful firewall.

The Cisco 70 series DSL routers and the CRWS tool support Cisco Easy VPN, enabling the setup of VPNs with static or dynamic IP addresses without router preconfiguration or remote-site technicians. Users in remote locations can use the graphical user interface to provide VPN configuration information, similar to using a VPN software client on a PC. After the VPN connection is set up, updated policies can be pushed to the remote offices, easing remote VPN connection management.

All Cisco routers support Cisco Configuration Express, in which routers can be shipped directly from the Cisco factory with custom configurations provided by customers when they order products from the Cisco web site (www.Cisco.com). These preconfigured routers are then shipped directly to the end-user site.

The SOHO 70 series comprises these models:

- SOHO 71
- SOHO 76
- SOHO 77 and SOHO 77H
- SOHO 78

Each of these is discussed next.

SOHO 71

The SOHO 71 router is an Ethernet-to-Ethernet router that connects to a DSL or cable modem. It permits up to five users. It allows all users in a small office to share a secure broadband connection with an integrated stateful inspection firewall. Corporate teleworkers can also take advantage of the Cisco SOHO 71 router when using VPN software clients installed on individual PCs to connect securely to a corporate network. With IPSec passthrough supported, this connection is seamless to the Cisco SOHO 71 router. (You'll learn about IPSec and other software security capabilities in the next chapter.)

SOHO 76

The SOHO 76 provides asymmetric DSL (ADSL) over Integrated Services Digital Network (ISDN), allowing it to be deployed in environments where local loops support ISDN service. This combination will continue to take advantage of service providers' ISDN investments. The SOHO 76 router allows multiple PCs to connect to the Internet simultaneously with ADSL when connected to a simple hub using Network Address Translation (NAT) to translate a single external IP address. (You'll learn about NAT in the next chapter, along with other IP address management techniques.)

SOHO 77 and SOHO 77H

The SOHO 77H and its predecessor, the SOHO 77, support ADSL, both full-rate and half-rate DMT. Although both models support multiple users on a single DSL line using a single IP address, the SOHO 77 has a single Ethernet connection. This requires multiple users to connect through a hub. The SOHO 77H integrates a four-port 10BASE-T hub. An additional external hub or switch can be cascaded from a LAN port on the SOHO 77H router, using a crossover button that determines if the device on port 1 is an active network component or a client. The integrated hub is an unmanaged hub, but Cisco IOS Software can provide detailed Ethernet statistics.

The Cisco SOHO 77H ADSL router supports the DSL Forum TR-048 specification. Interoperability had not always been achieved with DSLAMs using non-Alcatel chipsets. The Cisco SOHO 77H router now meets the DSL Forum's specifications for interoperability with

DSLAMs/IP-DSL switches that use other chipset vendors. The Cisco SOHO 77H model uses the Generation 5 chipset from Alcatel.

The SOHO 77H also supports the telecom industry-standard "dying gasp" feature, which sends an alert to the router if the box shuts down. For example, if there is power problem at the remote site, the router sends a message to the DSLAM/IP-DSL switch that it is going to be powered off.

SOHO 78

The Cisco SOHO 78 supports G.SHDSL, the worldwide standard for symmetric DSL service. It offers multiple connections through an integrated four-port Ethernet hub. An additional external hub or switch can be cascaded from the LAN port on the SOHO 78.

Cisco 820 Series Routers

The Cisco 820 series routers are designed for up to 20 users in a small office or as an enterprise telecommuting solution. They are IOS-based and can be managed with the graphical user interface CRWS. The 820 series enables PAP, CHAP, MS-CHAP, and Access Control Lists, which protect the network from unauthorized access. These security features, and others such as Secure Shell (SSH), which provides encryption for Telnet sessions, are described in the next chapter.

The Cisco 820 series also enables differentiated classes of service through quality of service (QoS) features.

The Cisco 820 series can be used to access popular European Internet services such as faxing, file transfer, and online banking. Cisco 820 series routers now include support for Common Application Programming Interface (CAPI) version 2.0, a feature required for specialized applications such as Deutsche Telecom's T-Online financial services and personal communication applications such as Symantec's WinFax Pro.

As with the Cisco 70 series, the Cisco 820 series of DSL routers also enables the web-based, graphical user interface tool known as CRWS (Cisco Router Web Setup).

Similar to the Cisco 70 series, the CRWS tool on the Cisco 820 series supports Cisco Easy VPN. This feature greatly eases remote users' installation and configuration of VPNs.

All Cisco routers support Cisco Configuration Express, allowing routers to be configured at the Cisco factory with custom configurations provided by customers when they order products from the Cisco web site (www.Cisco.com). These preconfigured routers are then shipped directly to the end-user site.

The Cisco 820 series of DSL routers comprises the following models:

- Cisco 826
- Cisco 827 and 827-4V
- Cisco 828

Cisco 826

Like the Cisco 76, the Cisco 826 provides ADSL over ISDN service (data only), allowing it to be deployed in environments where local loops support ISDN service. This combination will continue to take advantage of service providers' ISDN investments. Additionally, the Cisco 826 ADSL router supports the U-R2 specification for deployments in Deutsche Telekom's ADSL network. Another important feature of the Cisco 826 is its capability for the dying gasp message in the event of power loss, meaning that it sends a message to the central office monitoring device that it will be powering down. Connectivity for multiple users is through a single external IP address and a single ADSL connection, using NAT, when connected through a simple hub to the SOHO 76 router.

Cisco 827 and 827-4V

The Cisco 827H, with an integrated Ethernet hub, and its predecessor, the Cisco 827 with a single Ethernet port, are data-only models. The Cisco 827-4V, with four voice connections, supports Voice over IP (VoIP) and Voice over ATM (VoATM). The Cisco 827 models support the dying gasp feature.

The Cisco 827H and Cisco 827-4V support ADSL over POTS lines. All the individual models in the Cisco 820 series look very similar to each other and are labeled generically "Cisco 800 Series."

Here are other characteristics of the 827 and 827-4V models:

- The Alcatel DMT chipset supports both full-rate and half-rate DMT.
- It's interoperable with Cisco and Alcatel DSLAMs.
- It's enabled for toll-quality voice (827-4V); the four voice ports are indicated in Figure 4-1.
- It supports VoIP on four Foreign Exchange Station (FXS) interfaces.
- All four FXS ports support G.711, G.729, and G.723.1 voice codecs.
- It has voice signaling with H.323.
- It's ready for VoATM (ATM Adaptation Layer 2 [AAL2]).
- It has optional Cisco IOS firewall support.

Cisco 828

The Cisco 828 is a data-only model supporting G.SHDSL, the worldwide standard for symmetrical DSL service.

Figure 4-1 *Cisco 827-4V Rear Panel*

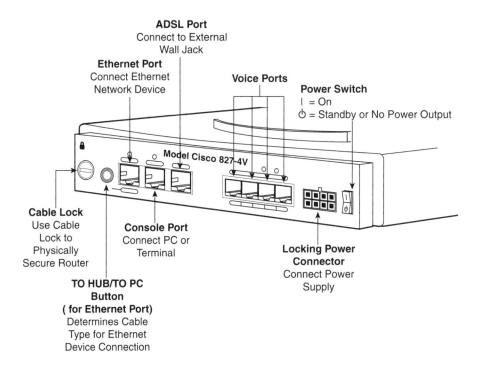

Concepts for Voice Signaling on the Cisco 827H and Cisco 827-4V

This section discusses vital concepts for voice signaling on the Cisco 827H and Cisco 827-4V, which are also valuable resources for all voice telephony.

Application-aware networking is made possible with the 827's various QoS capabilities. These ensure consistent response times for multiple applications by allocating bandwidth intelligently by classifying and prioritizing applications. The most important applications have priority use of the WAN line.

One basis for this classification and prioritization is low-latency queuing (often called LLQ or Priority Queuing Class-Based Weighted Fair Queuing [PQCBWFQ]). This lets service providers and resellers guarantee or differentiate bandwidth based on a specific application or user. For example, order-entry department traffic can be given priority over marketing department traffic, and voice traffic can be given priority over data traffic.

Another QoS feature is Resource Reservation Protocol (RSVP). This provides QoS admission control, resource reservation requests, and feedback to allow end-to-end bandwidth reservation and management.

In addition to IP QoS features, the Cisco 827H provides ATM QoS features. Per-virtual-circuit traffic shaping and queuing allow further optimization of the existing bandwidth between customers and various services. ATM QoS guarantees prioritization for real-time traffic, such as voice or video, with ATM-level shaping. It ensures that no head-of-line blocking can happen between circuits of different or equal traffic classes. (Head-of-line blocking means that in different queues, packets behind the first queue get blocked if the first one needs a resource that is busy.)

For the Cisco 827-4V, another important definition is the *Ringer Equivalence Number (REN)*. The REN is used to determine the number of devices that may be connected to the telephone company lines. Excessive RENs on the telephone line can result in the devices not ringing in response to an incoming call. Five RENs on each 827-4V port is the maximum allowed in most areas.

The Cisco 827-4V adheres to several ITU-T standards whose importance is vital to the continuing convergence of voice and data:

- G.711
- G.726 (ADPCM)
- G.729 (8 kbps)
- G.723 and G.723.1 (5.3, 6.3 kbps)
- H.323

G.711 is an audio compression standard used for digital telephones on a digital PBX/ISDN. In G.711, encoded voice is already in the correct format for digital voice delivery in the PSTN or through PBXs. G.711 uses a bandwidth of 64 kbps and is frequently chosen within enterprises or closed networks for its premium QoS. The benefit of G.711 is better audio quality, because there is no compression. *Pure* G.711-compliant devices can communicate with other G.711 devices, but not with G.723 devices. Communication between devices of different standards requires transcoding, in effect an IP-to-IP voice gateway service. A transcoding node can convert a G.711 voice stream into a low bit rate (LBR) compressed voice stream, such as G.729. This is critical for enabling applications such as integrated voice response, voice messaging, and conference calls over low-speed IP WANs. The 827 has transcoding functionality. Because G.711 uses 64 kbps, this can result in storage maintenance issues such as queuing delays.

G.723 describes a compression technique that can be used to compress speech or other audio signal components of multimedia service at a very low bit rate. This ITU-T standard coder has two bit rates associated with it—5.3 and 6.3 kbps. The higher bit rate is based on Multi-Pulse, Multi-Level Quantization (MP-MLQ) technology and has greater quality. The lower bit rate gives good quality and offers system designers additional flexibility.

G.726 ADPCM (adaptive differential pulse code modulation) encoding produces bit rates in the range of 16, 24, 32, and 40 kbps. G.726 is an LBR codec. The principal application of the 24 and 16 kbps rates is to handle temporary overloads in voice multiplexing equipment, whereas the 40 kbps is mainly intended to carry voice-band modem signals operating at data rates greater than 4.8 kbps. A reasonable assumption is that each G.726 call takes twice the resources of a G.729 call.

The G.729 codec has better bandwidth utilization and storage because it uses 8-kbps compression. This codec's LBR makes it ideal for deployments in which limited-bandwidth connections are required. This is especially important for dialup situations (for example, home access to a business). The G.729 encoded files are approximately one-eighth the size of the G.711 equivalent files. For example, a recorded message that is 1 MB in G.711 encoding is only 125 KB when recorded using G.729 encoding.

H.323 is an International Telecommunications Union (ITU) standard that describes packet-based video, audio, and data conferencing. H.323 is an umbrella standard that refers to a set of other standards (H.245, H.225.0, and Q.931) to describe its actual protocol. These contained standards include Registration, Admission, and Status (RAS), used to perform call registration, admission control, bandwidth changes, status, and disengage procedures for transmission. Basically, H.323 provides hardware-based voice compression to fit significantly more voice lines over a single copper pair without breaking the end-to-end delay budget.

The Cisco 827-4V router, with four analog voice ports, is an H.323 VoIP gateway. An H.323 gateway is an endpoint on the LAN that allows non-H.323 devices (such as analog phones and faxes) to make calls using the H.323 protocol suite. The Cisco 827 is software upgradable to VoATM (ATM AAL2).

The gatekeeper maintains a registry of devices in the multimedia network. The gatekeeper maps destination phone numbers to IP addresses, keeping track of what addresses or services are associated with a particular gateway. The devices register with the gatekeeper at startup and request admission to a call from the gatekeeper. The gatekeeper may provide other services to the H.323 terminals and gateways, such as bandwidth management and locating gateways.

Cisco H.323 version 2 upgrades Cisco IOS software to comply with the mandatory requirements and several of the optional features of the version 2 specification.

Central Office/Exchange Equipment

Central office/exchange equipment includes the IP DSL switch, the successor to the first-generation DSLAM, and the Cisco 6400 UAC.

IP DSL Switch

This section focuses on the network interface second generation (NI-2) family of IP DSL switches. This family of Cisco devices is also called the Cisco 6000 series. Before the NI-2 module's advanced functionality, the Cisco 6000 series were exclusively called DSL Access Multiplexers (DSLAMs). The NI-2 module provides FCAPS functionality (fault, configuration, accounting, performance, and security). This latest generation of DSLAMs allows Layer 3 intelligence for IP switching, as well as Layer 1 multiplexing.

In addition to management, the NI-2 card provides network uplink and downlink connectivity through the options described next. The NI-2 card allows linking of multiple peers through a technique called subtending (described later in this section), in which up to 12 other IP DSL switches share a single network uplink with fair and balanced queuing of traffic through that uplink from the linked devices.

Network connectivity includes IMA. Inverse multiplexing divides traffic from a single, large connection into carefully balanced smaller connections and then recombines the traffic onto a larger connection. As described next, IMA on the Cisco IP DSL switch makes efficient use of an existing T1/E1 infrastructure in the field, allowing the larger DSL network OC-3 or STm1 optical fiber connection to be carried over multiple T1s/E1s that are already installed.

DSL subscribers are connected directly to DSL modem cards in the DSLAM/IP-DSL switch. These DSL modem cards have varying numbers of ports, currently either four or eight ports depending on the card type. These modem cards are also called line cards, because each port on a line card terminates a single DSL subscription line, the wire pair extending to the customer premises. This termination of the wire pair is the end of the OSI Layer 1 DSL connectivity.

The Cisco 6000 series of DSLAMs/IP-DSL switches has these characteristics:

- Depending on line card port density, up to 256 DSL subscriber ports VCCs supported by a single DSLAM
- 3-Gbps point-to-point backplane
- ATM WAN interface OC-3c/STM1 (both single-mode intermediate reach and multimode fiber), DS-3/E3, or T1/E1 with IMA
- Network Equipment Building Systems (NEBS) Level 3-compliant (6015, 6160)
- European Telecommunications Standards Institute (ETSI)-compliant (6015, 6260)
- Compatible with high-density POTS splitter chassis (PSC)
- Multiprotocol Label Switching/Virtual Private Network (MPLS/VPN)
- IP Security Virtual Private Network (IPSec VPN)
- WebCache awareness to conserve WAN bandwidth and speed the user experience in web browsing
- Multicast for video entertainment and education
- Firewall for enhanced security
- ATM CoS and DSL QoS support for unspecified bit rate (UBR), available bit rate (ABR), variable bit rate real-time (VBRrt), variable bit rate nonreal-time (VBRnrt), and constant bit rate (CBR)

Suppose that your network combines voice and data over the same wire pairs. As shown in Figure 4-2, ADSL lines are brought into the CO/exchange's main distribution frame (MDF).

Figure 4-2　*IP DSL Switch System Connections*

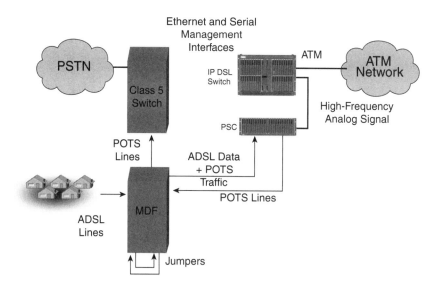

The line is then jumpered over to a cable block that runs to the PSC. The POTS signal is then split out and run back to the MDF. The ADSL signal is then connected to the ADSL modem parts within the IP DSL switch.

The PSC, provided by companies such as ADC and Corning, separates voice from ADSL signals in advance of the IP DSL switch, thereby preserving emergency calling protection (such as 911 service in the U.S.). The PSC itself is passive, requiring no power, and therefore is unaffected by power loss. Although there are still some MDF-mounted PSCs, the past few years of product development have concentrated on rack-mounted types.

Other successful network arrangements with ADSL do not require use of the PSC. The most common non-PSC architecture makes use of dedicated wire pairs for DSL signals, physically isolating data traffic from the wire pair carrying voice traffic. The DSL provider may be a separate company, or it may be just a department of the voice provider. Symmetric DSL (SDSL) service does not allow line sharing with voice service. As you read in Chapter 1's discussion of xDSL varieties, SDSL occupies all possible frequencies on the wire pair, even the low ones otherwise used by voice. Therefore, SDSL service does not require a PSC. The SDSL line cards on the IP DSL switch are called STU-Cs (Symmetric Transceiver Units-Central office). ADSL with its voice integration capability makes use of line cards also called Asymmetric Transceiver Units-Remote (ATU-Rs). Both of these card types can have eight ports, or more in the future.

Each Cisco 6160 supports up to 128 DSL modem ports (subscribers) with four-port cards and up to 256 subscribers with eight-port cards. Each Cisco 6260 supports up to 120 subscribers with four-port cards and 240 subscribers with eight-port line cards. The Cisco 6015 supports up to 24 direct subscribers with four-port line cards and 48 subscribers with eight-port cards. For ADSL with voice integration on the same wire pairs, the PSCs are generally designed to match these figures closely and to fit compactly onto the same racks as the IP DSL switches themselves.

NI-2-based systems also support *subtending*. This feature allows up to 12 other chassis to be subtended to a single host DSLAM/IP-DSL switch system, aggregating the subtended systems through a single network uplink. For implementations not fully using the ATM bus and network uplink, subtending can be used to further lower the cost per subscriber.

Subtending is accomplished through the use of WAN interfaces. In a subtending arrangement, each chassis is connected by one WAN interface to the chassis above it in the subtending hierarchy or, if it is at the top of the hierarchy, to the network trunk. Each chassis is connected by one or more WAN interfaces to those below it in the hierarchy. The distance allowed between subtended nodes is determined by the WAN interface used, whether optical fiber or coaxial cable.

The current, second generation of Cisco Smart DSLAM follows the first generation of simple DSLAMs. Today the Cisco 6000 IP DSL switch series integrates IP routing with ATM switching at the network edge.

This IP DSL switch family provides an evolution path from the first-generation DSLAM with a UBR-oriented Internet access service model to a varied CoS family of service levels with individual ATM QoS. The service variety makes use of traffic management and policing, extensive-output queue buffering, and virtual path shaping. Switch linking (daisy-chaining multiple IP DSL switches so that they share a common uplink trunk—also called subtending) allows support of up to 3328 ports, allowing network providers to extract maximum value from each network trunk connection without creating the "parking lot" problem encountered with first-generation DSLAMs.

NI-2

The NI-2 is found in these Cisco systems: 6160, 6260, later 6130s, and 6015. (The Cisco 6130 is now end of life [EOL], but many are still deployed around the U.S.) The NI-2 includes the following features:

- Console/craft Cisco IOS software and Ethernet SNMP management
- Processing and nonvolatile storage resources (memory)
- Timing and redundancy control
- Alarm interface for the IP DSL switch itself

Two WAN options also determine the subtending topology: the OC-3/STM1 creates a daisy-chain topology and the DS3/E3 WAN connection can be set up in a tree (pyramid) topology.

In order for each chassis in a subtended group to have fair access to the shared trunk, each chassis must have a unique ID number. The originating chassis places this ID number in the General Flow Control (GFC) field of the ATM header of each cell, and the ID number is used to forward cells up the tree toward the trunk in a fair manner. The daisy-chain scheme is shown in Figure 4-3.

Figure 4-3 *Cisco NI-2 OC-3/STM1 Subtending: Daisy-Chain Topology*

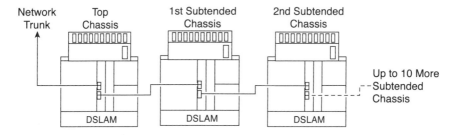

Two dual SC connectors are recessed into the NI-2 faceplate. The upper SC connector pair is an uplink; it can serve as either a network trunk port or, in a subtending arrangement, as the subtending interface to the chassis above this one in the hierarchy. The lower SC connector pair is for subtending only; it cannot serve as a trunk port. This means that a Cisco IP DSL switch equipped with the fiber-connected NI-2 has only one downlink for subtending (due to the circuitry size of the optical connections).

In a daisy-chain topology, the top chassis connects to a network trunk and to a subtended chassis. As you will learn in Chapter 6, "Cisco IOS Configurations," the network trunk is designated Interface ATM 0/1. It is also called the uplink or northbound trunk, although its actual direction may be anywhere. The subtending trunk is designated Interface ATM 0/2 and is frequently referred to as the downlink or southbound trunk. The subtended chassis can connect to another subtended chassis, which can connect to another, and so on. Figure 4-4 shows the top half of the fiber-connected NI-2 card.

Figures 4-5 and 4-6 show the connectors and indicators on the lower half of the OC-3/STM1 NI-2 card.

Figure 4-4   *OC-3 NI-2 Card Faceplate (Top)*

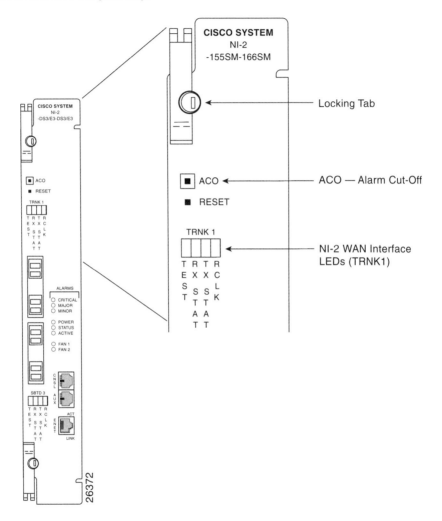

Figure 4-5 *OC-3/STM1 NI-2 Card Faceplate (Bottom)*

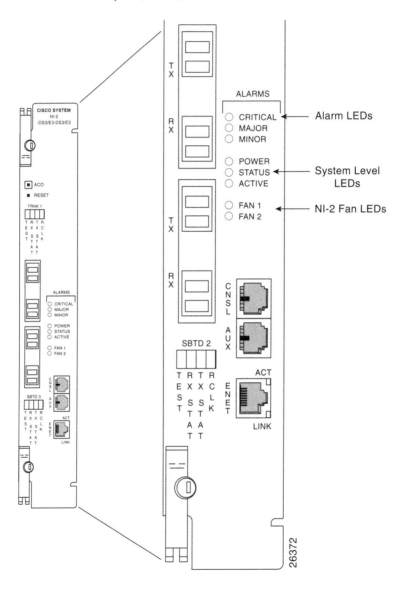

Figure 4-6   *OC-3/STM1 NI-2 Card Faceplate (Bottom, Continued)*

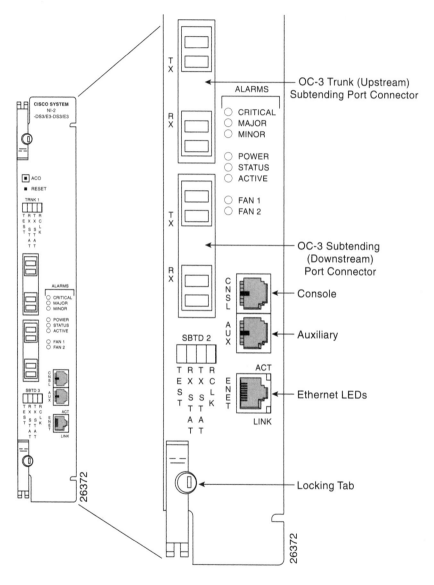

The components shown in these views are as follows:

- **Console port**—An RJ-48 connector that is an EIA/TIA-232 port configured as a DCE device. This is used for servicing by craft personnel. You will see in Chapter 6 that it is used briefly during the initial installation of the IP DSL switch to define basic settings. After the initial installation, maintenance and management are usually performed via Ethernet.

- **Auxiliary port**—An RJ-48 connector that is an EIA/TIA-232 port configured as a DTE device. When used, this usually connects a dialup (analog) modem to the IP DSL switch for management access redundancy. This port provides modem signaling that the console does not have. In other words, if the Ethernet and trunk connections fail, the service provider can dial in remotely to begin servicing the IP DSL switch.

- **Ethernet port**—An RJ-45 10BASE-T connector that complies with Ethernet standards. It is used to connect the Cisco IP DSL switch to its management LAN. Management can be performed through Telnet sessions or through SNMP communications, as you will learn in later chapters.

Although several of the LEDs are common to both the coaxial versions of the NI-2 (DS-3, E3) and the fiber-optic versions (OC-3, STM1), there are important differences between the two card versions. The most important consideration for subtending is that there are two available downlinks (subtending links) on the coaxial version of the NI-2 card. As you will learn in depth in Chapter 6's explanation of software configurations, the network trunk is designated Interface ATM 0/1, the first subtending trunk is designated Interface ATM 0/2, and the other subtending trunk is designated Interface ATM 0/3. This means that subtending can take the form of a pyramid, or tree, as shown in Figure 4-7.

In a tree topology, the top chassis connects to a network trunk and to two subtended chassis. Those two chassis each connect to two more subtended chassis, which in turn connect to one or two more chassis.

As the coaxial NI-2 offers three coaxial connections, three identical sets of LEDs report the status of the trunk and subtending WAN interfaces. These LED sets are labeled TRNK 1, SBTD 2, and SBTD 3, as shown in Figure 4-8.

Both NI-2 cards' connectivity versions, optical fiber and coaxial cable, permit module redundancy for the NI-2. Understanding NI-2 redundancy requires understanding two sets of terms. The basic designation for two NI-2s describes their location in the chassis as seen from the front of the Cisco 6000 chassis. The NI-2 card on the left is always the primary card, and its twin on the right is always the secondary one.

Figure 4-7   *Cisco NI-2 DS-3/E3 Subtending: Tree Topology*

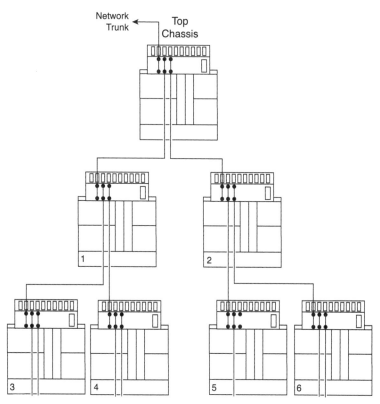

Either the primary (left side) or secondary (right side) NI-2 can be the active one. The terms *active* and *standby* refer to the status of the NI-2s rather than their placement in the chassis. The active (online) NI-2 can be either the primary card or the secondary card. Complementarily, the standby (inactive) NI-2 can be either the primary or secondary card. The standby unit's boot process is suspended before completion, remaining at standby. There is no CLI access to the standby NI-2. On the standby unit, there is no access to or from Ethernet or console ports. Nor is there access to line cards. Alarms can be asserted, but they are reported via the active NI-2 card.

The active unit offers full access to line cards, full access to system buses, and full access to and from Ethernet and console ports. The active unit uses the Ethernet MAC address on the system I/O board (electrically erasable programmable read-only memory [EEPROM]).

Figure 4-8 *Cisco NI-2 DS-3/E3 Card Faceplate (Top)*

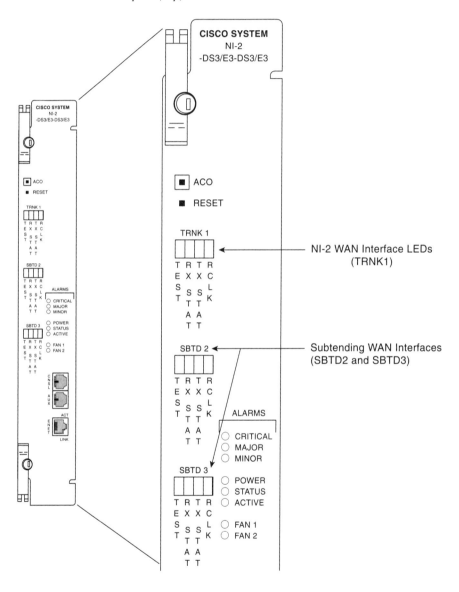

Initial CLI configuration is required after you install a new or replacement standby NI-2. Flash memory and configuration must be manually synchronized before you enable auto-sync. There is no auto-sync immediately after you install a standby card. After initial manual sync, and after auto-sync is enabled, the standby NVRAM mirrors the active unit's NVRAM. In this auto-synch configuration, the standby unit receives config updates from the active card.

Automatic Protection Switching (APS) is a standard method of providing link redundancy on SONET/SDH interfaces, providing link redundancy for OC-3 and STM1 ports. Redundancy is available for both trunk and subtended fiber-optic ports. Switchover occurs in response to loss of signal (LOS) or loss of frame (LOF), which are SONET/SDH failure conditions. As per industry standards, there is a maximum 10-millisecond LOS/LOF detection interval, followed by a maximum 50-millisecond switchover. The switchover applies to the receive path only. Both NI-2 cards transmit the same data simultaneously. APS link redundancy provides for a single OC-3 link, shared by both primary and secondary NI cards. This is done via intercard buses only. An optical Y-cable cannot be used on NI-2 OC-3 interfaces. As per telecommunications industry standards, the default status of link redundancy is nonrevertive. This means that the switched link does not revert to the former primary link without manual intervention. This prevents premature switching to a still-faulty connection, which could result in a flapping interface.

There are two types of NI-2 redundancy—cold and hot. *Cold redundancy* is when the standby unit does not completely mirror the state of the active unit. In DSL applications, this means that line-trained rates are not maintained in both the active and standby units. A switchover requires that DSL lines be retrained. Cold redundancy may be planned when a single, regional spare backs up more than one IP DSL switch. The regional spare may be minimally configured for transportability.

Hot redundancy is the state in which the standby unit mirrors the state of the active unit. In DSL applications, this indicates that all line-trained rates are maintained as dynamic information in both the active and standby units. This allows very fast switchovers.

The switchover process is as follows:

Step 1   Standby detects a failure of the active unit, typically a loss of keepalive messages.

Step 2   Standby NI-2 resets and boots.

Step 3   Standby attempts the following functions as part of the sequence to online status:

Step 4   The system syncs the running config if possible.

Step 5   The system syncs Flash memories if possible.

Switchover can be prompted by any failure that interrupts IOS program execution. There is minimal verification of standby unit functionality before failover.

Manual switchover can be made via the command-line interface (CLI) prompt. The system asks for a confirmation and then switches sides. The standby NI-2 resumes and completes the boot sequence, and the previously online NI-2 reboots to standby state.

The green STATUS LED shows the online NI-2. Only the online NI-2 lights this LED.

Redundant data is transmitted and received simultaneously on both the primary and secondary NI-2 OC-3 trunk 0/1 interfaces. If both interfaces are working correctly, OC-3 switchover occurs instantly, as the same data is transmitted simultaneously on two links. The far end also transmits simultaneously on two links. Either of the two incoming data streams may be selected as the active received traffic source, regardless of which NI-2 is online.

If the standby NI-2 receive path is defective, a manual switch from active to protect status is not allowed.

Physical trunk connections are located on the system I/O card. The common backplane I/O board serves as a DS-3 Y-cable, connecting the online NI-2 trunk ports to a common DS-3 coaxial cable.

There is no DS-3 link redundancy—only a single physical link.

The active and standby DS-3 NI-2 cards share a common physical interface for ports 0/1, 0/2, and 0/3. The coaxial ports can be accessed by either the primary or secondary NI-2 card, but only by the online card.

Line Cards

As you read earlier, individual ports on DSL modem cards are the termination of the DSL connection itself. The modem cards may be asymmetric or symmetric types and are frequently called line cards. The line cards convert xDSL modulation into digital data streams to and from the NI-2 card and negotiate the line rate with the CPE. All Cisco IP DSL switches have three prevailing types of line cards. Not all line cards are available on all DSLAM models due to chassis differences. The three main types of line cards are as follows:

- The four-port Flexi line card, also called an Asymmetric Transceiver Unit-Central office (ATU-C), not only can provide full-rate and half-rate DMT, but also can be programmed to support the legacy Carrierless Amplitude Phase modulation (CAP) technology. Although it is increasingly being displaced by the worldwide standards of DMT, CAP was widely deployed around the world several years ago. Therefore, the Flexi offers a migration for service providers to the newer, standardized technologies on the same IP DSL switch platform.

- ADSL line cards (ATU-Cs) come in both four- and eight-port versions. These cards automatically recognize and adapt to either the ANSI DMT2 standard (T1.413.2) or the ITU standards for both full-rate (256 tones) and half-rate (128 tones) DMT.

- The G.SHDSL Symmetric Transceiver Unit-Central office (STU-C) is an eight-port line card providing the ITU symmetric service standard.

All line cards except the Flexi are automatically discovered by the NI-2. The NI-2 first queries the card to determine its validity for the particular chassis type. Then the NI-2 analyzes the line card's software image. If the image on the new line card is not the same version as the image for the card type contained on the NI-2, the NI-2 automatically downloads its own copy of the software image directly to the line card. This takes about 2 or 3 minutes, depending on the particular line card.

As shown in Figure 4-9, the Flexi card's LEDs indicate what type of DSL service is in place.

Figure 4-9   *Flexi Line Card LEDs*

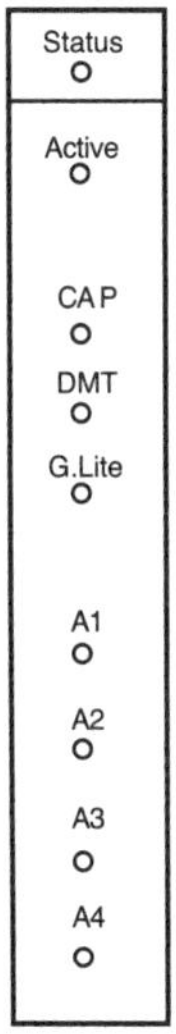

Status	Blink Red	-	POST Errors
	Solid Green -		Running Application Image (No POST Errors)
	Blink Green -		500 msec On/Off - Downloading Image
Active	Green	-	InterProcess Communication (IPC) Connection Established
CAP	Green	-	Provisioned as CAP
DMT	Green	-	Provisioned as DMT
G.Lite	Green	-	1 or More DMT Ports Is Connected to CPE in G.Lite Mode. Always in Conjunction with DMT LED Lit Green
A1-A4	Green	-	Green -Trained
			Off - No CPE Detected
			Blinking - Training

The panel on the left shows LEDs labeled: Status, Active, CAP, DMT, G.Lite, A1, A2, A3, A4.

The Flexi is autodiscovered by the NI-2, but the software image upgrade requires manual intervention by the carbon-based unit to configure that Flexi for either DMT or CAP. In other words, the line card cannot fit both the DMT and CAP images onboard itself and has no way of autosensing the particular modulation desired or connected. Although the Flexi card must be configured manually in advance to accommodate either DMT or CAP, the card recognizes and adapts to G.Lite from a DMT configuration.

The Flexi card may mix full-rate and half-rate DMT on neighboring ports on the same card, but at this time it is not recommended to mix CAP with DMT on the same Flexi card. Spectral incompatibility is especially a factor with 2B1Q line coding. This coding is used in CAP, ADSL over ISDN, ISDN itself, and legacy, nonstandard symmetric DSL service. The danger to performance lies primarily with coaxial cable proximity on the backplane and, to a lesser degree, the line card itself.

The 4DMT line card provides four DMT ATU-C modem ports, and the 8DMT version has eight ports. The only difference between the four-port version and the eight-port version is the presence of four more LEDs aligned vertically. The card supports maximum data rates of 8032 Mbps downstream and 864 Mbps upstream on all four ports simultaneously. It also provides the ability to obtain and report the actual acquired modem rate if the desired rate cannot be achieved.

Two DMT operating modes are supported:

- Automatic mode, in which the CO line card autodetects the CPE capabilities and starts in the appropriate mode. Modes can be T1.413, G.992.1, or G.992.2.
- Splitterless, in which the ATU-C offers only G.992 operating mode.

When configured for G.dmt operation, the ATU-C supports these rates:

- **Upstream line rates**—32 to 864 Kbps in increments of 32 Kbps
- **Downstream line rates**—32 to 8032 Kbps in increments of 32 Kbps

When configured for G.Lite operation, the ATU-C supports these rates:

- **Upstream line rates**—32 to 512 Kbps in 32 Kbps increments
- **Downstream line rates**—32 to 1536 Kbps in 32 Kbps increments
- **Symmetric line rate**—Matches upstream and downstream rates

Figure 4-10 shows the DMT line card LEDs.

Figure 4-10 *DMT ATU-C Card LEDs*

Status	Blink Red	-	POST Errors
	Solid Green	-	Running Application Image (No POST Errors)
	Blink Green	-	500 msec On/Off - Downloading Image 250 msec On/Off Is Downloading in Boot Code, Never Done Intentionally in the Field
Active	Green	-	InterProcess Communication (IPC) Connection Established
A1-A4	Green	-	Trained

NOTE   The eight-port STU-C supports the ITU standard symmetric DSL service. Its LEDs are in the same relative place and are triggered by the same conditions as the other two line cards. Therefore, that information is not repeated here.

For all these line cards, you should never remove any line card from the chassis if the card's active LED is blinking, indicating that the card is loading microcode. If a line card is removed while it is loading, there is a slight chance that the card's Flash memory might be damaged, making it necessary to replace the card.

During normal operations, any or all Cisco IP DSL switch line cards can be installed and removed while the rest of the system continues to operate.

Following is a depiction of the LEDs on the coaxial NI-2, either the North American DS-3 or the worldwide E3.

North American 6160

The Cisco 6160 has 32 line card slots. It accommodates all ports on either four-port or eight-port cards. At quad density, there are 128 ports. At octal density, there are 256 ports. There are two network interface slots for the optionally redundant NI-2 cards (primary/secondary). The 6160, shown in Figure 4-11, has two NI-2 cards.

Figure 4-11 *Cisco 6160 with DS-3/E3*

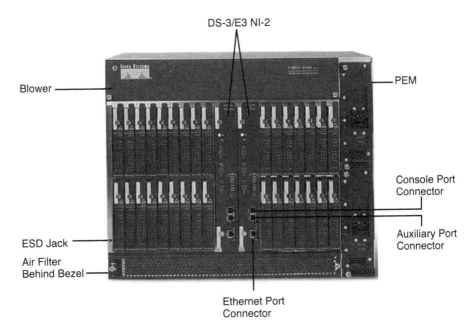

The whole DSLAM chassis is only 10.5 rack units (RUs) high, with dimensions of 18.38 inches high by 23 inches wide by 12 inches deep. It is fully compliant with NEBS-III standards.

The 6160 features integrated Power Entry Modules (PEMs) and cooling. Routine maintenance requirements specify monthly cleaning of the fan filter at the bottom of the chassis.

There is presently hardware and software support for NI-2 redundancy and hardware support for N:1 line cards (software support is pending).

The backplane includes 11 RJ-21 connectors for DSL traffic. The wire wrap connector may be used for out-of-band alarm delivery and BITS clock connectivity for two more facets of communication and management connectivity redundancy. (BITS stands for Building Integrated Timing Supply, meaning a commonly accessible, highly accurate clocking signal.)

All trunk interfaces may be addressed by either NI-2 card when the latter are configured for redundancy.

The backplane of the Cisco 6160 is the same, regardless of what NI-2 card is used, whether fiber-optic or coaxial, as you can see in Figure 4-12.

Figure 4-12 *Cisco 6160 Rear Cable Access*

As per North American standards, all fiber connections are on the front, and coaxial connections are on the rear plane. In both cases for the 6160, DSL data line connections are on the backplane. These rear Amphenol connectors are clearly labeled for easy troubleshooting.

The PEMs do not actually supply power. They merely regulate and distribute the –48 volts DC supplied from a standard telco power bar. Cisco can recommend approved AC power supplies from third-party suppliers, but these are rarely used with the Cisco 6160 IP DSL switch, because North American central offices use a common DC power bus.

Worldwide 6260

As you can see in Figure 4-13, the 6160's PEMs are located below the line cards, not beside them as with the Cisco 6160. This is to accommodate the European-standard 19-inch telco rack width. (North America uses 23-inch racks.) This width also allows only 30 line cards per 6160, meaning that the Cisco 6260 supports up to 120 ADSL subscriber connections on one WAN trunk. Using subtending, up to 13 6260s can be daisy-chained onto a single WAN trunk (1560 total subscribers). The chassis design, as used throughout Europe and other parts of the world, provides for complete front access for cabling and maintenance. This front access includes the coaxial connections for E3 cables if that NI-2 version is what you want.

The front access includes connections for coaxial E3 cables, attached via a floating I/O plane at the top of the 6260 chassis, as shown in Figure 4-14.

There are redundant power units and two-speed, software-controlled cooling fans.

Some early 6260 backplanes might require an update to support redundancy, so you should check the product notes for details.

The Cisco 6260 with either the OC-3c or STM-1 fiber-optic interface provides all trunk and subtending connectors on the NI-2 card itself.

Figure 4-15 shows the Cisco 6260 chassis slot numbering. Slots 10 and 11 hold the NI-2 cards. Slots 1 to 9 and 12 to 32 hold the line cards.

The wire wrap connector, located near the top of the 6260 chassis and shown in Figure 4-16, provides a total of 36 posts for wire wrap connections. These contacts are for alarm relay and BITS clock connections. Both the alarm relays and the BITS clock connections are optional.

Figure 4-13 *Cisco 6260 with an OC-3c/STM-1 Interface*

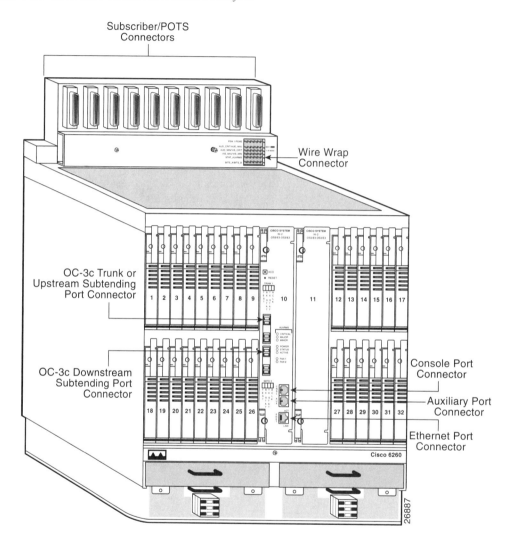

Figure 4-14 *Cisco 6260 E3 I/O Module*

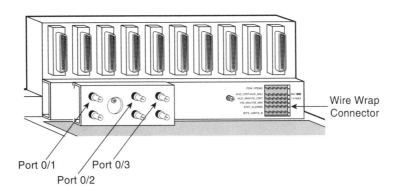

Port 0/1   Port 0/3
        Port 0/2

Figure 4-15 *Cisco 6260 Chassis Slot Numbering*

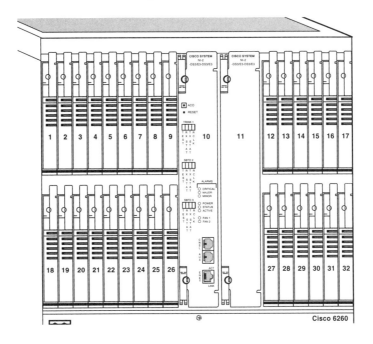

Figure 4-16 *I/O Module Wire Wrap Connector*

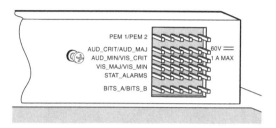

If you connect the alarm relays, they transmit critical, major, and minor alarms to a separate, external alarm device. The alarm device uses a bell, light, or some other signal to alert for the change in status.

The BITS interface lets the 6260 receive a clock signal from a T1/E1 line.

The connector provides contacts for the following features, all of which can be used (or not used) separately:

- **Audible alarms**—Wire pins whose signals begin with AUD (audible)
- **Visible alarms**—Wire pins whose signals begin with VIS (visible)
- **Power alarms**—Wire pins whose signals begin with PEM (Power Entry Module)
- **BITS clock**—Wire pins whose signals begin with RX_BITS (Receive-Building Integrated Timing Supply)

The fans have two speeds. By default, they run at low speed. The system turns up the fan speed when

- It senses high temperatures within the chassis.
- One or more fans fail.
- The other fan tray is removed.

The fan speed returns to normal (low speed) when

- Temperatures within the chassis fall to acceptable levels.
- A missing fan tray is returned to the chassis.

LEDs that report the status of the fan trays are located on the PEMs. Facing the chassis, fan tray 1 is on the left, and fan tray 2 is on the right. The cooling fans in both fan trays must run continuously. The system might suffer thermal damage if the fans in either tray stop for more than 5 minutes.

The following are some details about the PEM:

Each 6260 is equipped with two –48 VDC PEMs, which distribute DC power within the chassis. The 6260 needs only one active PEM to operate. If two PEMs are installed, the second PEM serves as a hot backup to the first.

Each PEM should be connected to a single DC power source. For full power redundancy with two PEMs, two separate DC power sources must be connected to the chassis. Each PEM is held in place by the overhanging lip of the fan tray above it. As shown in Figure 4-17, you must remove the fan tray before you can remove the PEM. In a system with two PEMs, you can remove and replace each PEM while the system continues to operate. However, a system with a single PEM must be powered down before you remove the PEM.

Figure 4-17 *Installing the Cisco 6260 Fan Trays*

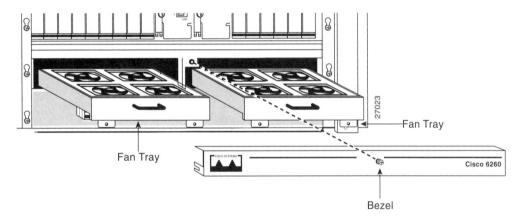

Remote Terminal and Small CO 6015

The Cisco 6015 is designed for worldwide use in remote terminals, small central offices, and multidwelling units (MDUs) and multitenant units (MTUs), sometimes combined to form the umbrella abbreviation MXUs. It meets both NEBS and ETSI standards. Its small form factor is due to the design for horizontal cards, standard to the other DSLAMs. Its most popular NI-2 connectivity is for eight T1s or E1s and one DS3, making use of IMA. With either a fiber-optic or coaxial cable NI-2 version, the Cisco 6015 supports six line cards, all of which can have eight DSL ports.

With MXUs, AC power is used. In both MDUs/MTUs and small central offices, POTS integration is an option. For remote and/or unmanned use, the 6015 is environmentally hardened to withstand a wide range of temperatures. In these situations, the 6015 draws on DC power.

As shown in Figure 4-18, the 6015's compact chassis occupies three RUs, with compact PSCs supplied by companies such as ADC and Corning (formerly known as Siecor Products).

Figure 4-18 *Cisco 6015*

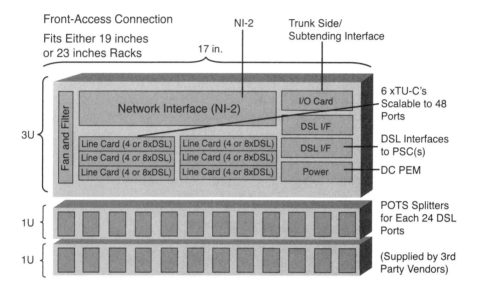

In all respects except the number of DSL subscribers, the Cisco 6015 is equal in capability to the larger CO/exchange DSLAMs/IP-DSL switches.

Inverse Multiplexing Over ATM

Because the remote terminals into which the Cisco 6015 fits are typically saturated with T1/E1 connections, the first and most prevalent network connectivity of the 6015 is via Inverse Multiplexing over ATM (IMA). The various T1s/E1s can be configured as either the WAN trunk or subtending trunks. The eight T1/E1 interfaces can be configured in up to four IMA groups.

The T1/E1 IMA feature uses IMA technology to aggregate multiple low-speed links (T1/E1) into one or more IMA groups at speeds between 1.5 Mbps and 16 Mbps. IMA breaks up the ATM cell stream and distributes the cells over the multiple physical links of an IMA group and then recombines the cells into a single stream at the other end of the connection, as shown in Figure 4-19. The multiple links of an IMA group increase the logical link bandwidth to approximately the sum of the individual link rates.

Figure 4-19 *Inverse Multiplexing Over ATM*

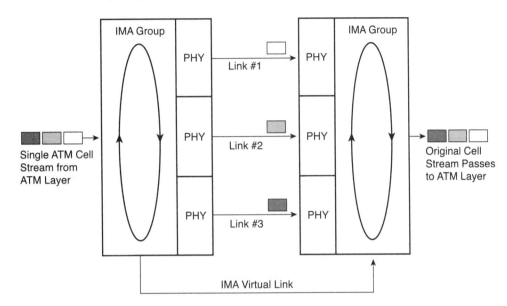

IMA links transmit IMA control protocol (ICP) cells, which enable the reconstruction of the original ATM cell stream. ICP cells define and separate IMA frames passing through each physical link in an IMA group. ICP cells also control IMA's operation by accounting for cell delay variation (CDV), which is introduced by ICP cells, and the link differential delays on physical links to ensure the proper reassembly of IMA frames. Using an IMA frame length of 128 cells, one out of every 128 cells on a physical link is an ICP cell. In this scenario, a frame containing fewer than 128 cells is injected with filler cells. The receiving end of an IMA group extracts the ICP and filler cells as the IMA stream is reconstructed into an ATM cell stream and passed to the ATM layer. IMA operation is transparent to ATM layer protocols. Therefore, the ATM layer operates as if a single physical interface is being used.

Aggregator/Concentrator: Cisco 6400

The Cisco 6400 is a UAC. When optimally configured with hardware components, it combines the functionality of the Catalyst 8500 ATM switch (Lightstream 1010) and the Cisco 7200 series router with Gigabit Ethernet and a wide variety of other connectivity options. The 6400 provides high-density integration of ATM transport and IP routed services, including security and service selection. There is handoff to service provider(s) and QoS enforcement for both IP and ATM. There are potentially tens of thousands of sessions per system. This UAC is compatible around the world, because it meets both North American and other standards (19-inch form factor, NEBS and ETSI compliance, and so on). The 6400 UAC can be configured and managed with either Cisco IOS or the Service Connection Manager (SCM) graphical user interface.

As you can see in Figure 4-20, the 6400 in its most effective configuration provides aggregation, switching, and forwarding of DSL traffic from and to the ATM network. In the center of the figure, the 6400 is connected to two IP DSL switches and to a local ATM access network. The network could include the Cisco (Cat) 8500, (BPX) 8600, or core router, Gigabit Switch Router (GSR), 12000 series, and so on. The 6400 runs the integrated Service Selection Gateway, Cisco cache engine, WebCache coordination protocol, and the Cisco User Control Point (UCP).

Figure 4-20 *6400 System Connections*

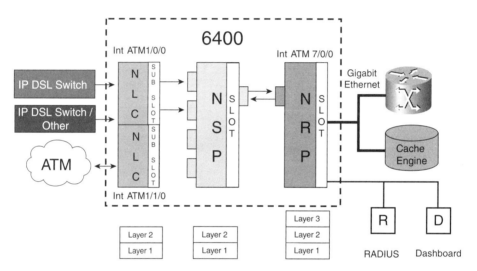

Hardware Overview

In summarizing the 6400 hardware, bear in mind that the best use of the 6400 includes the hardware modules that deliver Layer 3 services such as IP address management through NAT/PAT, standard routing, and even basic security.

You will read about the details of these hardware components in the next few pages. The second-generation node route processor (NRP2) receives traffic from OC-12/STM3 interface ports via the node switch processor (NSP) ATM switch. (The predecessor first-generation NRP has OC-3/STM1 ports.) The NRP2 reassembles the ATM cells into packets, processes them, segments them, and sends them back to the ATM switch for transmission out another high-speed interface. The NSP also transmits the configuration for the NRP2. The Cisco 6400 UAC can contain multiple NRP2 modules, configured to operate independently or as redundant pairs (1+1). The Gigabit Ethernet interface can be used to either switch traffic or connect high-capacity Internet applications such as RADIUS or Dynamic Host Configuration Protocol (DHCP) servers. The default ATM interface type for each NRP2 is User-Network Interface (UNI).

The 6400 UAC supports a variety of configurations, including Point-to-Point Protocol (PPP) over ATM (PPPoA), RFC 1483 bridging, Layer 2 Tunneling Protocol (L2TP), virtual LANs, and so on. The 6400 can be configured in a number of ways to accommodate different high-speed access concentrator arrangements.

The chassis shown in Figure 4-21 shows that there are ten vertical slots in the 6400 system. The two center slots are reserved for the optionally redundant node switch processor(s) [NSP(s)]. These are the ATM switching engines with per-flow queuing logic. The other eight slots, four on each side of the two center slots, are reserved for either NRP2s or node line cards (NLCs). NLCs are half-slot, fitted into full-height sheet metal sleeves that fill the entire slot. A single slot can be populated with either one or two half-slot NLCs.

Figure 4-21 *6400 Hardware Components*

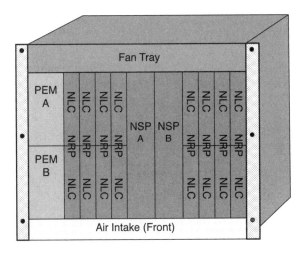

The blower assembly is on the top of the system. The PEMs are on the left of the system, as shown in Figure 4-22. This figure shows the power distribution of the 6400. These are DC PEMs. There are also two battery feeds for use with optional batteries, one connected to each of the PEMs. The two PEMs are wired to the backplane and provide 48 volts to all the components in the system. The system is a distributed power conversion system in which each card converts from 48 volts to whatever voltage is needed on the cards. The system operates with only one active PEM. Currently, if you need AC power to the system, an external shelf is required.

Due to the size of the OC-12/STM3 circuitry, each of these cards has only one trunk port.

Figure 4-22 *Cisco 6400 Power Distribution*

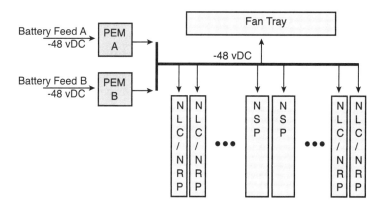

On the 6400, optical interfaces are on the front of the system on line cards. On the rear of the system are the copper and coaxial interfaces. Backplane connections include the following:

- Rear 50-pin RJ-21 connectors for T1
- Rear coaxial connectors for DS-3s
- Telco alarm terminal block
- Redundant battery feed terminal blocks
- Redundant BITS clock terminal blocks

The 6400 rack system has a 12-inch depth that allows for installation in most telco office frame rooms. It is designed to fit three 19-inch shelves in a 7-foot rack.

To add PVC termination capability, additional NRP2s can be installed. Although there are eight possible slots for NRP2s, the physical maximum number of NRP2s would leave no room for NLCs. Without NLCs, network traffic connectivity is exclusively via the Gigabit Ethernet interfaces on the NRP2(s).

The system can have up to 16 half-height NLCs, one or two per full slot. This all-NLC configuration would create a solely Layer 2 device, for simple aggregation and switching, as shown in Figure 4-23.

In this example, ATM traffic (virtual path [VP] and virtual circuit [VC]) is being switched between the node line card and the NSP, then out to another node line card with no Layer 3 processing.

The various modules within the 6400 present different types of control and data interfaces. The console port appears on the NSP, just as it does on regular Cisco routers, along with the auxiliary port. The console port provides a serial connection for a command-line interface to the vital NSP operating system.

Figure 4-23 *Cisco 6400 Used Solely for ATM Concentration*

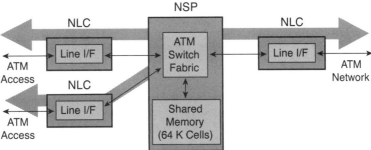

There is a special management Ethernet on the chassis called backplane Ethernet (BPE). It can be used to manage and configure the system. The internal Ethernet provides for intermodule communication. There is an external 10BASE-T Ethernet port to connect external system management applications (Telnet/SCM).

The Gigabit Ethernet interface is fully routable from the NRP2. It can be used to connect to upstream caching servers, service selection gateways, or within a Layer 3 point of presence (POP). Finally, the node line cards present the actual ATM interfaces. These may be used as either downlinks to an ATM access network or as uplink interfaces into an ATM core.

Node Switch Processor

The NSP is the centerpiece of the 6400 system. It has the following features:

- 4700 RISC processor (100 MHz)
- Standard: 64 MB DRAM, 32 MB Flash Disk, 8 MB BootFlash
- Optional: 128 MB DRAM, 350 MB Flash Disk
- Dual PCMCIA (Personal Computer Memory Card International Association) slots for Flash Card and Flash Disk
- 64 K cell buffer Static Random Access Memory (SRAM)
- Per-flow queuing (PFQ) control by processor
- Controls SONET/SDH APS port redundancy
- Alarm reporting
- Backplane Ethernet interprocessor communication
- 32-port, 5 Gbps ATM switch fabric
- Traffic shaping and queuing functions

The NSP configures, controls, and monitors the whole 6400 unit. More specifically, it configures the switch fabric and feature cards, the NLCs and the NRP2s. (The predecessor first-generation NRP has its own software image and must be configured individually.) The NSP detects the presence of NLCs/NRP2s in the system, brings them online, and continually monitors the status of each NLC/NRP2, as well as system and environmental status (PEM status, temperature, and so on).

The NSP performs the ATM switching and per-flow queuing for the ATM virtual circuits. It performs traffic management and signaling, including Cisco's hierarchical Private Network Node Interface (PNNI). The NSP consists of an ATM switching board, controller board, and PFQ logic. Three separate printed circuit boards (PCBs) are folded in upon themselves within the NSP.

The NSP can be operated in nonredundant or redundant mode. In redundant mode, NSPs occupy both center slots (0A and 0B), with one operating as the primary NSP and the second one in standby. If the primary fails, the second automatically takes over. NSPs are hot-swappable (also called Online Insertion and Removal [OIR]). The redundancy is governed by Extended High Signal Availability (EHSA) interboard signaling.

As shown in Figure 4-24, the NSP supports standard telco alarm functionality. Three levels of defined alarms are indicated by LEDs—minor, major, and critical—in increasing order of importance. These alarms are signaled by relays that connect at the back of the 6400 chassis to the LEDs on the faceplate.

Figure 4-24 *NSP LED Indicators*

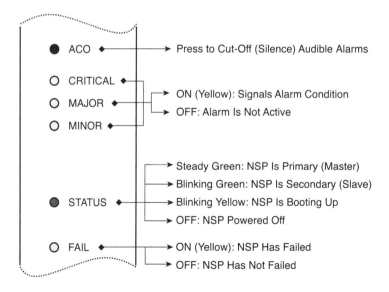

Node Route Processor, Second Generation

Cisco's NRP2 module for the Cisco 6400 carrier-class broadband aggregator aggregates and terminates large numbers of broadband subscribers.

The NRP2 provides the Cisco 6400 with a maximum capacity of 96,000 sessions (with six NRPs), because each blade can support up to 16,000 subscriber sessions. (The follow-on NRP2SV [NRP2 with Shaped Virtual Circuits] can support 48000 sessions.)

Overall 6400 configuration storage, console traffic, and network management traffic are now controlled by the existing NSP, providing a manageable and integrated platform to the user. The NSP provides a single console port and a single management Ethernet interface to configure and monitor all NRP2s in the chassis. The NRP2 itself has no console port for direct management access.

Hardware features of the NRP2 include the following:

- Dual RM7000 processors with a 270-MHz internal clock
- 2x256-MB ECC-protected SDRAM memory, with an optional upgrade to 2x512-MB ECC-protected SDRAM
- 2-MB external cache per processor
- 622-Mbps forwarding capacity derived from Cisco 7200 technology (Networking Processing Engine [NPE] 300)

The forwarding (switching) plane and control (management) planes are separated, improving the performance of each. The control plane creates and maintains sessions and tunnels, and the forwarding plane switches packets.

In the optional redundancy configuration, two NRP2s use EHSA signals, as shown in Figure 4-25. These signals allow the two NRP2s to negotiate which is the master and which is the secondary. The NRP2s determine which is the primary and then communicate that information to the NSP. The NSP chooses to transmit to and receive from that specific NRP2.

The NRP2 has these capabilities:

- OIR
- Virtual routers or multidomain PPP termination aggregation (PTA) to provide connectivity to up to 500 simultaneous domains
- Full multiprotocol label switching (MPLS) support
- Integrated Layer 3 service selection with web-based dashboard

Figure 4-25 *Node Route Processor Card Redundancy*

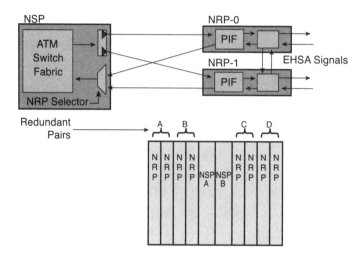

The Gigabit Ethernet port on the NRP2 uses existing Cisco Gigabit Interface Converter (GBIC) technology. It is compliant with the IEEE 802.3z standard. It has a variety of fiber options, including support for short/medium/long-haul types, including these:

- Short-wavelength (SX) fiber 500 m

- Multimode (MM) fiber

- Long-wavelength/long-haul (SX/LH)—5 km to 10 km single-mode (SM) fiber

- Extended wavelength ZX—10 km up to 70 km single-mode (SM) fiber

Node Line Card

The 6400's NLC is a simple module with these connectivity options:

- 2xOC-3

- 2xSTM-1

- 2xDS3 (backplane connection)

- 2xE3

- 1xOC-12

- 1xSTM-4

- All fiber-optic connections are single-mode, intermediate reach

- SONET/SDH APS 1+1 redundancy support

Just as the NLC is a simple module without its own memory or processor, the LEDs are simple as well. As shown in Figure 4-26, there are three indicators on the front panel for NLCs: the Fail LED, the Status LED, and the TX/RX LEDs. There are two status LEDs on the line card. The blinking green LED is seen only if the port is being configured as a redundant pair. There are two sets of transmit and receive LEDs.

Figure 4-26 *Node Line Card LED Indicators*

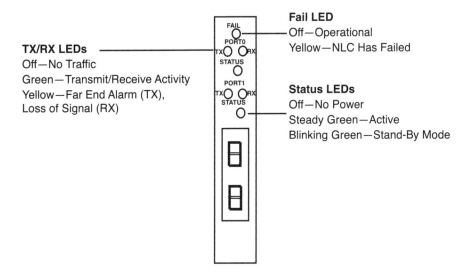

Fail LED
Off—Operational
Yellow—NLC Has Failed

TX/RX LEDs
Off—No Traffic
Green—Transmit/Receive Activity
Yellow—Far End Alarm (TX),
Loss of Signal (RX)

Status LEDs
Off—No Power
Steady Green—Active
Blinking Green—Stand-By Mode

Figure 4-27 shows how the NLC performs its redundancy. On the left is an NSP communicating with two NLCs. The driver transmits the same information to two NLCs at the same time. The NLCs then transmit that information to the fiber. Redundant signals are received by two NLCs. The NSP determines which line card it listens to—that is, which is the primary card. This can be based on bit error rates, line outage, or any status selected to trigger the NLCs' switchover.

Figure 4-27 *Node Line Card Redundancy*

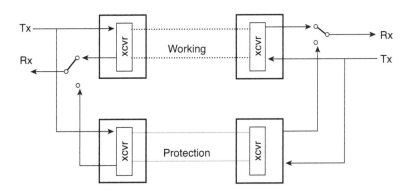

NLCs must be adjacent to be configured as redundant pairs. For example, if data transmissions to a line card located in slot 1 subslot 0 fail, slot 2 subslot 0 picks up the load.

Summary

Cisco DSL hardware, starting with the customer premise equipment (CPE) lines of the Cisco 70 and 820 DSL routers, is presented. Central office (exchange) equipment is also explored. The CO/exchange multiplexers includes the Layer 2 functionality of DSL Access Multiplexers (DSLAMs), as well as the Layer 3 sophistication leading to the designation of IP/DSL Switches, which are all known as the Cisco 6000 series. The Cisco 6000 series permits linking up to 13 units in a technique called subtending. A particular hardware configuration on the IP/DSL Switch also permits Inverse Multiplexing over ATM (IMA) to leverage an existing T1/E1 wiring infrastructure. Finally, the Cisco 6400 Universal Access Concentrator (UAC), that combines high-speed interfaces with L2 switching and L3 routing intelligence, is discussed.

For all these hardware items, this chapter describes individual components and capabilities, physical connectivity, and redundancy where available. Overall, you should now grasp the interconnectedness of these devices within the DSL provider network.

Review Questions

1 What is the NSP switch default ATM protocol?

   A LAPD

   B X.25

   C UNI 4.0

   D ISDN

2 Which of the following best describes SONET APS on the 6400 system?

   A Redundant NLC cards supplying OC-3 traffic to the NSP

   B Redundant NRP2 ports supplying OC-C traffic to the NSP

   C The 6400 system does not support SONET APS

   D Redundant NSP configured for failover

3 When two NRP2s are configured in a redundant configuration, which of the following is true?

   A Both NRP2s provide redundant traffic to the NSP

   B Both NRP2s provide redundant traffic to the NLC

   C Both NSPs provide redundant traffic to the NPP

   D None of the above

4 What is the maximum card load that the present Cisco 6260 chassis supports?

A 28 DMT cards and four NI-2 cards

B 30 DMT cards and one NI-2 card

C 30 DMT cards and two NI-2 cards

D 32 DMT cards and two NI-2 cards

5 Which function is *not* provided by the NI-2 card?

A Cisco IOS Software support

B SNMP Agent

C ATM switch fabric

D Four ATU-C modems

E Subtending

6 The present Cisco 6160 chassis can support which of the following maximum card loads?

A 28 DMT cards and four NI-2 cards

B 30 DMT cards and one NI-2 card

C 30 DMT cards and two NI-2 cards

D 32 DMT cards and two NI-2 cards

7 The out-of-band alarm relay functions on the 6260 are provided by what?

A The NI-2 card

B The lead DMT card

C The power supply

D The wire wrap connector

8 True or false: The 6260 fan tray must be installed before the PEMS.

9 On the IP DSL switch, the DS-3 trunk is connected on which of the following?

A The DS-3 NI-2 card

B The DS-3 I/O module

C The network line card

10   What is the function of the CO splitter?

   A   Equalize the circuit

   B   Generate ringing voltage

   C   Manage ADSL signaling

   D   Separate low and high frequencies

   E   None of the above

11   In the NI-2-equipped IP DSL switch system, how is the splitter function performed?

   A   By the network interface module

   B   In the line module

   C   In the system controller card

   D   In the PSC

   E   None of the above

12   All subscribers in a subtended IP DSL switch report that their CPE trains up OK, but no one can access the Internet. Subscribers in the host switch are not experiencing a problem. Both DIP DSL switches are equipped with OC-3 NI cards. Which of the following could cause this error?

   A   A defective OC-3 patch cord is connected to the transmit output of ATM port 0/1 on the host system.

   B   ATM port 0/1 in the host system is out of service (shut down).

   C   ATM port 0/1 in the subtended system is out of service (shut down).

   D   A defective OC-3 patch cord is connected to the receive input of ATM port 0/2 on the subtended system.

13   A DSLAM is equipped with two PEMs, and –48 VDC is connected to each PEM. The circuit breaker on the right-side PEM is switched to the off position. What is the effect on customer service or system operation?

   A   Subscribers served by ATU-C slots 12 to 17 and 27 to 32 are out of service.

   B   Subscribers served by ATU-C slots 18 to 26 and 27 to 32 are out of service.

   C   There is no effect on customer service.

   D   Subscribers on systems subtended from this DSLAM are out of service.

CHAPTER 5

Security: AAA/SSG/RADIUS

In both business and residential environments, DSL's always-connected status presents a potential access point for illegitimate use. Unlike the session-by-session access through a dialup analog modem, DSL is always on.

How can providers and users be assured of reasonable security for DSL's always-on vulnerability? Furthermore, how can users easily but assuredly manage privileges and control usage?

Visualize DSL's use in a home with a typical family's different needs. In a home, parents would probably want to control their children's Internet usage, giving them easy access to age-appropriate sites.

Now bear in mind a telecommuter's use of DSL. A telecommuter needs security for work-related traffic, protection for private business files, as well as ease of access to desired sites. Add the consideration for DSL's use by different levels of users within a small business setting. The company's management would be wise to define Internet access to prevent inappropriate use of company resources, and enhance productivity.

DSL can be managed for all these purposes and audiences. This chapter begins with a short review of basic security tools, not unique to DSL. Tools include access control lists (ACLs), and authentication protocols such as CHAP (Challenge Handshake Authentication Protocol). The book continues with a definition of authentication, authorization and accounting (AAA) functionality. The review of standard security components concludes with the most common AAA security protocol for DSL, which is RADIUS (Remote Authentication Dial-In User Service. Readers with Cisco Certified Network Associate (CCNA) or higher experience may choose to treat the first few sections as review.

The chapter then describes DSL-specific management tools. These are based on some model of Service Selection Gateway (SSG). This suite of functionality affords productive and healthy use. Topics include authenticating individual users, variable account account options, which can produce revenue from the provider's channels.

This chapter includes descriptions of techniques and protocols for the most user security in current DSL networks. Although these topics, Virtual Private Networking (VPN) and tunneling, are used outside the last mile DSL network, they are vital to aggregated traffic such as dial-up connections and DSL. Therefore, the chapter ends with descriptions of current internetworking cloud traffic management.

Upon completing this chapter, you will be able to do the following:

* Relate the AAA functions to each other in service of the dial-in user model
* Describe the two protocols that enable AAA—RADIUS and TACACS+
* Describe typical applications for RADIUS in the DSL environment
* Trace the RADIUS server-client transmission and accounting flow
* Describe the function of SSG/SSD/RADIUS in the DSL environment
* Describe RADIUS transmission and accounting flow in terms of the packets exchanged between client and server
* Identify the components of the user profile
* Identify the components of the service profile
* Identify the components of the client profile
* Describe the advantages to the service provider and to the DSL user of the service selection application
* Describe the two levels (Layer 2 and Layer 3) of service selection and give examples of each
* Define the concept of VPNs and describe their use for secure connectivity

Basic Network Security

Basic network security in the DSL environment includes industry-standard techniques and protocols that are not unique to DSL. Cisco IOS Software enables several security features, including ACLs for packet filtering, router authentication, network address translation (NAT), and choices of security standards such as RADIUS and TACACS. These features are the building blocks of DSL network security.

Access Control Lists

Both standard and extended ACLs are supported with the standard IOS configuration. As you should know from prior experience with Cisco internetworking, access lists are packet filters that can restrict access but that provide no challenge mechanism.

Access Protocols

The following access protocols are typically configured on the Layer 3 device, whether the IP DSL switch or the Cisco 6400's node route processor (NRP) device or some other router.

Password Authentication Protocol (PAP) requires a remote router to send an authentication request when attempting to connect to a local router. The PAP request comprises an identification and a password. This pair of account data is repeatedly sent by the remote device to the authentication device. This is done until authentication is acknowledged by the authentication device or the connection is terminated.

However, PAP provides only a basic authentication level. Because PAP sends passwords in clear (unencrypted) text, there's some risk that the connection's security might be compromised. For example, a hacker could record the legitimate user's PAP login sequence and then play back the recorded login later to gain access to the network. Because PAP has no timeout function, the hacker is free to use repeated trial-and-error attempts. PAP is supported only on Point-to-Point Protocol (PPP) lines, so both the remote and local routers are PPP peers.

Challenge Handshake Authentication Protocol (CHAP) uses a challenge-response mechanism with one-way encryption on the response. It allows the CiscoSecure ACS (Access Control Server) to negotiate downward from the most-secure to the least-secure encryption mechanism, and it protects passwords transmitted in the process. CHAP passwords can be reused.

A more secure authentication protocol, CHAP is also supported only on PPP connections. The CHAP algorithm depends on a calculated value, or secret, that is at least one octet in length and is known only to the authenticator and the remote-access device. Because the CHAP secret is never sent over the link, it is highly effective against playback and trial-and-error attempts.

Instead of sending the secret, CHAP sends a challenge to the remote unit attempting to connect to the network. The remote unit responds with a value calculated by a common algorithm used by both devices. The authentication device checks the response against its own calculation of the expected value. If the values match, the authentication is acknowledged; otherwise, the connection is terminated. Each new challenge value is unique, which prevents an attacker from using a previously intercepted response to obtain network access.

CHAP and PAP help ensure that the correct remote device has dialed in to the network. Bear in mind, however, that both protocols authenticate only the remote device. They do not authenticate the user. Therefore, they should always be used in combination with other security methods (which are described next.)

Another technique that is frequently overlooked as part of security is *network address translation (NAT)*. Although NAT's main benefit is usually considered conservation of global (registered) IP addresses, NAT fulfills a vital security role in hiding an internal network's IP addresses. NAT translates one or more outside, global, registered IP addresses to one or more internal, private IP addresses. In other words, either a single external address or a pool of different external addresses is shared by a large number of internal hosts. NAT eliminates the need to readdress all hosts with existing private network addresses. For businesses that want to allow selected access to the network, NAT can be configured to allow only certain types of data requests, such as web browsing, e-mail, or file transfers.

Cisco CPE devices enable both NAT and *port address translation (PAT)*, also called *overloaded NAT,* which translates one external address into multiple internal addresses.

Cisco IOS Firewall

The Cisco IOS Firewall suite is included with more-sophisticated CPE devices' standard software images, such as on the Cisco 800 routers. The Firewall suite might be available as an addition for other devices' configurations. The Cisco IOS Firewall parameters can be determined and managed remotely by an IT manager or service provider.

The previously discussed techniques and technologies are considered the main components of basic, generic network security. The following sections are related more directly to the DSL network. They describe both industry-standard protocols and Cisco DSL-specific security components.

AAA Overview

This section describes the combined functionality of AAA as it relates specifically to the DSL environment. A very common real-life example of AAA is providing secure access to different network services from the same DSL connection, which must be a PPP connection to use AAA. A user might have one login account for corporate access and a different account for Internet access. Each of these accounts is identified by a unique username and password. In this way, a home office user can access a corporate network with one account while allowing his children to access the Internet with another.

AAA's three component functions are specified in different Requests For Comments (RFCs). AAA is defined in four sequential RFCs, all dating from August 2000:

- RFC 2903, "Generic AAA Architecture"
- RFC 2904, "AAA Authorization Framework"
- RFC 2905, "AAA Authorization Application Examples"
- RFC 2906, "AAA Authorization Requirements"

You can review these and all other RFCs by going to www.ietf.org/rfc.html.

Following is a summary of the three AAA components:

- *Authentication* is the process of validating the claimed identity of an end user or device, such as a host, server, or switch. The end user is identified by a username and password provided during the PPP login negotiation with the network access server (NAS).
- *Authorization* is the act of granting access rights to a user or group of users to specific network services. The AAA server maintains a user profile with services available to the user. These services typically include corporate networks, the Internet, and gaming network servers. From the service provider's point of view, authorization for various online services is usually translated into specific marketing plans.

- *Accounting* is the function that keeps track of the actions performed. Both the current AAA protocols record not only the owner and duration of each remote-access session, but also the service and protocol used, NAS and port identifiers, addresses, octets transferred, and cause of session termination. Together, these variables offer a detailed record of each remote-access session, useful in both auditing and billing functions.

As shown in Figure 5-1, two protocols implement AAA—Terminal Access Controller Access Control System Plus (TACACS+) and Remote Authentication Dial-In User Service (RADIUS). These protocols enable the AAA functionality, and several products are available that conform to the protocols.

Figure 5-1   *Function, Protocols, and Products*

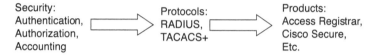

Both of these AAA-enabling protocols allow a service provider to maintain user profiles in a central database that all remote servers can share. They allow the service provider to define and apply a policy at a single administered network point. Having a central service also means that it is easier to track usage for billing and for keeping network statistics. Both RADIUS and TACACS are described in RFC 1492. The current RADIUS specifications are defined in RFC 2865.

Cisco supports both protocol standards to provide the AAA solution. TACACS+ uses Transmission Control Protocol (TCP), and RADIUS uses User Datagram Protocol (UDP). Some administrators recommend using TACACS+ because TCP is seen as a more reliable protocol. Whereas RADIUS combines authentication and authorization in a user profile, resulting in a less complex but less robust protocol, TACACS+ separates the two operations. Although TACACS+ is considered more versatile, RADIUS is used more widely because it requires fewer CPU cycles and is less memory-intensive.

Within the DSL environment, proxy authentication could be used in very large-scale DSL networks, enabling access servers in virtually any location to query independently maintained user databases. The disadvantage of this scheme is that transmitting authentication packets across public networks poses a distinct security risk. RADIUS (and TACACS+ as well) encryption is based on static keys, and usernames, passwords, and authentication server information are conveniently contained in a single packet. Both RADIUS and TACACS+ encrypt passwords as they traverse the network between the NAS and the authentication server. (RADIUS encrypts only the password, and TACACS+ encrypts the entire packet.) Likewise, both protocols support CHAP for added security, preventing passwords from traversing the entire link.

Both RADIUS and TACACS+ were originally engineered for small network devices supporting just a few end users requiring simple server-based authentication. DSL and dialup providers must now provide AAA services for hundreds or thousands of concurrent end users accessing network services over a variety of technologies. They must also support AAA services across ISP boundaries in a secure and scalable manner. This is beginning to place a burden on the functional capabilities of the existing AAA protocols. Therefore, the Internet Engineering Task Force (IETF) has undertaken an effort to develop a next-generation AAA protocol.

A certain combination of features creates a problem for RADIUS and TACACS+. This situation arises when CHAP is combined with a back-end user directory such as a Novell Directory Services (NDS) tree or Microsoft NT domain. To generate the client challenge, CHAP requires access to the cleartext password. However, NT, NDS, and other user directories store a one-way hash of the password—that is, an encrypted version, not the cleartext password itself. This hashed value prevents CHAP from performing the challenge-response interchange, which in turn prevents RADIUS or TACACS+ operations. There are at least three solutions in this scenario. When using RADIUS or TACACS+ with a user directory of passwords, you can ensure smooth operation by using a standard NAS login prompt or PAP. PAP obtains the user's password in clear text, where it can be verified against the back-end directory. Because cleartext transmissions of long-term authentication secrets contradict advanced security, the third solution is to use Cisco's Secure ACS (Access Control System). ACS supports both RADIUS and TACACS+ protocols and can use the NT domain user database for authentication.

RADIUS Overview

Learning the basic operation of a RADIUS server in a dialup environment helps you understand its role in the SSG environment. RADIUS features are shown in Figure 5-2.

Figure 5-2   *RADIUS Features*

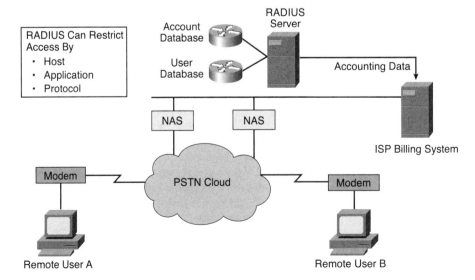

RADIUS allows access control to a single host, to a single application such as Telnet, or to a single protocol such as PPP. RADIUS is used in the following types of DSL network environments. Note that each requires high levels of security while maintaining network access for remote users:

- Networks with multiple-vendor access servers, each supporting RADIUS server-based AAA. Each uses the same RADIUS server-based access database.

- Networks that require resource accounting. Accounting data can be sent at the start and end of the service to meet an ISP's security and billing needs.

- Networks in which the user must access only a single service, such as corporate employees who have telecommuting dialup access to the corporate intranet.

For example, service providers prefer to maintain their access database in a central location rather than distributed into individual devices throughout the network (NASs). This permits easier updating of the database as new users are added, older users are deleted, and service access features are changed. Through a shared RADIUS database, changes to access security can more easily and quickly be implemented in the network.

RADIUS Client/Server Model

RADIUS uses a client/server model, with the RADIUS client represented by the NAS. The RADIUS server is usually a dedicated server. The NAS itself can be any Layer 3-capable router, such as Cisco's AS5xxx family of access servers for dial-in access or the NRP card in the Cisco 6400 Universal Access Concentrator (UAC). The RADIUS client function is a software service of the NAS hardware device. This software function provides access to corporate network services. The NAS and RADIUS server share an authentication secret password in order to ensure the integrity of their mutual transactions.

RADIUS and TACACS+ authorize users for specific rights by associating attribute-value pairs (AVPs), which define those rights with the appropriate user. RADIUS allows the definition of vendor-specific attributes (VSAs) in addition to a base set of dictionary attributes. These VSAs allow vendors to add new features in their NASs that differentiate their products.

RADIUS servers are required to have the following:

- Extensive dictionaries and the capability to provide multivendor support

- Integration with existing user/password databases, such as Lightweight Directory Access Protocol (LDAP), Novell Directory Services (NDS), or other user directories

- The capability to track individual user sessions and provide output to standard spreadsheet or accounting applications to track usage for billing and capacity planning

Communications between the RADIUS client and the RADIUS server are based on UDP. The RADIUS packet contains a code field that identifies the type of packet (such as Access-Request or Access-Accept) and a list of AVPs that describe the parameters to be used in the session.

The RADIUS server is generally a daemon process running on a dedicated UNIX workstation or Windows network machine. The RADIUS server provides these functions:

- It receives access requests for access from multiple RADIUS clients.

- It authenticates users against authorized access lists stored on the database of users and passwords.

- It returns access acceptance packets containing all configuration information needed by the client to deliver service to the end user—that is, the specific AVPs that complete the end user's DSL profile.

In summary, the Cisco 6400 or IP DSL switch serves as the RADIUS client, delivering network access services to the DSL users upon approval from the RADIUS server. The next section details how the RADIUS traffic flows among these devices.

RADIUS Transmission Flow

Bear in mind that RADIUS (and AAA, the functionality that the RADIUS and TACACS+ protocols deliver) is valid only for the two, more-complex DSL network architectures, PPP over Ethernet (PPPoE), and PPP over ATM (PPPoA), as shown in Figure 5-3.

Figure 5-3   *RADIUS Operation Flow*

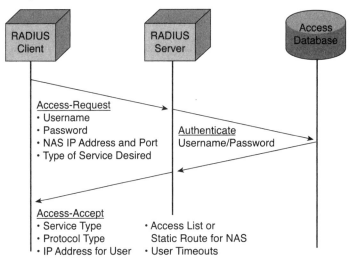

When a user attempts to log in and authenticate at an access server using RADIUS, these steps occur:

Step 1   In the case of PPPoE, the username and password are typically requested and supplied through the PPPoE client software on the user's PC, such as WinPoET. If the ATU-R itself has been configured as the PPPoE client, this is where the username and password are defined and requested.

NOTE   According to "dslReports" of March 2002, WinPoET is the most common default PPPoE software. It was developed by the iVasion Group of RouterWare, Inc., which was acquired by Wind River Systems in 1999. Another PPPoE login client is Enternet, used in the U.S. by SBC Communications, Inc., and its regional operating companies. Enternet was developed by Network TeleSystems (NTS), acquired by Efficient Networks, Inc., in 2000 and now part of Siemens.

In the case of PPPoA, the ATU-R generates the service request when the ATU-R is powered on. Because PPPoA does not use client software, the username and password are configured inside the ATU-R, to be passed to the RADIUS client.

Step 2   When the RADIUS client receives this service request (the PPP login request) from the end user, it creates the Access-Request packet and inserts the user information, including these minimum attributes:

— Username

— Encrypted user password

— NAS IP address and port

— Type of session requested (such as Exec-User or Framed-PPP)

Step 3   The RADIUS client sends the Access-Request to the RADIUS server.

Step 4   When the RADIUS server receives the Access-Request, it searches the access database to compare user details with the stored information. If a match is found, the RADIUS server returns an Access-Accept packet containing these Return-List-Attributes:

— Service type (shell or framed)

— PPP

— Exec

— Telnet

— Protocol type

— Internet protocol (IP) address to assign to the user (static or dynamic)

— Access list to apply to NAS

— Static route to install in the NAS routing table

— User timeouts

This is called the *authentication phase*. If the Access-Accept packet contains Return-List-Attributes that customize the user's session, it is also called the *authorization phase*.

RADIUS can also send one of these responses:

— **Reject**—The user is not authenticated and is prompted to reenter the username and password, or access is denied.

— **Challenge**—A challenge is issued that collects additional data from the user before authentication.

— **Change Password**—The user is asked to select a new password.

Step 5 The client acts on the response sent by the RADIUS server. The action may be an acceptance, rejection, challenge, or request to change the password.

RADIUS Accounting Flow

The next phase of RADIUS operation is called the *accounting phase*. It is shown in Figure 5-4.

Figure 5-4   *RADIUS Accounting Flow*

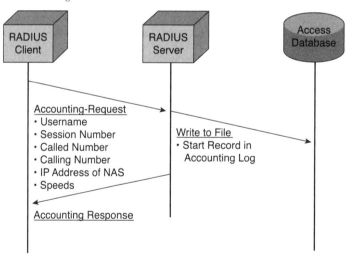

After the Access-Accept is received, the NAS sends an Accounting-Request to the RADIUS server. The request contains specific information about the call. The two most common accounting types are *call start* and *call stop*. A start Accounting-Request is sent when a dial-in session begins, and a stop record is written to the RADIUS server when the session ends.

The Accounting-Request can include such information as

- Username
- Session number
- NAS's IP address
- Transmit and receive speeds

The Accounting-Request causes the RADIUS server to write the accounting record to a file and to create a start record in the server's accounting log. The server acknowledges creation of the start record by sending an Accounting-Response to the client. Accounting information in the user access database is then transferred to the ISP billing system for generation of service or usage billing.

RADIUS Profiles

This section explains the parameters of user access and restrictions, which are grouped into RADIUS profiles. These profiles are individualized based on the user's preceding RADIUS AAA validation.

As you can see in Figure 5-5, the service selection model uses three different RADIUS profiles to control the service selection process:

- Service profile
- Client profile
- User profile

Each of these is discussed in the following sections.

Figure 5-5   *RADIUS Parameters Grouped into Profiles*

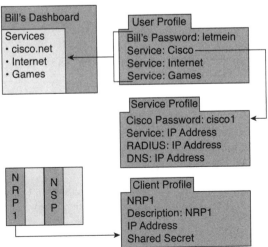

Service Profile

Each possible online service has its own service profile, which defines that service's associated parameters. There must be a corresponding service profile for each service identified in the user profile. The service profile defines such parameters as how to access the service, how to authenticate a user on the service, and how long a user can remain connected to the service.

The service profile attributes describe such things as the label for the dashboard button, the network address of the destination service, and the IP address of the RADIUS server. The service profile might also contain the Domain Name Service (DNS) server address. For a comprehensive list of all possible attributes in the service profile, consult the documentation for the particular Cisco device to be configured.

Client Profile

RADIUS also contains a client profile that identifies any RADIUS client that is permitted to access the RADIUS server. This profile contains the security key that must be exchanged between the RADIUS clients and RADIUS servers to authorize RADIUS client access.

When the RADIUS server receives an Access-Request packet, it verifies the RADIUS client against an existing client's profile. For a comprehensive list of all possible attributes in the client profile, consult the documentation for the particular Cisco device to be configured. Among other values, the client profile attributes include the following:

- Profile name
- Profile description
- Client IP address (must match the client IP address in the Access-Request packet)
- Shared secret password for RADIUS communication
- Type of client (such as a NAS)

User Profile

The user profile authenticates a user and authorizes the appropriate service(s). The contents of the user profile determine the services that are available on the service selection screen. The screen can be customized for individual users or, more likely, any one of several subscriber classes of service.

RADIUS checks for a user profile that has the same username. If the profile is found, RADIUS checks the password for proper authentication. If the user profile is not found, the user login fails.

As soon as authentication occurs, the user must be authorized to access specific services. This is done through a list of services in the user profile, which determines the online services available to the user. It also defines the service buttons that appear on the user's service selection screen. Each entry in the service list is actually a pointer to a service profile that describes that service.

A user profile can also contain both session and idle timeout values. These define the maximum amount of time (in seconds) a user can remain logged in to the dashboard (session timer) or the maximum amount of time the user can remain idle before being automatically logged out of the dashboard. For a comprehensive list of all possible attributes in the user profile, consult the documentation for the particular Cisco device to be configured. An individual user profile must be created for each unique user accessing the SSD. Guest accounts can be created to facilitate trial access by potential SSD customers or to cover any delay in creating a specific user account.

A typical user profile might include the following:

- User's password
- Defined access to a corporate network
- Defined subscription access to the Internet
- Defined access to a specialty network, such as an academic or gaming network

In summary, three profiles categorize the RADIUS values. These profiles, and RADIUS itself, are not unique to DSL networking, but they can be leveraged to provide a more customized user interface, Internet gateway, and accounting engine for DSL users. This is called a *Service Selection Gateway (SSG)*. As the name implies, the SSG builds on the AAA functionality by adding user selection options in a provider-defined Internet portal in a mutually beneficial way for both the DSL user and the service provider. The SSG is explained in the next section.

Service Selection Gateway Overview

In the first implementations of DSL before the SSG, DSL users would typically be sent to a single service, such as the Internet, corporate intranet, or extranet, through a single virtual circuit to that particular network. Any need for additional networking required another circuit. This additional DSL networking required days, if not weeks, to provision the circuit, adjust billing details, and so on, much like changing voice service not so many years ago.

Now network providers can offer various selection options according to the DSL subscriber's class of service and subscription. There are service provider options for both simpler OSI Layer 2 SSGs and more complex and more robust Layer 3 SSGs.

In the most robust implementations of the SSG, the provider can market different domains and different qualities of service with varying bit rates. A creative marketing plan could even offer temporary service changes, such as for on-demand events, and should be able to make service changes almost immediately. For instance, suppose a business subscriber is participating in a project that requires extensive online collaboration with a remote client.

In a residential scenario, suppose that children are on school holiday; parents could select an additional, child-focused domain for age-appropriate entertainment. In both scenarios, the SSG could allow the subscriber to increase bandwidth for a particular period of time and then resume the previous rate, all with easy and accurate billing changes. RADIUS accounting records keep track of the service selected and the connection time. The SSG's refinement to RADIUS gives the transport provider detailed station usage records for accurate billing.

The SSG can provide universal VPN control as well for on-demand telecommuting security. (VPNs are explained in more detail later in this chapter.)

The service selection feature is composed of three components that interact to provide the required service. As shown in Figure 5-6, the three components that make up the service selection are the SSG, the SSD, and the RADIUS server. Because we've already discussed the RADIUS server, the following sections cover SSG and SSD.

Figure 5-6 *Service Selection Components*

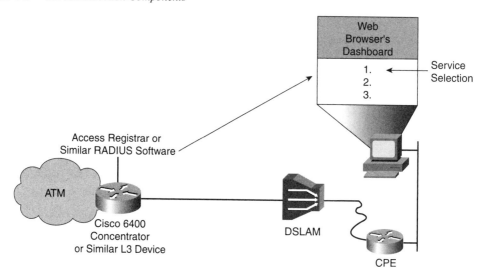

Service Selection Gateway

SSG is the software running on the Cisco 6400's NRP or another Layer 3- (L3) capable device. SSG is a component of all Cisco IOS images from 12.05 and above.

The SSG software binds the user connection to an IP address of the destination service. The SSG communicates with the RADIUS server to acquire authentication and authorization information on the end user. It also communicates with the SSD to identify services selected and functions requested by the user. The SSG has a unique RADIUS key that identifies it to the RADIUS server and a unique service key that identifies it to the SSD.

Service Selection Dashboard

The SSD is a web server that controls the user interface for selecting access to various services. The SSD serves as an interface to the AAA functionality of the RADIUS or TACACS+ server, as well as the DSL-specific operation of the SSG itself. To authenticate a user, the SSG uses a user profile that is stored in the RADIUS server. When a user logs in to the dashboard, the username and password are placed in an Access-Request packet that is sent to RADIUS. From the user's point of view, the SSD facilitates direct access to the contracted services without making the user type Internet addresses. From the service provider's point of view, the SSD can provide additional revenue through advertising on its web interface.

The SSD web address is programmed into the user's web browser as the home page. The SSD itself is software implemented in Java using servlets that can be run on a wide variety of network operating system platforms. The dashboard uses HTML pages to display the web selection screen at the user's web client. When the DSL service is first brought up, the user can only access the dashboard. The user then can select a service by clicking the corresponding service button.

The different individual dashboard logins can determine the screen offering of a unique menu of services. The SSD translates the username and password received via HTTP into a RADIUS authentication packet and sends it to the SSG server. This permits personalized services for each member of the family, such as corporate intranet access for telecommuting adults and age-appropriate entertainment and education services for children.

From this web selection page, the user can do the following:

- Log in to or out of sessions from the dashboard logon screen
- View a service list
- Log in to or out of services by clicking dashboard buttons
- View session status of any active connection
- View messages for diagnostic support

Layer 2 Service Selection

Layer 2 service selection depends on a structured username that selects the desired service. In particular, *PPP Termination Aggregation (PTA)* is a PPP selection method based on a structured domain name (username@service.com) that supports a single service at a time. With Layer 2 service selection, the following occurs:

Step 1   A user initiates a PPP session with a structured username in the format of user@serviceA.com. This can be configured into the DSL modem (especially for PPPoA) or entered into the PPPoE client login screen.

Step 2   The PPP session terminates at the NRP of the Cisco 6300 access
concentrator that is running the SSG software. The SSG examines the
username of the PPP session and accesses a service profile for the
requested service. The service profile's parameters include the service's
destination IP address.

A connection is now made in the SSG between the user in the downlink direction and the
service in the uplink direction.

If the user wants to access a different service, he or she must first disconnect from the
present service. Using a different username (user@serviceB.com, for example), the user
can initiate a new connection to the second service.

Layer 2 service selection (PTA) has these characteristics:

- The user can access only one destination at a time.
- It is implemented without SSD.
- It can be used only by PPP-type users, because it is based on the PPP username.

Layer 3 Service Selection

As shown in Figure 5-7, Layer 3 service selection lets a Cisco DSL user control service
access through a web interface. This service-selection capability allows service providers
to customize services to meet the individual needs of their client base.

Figure 5-7   *Full-Featured Service Selection*

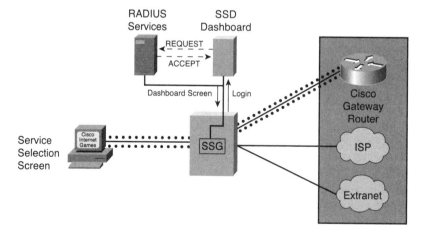

Layer 3 SSG service selection is done using a web browser to display a dashboard of available services. This method of service selection is independent of Layers 1 and 2. Web-based service selection may be used over these TCP/IP architectures:

- RFC 1483 bridged (Integrated Routing and Bridging [IRB])
- RFC 1483 routed (Route Bridge Encapsulation [RBE])
- PPPoA
- PPPoE

When a connection is established to the L3 authentication source, the user is given access to the dashboard server (SSD) by default, and these steps occur:

Step 1 The user opens the web browser, whose home page is the dashboard server. The user sees an SSG login screen.

Step 2 The user logs into the dashboard service with a unique SSG username and password.

Step 3 The SSG sends the username and password to the dashboard server (the SSD) in the form of an HTML request containing the username and password.

Step 4 When the web dashboard server receives the request, it triggers an Access-Request packet to the RADIUS server. If the user is authenticated, RADIUS sends back an Access-Accept packet with a list of services for that user.

Step 5 The dashboard server constructs a web page that contains buttons for the authenticated services.

Step 6 The user selects a service or feature by clicking the corresponding dashboard button.

Layer 3 service selection has these characteristics:

- Because it uses HTML code, it can be used with any web browser
- Advertising can be sold on the web page
- Services can be turned on and off without having to disconnect the end user's service
- A user can select multiple destinations simultaneously or sequentially
- Users can have personalized service through a unique web selection screen

In summary, the RADIUS service of authentication, authorization and accounting (AAA) is extended in the DSL environment through the customization of service selection for individual users and service levels. The next section describes virtual private networking, which can be available as a security option through the service selection gateway or enabled as a standalone functionality.

Virtual Private Networks, Virtual Private Dialup Networks, and Layer 2 Tunneling Protocol

Telecommuting business users who need to connect to a corporate network over the Internet usually require more security than authentication of their own remote device enabled by PAP or CHAP. Additional security is afforded by data encryption with IPSec for VPNs. A VPN means customer connectivity deployed on a shared (public) infrastructure with the same policies as a private network, where users expect the same application behavior, performance, and connectivity. A VPN can be built on the Internet or on a service provider's IP, Frame Relay, or ATM infrastructure.

In terms of security, VPNs let IP traffic travel securely over a public TCP/IP network by encrypting all traffic from one network to another. A VPN uses tunneling to encrypt all information at the IP level.

VPNs are classified differently by different equipment providers. Among the other Cisco VPN types, such as intranet and extranet VPNs, the access VPN applies most directly to the DSL world. Access VPN services are most popular with mobile users and telecommuters who require remote-access connectivity through DSL, as well as other access methods such as dialup, wireless, and cable technologies.

A key building block for access VPNs is Layer 2 Tunneling Protocol (L2TP), an extension of the PPP protocol and a fundamental building block of virtual private dialup networks (VPDNs). VPDNs are networks that extend dialup access to users over a shared infrastructure. They are a cost-effective method of establishing long-distance point-to-point connections between remote users and a private network. With VPNs, organizations do not have to use expensive leased or frame relay lines and can connect remote users to their corporate networks via a local Internet service provider (ISP) instead of via expensive 800-number or long-distance calls to resource-consuming modem banks.

L2TP merges the best features of two other tunneling protocols: Layer 2 Forwarding (L2F) from Cisco Systems and Point-to-Point Tunneling (PPTP) from Microsoft.

L2TP by itself does not offer protection from typical Internet security threats. IPSec's goal is to minimize all these threats in the existing network infrastructure without requiring expensive host and application modifications to the existing VPDNs. In a DSL context, an ISP partners with one or more of its enterprise customers to add IPSec encryption to an existing VPDN.

In an encryption environment, support can be challenging because of the extra delay introduced by the cryptographic process. Cisco has VPN hardware encryption modules on various router families to offload the encryption tasks. Encryption is rarely used with voice traffic because voice sessions are less prone to attacks because of their real-time nature. This means that wiretapping the packetized voice connection requires very specialized equipment in the voice traffic path. The difficulty of tapping into real-time packetized voice traffic is unlike analog voice traffic, which can be tapped by very simple means, and unlike IP data traffic, which can be received and stored for later review.

Summary

RADIUS is one of two industry-standard protocols used to implement AAA functions in addition to TACACS+.

RADIUS is used in network environments that require high levels of security while maintaining network access for remote users. The RADIUS protocol is based on the client/server model.

RADIUS supports access to a central database of remote users and their authorized services. RADIUS allows the definition of VSAs in addition to a base set of dictionary attributes.

Service selection is controlled by three profiles in the RADIUS server—the user, service, and client profiles. The user profile authenticates the user and identifies the services that the user is authorized to access. The service profile contains the attributes that describe the service. These attributes allow the SSG to bind the user to the selected service. The client profile allows the RADIUS server to authenticate a remote RADIUS client.

Service selection allows the user to dynamically select services and service quality. The operation of the service selection requires careful coordination between the SSG, the SSD, and the RADIUS server. Both the SSD and SSG request information from RADIUS that is stored in specific profiles.

Layer 2 service selection uses a structured username to map to a requested service. Layer 3 service selection uses a web selection screen to allow users to click the desired service.

Review Questions

1 Which of the following typically controls end-user access through AAA to a specific network service?

   A Dial-in access number

   B PPP login

   C Network profile

   D Service profile

2 Which of the following statements about RADIUS are true?

   A RADIUS can collect accounting data for transfer to the ISP billing system.

   B RADIUS is a less-complex AAA protocol than TACACS+.

   C A single common RADIUS server can be accessed by many different NASs.

   D Each NAS authenticates with RADIUS using a secret authentication password.

   E All of the above.

3 Which parameter is contained in the Accounting-Request packet?

  A Username

  B IP address of the RADIUS client

  C Unique session number

  D Calling number

  E All of the above

4 In the DSL environment, what could be the RADIUS client?

  A ATU-R

  B DSLAM

  C NRP

  D Home hub

5 Which attribute is *not* returned in an Access-Accept packet from the RADIUS server?

  A User authentication password

  B End user's IP address

  C Static route to the NAS

  D Service type

  E Access list

6 RADIUS uses VSAs to do what? (Select all that apply.)

  A Add extra security features

  B Replace base dictionaries

  C Differentiate vendor products

  D Make RADIUS interoperable with older software

7 The Start Accounting-Request is sent from the NAS to the RADIUS server at what point?

  A When the access device is powered on

  B After the Access-Reject is received

  C After the Access-Accept is received

  D Upon logout of the session

8 Which function is performed by the RADIUS client?

A Creates an Access-Request packet

B Returns an Access-Reject packet

C Initiates the service request

D Returns an Access-Accept packet

9 Which of the following is *not* a valid response from the RADIUS server to an Access-Request packet?

A Access-Accept

B Access-Reject

C Challenge

D Access Restricted

E Change Password

10 With Layer 3 SSG, if a dashboard (SSD) user requests a connection to the user's corporate network, which of the following profiles contains the IP address of the corporate gateway?

A User profile

B Service profile

C Client profile

D Dashboard profile

11 Which attribute(s) is/are contained in the user profile?

A The username and password

B The attributes that describe a particular service

C The type of RADIUS client

D The IP address of the RADIUS server

12 Which of the following is *not* part of the service profile?

A The IP address of the RADIUS server

B The IP address of the DNS server

C The IP address of the RADIUS client

D The labels for the service buttons

13 Which attribute is contained in the client profile?

A The IP address of the DNS server

B The username and password of the dashboard user

C The service network address

D The IP address of the RADIUS client

14 Which profile contains a list of services to be displayed on the service selection screen?

A User profile

B Service profile

C Client profile

D Dashboard profile

15 Why can Layer 2 service selection connect to only one service at a time?

A It can store only one service profile.

B It is linked to the PPP username.

C It requires SSD support for multiple connections.

D It uses a web interface.

16 Why does Layer 3 service selection provide personalized services?

A It is based on the PPP login.

B It is preconfigured for each user.

C It is sold at a higher price.

D It is based on a unique SSG login.

17 Which service selection component authenticates the user login at the SSD?

A Web interface

B User profile

C Dashboard server

D RADIUS server

18 Which service selection component is responsible for sending the RADIUS Access-Request packet?

A   ATU-R

B   SSD

C   RADIUS client (NRP)

D   RADIUS server

19 Which of the following initiates Layer 2 service selection?

A   DSL profile

B   RADIUS profile

C   Structured PPP username

D   The web selection screen

20 Layer 3 service selection offers which of the following benefits? (Select all that apply.)

A   Sell advertising space on the web selection screen

B   Dynamically select from a list of available services

C   Dynamically select service quality

D   Prevent unwanted telemarketer calls

CHAPTER 6

Cisco IOS Configurations

This chapter presents the configurations of the four basic TCP/IP architectures for DSL that were described in Chapter 3, "TCP/IP Over ATM." These include three architectures based on RFC 2684 (which made obsolete RFC 1483): Integrated Routing and Bridging (IRB), Routed Bridge Encapsulation (RBE), and Point-to-Point Protocol over ATM (PPPoA). Additionally, both Chapter 3 and this chapter explain Point-to-Point Protocol over Ethernet (PPPoE, RFC 2516). Virtual Private Networks (VPNs) are also described in this chapter, but they are configured beyond the actual DSL network.

In DSL networking, PPPoE is the most popular, although exact market shares of these architectures have not been defined. IRB was the first common architecture in the DSL world and is generally considered obsolescent, although it is still present in legacy networks around the world. RBE is more secure and scalable than IRB while still allowing for the simple, low-cost equipment found in legacy networks. PPPoA is the author's favorite, enabling optimal scalability for provider network expansion and increased end-user sophistication, combined with better security for all parties. All these architectures are encountered in today's DSL networks, and all are covered on the Cisco certification examinations.

This chapter starts with configurations for the Cisco 827 CPE router and then describes the configurations for the Cisco 6000 series of IP/DSL Switches. It finishes with the configurations for the Cisco 6400 Universal Access Concentrator (UAC). You might need to refer to Appendix B, "ATM Overview," to review the details of ATM.

Cisco 827 DSL Configurations

Setting up voice service on the Cisco 827 router is more demanding than just enabling the port(s). Voice activation actually includes two configurations: one for data and one for voice. When you have completed the configuration for the data scenario, you can add voice by configuring the voice ports and dial peers for both analog voice service and Voice over IP (VoIP). The first part of this chapter shows the configuration for data traffic only. Each architecture configuration is explained in its own section. Voice configurations for the 827 are shown in the second half of this chapter.

The data configurations section first lists the configuration commands that are common to all the TCP/IP architectures, such as interface configuration commands. If you understand and can apply those common commands, you can see more quickly the specific commands for each type of architecture. These architecture-specific commands are described in a different section for each type. Beyond learning the commonalities of all the architectures, you only need to learn the architecture-specific commands for Cisco certification testing, because no DSL service provider would combine all four types simultaneously. Therefore, in the real world, you probably would read about a certain architecture and its configurations, (optimally) try out that configuration or evaluate it for your own network needs, and return to read about alternatives at your convenience.

Interface Commands Common to All DSL Architectures

These configuration commands apply to the ATM and Ethernet interfaces of the Cisco 827, where the ATM interface is also the DSL interface facing the DSL network itself. ATM commands are listed and explained, followed by the Ethernet commands, including enabling basic Network Address Translation (NAT) and Port Address Translation (PAT). After the interface commands, Challenge Handshake Authentication Protocol (CHAP) security commands are listed and explained. Finally in this section of common Cisco 827 commands, basic IP routing commands are listed and explained.

ATM Interface Commands

On the Cisco 827 ADSL router, here are the ATM interface configuration commands you will use most frequently, regardless of the type of TCP/IP architecture:

- **interface ATM0**—Begins interface configuration mode on the main ATM interface, the ADSL port.

- **no shut**—For new routers, the only configuration that is necessary to activate the ADSL port (the ATM interface) is to perform a **no shut** on the ATM interface. If the ADSL trainup is successful, you see the ATM interface line and line protocol become active. If not, use the **debug** command to debug the trainup sequence, as explained throughout other Cisco documentation but not repeated here.

- **no ip address**—Conserves IP addresses by not assigning an address to this main ATM interface.

- **dsl operating-mode auto**—This value might be the default, depending on your version of Cisco IOS Software. Cisco recommends using this command if you are unsure what discrete multitone (DMT) technology the ISP is using. It provides for automatic analysis and synchronization for either of the ITU-defined DMT standards (G.992.1 and G.992.2). If the DSLAM/IP-DSL Switch is using a Cisco 4xDMT ADI-based card with the ANSI-defined DMT2 standard, you should enter the command **dsl operating-mode ansi-dmt**.

- Depending on the version of Cisco IOS Software, you might or might not see the command **no atm ilmi-keepalive** in the configuration, because this is now a default value. When you enable Integrated Local Management Interface (ILMI) keepalives on a dual ATM module, periodic ILMI keepalive messages are sent to the ATM switch on the active. The ATM switch responds to the ILMI keepalives. If the ATM switch fails to respond to four consecutive keepalives, the dual switches from the active to the backup. The ILMI keepalives feature is useful only if the module is connected to two different ATM switches.

- **bundle-enable**—ATM Permanent Virtual Circuit (PVC) bundles allow you to configure multiple PVCs that have different quality of service (QoS) characteristics between two devices. The purpose is to bind a PVC from the bundle to one or more precedence values. To determine which VC in the bundle will be used to forward specific traffic, the ATM VC bundle management software matches precedence levels between packets and VCs.

   The ATM virtual bundle acts as a single routing link to the destination router. The Operation and Maintenance (OAM) polling mechanism monitors each circuit's integrity individually. For more information, see Appendix B.

- **hold-queue**—Each network interface, including this ATM interface, has a hold-queue limit. This limit is the number of data packets that the interface can store in its hold queue before rejecting new packets. When the interface empties the hold queue by one or more packets, the interface can accept new packets again.

   The command **no hold-queue** with the appropriate keyword restores an interface's default values. The keyword **in** specifies the input queue, and the keyword **out** specifies the output queue. The default input hold queue is 75 packets. The default output hold-queue limit is 100 packets. A queue size has no fixed upper limit. The input hold queue prevents a single interface from flooding the network server with too many input packets. Further input packets are discarded if the interface has too many input packets outstanding in the system. This limit prevents a malfunctioning interface from consuming an excessive amount of memory. For slow links, use a small output hold-queue limit. This approach prevents storing packets at a rate that exceeds the link's transmission capability. For fast links, use a large output hold-queue limit. A fast link might be busy for a short time (and thus require the hold queue), but it can empty the output hold queue quickly when capacity returns.

- **interface ATM0.1 point-to-point**—Configures a virtual ATM subinterface and defines it as a point-to-point type; this command opens subinterface configuration mode. Subinterfaces are handy for differentiating virtual connections by DSL QoS and/or ATM class of service. For instance, priority business DSL subscribers' virtual connections might be configured on one subinterface, and standard residential DSL subscribers' virtual connections would be configured on another subinterface. There might be hundreds, or even thousands, of subinterfaces, so there might be two, three, or more digits after the **ATM0.** prefix. In practice, good DSL network design limits the number of subinterfaces, just as different service-level agreements are limited to a reasonable number that can be easily marketed and configured. Last but not least regarding subinterfaces, an enormous number of subinterfaces would eventually hamper CPU performance.

- **pvc 1/32**—Begins to configure this PVC, as assigned by the DSL network provider, as virtual circuit 32 on virtual path 1 (or any other valid combination) on this interface or subinterface; this command opens PVC configuration mode.

- If NAT is used, the command **ip nat outside** enables external network address translation and establishes this subinterface (the ADSL interface on the 827) as the outside interface.

Ethernet Interface Commands

- On the Cisco 827 ADSL router, the Ethernet interface is the one facing the user network. Here are the Ethernet interface configuration commands you will see and use most frequently. They apply to most types of TCP/IP architectures.

- If NAT is used, the command **ip nat inside** establishes the Ethernet interface as the inside interface for translation direction.

- The command **ip address negotiated** indicates that Internet Protocol Control Protocol (IPCP, RFC 1332) is being used rather than a static IP address. IPCP is an efficient way to obtain the baseline IP address for the Ethernet interface. It is frequently used to enable distribution of IP addresses to the user's LAN devices through Dynamic Host Configuration Protocol (DHCP), where IPCP provides a valid starting address to acquire the range of DHCP addresses.

- Alternatively, a command such as **ip address 192.168.1.1 255.255.255.0** assigns an IP address and subnet to the Ethernet interface.

- The command **mtu** *size* applies to the Maximum Transmission Unit (MTU). Each interface has a default maximum packet size or MTU size. This number generally defaults to the largest size possible for that type of interface. The default MTU size is 1500 on the Ethernet interface. As you will learn later in this chapter, the PPPoE configuration requires changing this Ethernet default. Other architectures and interfaces might require specific MTU configuration as well.

Challenge Handshake Authentication Protocol (CHAP) Commands

The command **ppp authentication chap callin** is one of three commands in typical configurations that together specify CHAP parameters for multiple scenarios. Normally, when two devices use CHAP, each side sends a challenge to which the other side responds, and it is authenticated by the challenger. Each side authenticates the other independently. If you want to operate with non-Cisco routers that do not support authentication by the calling router or device, you *must* use the command **ppp authentication chap callin**.

When you use the **ppp authentication** command with the **callin** keyword, the access server authenticates the remote device only if the remote device initiated the call—that is, if it is the remote device that is calling in. In this case, authentication is specified on incoming (received) calls only.

The second and third CHAP commands configure the central site with a single username and shared secret. These values can be used to authenticate multiple dial-in clients.

For example, consider a situation in which multiple remote devices dial into a central site. Using normal CHAP authentication, the username (which would be the host name) of each remote device and a shared secret must be configured on the central router. In this scenario, the configuration of the central router can get lengthy and cumbersome to manage; however, if the remote devices use a username that is different from their host name, this can be avoided. The username configuration command is **ppp chap hostname** *username1*.

The third CHAP command is **ppp chap password** *password*. It lets the 827 call one or more routers that do not support CHAP as it is defined in up-to-date Cisco IOS Software versions on the 827 router. This configures a common CHAP secret password to use in response to challenges from an unknown peer.

For example, your Cisco 827 might call a rotary of routers (either from another vendor, or running an older version of the Cisco IOS Software) to which a new (that is, unknown) router has been added. The **ppp chap password** command allows you to replace several username and password configuration commands with a single copy of this command on any dialer interface or asynchronous group interface. This command is used for remote CHAP authentication only (when routers authenticate to the peer). It does not affect local CHAP authentication.

Additional Common Commands

The command **ip route 0.0.0.0 0.0.0.0 192.168.2.254** configures the default gateway, pointing the way through the interface address 192.168.2.254 to the rest of the networked world. The commands discussed previously, starting with the interface configuration commands and including NAT, CHAP, and other common commands, are the basis of the following sections concerning architecture-specific commands.

PPPoA Configuration

Figure 6-1 shows the role of a Cisco 827 router configured with PPPoA.

Figure 6-1   *Cisco 827 Using PPPoA with Dialer Interface, IPCP Negotiation, and NAT Overload*

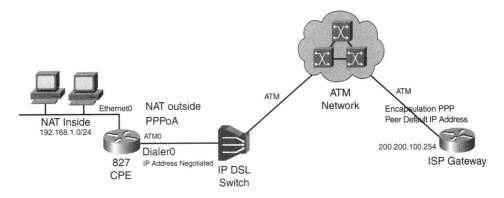

The following configuration output enables the functionality shown in Figure 6-1. In this configuration, first the Ethernet interface is configured with its IP address and subnet mask. Then the ATM interface (ATM0) is configured, as explained earlier in the "ATM Interface Commands" section, and an ATM subinterface is defined on which PVC 1/32 is configured. The

PPPoA-specific commands begin after the PVC definition. Those commands are explained following this configuration listing:

```
version 12.2
!
interface Ethernet0
    ip address 192.168.1.1 255.255.255.0!
interface ATM0
!(lines omitted)
    interface ATM0.1 point-to-point
      pvc 1/32
        encapsulation aal5mux ppp dialer
        dialer pool-member 1
    interface Dialer1
      ip address negotiated
      ip nat outside
      encapsulation ppp
      dialer pool 1
!
 ip route 0.0.0.0 0.0.0.0 Dialer1
!
hold-queue 224 in

    ppp authentication chap callin
    ppp chap hostname <username1>
    ppp chap password <password1>
!
```

Here are descriptions of the commands:

- **encapsulation aal5mux ppp dialer**—Specifies the encapsulation type for the PVC as aal5mux with Point-to-Point Protocol (PPP) characteristics. It also points back to the dialer interface, which is the ADSL interface on the Cisco 827.

- **dialer pool-member 1**—Specifies that this PVC is a member of dialer pool 1. There can be more than one dialer pool on the physical dialer interface, which is the ADSL interface. Each dialer pool connects to a specific destination subnetwork. That subnetwork usually represents the Cisco IP/DSL Switch.

- **interface Dialer1**—A dialer interface assigns PPP features (such as authentication and IP address assignment method) to a PVC. Dialer interfaces are used when configuring PPP over ATM. This value can be any number in the range 0 through 255. No dialer rotary groups are predefined. This command also opens interface configuration mode for the ADSL interface, which is designated the dialer interface. A dialer interface is not a physical interface, but a logical grouping of physical interfaces with the same configuration. Dialer interfaces allow you to apply a single interface configuration, such as an access control list, to one or more physical interfaces. This standardizes the configuration on those interfaces and reduces configuration labor.

- **ip address negotiated**—Rather than assigning an IP address to this dialer interface, IPCP is used to obtain an IP address as needed upon startup.

- **ip nat outside**—This dialer interface (the ADSL interface, also the ATM interface) is the interface that translates external IP addresses through NAT.

- **encapsulation ppp**—Associates the PPP encapsulation with this dialer (ADSL) interface.

- **dialer pool 1**—Specifies on the dialer (ADSL) interface which dialer pool number to use to connect to a specific destination subnetwork. The number can be any number from 1 to 255. There is no default. This number must match the number used in the **dialer pool-member 1** under the physical interface.

- **ip route 0.0.0.0 0.0.0.0 Dialer1**—Configures the default route available through this dialer (ADSL) interface.

Now suppose that the provider has assigned a single, external IP address. In addition to the configuration shown previously, you can proceed to add the commands for NAT overload, also called PAT, as shown in the following:

```
interface Ethernet0
  ip address 192.168.1.1 255.255.255.0
  ip nat inside
interface Dialer1
    ip address negotiated
    encapsulation ppp
    dialer pool 1
!   (lines omitted)
    ip nat outside
!

ip route 0.0.0.0 0.0.0.0 Dialer0

access-list 1 permit 192.168.1.0 0.0.0.255
!
ip nat inside source list 1 interface Dialer1 overload
```

- **ip nat outside** establishes the interface Dialer1, the ADSL interface, as the NAT outside interface.

- **access-list 1 permit 192.168.1.0 0.0.0.255** defines a standard access list, matching the number 1 of the **list 1** in the next command, permitting addresses that need translation.

- **ip nat inside source list 1 interface Dialer1 overload** enables PAT using the Dialer1 IP address as the inside global address for source addresses that match **access-list 1** in the previous command.

The final set of modifications to the original, simple PPPoA configuration lets the 827 deliver IP addresses to the user workstations and other client devices using DHCP:

```
interface Ethernet0
  ip address 192.168.1.1 255.255.255.0
  ip nat inside
interface Dialer0
    ip address negotiated
    encapsulation ppp
    dialer pool 1
!   (lines omitted)
    ip nat outside

!(lines omitted)

ip dhcp pool POOL-DHCP
      network 192.168.1.0 255.255.255.0
      domain-name cisco.com
      dns-server 192.168.3.1
      default-router 192.168.1.1
```

In this configuration, the command **ip dhcp pool POOL-DHCP** defines the range of IP addresses that can be assigned to the DHCP clients. Note that rather than specify a beginning address and an ending address in the pool, subnetting is used for the entire subnet 192.168.1.0.

The command **domain-name cisco.com** simply configures the domain name—in this case, with the variable **cisco.com**. The command **dns-server 192.168.3.1** defines the DNS server with that IP address. The command **default-router 192.168.1.1** designates the 827 router as the default router and specifies an IP address.

RFC 2684 Bridging (Formerly RFC 1483 Bridging)

Figure 6-2 shows the role of the 827 device in a bridged network.

Figure 6-2   *Cisco 827 Using RFC 2684 Bridging (IRB) with NAT*

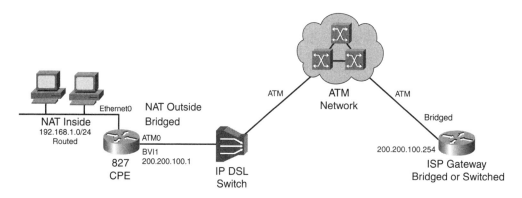

RFC 2684 bridging is possible on the Cisco 827, as shown in this section's configuration and explanations. The 827 is capable of more-sophisticated configurations than bridging. Therefore, its use in bridging would probably be as an interim solution for a DSL provider who is migrating to a more-sophisticated model, such as PPPoE or PPPoA. When the 827 router is in bridge mode, the Ethernet and ATM interfaces can have the same IP address. That would be the MAC address of interface ethernet0, displayed with the Cisco IOS Software command **show interface ethernet 0**. Following is the configuration for RFC 2684 bridging:

```
bridge irb
!
interface Ethernet0
 ip address 192.168.1.1 255.255.255.0
!
interface ATM0
 (lines omitted)
 bundle-enable
!
interface ATM0.1 point-to-point
 pvc 1/32
```

```
!
  encapsulation aal5snap
!
 bridge-group 1
!
interface BVI1
!
 ip address 192.168.2.1 255.255.255.0
 no ip directed-broadcast
!
ip route 0.0.0.0 0.0.0.0 192.168.2.254
!
bridge 1 protocol ieee
 bridge 1 route ip
```

Here are the explanations for the pertinent commands in this configuration:

- **bridge irb** enables IRB as opposed to the Cisco 827 default of routing.

- **encapsulation aal5snap** specifies the encapsulation type for this particular PVC. **aal5snap** means ATM Adaptation Layer 5 Subnetwork Access Protocol, the standard for RFC 2684-based bridging.

- **bridge-group 1** specifies the bridge-group number to which the point-to-point ATM0.1 interface belongs. This corresponds to the **bridge protocol** command.

- **interface BVI1** defines a bridge group virtual interface (BVI) on the existing routed interface from the WAN bridge group to the nonbridged LAN interface—that is, from the DSL provider to the internal LAN. Each bridge group can have only one corresponding BVI. When you configure the BVI and enable routing on it, as shown in the preceding command, packets that come in on a routed interface destined for a host on a segment that is in a bridge group are transferred from Layer 3 routing to Layer 2 bridging across this interface.

- **ip address 192.168.2.1 255.255.255.0** assigns an IP address and subnet to the BVI within interface configuration mode on BVI 1.

- **bridge 1 protocol ieee** enables the Cisco 827 router's bridging engine, identifies the bridging process with a bridge-group number, and specifies the particular spanning tree algorithm used to avoid bridging loops. All routers on the network that expect to bridge between each other need to share the same bridge-group number. The selected spanning-tree protocol must also be consistent on each router. In this example, the IEEE spanning-tree algorithm is specified (as it invariably is) rather than the DEC option.

- **bridge 1 route ip** enables IP routing to and from bridge group 1.

RFC 2684 Bridging with PAT

Beyond the simplest configuration for RFC 2684 bridging, you can also configure the Cisco 827 to include NAT and PAT. As described previously for the basic IRB configuration, the Cisco 827 might be used as a bridging device in a legacy DSL network situation. In this scenario, only one registered IP address might be assigned by the service provider, indicating the benefit of PAT, which translates one-to-many IP addresses. This is shown in the following configuration:

```
bridge irb
! (lines omitted)
interface Ethernet0
   ip address 192.168.1.1 255.255.255.0
   ip nat inside
! (lines omitted)
interface BVI1
 ip address 192.168.2.1 255.255.255.0
   ip nat outside
!
ip nat inside source list 1 interface BVI1 overload
!
! (lines omitted)
access-list 1 permit 192.168.1.0 0.0.0.255
```

The explanations for the new commands, enabling PAT, are as follows:

- Together, the following three lines in sequence open interface configuration mode for the primary Ethernet interface, assign an IP address to it, and establish the Ethernet interface as the inside (customer-facing) interface:

  ```
  interface Ethernet0
     ip address 192.168.1.1 255.255.255.0
     ip nat inside
  ```

- Together, the following three lines in sequence open interface configuration mode for the BVI, assign an IP address to it, and establish the BVI interface as the outside (DSL network-facing) interface:

  ```
  interface BVI1
     ip address 192.168.2.1 255.255.255.0
        ip nat outside
  ```

- **ip nat inside source list 1 interface BVI1 overload** enables dynamic translation of addresses permitted by the access list to the address specified in the BVI.

- **access-list 1 permit 192.168.1.0 0.0.0.255** defines a standard access list permitting addresses that need translation with PAT.

RFC 2684 Bridging with NAT

Continuing the scenario of the Cisco 827 in bridging mode, suppose that the DSL provider has assigned a block of IP addresses instead of a single address as defined previously. For multiple IP addresses, NAT can be used to translate many-to-many IP addresses. Like PAT, NAT provides privacy for the internal, client-side IP addresses on the internal LAN. These additions are shown in the following configuration snippet. The pertinent commands are followed by the explanations for the commands that amplify the original RFC 2684 bridging configuration.

```
bridge irb
! (lines omitted)
interface Ethernet0
   ip address 192.168.1.1 255.255.255.0
   ip nat inside
```

```
!
interface ATM0
! (lines omitted)
!
interface ATM0.1 point-to-point
   pvc 1/35
!
ip address 192.168.2.1 255.255.255.0
   ip nat outside
!
ip nat pool POOL-A 192.168.2.2 192.168.2.10 netmask 255.255.255.0
!
ip nat inside source list 1 pool POOL-A overload
!
access-list 1 permit 192.168.1.0 0.0.0.255
```

Following are the explanations that add to the original RFC 2684 bridging configuration to permit NAT:

- Together, the following three BVI-related commands open configuration mode for this BVI, assign an IP address and subnet to it, and then establish the BVI as the outside (DSL network-facing) interface:

  ```
  interface BVI1
     ip address 192.168.2.1 255.255.255.0
     ip nat outside
  ```

- **ip nat pool POOL-A 192.168.2.2 192.168.2.10 netmask 255.255.255.0** creates a pool named POOL-A of global (registered) IP addresses for NAT, from addresses 192.168.2.2 through 192.168.2.10, with appropriate subnet masks.

- **ip nat inside source list 1 pool POOL-A overload** enables dynamic translation of addresses permitted by the access list numbered 1 to one of the addresses specified in the pool.

- **access-list 1 permit 192.168.1.0 0.0.0.255** defines a standard access list permitting addresses that need translation.

RBE Configuration

RBE is set up on the Cisco 827 router exactly like its more-basic cousin, IRB. Remember from the descriptions of the TCP/IP architectures in Chapter 3 that RBE is a more-efficient implementation of RFC 2684 bridging than simple IRB. For RBE, the difference consists of only a few different commands configured on the IP DSL Switch, Cisco 6400, or a comparable Layer 3 device. In the DSL environment, RBE actually routes IP over bridged RFC 2684 Ethernet traffic from a stub-bridged LAN. Bridged IP packets received on an ATM interface configured in route-bridged mode are routed through the IP header. These interfaces on the IP/DSL Switch or a similarly-capable device offer increased performance and flexibility over IRB. In addition, RBE reduces the security risk associated with IRB by reducing the size of the unsecured network. By using a single virtual circuit (VC) allocated to a subnet (which could be as small as a single IP address), ATM RBE limits the "trust environment" to a single customer premises using IP addresses in the subnet.

PPPoE Configuration

The PPPoE feature allows a PPP session to be initiated on a simple bridging Ethernet-connected client. The session is transported over the ATM link via encapsulated Ethernet-bridged frames. With PPPoE, multiple PCs can be installed behind the Cisco 827. As with PPPoA, traffic from these clients can be filtered, NAT can be run, and so on.

In Cisco IOS Software Release 12.1(3)XG, a PPPoE client feature was introduced for the Cisco 827, allowing the PPPoE client functionality to be moved to the router.

When the Cisco 827 itself is the PPPoE client, the 827 PPPoE configuration uses Virtual Private Dialup Networking (VPDN). The following configurations show this scenario. This requires Cisco IOS Software version 12.1(3)XG or later. Multiple PCs can be installed behind the Cisco 827. The Cisco 827 performs routing in this case, and it can be set up as the DHCP server and can perform NAT/PAT, as in the PPPoA configuration example.

The following is the configuration of the PPPoE client on the 827. It is followed by detailed explanations of the important commands.

```
vpdn enable
!
vpdn-group pppoe
        request-dialin
        protocol pppoe
!
interface Ethernet0
        ip address 10.92.1.182 255.255.255.0
        ip nat inside


!

interface ATM0
!(lines omitted)
!

interface ATM0.1 point-to-point
        pvc 1/32
                pppoe-client dial-pool-number 1

interface Dialer1
        ip address negotiated
        mtu 1492
        ip nat outside
        encapsulation ppp

         dialer pool 1
        ppp authentication chap callin
        ppp chap hostname client1
        ppp chap password 7 020508520E081B70


ip nat inside source list 1 interface Dialer1 overload
ip classless
ip route 0.0.0.0 0.0.0.0 dialer1
no ip http server
!
access-list 1 permit any
```

The command **vpdn enable** turns on VPDN on the router. PPPoE runs on top of AAL5SNAP, but the **encap aal5snap** command is not used on the interface, as it is with simple RFC 2684 bridging.

The command **vpdn-group pppoe** associates a VPDN group with a VPDN profile. Then the command **request-dialin** means that this endpoint, the 827, represents the PPPoE client requesting to establish a PPPoE session with the aggregation unit (6400 UAC).

The third command in this group, **protocol pppoe**, characterizes this VPDN group as a PPPoE protocol type.

After the ATM subinterface command and the PVC definition, the command **pppoe-client dial-pool-number 1** indicates that the PPPoE client is linked to a dialer interface upon which a virtual-access interface is cloned.

The command **mtu 1492** applies to the MTU, as introduced at the start of this chapter in the Ethernet interface commands. The default MTU size is 1500 on the dialer interface. Because the PPPoE header is 8 bytes long, you must lower the maximum MTU size to 1492 bytes (1500 minus 8) to allow the 8 bytes of PPPoE header overhead.

If an 82X router terminates the PPPoE traffic, a computer connected to the Ethernet interface might have problems accessing web sites, because the default MTU configured on the PC(s) might be too high. The default MTU on the computer is 1460. The solution is to let the router automatically reduce the value of the Maximum Segment Size (MSS) inside the Transmission Control Protocol (TCP) Synchronization (SYN) packets transmitted by the PCs by entering the following command on the router's Ethernet interface:

```
ip adjust-mss mss
```

where *mss* must be 1452 or less to fix the computer-82X PPPoE MTU problem. This command works only if NAT is configured.

NOTE   It is vital to note that all devices on a physical medium must have the same protocol MTU to operate.

The command **encapsulation ppp** is self-explanatory. The PPP encapsulation provides for multiplexing of different network-layer protocols simultaneously over the same link. The PPP encapsulation has been carefully designed to retain compatibility with the most commonly used supporting hardware.

To support high-speed implementations, the default encapsulation uses only simple fields, only one of which needs to be examined for demultiplexing. The default header and information fields fall on 32-bit boundaries, and the trailer may be padded to an arbitrary boundary. The packets to be encapsulated consist of a protocol field, followed by the payload and optionally followed by padding.

The command **ip nat inside source list 1 interface Dialer1 overload** enables dynamic translation of addresses permitted by the access list to the address specified in the Dialer interface.

The command **ip route 0.0.0.0 0.0.0.0 Dialer1** configures the default route. For NAT you can overload on the Dialer1 interface and add a default route out to the Dialer1 interface, because the dialer's IP address can change.

The command **access-list 1 permit any** permits any source address to be translated.

When a packet leaves via this Ethernet interface for a multicast routing table entry, the packet is process level-switched for this interface but may be fast-switched for other interfaces in the outgoing interface list. When fast switching is enabled (such as in unicast routing), debug messages are not logged. If you want to log debug messages, you must disable fast switching, as was done in this configuration.

VPN Configuration

A VPN carries private data over a public network, extending remote access to users over a shared infrastructure. VPNs maintain the same security and management policies as a private network. They are the most cost-effective method of establishing a point-to-point connection between remote users and a central network.

A benefit of access VPNs is the way they delegate responsibilities for the network. The customer outsources the responsibility for the IT infrastructure to an Internet service provider (ISP). The ISP maintains the modem pools into which the remote users dial, the access servers, and the internetworking expertise. The customer is then responsible only for authenticating users and maintaining its network. VPNs also allow separate and autonomous protocol domains to share common access infrastructure, including modems and access servers, enabling service provider resource sharing among clients.

Instead of connecting directly to the network by using the expensive Public Switched Telephone Network (PSTN), access VPN users only need to use the PSTN to connect to the ISP local point of presence (POP), constituting a VPDN. The ISP then uses the Internet to forward users from the POP to the customer network.

Forwarding a user call over the Internet provides dramatic cost savings for the customer. Access VPNs use Layer 2 tunneling technologies such as Layer 2 Tunneling Protocol (L2TP) to create virtual point-to-point connections between users and the customer network. These tunneling technologies provide the same direct connectivity as the expensive PSTN by using the Internet. This means that users anywhere in the world have the same connectivity as they would have at customer headquarters.

Using L2TP tunneling, an ISP or other access service can create a virtual tunnel to link a customer with remote sites or remote users with corporate home networks. In particular, a network access server (NAS) at the ISP POP exchanges PPP messages with the remote users and communicates through L2TP requests and responses with the customer tunnel server to set up tunnels.

L2TP passes routed protocol packets through the virtual tunnel between endpoints of a point-to-point connection. Frames from the remote users are accepted by the ISP POP, stripped of any linked framing or transparency bytes, encapsulated in L2TP, and forwarded over the appropriate tunnel. The customer tunnel server accepts these L2TP frames, strips the Layer 2 encapsulation, and processes the incoming frames for the appropriate interface.

Cisco 827 Configurations for Voice Service

Figure 6-3 shows a theoretical network with VoIP configured on the 827-4V. The voice capability of the 827-4V starts with the same configurations as for the 827 without voice ports.

Figure 6-3   *Cisco 827-4V with Basic VoIP*

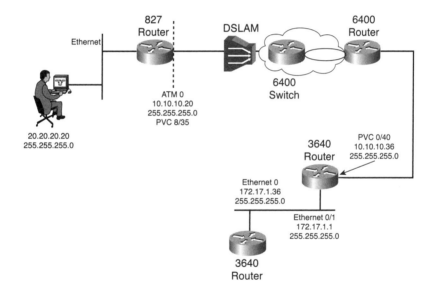

As discussed earlier, setting up voice on the router actually includes two configurations—one for data and one for voice. This section leads you through the data configurations first and then the voice configurations. These consist of the following steps:

Step 1   Configure the data network:

— Configure the class map, route map (optional), and policy map

— Configure the Ethernet interface

— Configure the ATM interface

— Configure Enhanced IGRP

Step 2   Configure the voice network:

  — Configure the POTS (plain old telephone service, or basic telephone service) dial peers

  — Configure VoIP dial peers for H.323 signaling

The following sections discuss the details of each of these steps.

Configuring the Data Network

The data network depends on a specific traffic classification policy that allocates bandwidth and interface access by priority according to traffic type. Traffic types include digitized voice service, standard IP-type packets, and various traffic types whose priorities fall between high-priority voice traffic and standard-priority routine data traffic. Defining the traffic policy determines how many types of packets (number of classes) are to be differentiated from one another. Packets are matched to each other, forming classes based on protocols, access control lists, and input interfaces. These three are the usual match criteria. Before starting the configurations themselves, you must understand the class options.

To characterize a class, you can specify the queue limit for that class, which is the maximum number of packets allowed to accumulate in the class's queue. Packets belonging to a class are subject to the bandwidth and queue limits that characterize the class.

Queuing Considerations

After a queue has reached its configured queue limit, enqueuing additional packets to the traffic class causes either *tail drop* or weighted random early detection (WRED) drop to take effect, depending on how the service policy is configured.

NOTE   Tail drop is a means of avoiding congestion that treats all traffic equally and does not differentiate between classes of service. Queues fill during periods of congestion. When the output queue is full and tail drop is in effect, packets are dropped until the congestion is eliminated and the queue is no longer full.

WRED drops packets selectively based on IP precedence. Packets with a higher IP precedence are less likely to be dropped than packets with a lower precedence. Thus, higher-priority traffic is delivered with a higher probability than lower-priority traffic in the default scenario. However, packets with a lower IP precedence are less likely to be dropped than packets with a higher IP precedence in certain WRED configurations.

Flow classification is standard weighted fair queuing (WFQ) treatment. That is, packets with the same source IP address, destination IP address, source TCP or User Datagram Protocol (UDP) port, or destination TCP or UDP port are classified as belonging to the same flow. WFQ allocates an equal share of bandwidth to each flow. Flow-based WFQ is also called fair queuing because all flows are equally weighted. WFQ can speed up handling for high-precedence traffic at congestion points.

There are two levels of queuing: ATM queues and IOS queues. Class-based weighted fair queuing (CBWFQ) is applied to IOS queues. It extends the standard WFQ functionality in support of user-defined traffic classes. For CBWFQ, you define traffic classes based on match criteria including protocols, access control lists (ACLs), and input interfaces. Packets satisfying the match criteria for a class constitute the traffic for that class.

Each class has a weight derived from the bandwidth you assigned to the class when you configured it. The weight specified for the class becomes the weight of each packet that meets the class's match criteria. Packets that arrive at the output interface are classified according to the match criteria filters you define, and then each one is assigned the appropriate weight.

After a packet's weight is assigned, the packet is enqueued in the appropriate class queue. CBWFQ uses the weights assigned to the queued packets to ensure that the class queue is serviced fairly.

Tail drop is used for CBWFQ traffic classes unless you explicitly configure a service policy to use WRED to drop packets as a means of avoiding congestion. Note that if you use WRED packet drop instead of tail drop for one or more traffic classes making up a service policy, you must ensure that WRED is not configured for the interface to which you attach that service policy.

If a default class is configured, all unclassified traffic is treated as belonging to the default class. If no default class is configured, by default the traffic that does not match any of the configured classes is flow-classified and given best-effort treatment. As soon as a packet is classified, all the standard mechanisms that can be used to differentiate service among the classes apply.

A first-in, first-out (FIFO) IOS queue is automatically created when a PVC is created. If you use CBWFQ to create classes and attach them to a PVC, a queue is created for each class.

CBWFQ ensures that queues have sufficient bandwidth and that traffic gets predictable service. Low-volume traffic streams are preferred; high-volume traffic streams share the remaining capacity, obtaining equal or proportional bandwidth. Bandwidth for the policy map may not exceed 75 percent of the total PVC bandwidth.

Resource Reservation Protocol (RSVP) can be used in conjunction with CBWFQ. When both RSVP and CBWFQ are configured for an interface, RSVP and CBWFQ act independently, exhibiting the same behavior that they would if each were running alone. RSVP continues to work as it does when CBWFQ is not present, even in regard to bandwidth availability assessment and allocation.

RSVP works well on PPP, HDLC, and similar serial-line interfaces. It does not work well on multiaccess LANs. RSVP can be equated to a dynamic access list for packet flows. You should configure RSVP to ensure QoS if the following conditions describe your network:

* Small-scale voice network implementation
* Links slower than 2 Mbps
* Links with high utilization
* You need the best possible voice quality

Configuring the Traffic Policy: Traffic Precedence, Class Maps, Policy Maps

After considering the queuing and prioritization techniques explained previously, you can begin designing the traffic policy configuration for the Cisco 827. Starting with the classification of traffic types, there are two principal aspects to configuring the traffic policy:

* Class maps, which define the traffic classes
* Policy maps, which associate the policies (traffic classes) with interfaces

Traffic Precedence

The first step in building the class map is to configure the access list, including setting an IP precedence, to associate with the class map. As per RFC 791, there are eight classes of service, although later RFCs provide more independence in proprietary precedence definitions. Cisco Systems endeavors to conform to RFC 791, meaning that you can partition traffic in up to six classes of service using IP precedence; two others are reserved for internal network use. The network queuing technologies then use this IP precedence definition to expedite traffic handling. The original, RFC 791-defined classes are as follows, in order from lowest priority to highest priority:

* **Traffic class (TC) = 0: Routine (uncharacterized traffic)**—If otherwise undefined, these packets are assigned the lowest-priority value and are delivered based on the available bandwidth. Non-TCP/IP traffic is assigned to this traffic class. There is a very high possibility of packet drop in the event of congestion.
* **TC = 1: Priority**—There is a high possibility of packet drop if congestion is encountered.
* **TC = 2: Immediate**—There is a medium possibility of packet drop in the event of congestion.
* **TC = 3: Flash**—There is a low possibility of packet drop in the event of congestion.
* **TC = 4: Flash-override**—There is a very low possibility of packet drop compared to the lower-priority classes.
* **TC = 5: Critical**—Cisco recommends this class for voice traffic.
* **TCs 6 and 7**—For Internet and network traffic, respectively. Examples include signaling protocols.

IP precedence is not a queuing method, but it gives other queuing methods (WFQ, WRED) the capability to prioritize based on the packet's IP precedence. The network gives priority (or some type of expedited handling) to the marked traffic through the application of WFQ or WRED at points downstream in the network.

The mapping from keywords such as **routine** and **priority** to a precedence value is useful in only some instances. In other words, the use of the precedence bit is evolving. Bear in mind that IP precedences can be used to establish classes of service that do not necessarily correspond numerically to better or worse handling in the network.

The **ip precedence** command is used by the Cisco 827 router to differentiate voice traffic from data traffic and to assign voice packets a higher priority. Here is an example of this command applied on a Cisco 827 DSL router for voice service:

```
Router (config)#access-list 101 permit ip any any precedence 5
```

This command builds an extended access list numbered 101, which permits IP traffic from any source to any destination and then assigns this permitted traffic the IP precedence of 5 for voice packets. You can also use the plain-text priority designations themselves rather than the numbers:

```
Router (config)#access-list 101 permit ip any any precedence critical
```

Features such as policy-based routing and committed access rate (CAR) can be used to set precedence based on extended access lists.

Class Maps

The next step in building the voice configuration on the 827 is to configure the class map called *voice*. The command **class-map voice** defines a traffic class and the match criteria that are used to identify traffic as belonging to that class. **match** statements can include criteria such as an ACL, an IP precedence value, or a Differentiated Services Code Point (DSCP) value.

The DSCP is a designation by the Internet Engineering Task Force (IETF) of the 6 most significant bits of the 1-byte IP Type of Service (ToS) field. The match criteria are defined with one **match** statement entered in class-map configuration mode.

Here is an example of what might be in the class-map VOICE definition:

```
Router(config)#class-map VOICE
Router(config-cmap)#match ip rtp 16384 16383
Router(config-cmap)#match access-group 101
```

In the first command, IP Real-Time Protocol (RTP) ports 16384 and 16383 (possible values through 32767) are configured as the match criteria. In the second command, access list 101 is matched with the class map. That is, the class map is now associated with IP packets whose IP precedence is 5, the recommended voice packet precedence you defined earlier with the command **access-list 101 permit ip any any precedence 5**.

Policy Maps

Policy maps group one or more class maps, up to 64 different classes of service, for later association with a particular interface. The policy map thereby confers all its referenced class map values onto the interface. In the commands discussed in the preceding section, you first defined an access list and assigned permitted traffic the priority of 5. Then you referenced that access list, 101, in defining the class map called VOICE. The class map is also related to traffic only on ports 16383 and 16384. Because that is a relatively narrow definition, the policy map should also contain a class for other types of traffic, although this is more of a security consideration than a voice configuration consideration.

The commands in the following listing define the policy map named MYPOLICY, which associates the class maps VOICE and class-default (the default for unreferenced traffic). As an example of one option, the command **Priority 176** guarantees 176 kbps of bandwidth for the priority traffic. Beyond the guaranteed bandwidth, the priority traffic is dropped in the event of congestion to ensure that the nonpriority traffic is not starved. Another option is to define the guaranteed bandwidth as a percentage of the overall interface bandwidth. A third option is to specify a maximum burst size in bytes to be tolerated before dropping traffic.

```
Policy-map MYPOLICY
      Class VOICE
            Priority 176
      Class class-default
```

You have finished configuring the class map and policy map, the first steps in configuring the data network, leading to final voice service configuration. Now you will adjust the interface configurations. You learned earlier about configuring the Ethernet interface for the TCP/IP architectures common to DSL. The ATM interface has some details beyond those earlier, basic ATM interface commands for the Cisco 827. These new ATM configuration commands provide for voice service and draw on the concepts already explained in this chapter, as well as some more specific details.

ATM Interface Configuration

The next step is to configure the ATM interface. Here are the commands to do so:

```
interface ATM0
     mtu 300
!
    ip address 192.168.2.1 255.255.255.0
    no atm ilmi-keepalive
    pvc 1/32
          service-policy out MYPOLICY
          vbr-rt 640 640 10
          encapsulation aal5snap
```

The first step in configuring the ATM interface is to adjust the size of the MTU. If you are configuring PPP, either PPPoA or PPPoE, you should decrease the ATM interface's MTU size so that large data packets are fragmented. It is recommended that you use 300 for the MTU size because it is larger than the size of the voice packets generated by the different codecs.

With multiclass multilink PPP interleaving, large packets can be multilink-encapsulated and fragmented into smaller packets to satisfy the delay requirements of real-time voice traffic. Small real-time packets, which are not multilink-encapsulated, are transmitted between fragments of the large packets. The interleaving feature also provides a special transmit queue for the smaller, delay-sensitive packets, enabling them to be transmitted earlier than other flows. Interleaving provides the delay bounds for delay-sensitive voice packets on a slow link that is used for other best-effort traffic.

Next, the policy map named MYPOLICY that you created earlier is associated with the PVC in the outbound direction.

You can then specify the PVC's service class. In this case, the command **vbr-rt 640 640 10** defines Variable Bit Rate Real Time with a peak cell rate (PCR) of 640 kbps, a sustained cell rate (SCR) of 640 kbps, and a Maximum Burst Rate (MBR) of ten cells in a single burst. You should configure the SCR to be at least four times the particular codec's bandwidth when the four voice ports are used. For example, if you have a 640 kbps upstream PVC running codec G.729, you could configure the PVC with an SCR of 176.

Finally in configuring the ATM interface, this PVC is assigned the encapsulation of aal5snap.

Enhanced IGRP Configuration

Continuing with configuring the data aspects of the Cisco 827, you should enter router configuration mode and enable Enhanced IGRP. The autonomous-system number identifies the route to other Enhanced IGRP routers and is used to tag the Enhanced IGRP information.

Specify the network number for each directly connected network.

The following configuration shows the Enhanced IGRP routing protocol enabled in IP networks 10.0.0.0 and 172.17.0.0. The Enhanced IGRP autonomous system number is assigned as 100:

```
Config#router eigrp 100
Config-router#network 10.0.0.0
Config-router#network 172.17.0.0
```

You can now proceed to the voice-specific configurations.

Voice Network Configuration

Following is the voice-specific configuration:

```
!(lines omitted)
voice-port 1
     timing hookflash-in 0
voice-port 2
     timing hookflash-in 0
voice-port 3
     timing hookflash-in 0
voice-port 4
     timing hookflash-in 0
!(lines omitted)
scheduler max-task-time 5000
```

```
dial-peer voice 1 pots
    destination-pattern 1001
    port 1
!
dial-peer voice 10 voip
    destination-pattern 2...
    session target ipv4:192.168.2.8
!
    codec g711ulaw (optional)
```

The commands **voice-port** *X* and **timing hookflash-in 0** turn off any hookflash indications that the gateway could generate on an FXO interface. Currently the Cisco 827-4V does not support hookflash indications, although that support is probably pending, because it is already available on other Cisco platforms with H.323 Version 2 Phase 2. On an analog phone, hookflash means pressing the switchhook for a moment (about one-half second) to produce a special stutter dial tone. This engages supplemental services, such as call waiting.

The command **scheduler max-task-time 5000** is not specific to the 827. It is how long, in milliseconds, a specific process is handled by the CPU before it reports debugging information—in this case, 5 seconds.

Dial Peer Configuration

Dial peers enable outgoing calls from a particular telephony device. All the voice technologies use dial peers to define the characteristics associated with a call leg. A call leg is a discrete segment of a call connection that lies between two points in the connection.

Bear in mind that these terms are defined from the router perspective. An inbound call leg means that an incoming call comes to the router. An outbound call leg means that an outgoing call is placed from the router.

Two kinds of dial peers can be configured for each voice port: POTS and VoIP:

- POTS associates a physical voice port with a local telephone device. The **destination-pattern** command defines the telephone number associated with the POTS dial peer. The **port** command associates the POTS dial peer with a specific logical dial interface, normally the voice port connecting the 827-4V to the POTS network. You can expand an extension number into a particular destination pattern with the command **num-exp**. You can use the **show num-exp** command to verify that you have mapped the telephone numbers correctly.

- The VoIP dial peer also associates a telephone number with an IP address. The key configuration commands are the same **destination-pattern** and **session target** commands that are used with the POTS dial peer. The former command is the same as with the POTS dial peer, defining a telephone number. The **session target** command specifies a destination IP address for the VoIP dial peer. This command must be used in conjunction with the **destination-pattern** command. Going further than the POTS dial peer, you can use VoIP dial peers to define characteristics such as IP precedence, QoS parameters, and codecs. For instance, you can optionally specify a different codec than the default codec of g.729.

For both POTS and VoIP, after you have configured dial peers and assigned destination patterns to them, you can use the **show dialplan** *number* command to see how a telephone number maps to a dial peer.

When a router receives a voice call, it selects an outbound dial peer by comparing the called number (the full E.164 telephone number) in the call information with the number configured as the destination pattern for the POTS peer. The router then strips the left-justified numbers corresponding to the destination pattern matching the called number. On POTS dial peers, the only digits that are sent to the other end are the ones specified with the wildcard character (.) with the command **destination-pattern** *string*. The POTS dial peer command **prefix** *string* can be used to include a dial-out prefix that the system enters automatically instead of having people dial it. If you have configured a prefix, it is put in front of the remaining numbers, creating a dial string, which the router then dials. If all the numbers in the destination pattern are stripped, the user receives (depending on the attached equipment) a dial tone.

For example, suppose there is a voice call whose E.164 called number is 1 (310) 555-2222. If you configure a destination pattern of 1310555 and a prefix of 9, the router strips 1310555 from the E.164 telephone number, leaving the extension number of 2222. It then appends the prefix 9 to the front of the remaining numbers so that the actual numbers dialed are 9, 2222. The comma in this example means that the router pauses for 1 second between dialing the 9 and dialing the first 2 to allow for a secondary dial tone.

Earlier, you defined a class called VOICE with the **class-map** command. You matched the access control list 101 with this class of service using the **match access-group** command. You also defined a policy map with the **policy-map** command. Those commands are shown here, along with some new options:

```
class-map VOICE
     match access-group 101
!
policy-map POLICY
     class VOICE
          priority 480

pvc 1/32
          service-policy out POLICY
          vbr-rt 640 640 10
          encapsulation aal5snap
!
bundle-enable
!
dial-peer voice 1 pots
     destination-pattern 1001
     port 1

dial-peer voice 10 voip
     destination-pattern 2...
!
     session target ipv4:192.168.2.8
!
     ip precedence 5
!
access-list 101 permit ip any any precedence critical
```

The command **priority 480** defines the priority of the VOICE class in terms of guaranteed bandwidth. In this case, if there is congestion on the network, even this priority traffic is dropped when it exceeds 480 kbps. This ensures that the nonpriority traffic is not starved.

The command **service-policy out POLICY** attaches the policy map to this particular PVC, 1/32. The policy map could also be attached to an interface, either inbound or outbound.

The command **vbr-rt 640 640 10** defines Variable Bit Rate Real Time (suitable for this voice traffic) with a PCR of 640 kbps, an SCR of 640 kbps, and an MBR of ten cells in a single burst.

This PVC's encapsulation type is aal5snap, suitable for either RFC 2684 bridging (IRB or RBE) or PPPoE.

The command **bundle-enable** creates ATM PVC bundles, about which you learned earlier. The command **dial-peer voice 1 voip** simply uses one of two options; this was explained earlier as well.

Two values at a minimum are required to configure a VoIP peer: the associated destination telephone number and a destination IP address. The command **destination-pattern** defines the destination telephone number. This specification is then associated with port 1. In this configuration example, the last digits in the VoIP dial peer's destination pattern are replaced with wildcards.

The **ip precedence** command defines precedence 5, preferred for voice.

Last, the **access-list** command clears the way through access list 101 for any IP traffic and sets that traffic's precedence as critical.

Returning to check the steps in configuring the 827-4V for data and voice, you are now ready for the last step, which completes the process by configuring the VoIP dial peers for H.323 signaling.

VoIP Dial Peers for H.323 Signaling

The H.323 signaling protocol was explained in Chapter 4, "Cisco DSL Products." Following is the configuration:

```
interface ATM0
    h323-gateway voip interface

h323-gateway voip id GATEKEEPER ipaddr 192.168.1.2 1719
!

h323-gateway voip h323-id GATEWAY
!
!(lines omitted:  define telephone number, specify port number)
!
dial-peer voice 10 voip
  destination-pattern +.T
session target ras

gateway
```

The first H.323-related command in this configuration, **h323-gateway voip interface**, identifies the interface ATM0 as the gateway interface.

The command **h323-gateway voip id GATEKEEPER ipaddr 192.168.1.2 1719** defines the name and location (IP address) of the gatekeeper for this gateway.

The next command, **h323-gateway voip h323-id GATEWAY**, defines the gateway's H.323 name, identifying this gateway to its associated gatekeeper.

The command **destination-pattern +.T** introduces a new value. The plus sign (+) indicates an E.164 standard number, and the T indicates the default route.

The command **session target ras** specifies the destination as having Registration, Admission, and Status (RAS) functionality, providing gateway-to-gatekeeper functionality.

Finally, the one-word command **gateway** defines this 827-4V as the H.323 gateway device.

Completing the 827-4V Configuration

You can now complete the configuration of the Cisco 827-4V. Figure 6-4 shows the use of the Cisco 827-4V configured for RFC 2684 bridging (IRB) and VoIP.

Figure 6-4   *Cisco 827-4V Using IRB for VoIP*

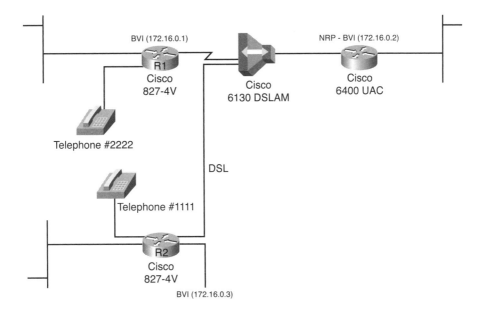

When the Cisco 827 replaces existing bridged DSL modems, the IRB configuration is a typical starting point. Although the Cisco 827-4V supports voice service in all the other previously discussed architectures in which the network scheme would be different, IRB is shown here simply as an example. The new commands are explained after the configuration listing.

Here is the configuration required for the 827-4V in this legacy replacement scenario:

```
version 12.1
service timestamps debug datetime msec
service timestamps log datetime msec
!
hostname R1
!
bridge irb
!
interface Ethernet0
no ip mroute-cache
!
interface ATM0
no ip address
no atm ilmi-keepalive
    pvc 1/150
        encapsulation aal5snap
bundle-enable
  bridge-group 1
  hold-queue 224 in
!
interface BVI1
      ip address 172.16.0.1 255.255.0.0
!
ip classless
ip route 0.0.0.0 0.0.0.0 BVI1
no ip http server
!
bridge 1 protocol ieee
      bridge 1 route ip
!

voice-port 1
    timing hookflash-in 0
!
voice-port 2
    timing hookflash-in 0
!
voice-port 3
    timing hookflash-in 0
!
voice-port 4
    timing hookflash-in 0
!
dial-peer voice 1 pots
    destination-pattern 2222
    port 1
!
dial-peer voice 2 voip
    destination-pattern 1111
    session target ipv4:172.16.0.3
!
```

The command **bridge irb** enables RFC 2684 bridging (IRB) for the whole Cisco 827-4V router.

The command **ip mroute-cache** configures IP multicast fast switching. In this Cisco 827-4V, it is disabled on the Ethernet interface. When packets arrive on this Ethernet interface for a multicast routing table entry with mroute caching disabled, those packets are sent at process level for all interfaces in the outgoing interface list.

When packets leave via this Ethernet interface for a multicast routing table entry, the packet is process level-switched for this interface, but it may be fast-switched for other interfaces in the outgoing interface list.

The command **bridge-group 1** specifies the bridge group to which the interface belongs.

The command **BVI1** creates a BVI and assigns a corresponding bridge group number to that BVI, as discussed earlier in this chapter.

The command **bridge 1 protocol ieee** is an IOS standard specifying Spanning Tree Protocol for bridge group 1.

The command **bridge 1 route ip** lets the BVI accept and route routable packets received from its corresponding bridge group. You must enter this command for each routed protocol (such as IPX) that you want the BVI to route from its corresponding bridge group to other routed interfaces.

You are now done configuring the Cisco 827-4V for IRB and VoIP. Look again at Figure 6-3 and consider the more-complex explanation of the use of your new, complete configuration. This figure shows a voice scenario configuration using the Cisco 827-4V router in an H.323 signaling environment. Traffic is routed through the 827 router and then is switched onto the ATM interface. The 827 router is connected through the ATM interface through one PVC, and it is associated with a QoS policy called mypolicy. Data traffic coming from the Ethernet must have an IP precedence below 5 (critical) to distinguish it from voice traffic.

NAT (represented by the dashed line at the edge of the 827 routers) signifies two addressing domains and the inside source address. The source list defines how the packet travels through the network.

Now that you have configured the 827-4V as a voice-carrying router, you need to configure the PVC endpoint. An interesting option is to use multiple PVCs. Multiple PVCs, separating voice and data, create an easily expandable, easily traced configuration, although this is not required for minimal functionality. Here is that configuration:

```
!(lines omitted)

interface ATM0.1 point-to-point
    ip address 192.168.2.1 255.255.255.0

    pvc 1/35
        protocol ip 192.168.2.2 broadcast

        vbr-rt 424 424 5
        encapsulation aal5snap
!
```

```
interface ATM0.2 point-to-point


    pvc 1/36 (data PVC)
              protocol ip 192.168.3.2 broadcast
              encapsulation aal5snap

dial-peer voice 1 pots
destination-pattern 1001
port 1


dial-peer voice 10 voip
destination-pattern 2...


session target ipv4:192.168.2.8
```

In this configuration, the first PVC is for voice service. It is configured on a point-to-point subinterface, ATM0.1. This IP PVC has a point-to-point IP address of 192.168.2.1, with a subnet mask of 255.255.255.0.

Then the service class of Variable Bit Rate (VBR) is set, with parameters of PCR of 424 kbps, SCR of 424 kbps, and MBR of five cells in a single burst. This voice PVC's encapsulation is aal5snap.encapsulation aal5snap.

Troubleshooting the Cisco 827

The first thing you should do when troubleshooting the Cisco 827 is check the front panel CD LED. If the light is not on, no ADSL carrier is detected. Usually this is a physical problem, probably due to a bad cable or a problem with an ADSL line or WAN service. You can try replacing the cable, but you will probably have to contact the DSL provider.

Another simple solution to 827 problems might lie with the ATM interface. To verify its status, you can enter the command **show interface ATM 0**. If the status is **up/down**, the Cisco 827 sees the ADSL carrier but cannot train up with the central office (CO)/exchange IP-DSL Switch properly. In this case, check the cable itself. The Cisco 827 uses pins 3 and 4 of the ADSL cable. The ADSL cable must be 10BASE-T Category 5 unshielded twisted-pair (UTP) cable. Using regular telephone cable can introduce line errors. Contact your ADSL line or service provider to determine if there is a problem.

If the Cisco 827 does not establish a satisfactory DSL circuit to the CO/exchange ADSL port, you can observe the process of DSL synchronization as the 827 trains up to help isolate the problem. Following are the normal stages of the synchronization so that you can verify which steps are occurring correctly to aid your troubleshooting. To observe the training process, you can enter the command **debug atm events** and observe the outputs, shown in the following:

Normal activation state changes are

STOP	In shutdown state
INIT	Initialization

DLOAD_1   Initialized and downloading first image

DLOAD_2   Downloading second image

DO_OPEN   Requesting activation with CO

In DO_OPEN state, look for the modem state for the progress information:

Modem state = 0x0   Modem down

Modem state = 0x8   Modem waiting to hear from CO

Modem state = 0x10   Modem heard from CO and now is training

Modem state = 0x20   Activation completed and link is up

SHOWTIME   Activation succeeded

Central Office/Exchange Equipment

This section discusses the configurations for the two pieces of CO/exchange gear in the DSL network—the Cisco 6000 series IP DSL Switch and the Cisco 6400 UAC.

IP DSL Switch/NI-2

The NI-2 Cisco IOS Software is based on the Catalyst 8500 (also known as the LightStream 1010) code, with added extensions for DSL. The IOS code supports ATM services such as ATM QoS and traffic management, PVCs and soft-PVCs, and ILMI and OAM cell support.

After the initial configuration, you can either continue to manage the DSLAM/IP DSL Switch with the Cisco IOS Software command-line interface (CLI) or use the Cisco DSL Manager (CDM) graphical user interface (GUI) software. Even if you choose to manage the device with CDM (this is covered in Chapter 7, "Cisco DSL Manager (CDM)"), you must still use a few Cisco IOS Software commands to prepare the device for CDM.

Basic Setup Commands

To start setting up the NI-2, you can access the CLI by connecting a terminal directly to the console port on the NI-2 card or by Telnetting to the management port if an IP address has been configured on the NI-2 Ethernet interface. Because the NI-2 runs a specific version of Cisco IOS Software, many commands are unique to the DSL service environment. The software image itself is designated with the letters DA. The D indicates that this is a Cisco IOS Software release for the DSL environment, and the A indicates that it is specifically for the NI-2. (As you will learn in the section "Aggregator/Concentrator: Cisco 6400," other specific software versions also start with D for DSL but have a different second letter.)

The System Configuration dialog and the CLI use the interface numbering scheme shown in Figure 6-5.

Figure 6-5   *Cisco 6160 Interfaces*

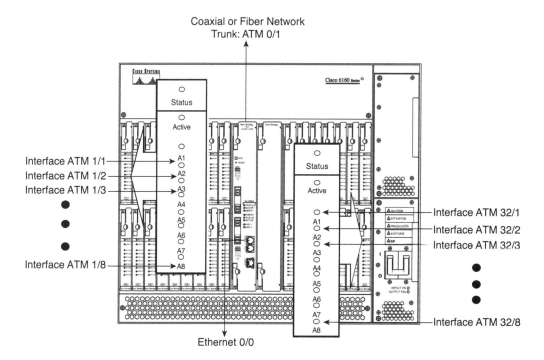

Interfaces whose names begin with ATM0 (ATM0/0, ATM0/1, and so on) are NI-2 card WAN interfaces. ATM0/0 is the ATM switch's interface with the processor. There is no need to configure ATM0/0 unless you plan to use in-band management. ATM0/1 is the trunk port, also called the upstream or network trunk. ATM0/2 and ATM0/3 (if present) are subtending interfaces.

Interfaces whose names begin with ATM1, including all the higher numbers after the ATM-designator, are xTU-C (line card) interfaces. The range of line cards is ATM1 through ATM6 on the compact 6015, ATM1 through ATM30 on the international 6260, or ATM1 through ATM32 on the North American 6160. ATM10 and ATM11, which would indicate the NI-2 slots, are omitted in the software configuration on the two larger IP DSL Switches, although these are labeled as slots 10 and 11 on the chassis itself.

Ethernet0/0 is the interface for the LAN that connects the Cisco IP DSL Switch to its management system.

For individual line card ports, the number before the slash indicates the slot number. The number after the slash indicates the interface or port number. For example, ATM6/4 is port 4 in slot 6.

The following steps show you how to configure the NI-2 for basic operations:

Step 1   Specify software codes. You should specify the source and filename of the configuration that will be used to boot the NI-2. Use the global configuration mode command **boot system flash:** *path filename* to specify the boot file. You can use the file system in Flash memory to copy files and troubleshoot configuration problems. Use the privileged EXEC command **dir flash:** to display the contents of Flash memory. This process might take a few minutes while Flash memory is being initialized.

```
DSLAM#dir flash:
Directory of flash:/
2   -rw-  4883532  Jan 01 2000  00:02:46  NI-2-dsl-mz.120-5.DA1
3   -rw-  5396464  Jan 02 2000  02:04:08  NI-2-dsl-mx.flexi.aluia
4   -rw-  345324   Jan 02 2000  02:06:13  flexd.bin.aluia
15990784 bytes total (413568 bytes free)
```

Step 2   Set the IP address on the primary Ethernet interface. You should set the IP address, and the subnet mask if you won't use the default, on the interface Eth 0/0. Use the interface configuration mode command **ip address** *XXX.XXX.XXX.XXX yyy.yyy.yyy.yyy,* where *X* represents the IP address and *Y* represents the subnet mask.

Step 3   Set the passwords. At a minimum, you will set three passwords:

A.   Console password—Set the console password using the standard Cisco IOS Software configuration command **password**.

B.   Telnet password—At the privileged EXEC mode prompt, enter the following commands:

```
NI-2#config terminal
NI-2 (config)#line vty 0 4
NI-2 (config- line)#password <TELNET PASSWORD>
NI-2 (config- line)#login
```

Exit, and then test by Telnetting into the device.

C.   Privileged EXEC password, also erroneously but popularly called the enable password—You set the privileged EXEC password using the standard Cisco IOS Software configuration command **enable secret** or **enable password**.

Step 4   Set the time, date, and host name. Although it isn't absolutely required, you can set several system parameters as part of the initial system configuration.

Step 5   Set the clocking options. Each port has a transmit clock and derives its receive clock from the receive data. You can configure transmit clocking for each port in one of the following ways:

— **Network derived**—Transmit clocking is derived from the highest-priority configured source, either from the internal clock (the default) or the public network.

— **Loop-timed**—Transmit clocking is derived from the receive clock source. The IP DSL Switch receives derived clocking, along with data, from a specified interface. Because the port providing the network clock source could fail, Cisco IOS Software lets you configure additional interfaces as clock sources with priorities 1 to 4.

If the network clock source interface stops responding, the software switches to the next-highest-configured priority network clock source.

NOTE   By default, the network clock is configured as nonrevertive. This is because the industry standard is to prefer a stable, if less-accurate, clock source over an unstable, even if more-accurate, clock source. Virtually every service provider's policy is to verify original clock source stability for a set period of several hours before reverting manually to that original source, while depending on the secondary, stable clock source in the interim.

The algorithm to switch to the highest-priority best clock runs only if you configure the **network-clock-select** command as revertive.

To configure the network clocking priorities and sources, use the following command in global configuration mode:

```
network-clock-select {priority} {bits} {atm} {system | card/port} [revertive]
```

The following example configures interface 0/0 as the highest-priority clock source to receive the network clocking, interface 0/2 as the second-highest priority, and interface 0/1 as the third-highest priority:

```
NI-2#config term
NI-2(config)#network-clock-select 1 atm 0/0
NI-2(config)#network-clock-select 2 atm 0/2
NI-2(config)#network-clock-select 3 atm 0/1
```

The following example shows how to configure the network clock to revert to the highest-priority clock source after a failure:

```
NI-2(config)#network-clock-select revertive
```

To configure the location from which an interface receives its transmit clocking, perform these tasks, beginning in global configuration mode:

Select the interface to be configured:

```
interface atm card/port
```

Configure the interface network clock source:

```
clock source {free-running | loop-timed | network-derived}
```

Network-derived means the highest-priority clock that is both configured and functional.

The following example configures ATM interface 0/1 to receive its transmit clocking from a network-derived source:

```
NI-2(config)#interface atm 0/1
NI-2(config-if)#clock source network-derived
```

Any module in a DSLAM chassis that can receive and distribute a network timing signal can propagate that signal to any similarly capable module in the chassis. The following entities can receive and distribute a Primary Reference Source (PRS) for synchronization:

— A Building Integrated Timing Supply (BITS) clock through the I/O card

— An OC-3/STM1 in an IP DSL Switch chassis

— A DS3/E3 module in an IP DSL Switch chassis that derives the clock from the trunk interface

The two trunk ports can propagate a clocking signal in either direction.

If you issue the **network-clock-select** command with the appropriate parameters, you can define any particular port in an IP DSL Switch chassis (subject to the previously discussed limitations) to serve as the clock source for the entire chassis or for other devices in the networking environment.

You can also use the **network-clock-select** command to designate a particular port in an IP DSL Switch chassis to serve as a master clock source for distributing a single clocking signal throughout the chassis or to other network devices. You can distribute this reference signal wherever the network needs to globally synchronize the flow of constant bit rate (CBR) data.

Step 6 Set the subtending numbers. If your DSL network will use subtending (subtending is discussed in Chapter 4), how can the network administrator guarantee adequate bandwidth and fairness of access for all subscribers in a subtended implementation?

The answer lies in leveraging the scheduler process on each IP DSL Switch that subtends another IP DSL Switch. (Incidentally, in a regular subtended tree configuration, there is automatic recovery from a failure of any node. In other words, a single failed node in the subtended family does not disrupt user traffic in the other, working IP DSL Switches.)

To guarantee that all subtended subscribers have equal access to the trunk port, the IP DSL Switch uses 13 numbered queues that are accessed in round-robin fashion. This approach keys off the **subtend-id,** which must be set in each subtended IP DSL Switch. This process is shown in Figure 6-6 and is described in more detail in the following list:

A. Each IP DSL Switch has 13 queues, starting with 0, which services the local (onboard) DSL subscribers for each IP DSL Switch.

B. When traffic comes from a subtended trunk, the General Flow Control (GFC) number determines the queue in which the traffic will be put.

C. The GFC number for subtended nodes is set equal to the subtend-id plus 3.

D. In Figure 6-6, the last node on the subtend tree has a subtend-id of 2. Local DSL subscriber traffic populates queue 0.

E. When that traffic is transmitted on the subtended trunk (0/1), it is assigned a GFC of 5 (subtend-id + 3).

F. In subtend node 1, that traffic populates queue 5. Local DSL subscriber traffic populates queue 0. The node services these two queues in a round-robin fashion.

G. When subtend node 1 traffic from queue 0 is sent up the subtended trunk, it is assigned GFC = 4 (subtend-id + 3) and populates queue 4. Traffic from queue 5 retains GFC = 5 and populates queue 5.

H. In the top-level node, local DSL subscriber traffic populates queue 0.

I. The top subtend node services queues 0, 4, and 5 in a round-robin fashion, thereby giving all DSL subscribers equal access to the network trunk.

You can set the subtend node identifier using the following global command:

```
subtend-id node#
```

where *node#* is the node for which the command sets the subtend node identifier. The range is 0 to 12.

In this example, the command sets the DSL subtend node identifier to node 12:

```
NI-2#conf t
NI-2 (config)subtend-id 12
```

Step 7 Configure Simple Network Management Protocol (SNMP) for CDM use or to direct SNMP traps to another system. Enter the following commands while in privileged EXEC mode:

```
NI-2#config terminal
NI-2 (config)#snmp-server community <PUBLIC> ro
NI-2 (config)#snmp-server community <PRIVATE> rw
NI-2 (config)#snmp-server host <CEMF Server IP Address> traps version 2c public
NI-2 (config)#snmp-server enable traps
```

Figure 6-6   *Subtending Queues*

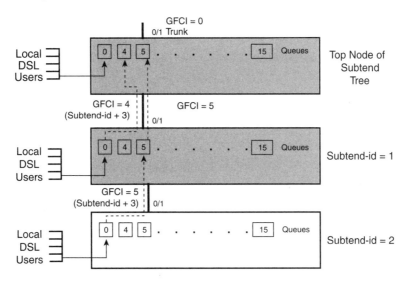

Step 8   After the basic NI-2 setup, you should verify that the NI-2 has autorecognized the line cards. Here is how that autodiscovery works:

The NI-2 autodiscovers all xTU-Cs (line cards) when they are installed. First the NI-2 verifies that the card is valid for that type of chassis. Second, for all but the Flexi card, the NI-2 compares the line card's installed software image to the particular software image that the NI-2 itself contains in its configuration. If the line card's installed image does not match the NI-2's image for that card type, the NI-2 automatically updates the line card with the software image that the NI-2 has available.

In the case of the Flexi card, the NI-2 can complete only the first step. As you saw in Chapter 4, the Flexi card offers connectivity for either the legacy Carrierless Amplitude Phase (CAP) modulation or the standardized DMT modulations (both full-rate and half-rate DMT). You must manually set the card to either CAP or DMT after initial recognition by the NI-2. (The Flexi card itself autorecognizes the difference between DMT2 and G.Lite coming from the CPE after the Flexi has been configured for DMT.) The NI-2 then completes its analysis of the Flexi line card's onboard image version and updates it as necessary. Here is the manual command format, starting in global configuration mode:

```
slot slot# cardtype
```

slot# is the slot number. For the 6160 IP DSL Switch, the range is 1 to 32. For the 6260 device, the range is 1 to 30. For the 6015, the range is 1 to 6.

cardtype is the modulation type for which you want to configure the slot.

Here's an example:

```
6160-94(config)#slot X atuc-4flexi{cap | dmt}
```

You cannot simply physically remove a line card from the chassis without changing the NI-2's configuration. To remove a line card from the NI-2's configuration, use the standard Cisco **no** option of the command for all card types, like this:

```
6160-94(config)#no slot X atuc-1-4dmt
```

At this point, after completing the previous eight steps (or the standard Cisco IOS Software startup configuration menu), with or without the optional subtending configurations, you could begin using the GUI CDM program. CDM lets you manage the IP DSL Switch, including provisioning the individual connections.

Continuing with Cisco IOS Software configuration of the NI-2, the next section describes configuring the NI-2 for redundant operations.

Redundancy Commands

Starting with Cisco IOS Software version 12.1(6)DA, NI-2 cards can be configured for redundancy in the IP DSL Switch. Synchronous Optical Network (SONET) and Synchronous Digital Hierarchy (SDH) NI-2s (OC-3 or STM1) have redundant physical links, and Automatic Protection Switching (APS) is in place. APS in the modern telecommunication equipment world is virtually hitless, because most modern fiber-equipped devices switch traffic in much less time than the APS-defined maximum 50 milliseconds. For instance, the NI-2 switches traffic in about 8 to 10 milliseconds. Because the human ear rarely detects gaps of 9 milliseconds or less in speech, even voice traffic is considered hitless. For data traffic, such a small interval is easily overcome by buffering and automatic retransmission if necessary.

For coaxial NI-2 cards, such as the DS3 and E3, if a physical link fails (the cable is cut), there is no switchover. Currently no redundant DS3/E3 physical links exist, so the NI-2 cannot overcome coaxial link failures. If a coaxial NI-2 card itself fails, there is protection, because the standby card takes activity automatically and takes over the coaxial ports on the IP DSL Switch I/O card on the backplane.

In cases of fiber- and coaxially-connected NI-2 failure, the secondary NI-2 assumes the configuration of the primary NI-2. All the ATM information stays the same, with the exception of the dynamically mapping switched virtual circuits (SVCs). These have to be reconfigured in the event of NI-2 failure.

The Ethernet IP address stays the same, but the MAC address might have to be reacquired through Reverse Address Resolution Protocol (RARP), depending on the degree of prior synchronization between the two NI-2 cards. Because the MAC address is stored on the I/O card, it can be shared between the NI-2s.

You must load the same redundancy-capable IOS image in both NI-2 cards. Do not install an NI-2 with IOS earlier than 12.1(2)DA in an IP DSL Switch with another NI-2 already in service. (A service interruption will result.)

APS-Related CLI Commands

The APS CLI commands include **show APS** and **show controllers**.

The **show APS** command displays APS state information.

The **show controllers** command is a classic IOS command that provides information on both the active and inactive OC-3/STM1 interfaces. You can use this command to determine which OC-3/STM1 NI-2 is online and which OC-3/STM1 interface is active. Following are seven examples of this command's output:

```
6160-1#show controller atm 0/1
IF Name: ATM0/1    Chip Base Address: B3809000
Port type: OC3  Port rate: 155000 kbps Port medium: SM Fiber

local            peer
                                (working)        (protection)

ACTIVE           INACTIVE

                                ---------------  ---------------
Port status                     Good Signal      Good Signal
Loopback                              None             None
Flags                               0x8300           0x8308
TX clock source                 loop-timed       loop-timed
Framing mode                        sts-3c           sts-3c
Cell payload scrambling                 On               On
Sts-stream scrambling                   On               On
TX Led:                                Off              Off
RX Led:                                Off              Off
TST Led:                               Off              Off
```

The output of the command **show controller atm0/1** reports that the secondary NI-2 (slot 11, protection) is online. The primary NI-2 (slot 10) is installed, functional, and in standby mode. The OC-3 datastream received by the secondary NI-2 port 0/1 is the datastream being processed by the system (active).

Controller terminology includes the following:

- **Local**—This is always the online NI-2, either slot 10 or slot 11.

- **Peer**—This is always the standby card, either slot 10 or slot 11.

- **Working**—This is always the card in slot 10. *Working* is an APS term that is the same as the term *primary* in redundant NI-2 systems.

- **Protection**—This is the same as *secondary* in NI-2 systems. It is always slot 11.

- **Active**—The OC-3/STM1 receiving datastream on this port is the one used by the system.

- **Inactive**—The OC-3/STM1 receiving datastream on this port is not being used as the active traffic source.

Following is different output for the **show controller atm0/1** command:

```
6160-1#show controller atm0/1
IF Name: ATM0/1    Chip Base Address: B3809000
Port type: OC3   Port rate: 155000 kbps   Port medium: SM Fiber

                               local           peer
                            (protection)     (working)
                              ACTIVE          INACTIVE
                            --------------   -------------
Port status                 Good Signal      Good Signal
Loopback                           None             None
Flags                            0x8300           0x8308
TX clock source              loop-timed       loop-timed
Framing mode                    sts-3c           sts-3c
Cell payload scrambling             On               On
Sts-stream scrambling               On               On
TX Led:                            Off              Off
RX Led:                            Off              Off
TST Led:                           Off              Off
```

In this case, the output from the command **show controller atm0/1** reports that the secondary NI-2 (slot 11, protection) is online. The primary NI-2 (slot 10) is installed, functional, and in standby mode. The OC-3 datastream received by the secondary NI-2 port 0/1 is the datastream being processed by the system (active).

Here is the third example of the command **show controller atm0/1**:

```
6160-1#show controller atm 0/1
IF Name: ATM0/1    Chip Base Address: B3809000
Port type: OC3   Port rate: 155000 kbps   Port medium: SM Fiber
Alarms:   Source: ATM0/1 protect
Severity: CRITICAL Description: 12   Loss of Signal

                               local           peer
                             (working)      (protection)
                              ACTIVE          INACTIVE
                            --------------   --------------
Port status                 Good Signal      SECTION LOS
Loopback                           None             None
Flags                            0x8300           0x8308
TX clock source              loop-timed       loop-timed
Framing mode                    sts-3c           sts-3c
Cell payload scrambling             On               On
Sts-stream scrambling               On               On
TX Led:                            Off              Off
RX Led:                            Off               On
TST Led:                           Off              Off
```

In this case, the output indicates a loss of signal (LOS) on the protect (secondary) NI-2 ATM0/1 port. The primary NI-2 (slot 10) is online, and the active OC-3 datastream is on slot 10.

Here is the fourth example of the command **show controller atm0/1**:

```
6160-1#show controller atm0/1
IF Name: ATM0/1    Chip Base Address: B3809000
Port type: OC3  Port rate: 155000 kbps  Port medium: SM Fiber

Alarms:
Source: ATM0/1 protect
Severity: CRITICAL
Description: 12 Loss of Signal

                                local            peer
                             (protection)      (working)
                               INACTIVE          ACTIVE
                             ---------------   ---------------
Port status                   SECTION LOS      Good Signal
Loopback                          None             None
Flags                            0x8300           0x8308
TX clock source               loop-timed       loop-timed
Framing mode                    sts-3c           sts-3c
Cell payload scrambling           On               On
Sts-stream scrambling             On               On
TX Led:                          Off              Off
RX Led:                           On              Off
TST Led:                         Off              Off
```

In this case, the output from **show controller atm0/1** reports a LOS on the protect (secondary) NI-2 0/1 port (slot 11), but the secondary NI-2 is online. The OC-3 datastream received by the NI-2 in slot 10 is being processed by the system (NI-2 in slot 11).

Here is the fifth of the seven examples of the command **show controller atm0/1**:

```
6160-1#show controller atm0/1
IF Name: ATM0/1    Chip Base Address: B3809000
Port type: OC3  Port rate: 155000 kbps  Port medium: SM Fiber

                                local            peer
                              (working)       (protection)
                               ACTIVE           INACTIVE
                             ---------------   ---------------
Port status                   Good Signal      Not available
Loopback                          None          Not available
Flags                            0x8300         Not available
TX clock source               loop-timed       Not available
Framing mode                    sts-3c         Not available
Cell payload scrambling           On           Not available
Sts-stream scrambling             On           Not available
TX Led:                          Off           Not available
RX Led:                          Off           Not available
TST Led:                         Off           Not available
```

The *Not available* status for peer (protection) in the output indicates that the standby NI-2 in slot 11 has not booted to a standby state. This is a normal status after switching from active to standby. *Not available* is reported for approximately 60 seconds after switchover, while the previously online card restarts.

Following is the sixth example of **show controller atm0/1**. In this case, it is for a coaxial (DS3) NI-2 variant:

```
6160-1#show controller atm0/1
IF Name: ATM0/1, Chip Base Address: B3809000
Port type: DS3 Port rate: 45000 kbps    Port medium: Coax
Loopback:None  Flags:8000 Port status: LOS
Source: ATM0/1
Severity: CRITICAL
Description: 6  LOS Detected
TX Led: Off    RX Led: On    TST Led: Off
TX clock source:  network-derived
DS3 Framing Mode:  m23 plcp
FERF on AIS is on
FERF on LCD is on (n/a in PLCP mode)
FERF on RED is on
FERF on OOF is on
FERF on LOS is on
LBO: <= 225'
```

The output shows a LOS on the DS3 trunk port 0/1. The status is reported by the online NI-2.

Finally, the following is the last output example for **show controller atm0/1**, following the command **redundancy switch-activity**. The online NI-2 reboots but does not complete the restart sequence, as evidenced by the following output:

```
Cisco Internetwork Operating System Software
IOS (tm) NI2 Software (NI2-DSL-M), Experimental Version 12.1(20000906:224310)
Copyright (c) 1986-2000 by cisco Systems, Inc.
Compiled Thu 21-Sep-00 14:54 by satrao
Image text-base: 0x800082B8, data-base: 0x80BD6000
*** This is the STANDBY unit. Initialization is being held. ***
```

This standby NI-2 completes its restart sequence and becomes the online unit. After the statement *Initialization is being held* is sent, the console port is inactive.

Secondary Unit Sync Commands

This section describes different levels of synchronization between the primary and secondary NI-2 cards and the commands to set up the synchronization. The NI-2 cards have different levels of memory and therefore different levels of synchronization of the memory contents. As with almost all Cisco IOS Software-based devices, there is bootflash memory, Flash memory, NVRAM memory, and the running configuration itself, which might not be saved in a particular moment in time.

For optimal redundancy preparedness, you should ensure that both NI-2s have the same running configuration and startup configuration. These two files are automatically synchronized between the two NI-2s when both NI cards are loaded with a redundancy-capable version of IOS, 12.1(6) or later (you should have identical IOS versions loaded on both cards). However, auto-sync can be enabled only when Flash itself is in sync. You must manually sync Flash before enabling auto-sync, because **auto-sync flash** is *not* enabled by default.

Here is the command to synchronize Flash, along with its related command to synchronize bootflash:

```
NI-2(config)#auto-sync flash
NI-2(config)#auto-sync bootflash
```

After you enter at least the first command, if not both, the configurations are automatically synchronized on an ongoing basis by default.

For verification, you can also directly enter the following commands to enable automatic synchronization:

```
NI-2(config)#auto-sync running-config
NI-2(config)#auto-sync config
```

You can also directly create synchronization for each type of memory on the NI-2 cards with the following commands:

- The **NI-2#secondary sync flash** command mirrors Flash on the secondary NI-2 by copying the contents of the primary NI-2 Flash to the secondary NI-2 Flash. This function is disabled by default.

- The **NI-2#secondary sync bootflash** command provides the same function as **sync flash**, but for bootflash. This function is disabled by default.

Verifying Memory Content

The following commands involve checking memory contents (don't overlook the ending colons!) from the privileged EXEC (enable) prompt.

The following two commands allow a quick comparison of which files are in Flash memory on the primary and secondary NI-2s:

```
NI-2#dir flash:
NI-2#dir secondary-flash:
```

The next two commands allow a quick comparison of the files in bootflash on the primary and secondary NI-2:

```
NI-2#dir bootflash:
NI-2#dir secondary-bootflash:
```

The next two commands allow a quick comparison of primary and secondary NVRAM, which is the simplest way to verify synchronization of the two NI-2 cards' configurations:

```
NI-2#dir nvram:
NI-2#dir secondary-nvram:
```

You can gain access to each NI-2 independently, which results in two different NI-2s unless auto-sync mode is in effect. You might use the following command if one of the NI-2s is being prepared for an upgrade or for use in another Cisco 6000 series IP DSL Switch or is a regional spare that happens to be housed onboard this device.

Disable split mode with the **NI-2#split-mode [enable | disable]** command to access each NI-2 independently.

Reload Redundancy Commands

The two redundancy commands that reload NI-2 cards are

- **NI-2#redundancy reload-peer**—Reloads the standby NI-2 card from Flash memory.

- **NI-2#redundancy reload-shelf**—Reloads both NI-2 cards (typically from Flash).

Changing Roles of NI-2 Cards

IOS commands can be used to manually switch the active receive port from primary to secondary and from secondary to primary. The first command is primarily used when neither NI-2 card is carrying traffic. The other commands are used to force a switch that might result in a loss of data. All the following commands are entered at the privileged EXEC (enable) prompt.

To manually switch from the active NI-2 to the standby NI-2, use the following command:

```
NI-2#redundancy switch-activity
6160-1#aps force atm 0/1 from working
6160-1#aps force atm 0/1 from protection
```

IOS commands and responses can also show an attempt to manually switch from a working interface to a faulty interface, as shown here:

```
NI-2#aps manual atm 0/1 from working
NI-2#ATM0/1 Protection link is not available
NI-2#
```

The **aps** command instructs the system to use the datastream from the named fiber interface. The **manual** option performs an audit before switching to ensure that the named datastream is available. The **force** option simply makes the switchover, even if no datastream is present on the named interface. The option **from protection** instructs the system to use the datastream received at the working interface instead of the protection interface. The option **from working** instructs the system to use the datastream received at the protection (standby) interface instead of the working interface. This configuration control allows maintenance on optical fiber systems without affecting traffic. The next step after switching the NI-2 cards is to shut down the NI-2 that is now inactive, as shown in the next command.

The **NI-2#shutdown interface configuration** command applies to both the active and protection OC-3/STM1 interfaces at the same time. The following command sequence shuts down all ATM traffic on the trunk port of both the active and standby NI-2 cards:

```
NI-2#config t
NI-2#[config-if]interface atm 0/1
NI-2#[config-if]shutdown
```

The next command disables automatic and manual APS. After entering this command, you can proceed to replace or otherwise work on the disabled unit:

```
NI-2#aps lockout
```

Verifying Redundancy States

The **NI-2#show redundancy states** command shows important information about NI-2 card and port status, used to show which card is online. Following are two sample outputs from this command:

```
NI-2#show redundancy states
        my state = 11 -ACTIVE
      peer state = 8  -STANDBY READY
            Mode = Duplex (The standby NI-2 is operational, otherwise this shows
   simplex)

            Unit = Primary (The on-line NI-2 is slot 10, the primary)


   Config  Sync = Enabled
 File Sys Sync = Enabled
      Bulk Sync = Enabled
 Dynamic Sync = Enabled

      Split Mode = Disabled
    Manual Swact = Enabled
 Communications = Up
```

This output shows that the NI-2 unit in slot 10 (primary) is online. The mode is duplex, indicating that a redundant NI-2 (slot 11) is installed and functional. (Note that state = 11 does not imply slot 11.) If the standby unit is not installed or not functional, the mode is simplex, as shown here:

```
barf1#show redundancy states
        my state = 11 -ACTIVE
      peer state = 8   -STANDBY READY
            Mode = Duplex
            Unit = Secondary

   Config  Sync = Enabled
 File Sys Sync = Enabled
      Bulk Sync = Enabled
 Dynamic Sync = Enabled

      Split Mode = Disabled
    Manual Swact = Enabled
 Communications = Up
```

This output shows that the NI-2 unit in slot 11 (secondary) is online. The mode is duplex, indicating that a redundant NI-2 (slot 10) is installed and functional.

With these commands, you can set up, manage, and display reports of redundancy on the Cisco IOS Software-based NI-2 cards on the 6000 series of IP DSL Switches. After you have configured the NI-2 cards for basic operations, you can proceed to configure them to perform DSL-to-ATM switching, which is explained in the next section.

Configurations for DSL-to-ATM Switching

DSL-to-ATM switching involves defining the DSL circuit parameters on the Cisco 6000 series IP DSL Switch and continuing the ATM circuit (PVC) through the NI-2 card to the ATM network. You can define the DSL circuit parameters and map the ATM circuits in either the Cisco IOS Software CLI or the CDM GUI software. This section discusses the Cisco IOS Software commands, and the next chapter discusses the CDM activities.

After you configure the Flexi line card to specify the precise ADSL type of traffic it will carry, and after the NI-2 cards automatically recognize the other line cards, you can proceed with the creation of subscriber profiles. Subscriber profiles provide various service levels for individual DSL subscribers. Profiles are discussed in the following sections.

Defining Profiles

A *profile* is a named list of specified values. To configure a subscriber, you attach a profile to that subscriber's port. You can change the configured items for a subscriber simply by changing that subscriber's profile.

There is a provided profile named *default*. You may configure the default profile with specific parameters, but you may not delete it. When you create new profiles, each new profile automatically takes on the values of the default profile unless you specifically override those values. This is useful when you want to modify one or two default parameters and apply the changes to every port in the system. This lets you avoid creating a new profile with minor changes and associating the new profile with every port in the system. Work smarter, not harder.

Except for a few dynamic operational modes, such as rate adaptation due to local impairments, port configuration takes place only through a configuration profile rather than by direct configuration. If you modify an existing profile, the change takes effect on every ADSL port linked to that profile, but only after all related connections are resynchronized (retrained).

To create or delete a DSL profile, or to select an existing profile for modification, use the following global commands:

- **dsl-profile profile-name**—Creates a new profile.
- **no dsl-profile profile-name**—Deletes an existing profile. A profile can be deleted only when it is no longer associated with any port.

profile-name is the name of the profile you want to create or an existing profile you want to delete or modify. Profile names are case-sensitive.

Remember that when you create a profile, it inherits all the configuration settings of the special profile named default. If you subsequently modify the special profile named default, the changes do not propagate to the previously created profiles.

The following command creates a profile called ALPHA_USERS:

```
c6260 (config)#dsl-profile ALPHA_USERS
```

Within this profile are many options for service parameters. In reality, you should not need the majority of these. In theory, you could define a unique profile for every subscriber, applying a different profile to each port. A typical service provider marketing plan would have no more than about a dozen profiles at most. For instance, the marketing department might offer both business and residential service profiles, each category of which might contain three different bit rates and other basic parameters, for a total of six levels of service. If you added a specialized service, such as for streaming video only, that might require one or two more profiles. You can see that unless the service provider's marketing department goes frantic after too much coffee in too many meetings, any DSL network should have no more than 10 or 12 profiles at most.

The following are examples of parameter options for profiles. These commands are entered in dsl profile configuration mode:

- **Setting the bit rate**—To set the maximum and minimum allowed bit rates for the fast-path and interleaved-path DMT profile parameters, use the following command:

  `dmt bitrate max interleaved downstream` *dmt-bitrate* `upstream` *dmt-bitrate*

  dmt-bitrate is a multiple of 32 kbps. If you enter a nonmultiple of 32 kbps, the Cisco IOS Software parser code rejects and aborts the command.

  In the following example, the command sets the maximum interleaved-path bit rate of the default profile to 8032 kbps downstream and 832 kbps upstream:

  ```
  NI-2#conf t
  NI-2(config)#dsl-profile default
  NI-2(config-dsl-profile)#dmt bitrate maximum interleaved downstream 8032
      upstream 832
  ```

- **Setting the margin**—To set upstream and downstream signal-to-noise ratio (SNR) DMT margins, use the following command:

  `dmt margin downstream` *dmt-margin* `upstream` *dmt-margin*

  dmt-margin equals the upstream and downstream SNR margins in decibels. Values must be nonnegative integers. The range is from 0 to 15 dB. The default is 6 dB in each direction; this default is recommended by the DSL Forum and was adopted by Cisco.

CAUTION   The margin command causes the port to retrain when you change the parameter. Setting a parameter to its previous value does not cause a retrain. If a port is training when you change this parameter, the port untrains and retrains to the new parameter.

In this example, the command sets the default profile's SNR DMT margins to 6 dB upstream and 3 dB downstream:

```
NI-2#conf t
NI-2(config)#dsl-profile default
NI-2(config-dsl-profile)#dmt margin downstream 3 upstream 6
```

- **Setting check bytes**—As discussed in Chapter 1, "DSL Primer," check bytes are the redundant, unaltered bytes that are used to verify DSL interleaving and deinterleaving. This interleaving process minimizes the impact of the inevitable bit errors, spreading out missed bits rather than losing a sequential string of bits. The higher the number of check bytes, the more accurately the algorithm can code and decode the straight bits, but a higher number of check bytes also means more overhead, reducing data throughput.

  Here is how to define the check bytes:

  ```
  NI-2#conf t
  NI-2 (config)#dsl-profile default
  NI-2 (cfg-dsl-profile)#dmt check-bytes interleaved downstream number check
    upstream number
  ```

  number is the number of redundancy check bytes per DMT frame. Values are from 0 to 16 bytes in increments of 2 (0, 2, 4, ... , 14, 16). You can set different values for both upstream and downstream, but you must reference (specify) both directions even if the number of check bytes is equal in both directions. The default is 16 (the maximum) in both directions. You can also set the number of check bytes by turning off check bytes. This means that the system determines and uses the optimal number of check bytes for that line.

  In general, you should probably use the default settings, unless and until the local transmission environment or the individual service-level agreement dictates otherwise.

- **Set the interleaving delay**—Presuming that this is not a fast-path service (see Chapter 1's discussion of fast and interleaved paths in DSL service), the interleaving delay helps protect against impulse noise and clipping. However, it adds delay, which might not be tolerable for some applications. To set the interleaving delay parameter, use the following command:

  ```
  dmt interleaving-delay downstream delay-in-usecs upstream delay-in-usecs
  ```

  delay-in-usecs is the interleaving delay in microseconds. The default interleaving delay is 16000 microseconds (16 milliseconds) for both upstream and downstream directions. Allowable values are 0, 500, 1000, 2000, 4000, 8000, and 16000 microseconds.

CAUTION   Like the **margin** command, this command causes the port to retrain when you change the parameter. Setting this parameter to its current value does not cause a retrain. If a port is training when you change the value, the port untrains and retrains to the new value.

In the following example, the command sets the default profile's interleaving delay to 2000 microseconds downstream and 4000 microseconds upstream:

```
NI-2#conf t
NI-2(config)#dsl-profile default
NI-2(config-dsl-profile)#dmt interleaving-delay downstream 2000 upstream 4000
```

The four parameters are not all the options available, but they are probably the most common settings made for typical DSL networks. You can even safely use the default settings, such as 6 dB for the margin, and just define the bit rate, for a very simple and quick beginning profile. The very simplest starting procedure is to keep using the default profile, possibly making a few changes to its parameters, which is already attached to every port until you specify a new profile.

In this case, after defining the new profile with the bit rates, margin, check bytes, and interleave delay, you can proceed to assign the profile to the port(s) desired. At this time you cannot attach a profile to a group or range of ports, so you must address each port individually.

Attaching and Detaching a Profile

To attach a profile to or detach a profile from a specific port, use the following interface commands:

- **dsl profile** *profile-name* (to attach)
- **no dsl profile** *profile-name* (to detach from the port)

profile-name is the profile you want to attach to or detach from the selected port.

In the following example, the command attaches the profile ALPHA_USERS to slot 20, port 1:

```
NI-2#conf t
NI-2(config)#int atm 20/1 (Enters interface configuration mode for port 20/1)
NI-2(config-if)#dsl profile ALPHA_USERS (Attaches ALPHA_USERS profile to this
  port)
```

In the following example, the command detaches the profile ALPHA_USERS from slot 20, port 1:

```
NI-2#conf t
NI-2(config)#int atm 20/1 (Enters interface configuration mode for port 20/1)
NI-2(config-if)#no dsl profile ALPHA_USERS (Detaches ALPHA_USERS profile from this
  port)
NI-2(config-if)#exit
```

The preceding commands detach this particular instance (application) of the profile from this particular port. However, the original definition of the profile, the class, still exists in the overall configuration. After you have detached the profile from the port, then and only then can you delete the original definition of the profile from the overall configuration, if you're sure you will never use this profile again. To do this, use the following command:

```
NI-2#conf t
NI-2(config)#no dsl-profile ALPHA_USERS
```

PVCs

Having defined and attached your profile, you can move on to creating an ATM connection from the line card port to the network trunk. The simplest type of connection is a PVC, which is the starting basis for the more-sophisticated soft-PVC and Permanent Virtual Path (PVP).

PVCs must be configured in both the IP DSL Switch and the ATM switch cloud. PVCs remain active until the circuit is removed from either configuration.

To create a PVC on an ATM interface, use the **atm pvc** interface configuration command. The **no** form of this command removes the specified PVC. The labor-saving news is that PVCs are bidirectional and need to be removed from only one direction or the other.

Here's the syntax:

```
atm pvc  vpi vci int atm [slot/port] vpi  vci
```

vpi is the virtual path identifier for this PVC. The *vpi* value is unique on only a single link, not throughout the ATM network, because it has local significance only. The *vpi* value must match that of the switch.

vci is the ATM network's virtual channel identifier. It is in the range of 0 to 1 less than the maximum value set for this interface by the ATM per-VC per-VP command. The *vci* value is unique on only a single link.

As an example, suppose that a DSL circuit is connected to DSL port 1 on line card 19. On that DSL side, it is configured as an ATM PVC using the virtual path of 0 and the virtual channel of 33. Here are the commands to switch that incoming connection to VPI 0, VCI 100 outbound on the network trunk, which is the ATM interface 0/1:

```
6260(config)#int atm 19/1
6260(config-if)#atm pvc 0 33 int atm 0/1 0 100
```

In a subtended configuration, you must configure the passthrough connections from the sub-tended trunk to the network trunk. In this case, you can build on the previous line card-to-trunk definitions to make the same PVC follow through to the host device's ATM trunk, 0/1 again. Bear in mind that the PVC definition turned the PVC 0/100 loose on this IP DSL Switch's incoming trunk 0/2. Here are the commands to switch the passthrough (subtended) PVC through this IP DSL Switch onto the network trunk, which is ATM 0/1:

```
6260(config)#int atm 0/2
6260(config-if)#atm pvc 0 100 int atm 0/1 0 200
```

Even if you use the same numbers for both ends of the connection, both the line card/port and the trunk or the trunk-trunk connection, you must specify the whole line, both incoming and outgoing identifiers.

You should be starting to realize that configuring each DSL subscriber's port on the IP DSL Switch with PVCs is quite labor-intensive. Remember also that you can configure multiple PVCs on the Cisco 827 DSL router—that is, one PVC for voice service and another for data traffic. You can also create two or more PVCs on each line card port on the IP DSL Switch.

Obviously, using nothing but PVCs would be inefficiently burdensome. In the interest of working smarter, not harder, consider the next two labor-saving ATM connections.

Soft-PVCs (SPVCs)

The SPVC is a combination of permanent circuits, manually configured at each end of the connection, and an SVC through the middle of the connection. The switched circuit depends on the ATM format's internal communications and routing protocols—specifically, the autoconfigured point-to-point signaling connection using VCI 5. (For more information, refer to Appendix B, "ATM Overview.")

Soft-PVCs have two main advantages. The first advantage is its flexible sustainability. If a particular link is unavailable, as with a cable cut, the SPVC takes advantage of the ATM network's other paths to reach its destination. This automatic PVC rerouting does not require human intervention, unlike the PVC in the case of connection unavailability. The second SPVC advantage is its efficiency in configuration labor. You can trust the ATM signaling protocols to automatically allocate available identifiers, both VPIs and VCIs, at each interface, eliminating the need to manually define each new connection.

However, these two advantages also suggest the SPVC's disadvantages. First, the SPVC requires more overhead to accommodate the signaling and updating required to maintain the network knowledge. Second, the SPVC is harder to trace, unlike the PVC, which is mapped to a known set of identifiers, because the SPVC takes on dynamic VPIs and VCIs at each interface.

Overall, many providers prefer to save human labor and tax the system itself, so you should know how to create a soft-PVC. You can use these steps:

Step 1   Find the target device's ATM address, such as the host IP DSL Switch in a subtending configuration, or the Layer 3 termination device, such as the 6400 UAC. You can do this with the IOS command **show atm addresses** on the target device. Just as obvious as the command is the listing of ATM addresses, with their own heading of *Soft-PVC Addresses* in the case of the 6400. The ATM address probably looks like this:

```
47.0091.8100.0000.0030.7b2d.0001.4000.0c80.0010.00
```

NOTE   For efficiency and to prevent human hand-copying errors, copy that ATM address to your computer's software clipboard.

Step 2   Telnet back (or otherwise connect) to the IP DSL Switch's NI-2. You cannot duplicate the existing PVC identifiers, so you must either remove the existing PVC or use a different set of identifiers. (Remember that you will have the same numbers of VCIs on differently-numbered VPIs as long as those combinations are still unique.)

Step 3   Map the new soft-PVC from the line card port to the target ATM address rather than out the DSLAM's network trunk interface as you would for a standard PVC. You specify that destination address rather than the outgoing network trunk. That is, the only interface you specify is the line card/port, *not* the network trunk interface. Following are the commands:

```
NI-2(config)#int atm 21/4 (for the 21st line card's fourth port)
NI-2(config-if)#atm soft-pvc 0 101 dest-address
    47.0091.8100.0000.0030.7b2d.0001.4000.0c80.0010.00 0 200
```

The command in interface configuration mode is actually all on one line. You can see why it's easier to paste the ATM address you obtained in the first step! Notice also that you must specify the exiting VPI and VCI—in this case, VPI 0 and VCI 200. That's how the circuit is identified at the other end, the target ATM device, although it takes on seemingly random identifiers in the ATM network between the two end devices. This is shown in Figure 6-7 (which is also repeated in Appendix B).

Figure 6-7   *Soft-PVC Mapping*

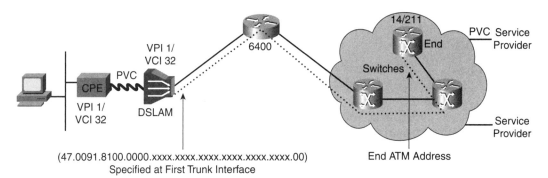

PVPs

Another type of labor-saving ATM connection is a PVP. As mentioned in Appendix B's discussion of basic ATM, a PVP is a manually configured connection that carries a bundle of virtual circuits. This is commonly implemented between ATM switches within an ATM network (node to node). The advantage of this type of connection is that a single VPI configured through several ATM switches carries thousands of VCs without the need to individually configure them. The common VPI means that any single channel with that VPI is automatically assimilated into the larger path without having to configure each circuit like adding threads.

Many service providers use a PVP to group the individual PVCs from a subtended IP DSL Switch so that the VPI highlights the common source as the subtended connections traverse the hosting devices. Another use of PVPs is to group connections with a common service-level agreement, according to an obvious mapping scheme that matches a VPI with a type of DSL service.

The first disadvantage of the PVP is that you cannot extract or work with a single PVC within the larger pipe without rebuilding the entire PVP. Among other considerations, this means that you must be careful when identifying the starting PVCs, because the system assimilates all the common VPIs regardless of whether you want to bundle them into that PVP. Second, as with the PVC, you must define the PVP at each interface through which it traverses (although defining a single element is still much easier than defining the thousands of separate PVCs). A third disadvantage is like the PVC's fragility: If a link is broken, as with a cable cut, the PVP must be manually reconfigured.

Following are the commands to configure a PVP:

- **NI-2(config)#int atm 0/2**—This command begins to configure the first subtending trunk interface, ATM 0/2.

- **NI-2(config-if)#atm pvp 0 int atm 0/1 0**—In the interface configuration command, notice that you specify only the VPI—0 in this case—on both ends, the subtending trunk of 0/2 and the network trunk of 0/1. This makes VPI 0 unavailable for any incoming connections on this host IP DSL Switch, and you must have previously identified all the desired incoming connections on the subtended IP DSL Switch with the common VPI of 0.

  You can repeat the PVP definition at the next ATM device, whether it is another IP DSL Switch in a subtended daisy chain or tree, or any other device. You can even change the PVP number as you did the PVC earlier, like this:

  ```
  Nextdevice(config)#int atm 0/2
  Nextdevice(config-if)#atm pvp 0 int atm 0/1 14
  ```

  In the second command, all the individual PVCs, which started their lives with the VPI of 0, are now grouped in the PVP numbered 14.

Configuring Inverse Multiplexing Over ATM (IMA)

As discussed at length in Chapter 4, IMA is most common on the Cisco 6015 IP DSL Switch, but it is available on the other switches in the 6000 series as well. As a very brief reminder here, the T1/E1 IMA feature aggregates multiple low-speed links (T1/E1) into one or more IMA groups. These multiple ATM links act as a single ATM physical layer element.

To enable IMA, you can configure any WAN interface (the DS3, any T1 link, any E1 link, or any IMA group) as the trunk. When you configure a T1 link or an IMA group as the trunk, the DS3 port is disabled. When you select the DS3 port as the trunk, the T1 links and IMA groups are all treated as subtended ports.

Configuring IMA involves three major processes:

- Configuring a trunk interface
- Configuring T1/E1 interfaces
- Configuring IMA interfaces

First, configure the trunk interface with the following command, which designates the interface to use as the trunk—in this case, the 0/1 (network) trunk:

```
6015(config)#atm ni2-switch trunk atm 0/1
```

Next, select the link's transmit clock source, which you learned about earlier:

```
6015(config-if)#clock source network-derived
```

Select the link's framing type, which must match on both sides of that link:

```
6015(config-if)#framing m23adm
```

Enable DS3 cell payload scrambling on the link; scrambling is required if you use ami line coding:

```
6015(config-if)#scrambling cell-payload
```

Specify the cable length line build-out (**short** or **long**), followed by mandatory values: the length following **short**, or the gain and margin value following **long**. You can view the acceptable lengths, such as 0 to 133 feet for **short**, by including the **?** option after the **long** or **short** commands. The default setting is long haul with gain36 and 0db (**lbo long gain36 0db**):

```
6015(config-if)#lbo short
```

Next, configure each T1/E1 interface that will go into the IMA group(s), starting in interface configuration mode for each interface in turn:

```
6015(config)#interface atm 0/2
```

If ami line coding is selected, as it is in the next command for this T1 link, you must have enabled cell scrambling on the link. T1 and/or E1 links have different, specific options, although ami applies to both T1 and E1 links. The defaults are b8zs for the T1s and hdb3 for the E1s.

```
6015(config-if)#linecode ami
```

Next, select the frame type for the T1 or E1 data links. The framing type must match on both sides of the link. The defaults are as follows:

E1—**pcm30**

T1—**esf**

DS3—**cbitadm**

```
6015(config-if)#framing esf (or framing pcm30 for the E1)
```

Specify the line build-out (LBO) length as either **short** or **long**, followed by the appropriate parameters, as you did earlier for the trunk interface. Here is an example of the **lbo** command in this case:

```
6015(config-if)#lbo short 133
```

Now you are ready for the third major step, which is to configure the IMA interfaces themselves. You repeat the following command sets for each IMA interface you want to configure:

```
6015(config)#interface atm 0/2 (first T1/E1 to be assigned to an IMA group)
```

Assign the ATM interface to an IMA group (numbered from 0 to 3, for a total of four possible IMA groups). After the interface is assigned to an IMA group, individual ATM functionality is no longer available on the link:

```
6015(config-if)#ima-group 2
```

Enable the individual link by canceling the shutdown state:

```
6015(config-if)#no shutdown
```

Now that you have created an IMA interface from the individual links, you can begin configuring the IMA interface as a whole:

```
6015 (config-if)#interface atm0/ima2
```

Select the transmit clock mode for the selected IMA group:

```
6015(config-if)#ima clock-mode independent
```

Enter the maximum differential delay in milliseconds for the selected IMA group. Although the ranges are different for T1s and E1s, the default for both is 25 milliseconds, which is the minimum delay for both these standards:

```
6015(config-if)#ima differential-delay-maximum 68
```

Enter the minimum number of links that need to be operational for the selected IMA group:

```
6015(config-if)#ima active-links-minimum 2
```

Enable the IMA group by canceling the shutdown state:

```
6015(config-if)#no shutdown
```

This completes the three major processes for configuring the NI-2 for IMA. The next section describes the commands to verify the configuration.

Verifying IMA Status

After you have configured IMA, you should verify the operational status of the IMA interfaces using these **show** commands:

- **6015#show ima interface**—Displays information about all IMA groups and the links in those groups.

- **6015#show interface atm0/ima2**—Displays interface configuration, status, and statistics for the IMA interface.

- **6015#show controllers**—Displays information about current settings and performance at the physical level. You saw detailed examples of this command earlier, in the section "APS-Related CLI Commands."

- **6015#show controller atm0/ima2**—Displays diagnostic information for the specified IMA group.
- **6015#show ima interface atm0/ima2**—Displays configuration information and operational status for the specified IMA group.
- **6015#show ima interface atm0/2**—Displays information for a single link in an IMA group.
- **6015#show ima counters**—Displays IMA statistics in 15-minute intervals, with 24-hour totals.

Now you can verify your work with sample configurations. The first sample configuration describes how to configure the topology shown in Figure 6-8, which consists of the following:

- An IMA group containing four links as a trunk interface
- Two IMA groups, each containing two links, connecting subtended Cisco 6000 series IP DSL Switch chassis

Figure 6-8 *IMA Trunk with IMA Subtended Chassis*

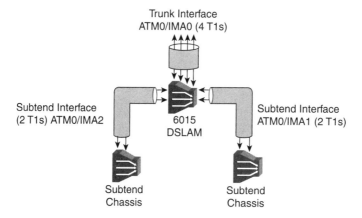

Here is the configuration, shown in the running config output:

```
atm ni2-switch trunk ATM0/IMA0 !Configures interface ATM0/IMA0 as the trunk!
!
interface ATM0/0
 no ip address
 no ip route-cache
 atm maxvp-number 0
 atm maxvc-number 4096
 atm maxvci-bits 12
!
interface Ethernet0/0
 ip address 192.168.1.1 255.255.255.0
 no ip route-cache
```

```
!
interface ATM0/1
 no ip address
 no ip route-cache
 shutdown
 no atm ilmi-keepalive
!
interface ATM0/2
 no ip address
 no ip route-cache
 no ip mroute-cache
 no atm ilmi-keepalive
 clock source loop-timed
 scrambling cell-payload
 linecode ami
 lbo short 133
 ima-group 0 !Adds this interface to IMA group 0!
!
interface ATM0/3
 no ip address
 no ip route-cache
 no ip mroute-cache
 no atm ilmi-keepalive
 clock source loop-timed
 scrambling cell-payload
 linecode ami
 lbo short 133
 ima-group 0 !Adds this interface to IMA group 0!
!
interface ATM0/4
 no ip address
 no ip route-cache
 no ip mroute-cache
 no atm ilmi-keepalive
 clock source loop-timed
 scrambling cell-payload
 linecode ami
 lbo short 133
 ima-group 0 !Adds this interface to IMA group 0!
!
interface ATM0/5
 no ip address
 no ip route-cache
 no ip mroute-cache
 no atm ilmi-keepalive
 clock source loop-timed
 scrambling cell-payload
 linecode ami
 lbo short 133
 ima-group 0 !Adds this interface to IMA group 0!
!
interface ATM0/6
 no ip address
 no ip route-cache
 no ip mroute-cache
 no atm ilmi-keepalive
 clock source loop-timed
 scrambling cell-payload
 linecode ami
 lbo short 133
 ima-group 1 !Adds this interface to IMA group 1!
!
interface ATM0/7
 no ip address
```

```
 no ip route-cache
 no ip mroute-cache
 no atm ilmi-keepalive
 clock source loop-timed
 scrambling cell-payload
 linecode ami
 lbo short 133
 ima-group 1 !Adds this interface to IMA group 1!
!
interface ATM0/8
 no ip address
 no ip route-cache
 no ip mroute-cache
 no atm ilmi-keepalive
 clock source loop-timed
 scrambling cell-payload
 linecode ami
 lbo short 133
 ima-group 2 !Adds this interface to IMA group 2!
!
interface ATM0/9
 no ip address
 no ip route-cache
 no ip mroute-cache
 no atm ilmi-keepalive
 clock source loop-timed
 scrambling cell-payload
 linecode ami
 lbo short 133
 ima-group 2 !Adds this interface to IMA group 2!
!
interface ATM0/IMA0 !IMA group 0 configuration!
 no ip address
 no ip route-cache
 no ip mroute-cache
 no atm ilmi-keepalive
 ima active-links-minimum 2
 ima clock-mode independent
 ima differential-delay-maximum 68
!
interface ATM0/IMA1 !IMA group 1 configuration!

 no ip address
 no ip route-cache
 no ip mroute-cache
 no atm ilmi-keepalive
 ima active-links-minimum 2
 ima clock-mode independent
 ima differential-delay-maximum 68
!
interface ATM0/IMA2 !IMA group 2 configuration!
 no ip address
 no ip route-cache
 no ip mroute-cache
 no atm ilmi-keepalive
 ima active-links-minimum 2
 ima clock-mode independent
 ima differential-delay-maximum 68
!
interface ATM0/IMA3
 no ip address
 no ip route-cache
 shutdown
 no atm ilmi-keepalive
```

This output shows the configuration for an IMA trunk with IMA-subtended chassis for the Cisco 6000 series IP DSL Switch. The next configuration is for the topology shown in Figure 6-9.

Figure 6-9   *DS3 Trunk with IMA and T1 Subtended Chassis*

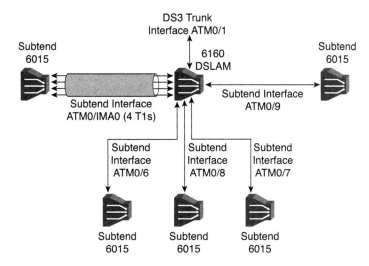

This configuration contains a combination of IMA, T1, and DS3 interfaces:

```
atm ni2-switch trunk ATM0/1 !DS3 is the default trunk!
!
interface ATM0/0
 no ip address
 no ip route-cache
 atm maxvp-number 0
 atm maxvc-number 4096
 atm maxvci-bits 12
!
interface Ethernet0/0
 ip address 192.168.1.1 255.255.255.0
 no ip route-cache
!
interface ATM0/1
 no ip address
 no ip route-cache
 no atm ilmi-keepalive
!
interface ATM0/2
 no ip address
 no ip route-cache
 no atm ilmi-keepalive
 ima-group 0 !Adds this interface to IMA group 0!
!
interface ATM0/3
 no ip address
 no ip route-cache
 no atm ilmi-keepalive
 ima-group 0 !Adds this interface to IMA group 0!
```

```
!
interface ATM0/4
 no ip address
 no ip route-cache
 no atm ilmi-keepalive
 ima-group 0 !Adds this interface to IMA group 0!
!
interface ATM0/5
 no ip address
 no ip route-cache
 no atm ilmi-keepalive
 ima-group 0 !Adds this interface to IMA group 0!
!
interface ATM0/6 !T1 configuration!
 no ip address
 no ip route-cache
 no ip mroute-cache
 no atm ilmi-keepalive
 clock source loop-timed
 scrambling cell-payload
 linecode ami
 lbo short 133
!
interface ATM0/7 !T1 configuration!
 no ip address
 no ip route-cache
 no ip mroute-cache
 no atm ilmi-keepalive
 clock source loop-timed
 scrambling cell-payload
 linecode ami
 lbo short 133
!
interface ATM0/8 !T1 configuration!
 no ip address
 no ip route-cache
 no ip mroute-cache
 no atm ilmi-keepalive
 clock source loop-timed
 scrambling cell-payload
 linecode ami
 lbo short 133
!
interface ATM0/9 !T1 configuration!
 no ip address
 no ip route-cache
 no ip mroute-cache
 no atm ilmi-keepalive
 clock source loop-timed
 scrambling cell-payload
 linecode ami
 lbo short 133
!
interface ATM0/IMA0 !IMA group 0 configuration!
 no ip address
 no ip route-cache
 no ip mroute-cache
 no atm ilmi-keepalive
 ima active-links-minimum 4
 ima clock-mode independent
 ima differential-delay-maximum 68
!
interface ATM0/IMA1
 no ip address
```

```
 no ip route-cache
 shutdown
 no atm ilmi-keepalive
!
interface ATM0/IMA2
 no ip address
 no ip route-cache
 shutdown
 no atm ilmi-keepalive
!
interface ATM0/IMA3
 no ip address
 no ip route-cache
 shutdown
 no atm ilmi-keepalive
```

Verifying NI-2 Processes with **show** Commands

Several general and DSL-specific **show** commands can help you verify proper operations on the NI-2. The first command is probably the most common Cisco IOS Software command. It produces output that is valuable for DSL and ATM troubleshooting. The other commands are more specific to DSL and/or ATM. These **show** commands are as follows:

- **show running-configuration**
- **show atm vc** (traffic and other options)
- **show hardware** (slot and chassis)
- **show dsl profile**
- **show facility-alarm status**
- **show environment**
- **show network-clocks**
- **show ATM Status**

Each of these is detailed in the following list. It includes the pertinent information you need to monitor DSL activity through the NI-2 card on the Cisco 6000 series of IP DSL Switches:

- **show running-configuration**

  This command tells you which ports are attached to each profile. You can obtain more-specific reporting for selected profiles by using the **show dsl profile** command.

  The following example shows the running configuration:

  ```
  alpha_c6260#show running-config
  Building configuration...
  Current configuration:
  !
  ! Last configuration change at 12:58:27 EDT Fri June 14 2002
  ! NVRAM config last updated at 14:13:58 EDT Thu June 13 2002
  !
  version 12.2 !Notice the more generic version designator!
  no service pad
  service timestamps debug uptime
  ```

```
service timestamps log uptime
no service password-encryption
service internal
!
hostname alpha_c6260
!
boot system flash:NI-2-dsl-mz.12-2.DA
slot 1 atuc-1-4dmt !These are the line cards, all four-port DMT cards in
  this chassis; remember that slots 10 and 11 are reserved for the NI-2
  card(s) and are ignored here!
slot 2 atuc-1-4dmt
slot 3 atuc-1-4dmt
slot 4 atuc-1-4dmt
slot 5 atuc-1-4dmt
slot 6 atuc-1-4dmt
slot 7 atuc-1-4dmt
slot 8 atuc-1-4dmt
slot 9 atuc-1-4dmt
slot 12 atuc-1-4dmt

no logging monitor
enable password lab
!
dsl-profile default !As with almost all Cisco show commands, if the default
  values have not been changed, no details are shown for any default
  parameters, such as this default profile. You can display the precise
  default values with the show dsl profile command.!
!
dsl-profile ALPHA_USERS
 dmt interleaving-delay downstream 3 upstream 6
 dmt bitrate maximum interleaved downstream 2048 upstream 256
!
dsl-profile test !This profile has not been defined yet beyond its name, so
  no values are shown.!
!
dsl-profile alpha_677
 dmt interleaving-delay downstream 0 upstream 0
 dmt bitrate maximum interleaved downstream 8032 upstream 864
!
dsl-profile alpha-677
 dmt bitrate maximum interleaved downstream 8032 upstream 864
!
dsl-profile jurgen
 dmt bitrate maximum interleaved downstream 8032 upstream 864
dsl-profile train
network-clock-select revertive !This clocking selection has been changed
  from the default value of non-revertive, which is much more typical in
  service provider environments.!
network-clock-select 1 ATM0/1
network-clock-select 2 system
ip subnet-zero
ip host-routing
ip host zeppelin 1.0.0.253
ip domain-name cisco.com
ip name-server 171.69.204.11
!
atm address 47.0091.8100.0000.0077.d0fe.4301.0077.d0fe.4301.00
atm address 47.0091.8100.0000.00e0.b0ff.b501.00e0.b0ff.b501.00
atm address 47.0091.8100.0000.0050.0fff.cc01.0050.0fff.cc01.00
atm router pnni
 no aesa embedded-number left-justified
 node 1 level 56 lowest
  redistribute atm-static
!
```

```
clock timezone EDT -5
clock summer-time EDT recurring
!
process-max-time 200
!
interface ATM0/0 !This is the backplane trunk, which you can think of as
  the backplane itself; unless you want to configure a PVC for in-band
  management, you need not configure this trunk at all, leaving the default
  values as they are.!
 no ip address

 no ip mroute-cache
 atm cac service-category abr deny
 atm maxvp-number 0
!
interface Ethernet0/0
 ip address 171.69.204.250 255.255.255.0

 no ip proxy-arp
 no ip mroute-cache
 no keepalive
!
interface ATM0/1
 no ip address

 no atm ilmi-keepalive
 atm cac service-category abr deny
 atm manual-well-known-vc
 atm pvc 0 5 pd on rx-cttr 3 tx-cttr 3  interface  ATM0/0 0 any-vci  encap
  qsaal
 atm pvc 0 16 pd on rx-cttr 3 tx-cttr 3  interface  ATM0/0 0 any-vci  encap
  ilmi
 atm pvc 0 18 pd on rx-cttr 3 tx-cttr 3  interface  ATM0/0 0 any-vci  encap
  pnni
 clock source loop-timed
!
interface ATM0/2
 no ip address

 shutdown !Shutdown is the default state of all interfaces, and in this
  case, the subtend trunk ATM0/2 is left shut down because there is no
  subtending on this chassis.!
 no atm ilmi-keepalive
 atm cac service-category abr deny
!
interface ATM1/1
 no ip address

 dsl subscriber RayBudge
 dsl profile alpha_676
 no atm ilmi-keepalive
 atm cac service-category abr deny
 atm pvc 0 35  interface  ATM0/1 0 101 !Here is the PVC that is designated
  0/35 as it enters from the DSL subscriber side and is designated 0/101
  as it leaves on the network trunk ATM 0/1.!
```

- **show atm vc**

  The details of this command and its output are explained after the output:

  ```
  6160-93#sho atm vc

  Interface  VPI VCI Type  X-Interface X-VPI X-VCI Encap Status
  ```

```
ATM0/0     0    35 PVC    ATM0/1     0     16   ILMI       UP
ATM0/0     0    36 PVC    ATM0/2     0     16   ILMI       DOWN
ATM0/0     0    37 PVC    ATM0/1     0      5   QSAAL      UP
ATM0/0     0    38 PVC    ATM0/2     0      5   QSAAL      DOWN
ATM0/0     0    39 PVC    ATM0/1     0     18   PNNI       UP
ATM0/1     0     5 PVC    ATM0/0     0     37   QSAAL      UP

ATM0/1     1    34 PVC    ATM1/1     1      1              UP
ATM0/1     1    36 PVC    ATM1/2     1      1              UP
ATM0/1     1    44 PVC    ATM2/2     1      1              DOWN

ATM1/1     1     1 PVC    ATM0/1     1     34              UP
ATM1/2     1     1 PVC    ATM0/1     1     36              UP
ATM2/2     1     1 PVC    ATM0/1     1     44              DOWN
```

This output displays statistics for all PVCs, both manually created and those that were autocreated by the system for ATM signaling and management. All ATM interfaces on the IP DSL Switch are reflected, although you can specify a particular interface's connections to display, such as a particular DSL port. The Status field is either UP or DOWN.

ATM VCs are shown twice, once on each interface. For instance, when you look a bit more than halfway down the second and third columns, VCC 1/34 is first shown on the network trunk interface ATM0/1, mapped to the Cisco 6400 from the line card interface ATM1/1, where it is connected to the CPE modem as 1/1. Then the line card interface itself is shown further down, as you see in the first column, mapping 1/1 to the interface ATM0/1.

To display all ATM virtual circuits (PVCs, soft-PVCs, and SVCs) and traffic information, you can use the **show atm vc** command. You can also use the command **show atm vc | interface** *interface-number,* where **interface** *interface-number* specifies the interface number or subinterface number of the PVC or SVC. This displays all VCs on the specified interface or subinterface.

In this example, ATM 0/2 is shut down, because subtending is not being used. Therefore, the signaling and OAM protocols in the reserved circuits are also down, such as PVC 0/36 in the second line of the list.

The following is an example of a more-specific display, using optional parameters where traffic displays the virtual channel cell traffic:

```
NI-2#show atm vc traffic int atm
Interface    VPI    VCI    Type    rx-cell-cnts    tx-cell-cnts
ATM0/0        0     35     PVC          43              38
ATM0/0        0     36     PVC           0               0
ATM0/0        0     37     PVC          27              29
ATM0/0        0     38     PVC           0               0
ATM0/0        0     39     PVC          64             144
ATM0/1        0      5     PVC          29              27
ATM0/1        0     16     PVC          38              43
ATM0/1        0     18     PVC         144              64
ATM0/1        0    100     PVC           0               0
ATM0/2        0      5     PVC           0               0
ATM0/2        0     16     PVC           0               0
ATM19/1       0     33     PVC           0               0
```

You can specify a particular interface to show the connections on that interface only. You can also use the command **show atm vp** if this is a subtended host with PVPs passing through it from the subtended system.

- **show hardware status**

You can display information about the chassis type and the physical cards in the chassis and determine whether the power supply and fan modules are present:

```
NI-2#show hardware (Displays all hardware, as shown here:)
Chassis Type: C6260
Slot 1 : ATUC-1-4DMT    Slot 17: ATUC-1-4DMT
Slot 2 : ATUC-1-4DMT    Slot 18: ATUC-1-4DMT
Slot 3 : ATUC-1-4DMT    Slot 19: ATUC-1-4DMT
Slot 4 : ATUC-1-4DMT    Slot 20: ATUC-1-4DMT
Slot 5 : ATUC-1-4DMT    Slot 21: ATUC-1-4DMT
Slot 6 : ATUC-1-4DMT    Slot 22: ATUC-1-4DMT
Slot 7 : ATUC-1-4DMT    Slot 23: ATUC-1-4DMT
Slot 8 : ATUC-1-4DMT    Slot 24: ATUC-1-4DMT
Slot 9 : ATUC-1-4DMT    Slot 25: ATUC-1-4DMT
Slot 10: NI-2-155SM-155SM    Slot 26: ATUC-1-4DMT
Slot 11: EMPTY  Slot 27: ATUC-1-4DMT
Slot 12: ATUC-1-4DMT    Slot 28: ATUC-1-4DMT
Slot 13: ATUC-1-4DMT    Slot 29: ATUC-1-4DMT
Slot 14: ATUC-1-4DMT    Slot 30: ATUC-1-4DMT
Slot 15: ATUC-1-4DMT    Slot 31: ATUC-1-4DMT
Slot 16: ATUC-1-4DMT    Slot 32: ATUC-1-4DMT
Fan Module 1: Present   2: Present
Power Supply Module 1:  Not Present   2:  Present
```

The **show hardware chassis** command shows the manufacturing data for the NI-2 motherboard and daughter card, I/O controller, power module, and backplane, plus the chassis type, chassis name, manufacturer's name, hardware revision, serial number, asset ID, alias, and CLEI code.

- **show dsl profile**

This command displays all profiles unless you use the option *profile-name* at the end of the command to specify a particular profile.

The following example displays the command profile named ALPHA_USERS:

```
NI-2#show dsl profile ALPHA_USERS

dsl profile ALPHA_USERS:
Alarms Enabled: NO
ATM Payload Scrambling: Enabled

DMT profile parameters
    Maximum Bitrates:
Interleave Path: downstream: 8032/kbs, upstream: 864/kbs
    Minimum Bitrates:
Interleave Path: downstream: 0/kbs, upstream: 0/kbs
    Margin: downstream: 3 db, upstream: 3 db
    Interleave Delay: downstream: 0 usecs, upstream: 0 usecs
    Check Bytes (FEC):
        Interleave Path: downstream: 16, upstream: 16
    R-S Codeword Size: downstream: auto, upstream: auto
    Trellis Coding: Disabled
```

```
        Overhead Framing: Mode 1
        Bit-Swap:      Enabled
        Bit-Swap From Margin:    3 dB
        Bit-Swap To Margin:    3 dB    Operating Mode:      Automatic
         Training Mode:        Standard

     SDSL profile parameters

     CAP profile parameters
```

The last two lines, for SDSL profile parameters and CAP profile parameters, are legacy provisions for these obsolescent modulations. In this case, no profile named ALPHA_USERS has been defined for SDSL or CAP, so these display areas are blank.

- **show facility-alarm status**

  This command shows the current major and minor alarms and the thresholds for all user-configurable alarms on a Cisco IP DSL Switch.

  The following are different examples of the output. The first example shows a single major alarm and a single informational notice:

  ```
  NI-2#show facility-alarm status
  System Totals  Critical: 0  Major: 1  Minor: 0
  Source: Fan Slot 0   Severity: MAJOR  Description: 1  Not detected or missing
  Source: Slot 19    Severity: INFO   Description: 4  Module was detected
  ```

  The next example of the **show facility-alarm status** command shows one critical alarm, one major alarm, and one informational notice:

  ```
  NI-2#show facility-alarm stat
  System Totals  Critical: 1  Major: 1  Minor: 0
  Source: NI-2 Module Severity: MAJOR  Description: 1  Loss of active clock sync
  Source: Slot 19    Severity: INFO   Description: 4  Module was detected
  Source: ATM0/1    Severity: CRITICAL Description: 6 Line RDI
  ```

- **show environment**

  This command displays temperature, voltage, and chassis status information. The **show environment** command has two valuable options—**all** and **table**.

  all lists temperature readings, fan status, and chassis status. **table** displays the temperature and voltage thresholds and lists the ranges of environmental measurements that are within the specified ranges.

  Here is an example:

  ```
  NI-2#show environment all
                    Slot 1     Slot 2
  Power/Fan Presence:
          Power Module:  No          Yes
             Fan Tray:  Yes         Yes

  Power Modules:
          48 VDC voltage:  0   volts    48 volts
          48 VDC current:  0   amps     1  amps
          24 VDC thresh.:  0   volts    20 volts
             Power Fault:  No          No

  Fans:
  ```

```
            Fan Number 0:  on         on
            Fan Number 1:  on         on
            Fan Number 2:  on         on
            Fan Number 3:  on         on

     Temperature readings:
             NI-2 inlet: 21C/69F
             NI-2 outlet: 27C/80F
      Slot 1 PM internal: 0C/32F
      Slot 1 PM external: 0C/32F
      Slot 2 PM internal: 23C/73F
      Slot 2 PM external: 15C/59F
```

- ## show network-clocks

  You can see which ports are designated as network clock sources with this command. For example:

  ```
  NI-2#show network-clocks
  PLL failed: 42; PLL Passed: 2741 !(PLL stands for Phase Locked Loop)!
  FAIL: 0; NCO: E391; REF: E390; ERR: 1; ERR_D: -1; MAG: 2;
  clock configuration is NON-Revertive
  Priority 1 clock source: ATM0/1
  Priority 2 clock source: No clock
  Priority 3 clock source: No clock
  Priority 4 clock source: No clock
  Priority 5 clock source: System clock
  Current clock source:System clock, priority:5
  Nettime Config Register Contents:
  SLOCK:0, TLOCK:0, NFAIL:0, E1:1, NSEL:0
  BITS Register Contents:
  CR1: C8, CR2: 0, CR3: 0, ICR: 0, TSR: C1, PSR: 11, ESR: 77, CR4: 0
  BITS Source configured as: E1 Short Haul, ITU G.703 pulse, 120 ohm TP/75
    ohm Coax, 12 db gain
  ```

- ## Confirming the interface status

  You can use the **show atm status** command to confirm the status of ATM interfaces.

  For example:

  ```
  NI-2#show atm status
  NUMBER OF INSTALLED CONNECTIONS: (P2P=Point to Point, P2MP=Point to
    MultiPoint, MP2P=Multipoint to Point)
  Type   PVCs SoftPVCs SVCs TVCs   PVPs SoftPVPs SVPs    Total
  P2P     1     0       0    0      0    0        0        1
  P2MP    0     0       0    0      0    0        0        0
  MP2P    0     0       0    0      0    0        0        0

  TOTAL INSTALLED CONNECTIONS =           1
  PER-INTERFACE STATUS SUMMARY AT 10:27:54 EDT Thu Jun 10 2002:
  Interface IF Admin  Automation :-Cfg ILMI Addr SSCOP Hello
  Name  Status Status  Status  Reg State  State State
  ------------- ------- ----------- ------- --------
  ATM0/0  UP    up      n/a  UpAndNormal Idle  n/a
  ATM0/1  UP    up      n/a  n/a         Idle  down
  ATM0/2  DOWN  down    waiting  n/a     Idle  n/a
  ```

Aggregator/Concentrator: Cisco 6400

The 6400 UAC provides both ATM switching and Layer 3 IP routing for the ATM signals coming from the DSL network. This section explains the 6400 configuration for a variety of scenarios, starting with redundancy commands and ending with sophisticated routing topologies.

You might want to review the 6400 hardware components that were discussed in Chapter 4 to refresh your memory and to help you better understand the Cisco 6400 ATM interfaces shown in Figure 6-10.

Figure 6-10 *Cisco 6400 ATM Interfaces Through the Node Switch Processor*

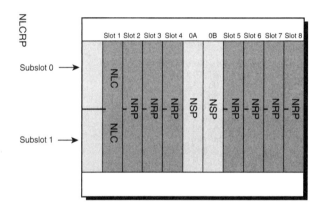

•Interface ATM0/0/0 Interface connected to backplane (not used for data traffic)
•Interface ATM1/0/1 NLC in slot 1, subslot 0, port 1
•Interface ATM5/0/0 NRP in slot 5
•Interface ATM6/0/0 NRP in slot 6

Bear in mind that there are eight full-height slots into which you can fit any combination of half-height node line cards (NLCs), full-height NLCs (the OC-12 variant), and/or full-height second-generation node route processors (NRP-2s).

The upper, half-height NLC is identified as subslot 0, as is the entire full-height NLC. A half-height NLC in the lower subslot is identified as occupying subslot 1. The first port on the half-height NLCs, and the only port on the full-height NLCs (OC-12/STM4), are designated as port 0.

The 6400 control is through the full-height, optionally redundant node switch processor (NSP), centered on the 6400 in a dedicated slot. Therefore, all interfaces are referenced from the NSP's point of view. The NSP is the only avenue to configure the NRP-2 and NLC. All 6400 cards are connected via the ATM backplane to the NSP. This interface is known as ATM INT 0/0/0 and can be thought of as the interface to the NSP, which itself is the interface to the entire 6400 device.

NRP-2

This section describes basic setup and initial configuration for the second-generation NRP blade on the Cisco 6400 (NRP-2), as well as redundancy options for all modules.

Cisco 6400 Redundancy Configurations

All the modules on the Cisco 6400 are optionally redundant. This section explains how to configure the 6400 for redundancy.

Memory Considerations for Redundancy

When you configure redundancy between two NRPs or two NSPs, the two cards must have identical memory capabilities and hardware specifications. Check each card in a redundant pair, and make sure they share the following parameters:

- DRAM size
- Flash memory size
- PCMCIA disk size (NSP only)
- Hardware version (module part number)

If redundancy is configured between two cards with different amounts of memory or disk capacity, the Cisco 6400 displays a warning message. Depending on which card is identified as the primary card, the Cisco 6400 performs the following actions:

- If the primary card has more memory than the secondary card, the Cisco 6400 shuts down the secondary card.
- If the secondary card has more memory than the primary card, the Cisco 6400 displays a message indicating that the secondary card has more memory than the primary card. This configuration causes redundancy to be disabled if the secondary card is activated.

Redundant NSPs

Both NSP slots are numbered slot 0 for consistent interface identification between primary and secondary devices. Nevertheless, the left NSP slot is labeled slot A and the right slot is labeled slot B to distinguish between the two slots when required. You do not need to explicitly specify redundancy between NSPs using slot identification. If two NSPs are installed in the Cisco 6400, they automatically act as a redundant pair.

You can use Enhanced High System Availability (EHSA) redundancy for simple hardware backup or for software error protection. Hardware backup protects against NSP card failure, because you configure both NSP cards with the same software image and configuration information. Additionally, you configure the system to automatically synchronize configuration information on both cards when changes occur.

Software error protection protects against critical Cisco IOS Software errors in a particular release, because you configure the NSP cards with different software images but use the same configuration. If you are using new or experimental Cisco IOS Software, consider using the software error protection method.

After you have installed the second NSP, you can verify NSP redundancy with the **show redundancy** command (the results might vary slightly with the Cisco IOS Software version):

```
Switch#show redundancy
!
NSP A:Primary
NSP B:Secondary
!
Secondary NSP information:
Secondary is up
Secondary has 131072K bytes of memory.
!
User EHSA configuration (by CLI config):
secondary-console = off
keepalive     = on
config-sync modes:
  standard  = on
  start-up  = on
  boot-var  = on
  config-reg = on
  calendar  = on
!
Debug EHSA Information:
!
Primary   (NSP A) ehsa state:SANTA_EHSA_PRIMARY
Secondary (NSP B) ehsa state:SANTA_EHSA_SECONDARY
!
EHSA pins:
peer present = 1
peer state   = SANTA_EHSA_SECONDARY
crash status:this-nsp=NO_CRASH(0x1) peer-nsp=NO_CRASH(0x1)
!
EHSA related MAC addresses:
this bpe mac-addr = 0000.0c00.0003
peer bpe mac-addr = 0000.0c00.0004
!
Switch#
```

To ensure that the configuration is consistent between redundant NSPs or NRPs, you can configure automatic synchronization between the two devices. You have the option of synchronizing just the startup configuration, the boot variables, the configuration register, or all three configurations. Boot variables are ROM monitor (ROMMON) environment variables used to control the booting process. The configuration register, stored in NVRAM, contains startup time parameters for the system. For more information about the booting process, see the *Cisco IOS Configuration Fundamentals Configuration Guide*. Frankly, though, you might as well use the default standard synchronization unless you have good reason to do otherwise.

After the configuration is complete, you can disable autoconfiguration using the **no** command. The default setting for individual synchronizable options is **no auto-sync**.

The following example shows how to synchronize the configurations on two redundant NSPs:

```
Switch#config term
Switch(config)#redundancy
Switch(config-r)#main-cpu
Switch(config-r-mc)#auto-sync standard
Switch(config-r-mc)#end
Switch#
```

NRP-1 Redundancy

Redundant first-generation NRPs use EHSA signals. These signals let the two NRPs negotiate which is the master and which is the secondary. After the NRPs determine which is the primary, they communicate that information to the NSP. The NSP then communicates with that specific NRP.

Configuring an NRP pair for redundancy starts with configuring the NSP, which is the controlling module for the Cisco 6400 UAC. Therefore, there are two sets of commands for NRP-1 redundancy:

- Configure NRP-1 redundancy on the NSP:

```
Switch(config)#redundancy
Switch(config-r)#main-cpu
Switch(config-r-mc)#associate slot 1 2 (You need specify only the first slot of
    the redundant pair, because redundant pairs must be adjacent. The second slot
    is assumed to be the adjacent slot. Specifying both slots is not harmful,
    though.)
Switch(config-r-a-sl)#prefer 1
```

- Configure auto-sync on the primary NRP-1:

```
Router(config)# redundancy
Router(config-r)# main-cpu
Router(config-r-mc)# auto-sync standard
```

NSP PCMCIA Disk Protection for NRP-2

NRP-2s do not support redundancy. However, an important aspect of NSP functionality affects the NRP-2 in the case of NSP failover. Bear in mind that the NRP-2 is controlled and configured entirely through the NSP, without direct access to the NRP-2 itself, and the NRP-2 depends on the NSP for image and file storage. The NRP-2 operation is ensured during switching from a failed NSP to a working NSP through disk mirroring of the PCMCIA disks on the redundant NSPs. Introduced in Cisco IOS Software Release 12.1(5)DB, PCMCIA disk mirroring enables automatic data synchronization between the PCMCIA disks of the two redundant NSPs. Disk synchronization is the act of copying data from one disk to another.

Without disk mirroring, there is no guarantee of NRP-2 support after an NSP failover. This means that you might have to manually restore the NRP-2 state to its status before the failover. With disk mirroring enabled, NRP-2 has continued support from the NSP, except during the relatively short NSP failover period.

When PCMCIA disk mirroring is enabled, as it is by default, disk synchronization is initiated in any of the following situations:

- The primary or secondary NSP boots or reloads
- The secondary NSP is inserted into the Cisco 6400 chassis
- A PCMCIA disk is inserted into disk slot 0 of the primary or secondary NSP
- The PCMCIA disk in disk slot 0 of either NSP is formatted
- A command is entered to
  - Re-enable disk mirroring (**mirror**)
  - Explicitly initiate disk synchronization (**redundancy sync**)
  - Modify or reorganize the files on the disks (**copy**, **rename**, **delete**, **mkdir**, **format**)

Cisco recommends that you use PCMCIA disks that have the same memory capacity.

PCMCIA disk mirroring is not supported in Cisco IOS Software Release 12.1(4)DB and earlier releases. Use the **dir**, **mkdir**, and **copy** EXEC commands to manually copy files from the primary NSP's PCMCIA disks to the secondary NSP's PCMCIA disks.

PCMCIA disk mirroring also introduced new labels for pairs of mirrored disks:

- **mir-disk0**—PCMCIA disks in disk slot 0 of both NSPs
- **mir-disk1**—PCMCIA disks in disk slot 1 of both NSPs

The mir-disk0 and mir-disk1 labels let you perform any integrated file system (IFS) operation (such as copy, rename, or delete) on the same file on both the primary and secondary disks.

Disk mirroring (automatic data synchronization between a pair of disks) is not supported between the following:

- Two disks on a single NSP
- Two disks with mismatched slot numbers (disk0: and disk1:)

You can initiate disk synchronization between disk0: and disk1: on the active NSP, even in a single-NSP system.

There are other uses for the PCMCIA disks aside from providing NRP-2 configuration redundancy. For instance, you can make full image and configuration backups if the disks are of sufficient size. Visit the appropriate online Cisco documentation for your version of Cisco IOS Software for other tips about these versatile disks.

NLC Redundancy and SONET APS

SONET APS provides a mechanism to support redundant transmission interfaces (circuits) between SONET devices. Automatic switchover from the working (primary) circuit to the protection (secondary) circuit happens when the working circuit fails or degrades.

The Cisco 6400 supports the following SONET APS operations:

- **1+1**—There is one working interface and one protection interface, and the payload from the transmitting end is sent to both the receiving ends. The receiving end decides which interface to use. The line overhead (LOH) bytes (K1 and K2) in the SONET frame indicate both status and action.

- **Linear**—A back-to-back connection (as opposed to a ring topology), as defined in the "Telcordia GR-253-CORE" document.

- **Unidirectional**—Transmit and receive channels are switched independently.

- **Nonreverting**—Nonreverting channels continue to operate after a failure has been corrected, thus preventing data from flowing back to the working channel.

- **Enabling and disabling SONET APS**—In the Cisco 6400, a pair of redundant ports is represented as a single interface. APS commands are accepted only for an interface that represents a pair of redundant ports.

For APS operation, the APS mode must be specified for each interface associated with a redundant pair of ports. To enable SONET APS, use these commands, beginning in global configuration mode:

```
Switch(config)#interface atm slot/subslot/port
```

You can use either NLC port number, 0 or 1. When an NLC is configured for redundancy, all ports on that card are automatically configured to operate in redundant mode using SONET APS.

```
Switch(config-if)#aps mode linear 1+1 nonreverting unidirectional
```

This command enables SONET APS on the interface. This command must be entered before any other **aps** commands. SONET APS is enabled by default when you install an NLC in a slot already configured for redundancy. Here is an example of a configuration with redundancy:

```
redundancy
 associate slot 1 2
!
interface ATM1/0/0
 no ip address
 no ip redirects
 no ip proxy-arp
 no atm auto-configuration
 no atm ilmi-keepalive
 atm uni version 4.0
 aps mode linear 1+1 nonreverting unidirectional
 aps signal-fail BER threshold 3
!
```

If you disable the redundant NLC configuration by using the **no associate slot** or **no associate subslot** redundancy configuration command, two interface configuration sections are created, one for each port, but all the APS configuration commands are removed. Here is an example of adjacent NLCs that are operating independently, not redundantly:

```
interface ATM1/0/0
 no ip address
 no ip redirects
 no ip proxy-arp
 no atm auto-configuration
 no atm ilmi-keepalive
 atm uni version 4.0
!
interface ATM2/0/0
 no ip address
 no ip redirects
 no ip proxy-arp
 no atm auto-configuration
 no atm ilmi-keepalive
 atm uni version 4.0
!
```

For two full-height (OC-12/STM4) NLCs to act as a redundant pair, they must be installed in adjacent slots, such as slots 1 and 2. By default, the NLC in the lower-numbered slot is the working device, and the NLC in the higher-numbered slot is the protection device.

To configure redundant full-height NLCs, use the **redundancy** and **associate slot** commands, as in the following example, where the OC-12s in slots 5 and 6 are configured for redundancy:

```
!
redundancy
 associate slot 5 6
!
```

For two half-height NLCs to act as a redundant pair, they must be installed in adjacent slot/subslot pairs. Here are some examples:

> 1/0 and 2/0, or 1/1 and 2/1
>
> 3/0 and 4/0, or 3/1 and 4/1
>
> 5/0 and 6/0, or 5/1 and 6/1
>
> 7/0 and 8/0, or 7/1 and 8/1

To configure redundant half-height NLCs, use the **redundancy** command as you have been doing, and use a variant of the **associate slot** command, **associate subslot**. In the following example, the OC-3s in subslots 3/0 and 4/0 are configured as a redundant pair:

```
!
redundancy
 associate subslot 3/0 4/0
!
```

Verifying NLC Redundancy

To verify NLC redundancy, use the **show aps** EXEC command on the NSP. The **show aps** command displays the status for all NLCs configured for port redundancy:

```
Switch#show aps

ATM7/0/0: APS Lin NR Uni, Failure channel: Protection
          Active Channel: CHANNEL7/0/0, Channel stat: Good
          Port stat (w,p): (Good, Good)
ATM7/0/1: APS Lin NR Uni, Failure channel: Protection
          Active Channel: CHANNEL7/0/1, Channel stat: Good
          Port stat (w,p): (Good, Good)
```

Verifying SONET APS

To verify that SONET APS is enabled, or to determine if a switchover has occurred, use the **show aps** EXEC command or the **show controller atm** *slot/subslot/port* command.

In the following example, slot 7 contains the working (primary) card, and slot 8 contains the protection (secondary) card:

```
Switch#show aps

ATM7/0/0: APS Lin NR Uni, Failure channel: Protection
          Active Channel: CHANNEL7/0/0, Channel stat: Good
          Port stat (w,p): (Good, Good)
ATM7/0/1: APS Lin NR Uni, Failure channel: Protection
          Active Channel: CHANNEL7/0/1, Channel stat: Good
          Port stat (w,p): (Good, Good)
```

In the following example, the OC-3 interface ATM 5/0/0 is not configured for redundancy:

```
Switch#show controller atm 5/0/0
Redundancy NOT Enabled on interface
IF Name: ATM5/0/0    Chip Base Address(es): A8B08000, 0 Port type: OC3
  Port rate: 155
Mbps     Port medium: SM Fiber
Port status:Good Signal    Loopback:None    Flags:8308
TX Led: Traffic Pattern    RX Led: Traffic Pattern  TX clock source:
  network-derived
Framing mode:  sts-3c
Cell payload scrambling on
Sts-stream scrambling on
```

Setting SONET APS Priority Requests: Preventing or Causing Automatic Protection Switching

APS priority requests are used to manually control the relationship between two APS ports from EXEC mode. The APS priority levels, lockout (1), force (2), and manual (5), are defined in the *"Telcordia GR-253-CORE"* document.

To set the APS priority requests, use the following commands in EXEC mode:

```
Switch#aps lockout atm slot/subslot/port
```

This APS priority level 1 request prevents a working interface from switching to a protection interface.

```
Switch#aps force atm slot/subslot/port from [protection | working]
```

This APS priority level 2 request manually forces the specified interface to the protection or working interface unless a request of equal or higher priority is in effect.

Use the **working** option to force operation from the working channel to the protection channel. Use the **protection** option to force operation from the protection channel to the working channel. For instance, in the following example, the system is forced to use the protection channel associated with ATM interface 1/0/0:

```
Switch#aps force atm 1/0/0 from working
```

The following APS priority level 5 request manually switches an interface to the protection or working interface unless a request of equal or higher priority is in effect. The **working** and **protection** options are available for this command as well:

```
Switch#aps manual atm slot/subslot/port from [protection | working]
```

The **Switch#aps clear atm** *slot/subslot/port* command manually clears all posted APS priority requests created by any of the APS priority commands.

To verify that you successfully set the APS priority requests, you can use the **show aps** EXEC command:

```
Switch#aps force atm 5/1/0 from working
Switch#show aps
    ATM5/1/0:APS Lin NR Uni, Failure channel:Working
    Active Channel:CHANNEL6/1/0, Channel stat:Force Switch
    Port stat (w,p):(Good, Good)
```

Setting SONET APS Signal Thresholds

You can configure the APS signal bit error rate (BER) thresholds at which the system announces signal degradation or signal failure.

The **Switch(config-if)#aps signal-degrade BER threshold** *value* command sets the interface's BER threshold value for signal degradation. This controls the BER value at which signal degradation is announced, indicating an unstable or error-prone connection. This BER threshold can be in the range of 10^{-5} to 10^{-9}. There is no default threshold, although the generally accepted telecom industry standard is 10^{-7}.

The **Switch(config-if)#aps signal-fail BER threshold** *value* command sets the interface's BER threshold value for signal failure. This controls the BER value at which a signal failure is announced, indicating a broken connection. This BER threshold can be in the range of 10^{-3} to 10^{-5}, with a default threshold of 10^{-3}.

The *value* argument represents the exponent of the BER threshold. For instance, a value of 5 sets the threshold to 10^{-5}. For example, here is how to set the APS signal degradation and signal failure thresholds for ATM interface 1/0/0:

```
Switch(config)#interface atm 1/0/0
Switch(config-if)#aps signal-degrade BER threshold 7
Switch(config-if)#aps signal-fail BER threshold 5
```

Verifying SONET APS Signal Thresholds

To display an interface's current BER threshold settings, use the **show interface atm** command:

```
Switch#show interface atm 1/0/0

interface ATM1/0/0
 description la1
 no ip address
 no ip redirects
 no ip proxy-arp
 no atm auto-configuration
 no atm ilmi-keepalive
 atm uni version 4.0
 aps mode linear 1+1 nonreverting unidirectional
 aps signal-fail BER threshold 3
 aps signal-degrade BER threshold 9
```

Primary and Secondary Role Switching

The Cisco 6400 allows you to manually force the primary and secondary devices in a redundant pair to switch roles. This capability can be important for upgrade or debug activities.

To reverse the primary and secondary roles in redundant modules, use the following command in EXEC mode:

```
Switch#redundancy force-failover {slot | slot/subslot | main-cpu}
```

This command forces the system to switch the current primary and secondary devices of the redundant pair.

Now that you have seen the redundancy commands, you can begin configuring the 6400 to accept and manage the incoming connections at the Layer 2 and Layer 3 levels.

Configurations for ATM Switching

Here is the most basic pair of commands that direct ATM connections through the Cisco 6400. To map PVC 1/100 coming from int NLC 1/0/0 to NRP 7/0/0, where it would change identification to become PVC 1/101, the 6400 commands would be

```
NSP(config)#int atm 1/0/0
NSP(config-if)#atm pvc 1 100 interface atm7/0/0 1 101
```

NOTE	You can also use PVPs to map whole groups of individual PVCs. Just substitute **pvp** for **pvc** and leave off the virtual channel identifier after the path number.

The first step is to address the ATM interface 1/0/0. This particular NLC identifier can relate to any of the following:

- A coaxial, half-height NLC (DS3 or E3) that addresses the BNC connectors on the 6400's backplane coaxial I/O board. The interface identification 1/0/0 would denote the connection in the first slot, the upper subslot, and the first of two ports for that upper subslot.

- A fiber-connected, half-height NLC (OC-3 or STM1) with optical fiber connections on the front of the card. The identifier 1/0/0 would denote the first slot's upper subslot's first port.

- A fiber-connected, full-height NLC (OC-12 or STM4) occupying the full first slot, obviously starting with the upper subslot, with one and only one port for the relatively large optical fiber connection on the front.

After addressing the NLC, the second command maps the VC to the ATM interface on the NRP card in slot 7/0/0 and renumbers the virtual channel identifier to 101 as it will be handled on the NRP. You can think of this mapping as across the 6400's backplane, after the NLC has stepped down the incoming high-speed signal (coaxial or optical).

Configurations for Layer 3 Terminations

After the PVC arrives at the NRP, more sophisticated coding is required to identify and manage the connection. This coding defines the Layer 3 terminations (bridging, PPPoE, PPPoA) as well as security options (AAA, RADIUS, or TACACS+) and address management options such as DHCP. Each of these is explained in the following sections with examples.

PPPoA

The following is the simple, manual configuration for a PPPoA connection on the 6400's NRP:

```
router(config)#username cisco password Cisco
router(config)#interface atm0/0/0.1 point-to-point
router(config-if)#pvc 1/101
router(config-if-atm-vc)#encapsulation aal5mux ppp virtual-template 1
router(config-if-atm-vc)#ubr 384
router(config-if-atm-vc)#exit
```

The **username cisco password Cisco** command identifies the remote ATU-R host name (cisco) and password (Cisco) used for PPP CHAP authentication.

The **interface atm0/0/0.1 point-to-point** command identifies the subinterface (logical division of a physical interface) atm0/0/0 as the target interface for the incoming connection. This subinterface is a point-to-point connection.

The **pvc 1/101** command addresses the connection that will terminate on this subinterface as a PVC, with the newly renumbered identification of VPI=1, VCI=101.

The **encapsulation aal5mux ppp virtual-template 1** command sets the encapsulation method for the PVC 1/101 as AAL5MUX. With AAL5MUX (as opposed to AAL5SNAP), multiple protocols (such as IP and IPX) can be carried inside the PPP frames and terminated on this interface. This command line also establishes that virtual template 1 will be used for additional configuration information for this PVC. You will see shortly the virtual template's labor-saving, commonly-shared parameters.

ubr 384 is a simple command that defines the unspecified bit rate (UBR) PCR as 384 Kbps bidirectionally (both upstream and downstream). The PCR is the only parameter that can be set with UBR, and it is optional. If no PCR is defined, each connection is theoretically free to occupy all the available bandwidth.

The previous example is an example of when a single VC within a subinterface is configured for PPPoA encapsulation (AAL5MUX). Although Template 1 is used to define AAA configuration for this VC, you can see that configuring each individual VC is not the best way to conduct large-scale implementations. Still, you should learn this simplest way so that you can appreciate the shortcuts shown later in this section.

The NRP's virtual templates assign PPP features (or other architecture characteristics) to a PVC. As each PPP session comes online, a virtual-access interface is cloned from the virtual template. This virtual-access interface inherits all the configuration specified in the virtual template. When the virtual template is changed, the changes are automatically propagated to all virtual-access interfaces cloned from that particular virtual template. Here is an example of a configured virtual template:

```
(lines deleted)
 pvc 1/101
   encapsulation aal5mux ppp Virtual-Template1

(lines deleted)

interface virtual-template1
 description PPPoATM
 ip unnumbered gigabit-ethernet0/0/0

 peer default ip address pool dsl
 ppp authentication chap
 !
 ip local pool dsl 192.168.40.20 192.168.40.50
```

In this configuration, it is assumed that all PPPoA VCs (DSL users) cloned from virtual template 1 will use CHAP authentication and will be allocated an IP address from the pool named dsl configured on the router. When the virtual template is changed, the changes are automatically propagated to all virtual-access interfaces cloned from that particular virtual template. To configure a different class of users on the same router, you can provision a separate virtual template interface. You can have up to 25 virtual templates.

An interesting characteristic of the virtual template is that the local end of the PPPoA connection runs without an explicitly-defined IP address. Instead, the IP address of the NRP-2's Gigabit Ethernet interface is used for addressability. This could also be the Fast Ethernet interface on the first-generation NRP or a loopback interface on either type of NRP. For reasons of memory allocation and addressing beyond the scope of this course, the virtual-access interface must have some sort of interface IP address linked with it syntactically. Therefore, this command essentially says, "Because we *must* link some sort of IP address to this virtual-access interface, but we do not want to waste a real IP address on it, just refer to it as having the same IP address as the already-designated Gigabit Ethernet interface."

In any case, do not use a static IP assignment within a virtual template; routing problems can occur, and you might end up working late if you forget this caution. Always use the **ip unnumbered** command when configuring a virtual template.

Following are explanations of the commands used:

- **interface virtual-template** *number*—Associates a virtual template with a virtual template interface.

- **description PPPoATM**—An optional plain-language description, which could also be the name of the marketed class of service, perhaps similar to "Business-class Gold" or "Residential-class Regular Plan."

- **ip unnumbered gigabit-ethernet 0/0/0**—Enables IP on the interface without assigning a specific IP address.

- **no ip directed-broadcast**—Depending on the Cisco IOS Software version, you might not see this command line, because it is now a default value. It is explained here only in the interest of completeness. This subcommand disables forwarding of directed broadcasts on the interface. The default is to forward directed broadcasts. A directed broadcast is a packet sent to a specific network or series of networks, whereas a flooded broadcast packet is sent to every network. A directed-broadcast address includes the network or subnet fields.

- **peer default ip address {pool [***poolname***] | dhcp }**—Specifies a dynamic IP address assignment method, in this case from a named pool of IP addresses. Another option is to assign addresses from a DHCP server.

- **ppp authentication {pap | chap} [pap | chap]**—Selects the authentication protocol, CHAP in this case, and an optional secondary protocol.

- **ip local pool dsl 192.168.40.20 192.168.40.50**—Defines the range of 31 IP addresses available through the pool named dsl. These addresses may be reused in instant succession as soon as one host device (DSL subscriber) relinquishes an address by logging off the DSL network.

Although instructive, this method is incredibly cumbersome, because you must define each PVC in turn, defining the encapsulation type for each PVC, referring to the same virtual template for each one, and so on. And this very simple example doesn't differentiate between service levels by bit rate, and so on.

How can you reduce the manual configuration for each PVC, saving labor costs and minimizing the chance of human error? You can group characteristics in a class of parameters and then reference the class repeatedly. Here is a configuration that does just that:

```
router(config)#vc-class atm ppp-atm !names the type of class, in this case, an ATM
   Point-to-Point Protocol over ATM class!
router(config-vc-class)#encapsulation aal5mux ppp
virtual-template 1
router(config-vc-class)#ubr 384
router(config-vc-class)#exit


router(config)#interface ATM 0/0/0
router(config-if)#class-int ppp-atm !Associates the new class with the interface
   ATM 0/0/0!
router(config-if)#pvc 1/101
router(config-if-atm-vc)#exit
router(config-if)#pvc 1/102
router(config-if-atm-vc)#exit
```

In this example, a virtual connection class (VC class) called PPP-ATM is defined that specifies how VCs will be encapsulated and secured. This VC class is then associated with the interface ATM0/0/0 on the NRP. Remember that ATM0/0/0 is the NRP's main (backplane) connection on the 6400. By associating the VC class with the interface, every individual PVC that is identified on that interface automatically takes on the characteristics of that class. This automation eliminates the need to repeat the characteristics line by line for each PVC.

This virtual class refers to the baseline virtual template, constituting a reference within a reference, meaning that when these VCs are assigned the values of the virtual class, they also inherit all the values of the virtual template. For instance, you already saw that the virtual template uses the PPP protocol CHAP to provide for AAA (Authentication, Authorization, and Accounting). This eliminates typing the same CHAP definitions for every PVC.

The VC class can be applied to an entire interface or subinterface, but there is still flexibility for different service levels. Even if the VC class is associated with an interface, an individual PVC on that same interface can be associated with a different VC class without affecting the overall association of the interface class for other PVCs.

It should be obvious that the VC class method of user configuration is much more efficient than repeated, individual VC configuration for large-scale service deployment. However, this method still requires manually identifying individual PVCs on a particular interface, even if no further definition is needed. Therefore, this is still a labor-intensive configuration to accommodate the tens of thousands of PVCs in a large DSL network. In the interest of working smarter, not harder, there should be a still-easier way. This easier way makes use of autodiscovery, as explained next.

This method does not require any individual definition of PVCs after they arrive on the NRP. With careful planning and precise advance configuration, the incoming PVCs are automatically switched to certain interfaces, according to the particular service levels, where the associated

VC class has been associated on that interface. Here is a simple example of the basic commands to establish this autodiscovery and routing:

```
router(config)#vc-class atm ppp-atm
router(config-vc-class)#encapsulation aal5mux ppp
virtual-template 1
router(config-vc-class) #exit

router(config)#interface ATM 0/0/0
router(config-if)#atm ilmi-enable
router(config-if)#atm ilmi-pvc-discovery sub-interface
router(config-if)#interface ATM 0/0/0.101
router(config-if)#class-int ppp-atm

router(config-if) #exit
```

Here are the steps required for this most efficient method of handling PVCs, in their suggested order of implementation:

Step 1 The individual PVCs must be configured with ordered VPIs that correspond to the individualized service levels. This can be done at the IP DSL Switch or when mapping the PVCs across the 6400 backplane. For instance, a very robust and well-differentiated marketing plan for the DSL service provider might offer six DSL service levels: regular, fast, and fastest for both business and residential customers. Therefore, the corresponding VPIs could be numbered 101, 102, and 103 for business-class customers, and the VPIs of the residential-class customers could be numbered 201, 202, and 203. As mentioned in Appendix B, the Network-Network Interface (NNI) topology has 4096 available VPI numbers.

Step 2 You must create NRP subinterfaces that correspond to the VPI numbers. In this example, these subinterfaces would be designated as follows:

int ATM 0/0/0.101	Regular business-class service
int ATM 0/0/0.102	Fast business-class service
int ATM 0/0/0.103	Fastest business-class service
int ATM 0/0/0.201	Regular residential-class service
int ATM 0/0/0.202	Fast residential-class service
int ATM 0/0/0.203	Fastest residential-class service

Step 3 In this example, you must define six virtual classes of service, each of which might reference as few as a single virtual template, as explained earlier. For simplicity, you could name each ATM VC class according to the marketed service level.

Step 4 Following this scenario, you would associate each of the virtual classes with the matching subinterface using the **int-class** command. This means that each of the six subinterfaces would have associated with it a particular VC class, with parameters varying by the end user's subscription.

Step 5 The fifth and suggested last step is to enable ILMI and **ilmi-pvc-discovery**. ILMI is one of ATM's internal signaling and control protocols.

As PVCs arrive on the NRP's main interface, int ATM0/0/0, they are discovered by the ILMI protocol. The incoming PVC's VPI is identified and matched with a corresponding subinterface that was configured in advance. In the present scenario with six different service levels and six different subinterfaces, the PVCs whose VPI is 101 would automatically be switched to subinterface 0/0/0.101, where they would be assigned the parameters that were associated with that subinterface through the VC class. The PVCs whose VPI is 102 would automatically be funneled to the subinterface 0/0/0.102, where the group characteristics would include a medium-fast peak cell rate. The PVCs from the business-class customers who had paid for the fastest service available, those whose PVCs came into the NRP with a VPI of 103, would automatically be steered by ILMI to the subinterface of 0/0/0.103. The continuous process of autodiscovery by ILMI and the assignment of the appropriate class characteristics is simultaneous, meaning that the residential customers' PVCs are also switched to their appropriate target subinterfaces, there to assume their own characteristics.

Consider this great news: You are not required to specify any individual PVC definitions, such as encapsulation and bit rate, for these tens of thousands of incoming connections! Of course, you should carefully define the VC classes and subinterfaces in advance and then test the ILMI discovery on a few sample PVCs in advance.

As many subinterfaces may be set up as there are VPIs. For instance, all incoming PVCs whose VPI is 2 would be routed automatically to subinterface 0/0/0.2, all incoming PVCs whose VPI is 3 would be routed automatically to subinterface 0/0/0.3, and so on. Each of these subinterfaces would presumably have a unique virtual class associated with it. However, in conformance with the good practice of a limited number of profiles on the IP DSL Switch, you should not need more than a dozen different service levels, and therefore, no more than a dozen different subinterfaces. This minimizes, to almost nothing, excessive ATM overhead and processing demands that could degrade performance if you had an unrealistically high number of subinterfaces, such as a different subinterface (and service level) for every PVC.

Now that you have configured the ultra-efficient autodiscovery of PVCs on the NRP, you must know how to verify the ATM traffic's status. You can do this with the command **show atm pvc**

ppp, which precisely displays the status of the ATM PVCs of the PPP type. Here is an example of this command's output:

```
NRP-1-8#sho atm pvc ppp
          VCD /
ATM Int.  Name VPI VCI Type   VCSt VA  VASt
0/0/0     17   1   34  PVC    UP   13  DOWN UBR 155000  UP
0/0/0     18   1   36  PVC    UP   10    UP UBR 155000  UP
0/0/0     19   1   38  PVC    UP   14  DOWN UBR 155000  UP
0/0/0     6    1   40  PVC    UP   8   DOWN UBR 155000  UP
0/0/0     1    1   42  PVC    UP   6   DOWN UBR 155000  UP
0/0/0     5    1   44  PVC-L  UP   7   DOWN UBR 155000  UP
0/0/0     8    2   36  PVC    UP   9   DOWN UBR 155000  UP
0/0/0     11   3   38  PVC-M  UP   11  DOWN UBR 155000  UP
0/0/0     10   3   40  PVC-L  UP   12  DOWN UBR 155000  UP
0/0/0.100 14 100  100  PVC-L  UP   21  DOWN UBR 155000  UP
```

This command also causes each PVC in turn to be analyzed in detail and reported, as shown for this single PVC:

```
Open: IPCP
  Bound to ATM4/0 VCD: 2, VPI: 0, VCI: 34
  Cloned from virtual-template: 1
  Last input 01:04:26, output never, output hang never
  Last clearing of "show interface" counters 5d02h
  Queueing strategy: fifo
  Output queue 0/40, 0 drops; input queue 0/75, 0 drops
  5 minute input rate 0 bits/sec, 0 packets/sec
  5 minute output rate 0 bits/sec, 0 packets/sec
     782 packets input, 30414 bytes, 0 no buffer
     Received 3 broadcasts, 0 runts, 0 giants, 0 throttles
     0 input errors, 0 CRC, 0 frame, 0 overrun, 0 ignored, 0 abort
     395 packets output, 5540 bytes, 0 underruns
     0 output errors, 0 collisions, 0 interface resets
     0 output buffer failures, 0 output buffers swapped out
     0 carrier transitions


NRP-1-8#
```

In this output, the router first displays the status of all PVCs configured for PPP in the ATM interface. The name of the VC, the VC VPI/VCI, the VC state (up/down, and the Virtual Access (VA) number are displayed, along with VA interface-specific configuration and status. Then the second portion (which shows only one PVC to avoid repetition) provides quick insight into the status of a particular PVC.

Overall, the **show atm pvc ppp** command's details might vary with the Cisco IOS Software version, so you should consult the particular version's release notes for full details of the columns.

Along with configuring the PVC mapping and verifying PVCs as needed, you also need to configure options for IP address management (DHCP) and security (AAA, RADIUS), as shown in the next section.

Configuring DHCP, AAA, and RADIUS

How can you configure the IP address allocation scheme, as well as security, which are required for PPPoA and the other, sophisticated topologies on the 6400?

To enable DHCP on the NRP, you can use this command set:

```
router(config)#ip dhcp-server <server name/ip> !the DHCP server IP address
  is the variable at the end of this line!
router(config)#interface virtual template-template 2
router(config-if)#ip unnumbered ethernet 1/0 !this is the management Ethernet port
  to be used as the address for the virtual template; this is also called the
  Backplane Ethernet (BPE)!

router(config-if)#peer default ip address dhcp
router(config-if)#ppp authentication chap
```

In this example, a DHCP server location (by IP address) and authentication method (CHAP) are defined under a virtual template (virtual template 2). The virtual template is then associated with a VC during the VC configuration process. Notice that the virtual template takes the address of the management Ethernet port. This is usually the next-hop gateway router address assigned to the CPE router during authentication.

Large-scale deployment of PPP user services requires the use of a central database such as RADIUS to ease the configuration burden. RADIUS servers, providing AAA functionality, contain the per-user configuration database, including password authentication and authorization information. To enable the functionality of AAA and define the application of the RADIUS protocol on the NRP, you can use the global config command set here:

```
aaa new-model
aaa authentication login default radius
aaa authentication ppp default radius
aaa authorization network radius
radius-server host 192.168.1.1 auth-port 1645 acct-port 1646 !These are the
  standard authentication and accounting ports for the RADIUS daemon!
radius-server timeout 20 !measure in seconds!
radius-server key root !the word root is the shared key between the Network Access
  Server (NAS) and the RADIUS server!

aaa new-model
aaa authentication login default none
aaa authentication ppp default local group radius
aaa authorization network default local group radius none
aaa accounting network default wait-start group radius

!
username cisco password 0 cisco
!

interface ATM0/0/0.132 point-to-point

 pvc 1/32
  encapsulation aal5mux
!
interface Virtual-Template1
 ip unnumbered FastEthernet0/0/0
```

```
 peer default ip address pool dsl-pool
 ppp authentication chap
!
radius-server host 192.168.2.20 auth-port 1645 acct-port 1646
radius-server key cisco
```

Following are the explanations for the pertinent commands:

- **aaa new-model**—Enables the AAA access control model.

- **aaa authentication login default none**—Ensures that if the user cannot be authenticated with the various methods defined in the next command, there is no default login. (All users must be authenticated according to at least one defined method.)

- **aaa authentication ppp {default | *list-name*} *method1* [*method2...*]**—Specifies one or more AAA authentication methods for use on interfaces running PPP. The *list-name* option refers to the name of this particular method list (or the default list, as in the previous example), and the *method* option is a list of methods to be tried in turn. You can use the command **aaa authentication ppp** with the *method* keyword **local** to specify that the Cisco router or access server should use the local username database for authentication. In this case, the local username database is used first, and then RADIUS.

- The **aaa authorization network radius** command sets RADIUS for network authorization, address assignment, and access lists. It follows the order of methods defined for individual PPP login.

  You can further control access and accounting by using the **wait-start** keyword, which ensures that the RADIUS security server acknowledges the start notice before granting the user's process request. In this case, it is applied only to network activities. To stop all accounting activities on this line or interface, use the **none** keyword.

- The RADIUS-specific commands in the second half of the configuration are as follows:

  — **radius-server host {*hostname* | *ip-address*} [*auth-port port-number*][*acct-port port-number*]**—Specifies a RADIUS server host.

  — **radius-server key cisco**—Sets the encryption key to match that used on the RADIUS server—in this case, the keyword **cisco**.

The AAA and RADIUS commands also apply to PPPoE, which is discussed in the next section.

PPPoE

As you learned in Chapter 3, PPPoE requires a PPP software client at the user location. The client (either the desktop PC or the Cisco 820 series router) initiates a PPP session by encapsulating PPP frames into a MAC frame and then bridging the frame (over ATM/DSL) to the gateway router. From this point, PPP sessions can be established, authenticated, addressed, and so on. VCs and associated PPP sessions can also be associated with VPDN groups, as shown here:

```
NRP-1(config)#username cisco password 0 cisco
NRP-1(config)#vpdn enable
```

```
NRP-1(config)#vpdn-group 1
NRP-1(config-vpdn)#accept dialin
NRP-1(config-vpdn)#protocol pppoe
NRP-1(config-vpdn)#virtual-template 1
NRP-1(config-vpdn)#pppoe limit per-vc 20

NRP-1(config)#int virtual-template 4
NRP-1(config-if)#ip unnumbered FastEthernet0/0/0
NRP-1(config-if)#ip mtu 1492

NRP-1(config-if)#peer default ip address pool pppoe-pool
NRP-1(config-if)#ppp authentication chap

NRP-1(config)#ip local pool pppoe-pool 192.168.5.100 192.168.5.150

NRP-1(config)#int atm 0/0/0.143 point-to-point
NRP-1(config-subif)#
NRP-1(config-subif)#pvc 3/143
NRP-1(config-if-atm-vc)#encapsulation aal5snap
NRP-1(config-if-atm-vc)#protocol pppoe
```

```
ip cef
!
```

In this example, the username and password (both **cisco**) are defined in the first line.

The following PPPoE termination command sets up VPDN:

```
vpdn enable
```

The following defines the VPDN group:

```
pppoe limit per-vc number
```

The command **vpdn-group 1** identifies the particular VPDN group whose characteristics follow. The command **accept dialin** configures the router to accept dial-in calls. The command **protocol pppoe** defines the VPDN's protocol as PPPoE. The command **virtual-template 1** associates this VPDN group with a particular virtual template, which is quite like the virtual template you created and referenced for PPPoA in the previous section. The optional command **pppoe limit per-vc 20** limits the number of PPPoE sessions that can be established on a virtual circuit. This limitation is a great help in managing the licensing of user accounts. The default is 100 sessions per VC.

Notice that the encapsulation type is aal5snap. This is the standard for both PPPoE and bridging.

The **interface virtual-template** *number* command selects the virtual-access interface to be configured.

The **ip unnumbered fastethernet 0/0/0** command enables IP on the interface without specifying a new address. In this case, the only address that might be associated with this virtual-template interface is the one already defined for the Fast Ethernet interface.

The **ip mtu 1492** command sets the IP MTU size to 1492, which is required for PPPoE.

The **peer default ip address pool pppoe-pool** command specifies that the dynamic IP addresses will come from the pool called pppoe-pool. Notice that the range of IP addresses in this pool, 51 in all, is defined in the following authentication definition line:

```
ppp authentication chap
```

This command sets the authentication protocol.

The **NRP-1(config)#interface ATM0/0/0.143 point-to-point** command defines a subinterface of the point-to-point type.

The **NRP-1(config-subif)#** subcommand disables the forwarding of directed broadcasts on the interface. The default is to forward directed broadcasts. A directed broadcast is a packet sent to a specific network or series of networks, whereas a flooded broadcast packet is sent to every network. A directed-broadcast address includes the network or subnet fields.

The **NRP-1(config-subif)#pvc 3/143** command defines a PVC on the subinterface.

The **NRP-1(config-if-atm-vc)#encapsulation aal5snap** command defines the type of encapsulation for PVC 3/143 as aal5snap, which is required for PPPoE (and RFC 2684 bridging as well, as you will see in the next section).

The command **NRP-1(config-if-atm-vc)#protocol pppoe** explicitly defines the protocol type as PPPoE, which avoids confusion with the much simpler bridging type of PVC, which is also based on RFC 2684.

The **ip cef** command enables Cisco Express Forwarding (CEF), because CEF is required for PPPoE.

This concludes the explanation of PPPoE on the Cisco 6400's node route processor.

RFC 2684 Bridging

This simplest type of architecture is frequently found in legacy DSL networks. It requires setting up a translation between the bridged network, the DSL users themselves, and the larger routed network, the Internet outside the local service area. This translation on the NRP is a bridge group virtual interface, meaning that you arbitrarily convert one of the Layer 3 interfaces to a Layer 2 bridging interface on the NRP. Here is an example of the configuration required:

```
router(config)#bridge irb
router(config)#bridge 1 route ip

router(config)#interface atm0/0/0.1 point-to-point
router(config-subif)#bridge-group 1
router(config-subif)#pvc 10/101
router(config-if-atm-vc)#encapsulation aal5snap
router(config-if-atm-vc)#ubr 384
router(config-if-atm-vc)#protocol bridge broadcast
router(config-if-atm-vc)#exit

router(config)#bridge 1 protocol ieee

router(config)#int bvi 1
router(config-if)#ip add 192.168.1.1 255.255.255.0
```

The following are explanations of the commands used in this example:

- **(config)#bridge irb**—Defines IRB. Usually for general Internet access, bridging may be combined with IRB to terminate the bridged traffic and route the traffic to an IP or IPX network. Issuing the **bridge irb** command enables the IRB feature in IOS, but you still need to specify the protocol to be used from the bridged domain to the routed domain. That is the result of the **bridge 1 route ip** command. When you configure **bridge 1 route ip**, a BVI is created. The BVI number corresponds to the bridge group. All other protocols are bridged. You can also route multiple protocols over a BVI.

- **(config)#interface atm0/0/0.1 point-to-point**—Defines a subinterface and specifies that it is a point-to-point type.

- **(config-if)#bridge-group 1**—Associates bridge group 1 with the subinterface.

- **(config-if)#pvc 10/101**—Creates a PVC on the subinterface.

- **router(config-if-atm-vc)#encapsulation aal5snap**—Defines the encapsulation type for this PVC as aal5snap, the same as for PPPoE.

- **router(config-if-atm-vc)#ubr 384**—(Optional) Sets the peak cell rate for this UBR connection at 384 Kbps or any other reasonable value.

- **router(config-if-atm-vc)#exit**—Exits PVC configuration mode.

- **Router(config)#bridge 1 protocol ieee**—Sets the Spanning Tree Protocol type as **ieee**, which is by far the most common type.

- **(config)#interface bvi 1**—Opens interface configuration mode, allowing you to define an IP address in the next line. When you intend to bridge and route a given protocol in the same bridge group, you must configure the network-layer attributes (Layer 3) of the protocol on the BVI. Do not configure protocol attributes on the BVIs. No bridging attributes can be configured on them.

  Although it is generally the case that all bridged segments belonging to a bridge group are represented as a single segment or network to the routing protocol, there are situations in which several individual networks coexist within the same bridged segment. To make it possible for the routed domain to learn about the other networks behind the BVI, configure a secondary address on the BVI to add the corresponding network to the routing process.

A more-scalable and less-insecure form of RFC 2684 bridging is available—RBE. Configuring the 6400's NRP for RBE is requires only the addition of the command **atm route-bridged** to the PVC's definition. As you can see in the following, you also might need to define host routes if you use unnumbered interfaces:

```
(config)#interface ATM0/0/0.133 point-to-point
  ip unnumbered Loopback0

    atm route-bridged ip
  pvc 1/33
    encapsulation aal5snap
```

```
! only need host routes when using unnumbered interfaces

ip route 172.168.1.2 255.255.255.255 ATM0/0/0.132
ip route 172.168.1.3 255.255.255.255 ATM0/0/0.133
```

This concludes the discussion of terminating PVCs with RFC 2684 bridging on the 6400's NRP.

VPN Configurations on the Cisco 6400

Configuring a virtual private network on the 6400's NRP requires more work outside the DSL network, and the 6400 itself, than any of the other architecture types. Although configuring the other end of the tunnel is far beyond the DSL network configuration, you have the opportunity now to learn these important procedures.

First, you should review these terms related to VPN:

- **Tunnel**—A virtual pipe between the LAC and the LNS that carries multiple PPP sessions. It consists of user traffic and header information necessary to support the tunnel. The tunnel profile can be in the local router configuration or on a remote RADIUS server.

- **L2TP access concentrator (LAC)**—The client directly connects to the LAC, which resides between the home network (Cisco in this example) and the remote user. Its job is to tunnel PPP frames through the Internet to the local L2TP network server (LNS). It may tunnel any protocol carried within PPP. The LAC initiates incoming calls and receives outgoing calls. For our examples, the LAC is typically the Cisco 6400's NRP.

- **L2TP network server (LNS)**—The termination point for the L2TP tunnel where the home LAN is located. It is the home LAN's access point where PPP frames are processed and passed to higher-layer protocols. An LNS can operate on any platform capable of PPP termination. The LNS handles the server side of the L2TP protocol, although it can initiate the outgoing call to create a tunnel.

- **Session**—A single tunneled PPP session. Also referred to as a call.

- **AAA**—The authentication, authorization, and accounting server, used to store domain and user information. At the LAC, the AAA server stores domain information necessary to identify and establish the tunnel to the remote LNS. At the LNS, the AAA server stores user information needed to authenticate the tunnel user.

L2TP can support either PPPoA or PPPoE encapsulation on the PVC coming from the CPE. The LAC accepts this PPP session and establishes the L2TP tunnel to the LNS. After Link Control Protocol (LCP) has been negotiated, the LAC partially authenticates the end user with CHAP or PAP but does not process PPP packets. The user is authenticated on the LNS where the call terminates. Information necessary to identify the remote LNS can be stored in the AAA server or can be entered directly into the LAC's configuration.

The username@domain name is used to verify that the user is a VPDN client and to provide a mapping to a specific endpoint LNS. The tunnel endpoints (LAC and LNS) authenticate each other, and the tunnel opens. As soon as the tunnel exists, an L2TP session is created for the end user. The LAC propagates the LCP negotiated options and the partially authenticated CHAP/PAP information to the LNS.

L2TP utilizes two types of messages—control messages and data messages. Control messages are used to establish, maintain, and clear a tunnel and to set up and clear sessions. Data messages are used to encapsulate PPP frames being carried over the tunnel.

L2TP guarantees the delivery of control messages through a control channel. Messages in the control channel have sequence numbers used to detect loss or out-of-order delivery. Lost control messages are retransmitted. Data messages may also use sequence numbers to reorder packets and detect lost packets.

To begin configuring VPDN, follow these steps:

Step 1 Start with configuring authentication for the L2TP tunnel. This causes the LAC to check for tunnel authentication using either a RADIUS server or a local database. To use local authorization, a local database of usernames and passwords can be defined on the LAC.

Step 2 Enable VPDN with the command **vpdn enable**. This extends remote access to a private network across a shared infrastructure, such as the Internet.

Step 3 Define a VPDN group, as you did earlier with PPPoE. You apply all VPDN attributes for the LAC through this group. You can use the command **vpdn-group** *number*. This VPDN group contains attributes for initiating the L2TP tunnel on the LAC. Typically, you need one VPDN group for each LAC. For an LNS that services many LACs, the configuration can become cumbersome. However, you can use the default VPDN group configuration if all the LACs will share the same tunnel attributes. An example of this scenario is an LNS that services a large department with many Windows NT L2TP clients that are colocated with the LAC. Each of the Windows NT devices is an L2TP client as well as a LAC. Each of these devices demands a tunnel to the LNS. If all the tunnels will share the same tunnel attributes, you can use a default VPDN group configuration, which simplifies the configuration process.

Step 4 Enable the LAC to initiate the L2TP tunnels using the **initiate-to** command. The configuration looks like this:

```
(config)#vpdn-group 2
 request-dialin
protocol l2tp
        domain Cisco.com
 initiate-to ip 192.168.2.2
 local name NRP-2
 l2tp tunnel password 7 060506324F41
```

In this example, the LAC is configured to initiate an L2TP tunnel to the LNS (whose IP address is 192.168.2.2) if the login contains the Cisco.com domain name. The LAC local host name and the shared secret password used for tunnel authentication between the LAC and the LNS can also be configured under the VPDN group.

Step 5   Move to the LNS and duplicate the security definitions, username, and password, as you did in Step 1 for the LAC.

Step 6   The next step on the LNS is to enable VPDN, again duplicating what you did on the LAC. You should also define a VPDN group to which you will apply all VPDN attributes for the LNS. This VPDN group contains attributes for accepting the L2TP tunnel on the LNS.

Step 7   Enable the LNS to accept L2TP tunnels, using the **terminate-from** command, as shown in the following, along with the other commands:

```
(config)#vpdn-group team1
 accept-dialin
 protocol l2tp
 virtual-template 1
 terminate-from hostname NRP-2
 l2tp tunnel password 7 0822455D0
```

The command **accept-dialin** specifies the local name to use for authenticating and the virtual template to use for cloning new virtual-access interfaces when an incoming L2TP tunnel connection is requested from a specific peer.

The command **terminate-from hostname NRP-2** defines the attributes needed to find the LNS for the given domain name. You can enter the LNS's IP address, or in this case, a predefined host name (NRP-2) instead of the IP address.

In the example, the LNS is configured to accept an L2TP tunnel from the LAC with a host name of NRP-2. The shared secret password used for tunnel authentication between the LAC and the LNS can also be configured under the vpdn-group. The virtual-template 1 interface is used for creating the virtual-access interface.

Step 8   A final task on the LNS, although not necessarily performed in strict order, is to define the virtual-template interface and an IP address pool for dynamic IP address assignment over IPCP, as shown in the following:

```
interface Virtual-Template1
    ip address 192.168.7.1 255.255.255.0
    peer default ip address pool L2TP_pool
    ppp authentication chap
 ip local pool L2TP_pool 192.168.7.100 192.168.7.120
```

You may continue to configure the virtual template interface with configuration parameters you want applied to the virtual-access interfaces.

Now that you have configured the LAC and LNS, you can use the **show vpdn** command to display information about active tunnels and message identifiers in a VPDN. Here is an example of the output:

```
lac1#show vpdn
L2TP Tunnel and Session Information
Total tunnels 1 sessions 1
```

```
LocID RemID Remote Name   State Remote Address Port Sessions
11984 36217 ciscoemp      est   172.30.248.10  1701 1

LocID RemID TunID Intf Username    State LastChg Fastswitch
9     5     11984 Vi6  joe@cisco.com est  00:31:39 enabled

%No active L2F tunnels

%No active PPPoE tunnels
```

This concludes the explanation of configuring L2TP on the Cisco 6400 and other devices in the larger network.

Summary

In this vital chapter, you configured all three components of the DSL network with the CLI Cisco IOS Software. Moving from the Cisco 827 and 827-4V, with their basic data and added voice configurations, you then followed the DSL traffic upstream to the Cisco 6000 series of IP DSL Switches. There you learned not only how to configure the IP DSL Switch for redundancy, but also how to map the incoming DSL traffic to outbound ATM traffic and to adjust configurations for particular models of IP DSL Switches and line cards. Finally, you learned how APS and other redundancy options work on the Cisco 6400 UAC, followed by configuration of the basic architectures, such as PPPoA on the NRP.

Review Questions

1 What does the command **ip unnumbered gigabit ethernet 0/0/0** accomplish?

   A It enables IP on the interface without assigning a specific IP address.

   B It selects the authentication protocol and an optional secondary protocol.

   C It associates a virtual template with a virtual template interface.

   D It specifies a dynamic IP address assignment method, from either an IP address pool or a DHCP server.

2 Which of the following apply to the NRP?

   A Layer 3 services

   B High-speed ATM switch

   C Central control for the 6400

   D Traffic shaping

3 Which of the following apply to the NSP?

   A Central control of the 6400

   B Layer 3 packet services

   C Terminates PPP

   D End-to-end transport authentication

4 Which of the following apply to the NLC?

   A Optical interface

   B Automatic protection switching

   C Layer 3 services

   D Terminates PPP

5 True or false: The 6400 must be configured with redundant NSP cards.

6 The IP address for the subscriber's PC can be provided by what? (Select all that apply.)

   A Static configuration

   B DHCP server on the ATU-R

   C DHCP server on the aggregation router

   D DHCP server on the RADIUS server

7 The interface designation **int atm 0/0/0** on the 6400 designates what?

   A ATM interface slot 0, subslot 0, card 0

   B Backplane connection, subslot 0, port 0

   C ATM interface port 0, subslot 0, slot 0

   D ATM interface slot 0, port 0, subslot 0

8 From the NSP, interface designation **atm 1/0/0** indicates what?

   A Interface to the card in port 1, subslot 0, slot 0

   B Interface to the card in slot 1, subslot 0, card 0

   C Interface to the card in slot 1, subslot 0, port 0

   D Interface to the card in slot 1, card 0, port 0

9 What is the NSP switch default ATM protocol?

   A LAPD

   B X.25

   C UNI 4.0

   D ISDN

10 Which of the following best describes a BVI?

   A It provides the interface between a bridge group and the routed network.

   B It assembles packets coming from the bridge group into FR frames.

   C It restricts broadcast messages within a bridge group.

   D None of the above

11 Which of the following best describes SONET APS on the 6400 system?

   A Redundant NLC cards supplying OC-3 traffic to the NSP.

   B Redundant NLC ports supplying OC-3 traffic to the NRP.

   C The 6400 system does not support SONET APS.

   D Redundant NSP configured for failover.

12 **ilmi-pvc-discovery** refers to the process of what?

   A The automatic discovery of configured PVCs on the NRP card

   B The automatic discovery of configured PVCs on the NLC card by the NRP card

   C The automatic discovery of configured PVCs on the NSP card by the NRP card

   D None of the above

13 When two NRP-1s are configured in a redundant configuration, which of the following occurs?

   A Both NRP-1s provide redundant traffic to the NSP.

   B Both NRP-1s provide redundant traffic to the NLC.

   C Both NRP-1s provide redundant traffic to the NPP.

   D None of the above

14 True or false: The function of the **encapsulation aal5mux ppp dialer** command is to specify the encapsulation type for the PPPoA PVC on the 827.

15 Which protocol contains information about higher-layer protocols, including IP and IPX, and their control protocols (IPCP for IP)?

   A NCP

   B LLC

   C PCP

   D NLP

CHAPTER 7

Cisco DSL Manager (CDM)

This chapter explains the GUI software element management system that supports all IP DSL Switches. This chapter starts with a CDM product overview and basic CDM concepts. It also explains deploying IP DSL Switches, configuration management, subscriber management, fault management, performance management, subtended topology configurations, and permanent virtual circuit (PVC) creation.

After completing this chapter, you will be able to do the following:

- Define CDM's key features

- Define CDM IP DSL Switch deployment

- Define CDM configuration management

- Define the concepts of subscriber management for the NI-2

- Determine how to set up CDM fault and performance management

- Define CDM subtended configuration and subtended PVC creation

CDM's Key Features and Concepts

CDM includes the following capabilities:

- Autodiscovery or manual configuration of Cisco IP DSL Switches and their components, such as line cards

- IP DSL Switch chassis mapping for graphical representations of the physical components

- Graphical and textual reporting of alarms and Simple Network Management Protocol (SNMP) traps

- Management for FCAPS (Fault, Configuration, Accounting, Performance, and Security) for the chassis and line cards

- Highly scalable, multiprotocol management package

- Analysis and reporting of performance statistics, including dynamically-updated graphics

The CDM also has labor-saving, human-error-reducing features:

- Predeployment of NI-2 chassis and line cards within CDM before the physical installation, ensuring uniform and verifiable configurations before operations

- Configuration backup and restoration

- Uploading (copying and reapplying) profiles and connection parameters

- Cisco IOS Software download onto the NI-2

CDM supports all the functionality of the Cisco IOS Software command-line interface (CLI). Subscriber management is a primary function of CDM. Through CDM, users can create and configure subscribers on the equipment. Users can create connection profiles on the NI-2 card, which you learned about in Chapter 6, "Cisco IOS Configurations." CDM has profiles specifically for discrete multitone (DMT) connections, as well as profiles for overall DSL connections and Asynchronous Transfer Mode (ATM) service levels.

CDM Release 3.4 supports 250 nodes (IP DSL Switches) and 30 operators logged on to the same network simultaneously. Future releases will support additional nodes and operators. Management support for these simultaneous operators of devices includes the most sophisticated functionality, such as Inverse Multiplexing over ATM (IMA) and eight-port line card support.

NOTE   Where possible in this chapter, version differences between CDM 3.3.x and CDM 3.4 are noted. In the case of a discrepancy, you should ultimately rely most thoroughly on the Cisco user documentation that came with your particular version of the CDM.

CDM itself is based on an underlying software platform that also supports GUI software for other Cisco devices. This platform is the Cisco Element Manager Framework (CEMF), which is described in the next section.

Cisco Element Manager Framework

CDM is a carrier-class element manager that plugs into the underlying platform, called CEMF. CEMF is required to install and operate CDM. The CDM Element Manager is launched from the CEMF Launchpad. You can deploy CDM in a number of different configurations, from a single hardware system to a multisite distributed management system, using Sun Solaris or Sun SPARC hardware with Solaris Release 2.6. It is vital to consult the software platform specifications provided by Cisco to be sure that your site is adequate for CEMF. For instance, memory and hard drive space requirements are quite demanding. (You should consult www.Cisco.com for installation requirements for your particular implementation.)

CDM's basis in CEMF ensures common communications with other element managers for different classes of Cisco devices. CEMF supports several different standards-based and proprietary management protocols. The CEMF system architecture provides a distributed network management solution designed to manage large-scale networks.

Every CEMF deployment has an installed CEMF server. Processes on the CEMF server keep track of the current state of the network model, user access, events, and so on. The ObjectStore database system is installed on this machine.

For CEMF's distributed management solution, additional clients can be added as required. All clients, such as CDM, run on the server, including all the client application GUIs, so no software client needs to be installed on the network nodes themselves, such as the IP DSL Switches.

For multiple clients, a CEMF deployment may have the client installation on separate work-stations, which are used to run CEMF applications to access objects on the server. A client installation contains only those parts of the CEMF system that are necessary for a CEMF user session. This user session communicates with the CEMF server when required to retrieve management information. The CEMF graphical user interface runs on the CEMF client machine, which frees system resources on the CEMF server machine to process network information.

The CEMF client installation process installs the client software on the local machine. Therefore, the files need not be mounted across a network.

The software stores a system log file (SysLog) and an event log file (EventLog) on the IP DSL Switch that you can view from CDM. These files log all CLI commands made by users on the IP DSL Switch and all events that affect the device. When viewing or printing log information, you can filter the information using specific search criteria, as discussed later in this chapter.

FCAPS Standards

The design rationale for element management is the FCAPS functional design, which is a standard for SNMP management systems. Users want a management system that handles faults, subscribers, and so on. CEMF was designed using the FCAPS feature, and its benefits are present in all versions of CDM.

Following are examples of CEMF/CDM capabilities that fulfill the FCAPS functions and that are integrated into the CDM navigation bar:

- The Faults tab (the F in FCAPS) is the most commonly used tab and therefore is positioned first on the navigation bar.

- The second component of FCAPS is represented by two tabs on the navigation bar—Configuration and More Configuration.

- Accounting is fulfilled by the logs, which you can view and print. This is explained later in this chapter.

- The FCAPS goal of performance is implemented by the Performance and Status tabs. These tabs not only provide operational statistics, but also permit viewing of system capacity information and more.

- Security is provided through CEMF's UNIX-powered user identification and password requirements.

In addition to FCAPS, CDM offers a variety of inventory data, such as chassis details and power supply, through the Inventory tab.

Cisco Architecture in CEMF/CDM

In CEMF and CDM, the most complete (although not mandatory) order of implementation starts with the creation of a site or region, according to your design for grouping the network elements to be created in the ensuing processes. For instance, a site is usually a central office/exchange containing one or more IP DSL Switches, and a region usually contains one or more sites. Within the site, you create a bay, which is equivalent to a rack of equipment. Some service providers skip the region creation and start with creating a site. A site is required to deploy a chassis.

When you deploy a Cisco 6000 series IP DSL Switch (or another Cisco device, such as the 6400 Universal Access Concentrator), CEMF automatically creates an entity called a *CiscoShelf*. The CiscoShelf resides under the bay entity.

Under the bay is a CiscoShelf, and under the CiscoShelf is a chassis. The CiscoShelf can be considered the container from which the user can view everything about the chassis.

In the element manager context, the Cisco device architecture consists of the chassis, module, and interface, which are supported by a set of Management Information Bases (MIBs).

The chassis defines the platform housing part of the device. The module is a replaceable unit within the chassis, such as a line card in the Cisco 6000 series of IP DSL Switches. The interfaces are technology-specific interfaces that normally reside on a module, such as the ATM trunk interface on the NI-2 card.

All the interfaces (and all other components) are reported and displayed through views, which are explained in the next section.

Views

Views model hierarchical relationships between objects.

Objects are organized into different views. They can exist in multiple views. Each object can have a number of parent and child objects.

Each view represents a different way of containing and grouping objects.

The CDM adds views to the standard views supplied by the CEMF during installation. The standard CEMF software provides Physical and Network views (overall IP DSL Switch Chassis and Connectivity views).

One of the CDM views is the Common (or Physical) view. When a shelf is selected, the Chassis view, including all the line cards, PVCs, and other entities, both actual and virtual, can be viewed as a bitmapped graphic. You can view more details by choosing the Chassis view.

After the chassis has been selected, any modules within or on the chassis can be right-clicked to launch menus. Each card in the rack has a color-coded box that identifies the card type, its position in the chassis rack, and its current alarm status.

In accordance with standard telecommunications industry color codes, each severity level has a corresponding color:

> Informational (white)
>
> Normal (green)
>
> Warning (cyan)
>
> Minor (yellow)
>
> Major (orange)
>
> Critical (red)
>
> Unmanaged, usually decommissioned (blue)

Names of network elements and subelements are also specified. You can use the default naming convention in CDM, or you can create and use your own naming conventions. Customized names are especially useful when you deploy elements manually instead of letting CDM autodiscover network elements and their components.

Polling for States

All CEMF element managers (EMs) use an internal state model. Each network device's behavior depends on the device's state. The device's (virtual) state machine files contain various tasks, and these tasks are run by the EM controller. For instance, error tasks are run every 5 minutes. Tasks can also run a multitude of different actions, such as subchassis discovery.

Tasks provide two types of polling functionality:

- **Presence polling**—Beyond the simple presence and status of a device, presence polling affects other tasks. For instance, when a device enters an errored state (down), tasks are shown as errored.

- **Performance polling**—NI-2 and ports have certain criteria that are examined for the reporting of several criteria, such as cells passed and so on.

In CDM, device states are shown at the bottom left of each window. There are five states:

- **Normal**—In the Normal state, the CDM polls the object every 60 seconds to determine if it is present. The default screen refresh period is every 10 seconds. Both of these periods can be modified. When the object is placed in commission, it is placed in the Normal state.

- **Perf Logging on**—When performance logging is enabled on a module or interface, that object's state at the bottom left of each window changes from Normal to Perf Monitoring.

- **Errored**—If the status is Errored, none of the displayed values can be queried. For example, if a chassis becomes unreachable for some reason, it moves into the Errored state.

- **Decommissioned**—When you want to replace an existing card or perform any kind of maintenance on an object, you should first decommission it. This is comparable to Maintenance mode in other software systems. When you decommission an object, the object is still present on the CDM map graphic, but the following three factors apply:

    — Active management stops.

    — All subobjects are also decommissioned (although you cannot directly decommission interfaces, such as the ATM interface ports on the NI-2 card).

    — Polling on the object stops.

- **Preprovisioned**—Preprovisioning is the process of reserving and configuring a space in the system for DMT line cards that have not yet been physically slotted into the system rack. If a DMT line card is in a preprovisioned state, it means that even though the card is not present, the system has been preprovisioned to hold that card.

    When you preprovision a chassis, the information is stored in CEMF and CDM in a Decommissioned state. When you preprovision subscribers or line cards, the information is stored on the DSLAM's NI-2 card and is reflected in the software as being in a preprovisioned state. This is not accessible through the CLI.

    Therefore, DMT line cards in the Cisco 6000 series chassis can exist in a state known as Preprovisioned, but the CDM does not monitor their status. When the actual cards are placed in the physical equipment, CEMF automatically detects them and moves the DMT card into the Normal state. However, you can manually move the DMT line card from the Preprovisioned state to the Commissioned state with a single click of the mouse.

CEMF/CDM Startup and Navigation

To start a CEMF user session, which is required before using CDM, go to the Solaris command line in the terminal window and enter the following:

```
CEMF_ROOT/bin/cemf session
```

Replace *CEMF_ROOT* with the root directory where CEMF is installed (for example, /opt/CEMF3). The splash screen appears, followed by the Login dialog box.

The CEMF Launchpad window contains two group boxes: CEMF Manager and Event Manager, in the upper and lower halves of the screen, respectively.

The CEMF Manager icon group contains the following icons:

- **Viewer**—Launches MapViewer, which was first launched by the CEMF session command.

- **Groups**—Launches the Object Group Manager.

- **Access**—Launches the Access Manager.

- **Events**—Launches the Query Editor and Event Browser.

- **Discovery**—Launches autodiscovery.

The Event Manager icon group contains the following icons:

- **Notify**—Launches notification profiles.

- **Thresholds**—Launches threshold regimes.

- **Event Groups**—Launches event groups.

CEMF's element managers have very similar windows.

There are three methods to quit a CEMF user session, all of which present the same user confirmation:

- In the Launchpad window, click the Close icon on the toolbar.

- Select File, Quit.

- Press Ctrl-Q. (You can close a single window anywhere in CEMF by pressing Ctrl-W.)

After you use one of these methods, a window appears, asking if you want to quit the session. Click Yes to quit. All active applications are closed, and the CEMF session terminates.

IP DSL Switch Deployment

This section describes the deployment of the Cisco 6000 series of IP DSL Switches in CDM. Each individual component of the switch, such as individual modules, must be brought online for the whole to be manageable in CDM. You can either deploy each component individually, as most service providers choose to do for a single switch or a single component of a switch, or you can use CDM's Deployment Wizard. The Deployment Wizard encompasses all individual components of the IP DSL Switch. The Deployment Wizard can deploy objects in CEMF before the actual deployment on a Cisco IP DSL Switch in the field. The Deployment Wizard is launched when the deploy option is selected. The wizard guides the user through the deployment process.

The CDM detects the presence of previously deployed network equipment as soon as that device is powered on or installed in a powered-on device.

Autodiscovery interrogates the network for Internet Protocol (IP) and SNMP devices and creates an object in the map for each new device discovered.

Bear in mind that predeployed objects are not monitored. Depending on your choice of technique, you can manually change the network element (IP DSL Switch) from a Predeployment state to a Commissioned state if it is not autodiscovered by the system for whatever reason, such as temporary Ethernet connectivity issues.

Preprovisioning allows line card modules to be deployed within the IP DSL Switch chassis before they are actually present in the hardware. Preprovisioned DMT line cards can be deployed only when the related Cisco IP DSL Switch chassis and NI-2 card are in a Normal state.

Configuration can be performed on the preprovisioned module. When the DMT card becomes physically available, it simply assumes all the configuration information that has already been set up for it. Like predeployed chassis, preprovisioned objects are also not monitored, meaning that alarm, status, and performance information is unavailable on a preprovisioned module. When the DMT line card is placed in the Cisco 6000 series IP DSL Switch chassis, it is automatically changed to a Commissioned state. Alternatively, you can move the card from the Preprovisioned state to the Commissioned state by clicking the Commission button.

When a preprovisioned module is commissioned, its status changes to Normal. The module is then continuously monitored as an existing module within CDM.

To deploy a manageable Cisco IP DSL Switch in CEMF, you must have a deployed site. You can open the Deployment Wizard for a new chassis from the site or bay from which you want to deploy the chassis. It's quite simple. Right-click the object (site or bay). From the resulting pop-up menu, select Deployment, and then select Deploy Objects. You'll read more about those steps later. The next section explains how to deploy an initial site by creating a new generic object.

Site Deployment

You can access the Deployment Wizard for an initial site through the Class Palette window. The Class Palette window provides a selection of network elements that can be displayed within CEMF. When you select an object, such as Site, from the Class Palette window, the Deployment Wizard is invoked.

This display of object types opens automatically when you select Edit Map from the pull-down menu of a selected object. The Map Builder window and the Class Palette window are displayed.

When the Class Palette window is open, follow these three steps to create the new site:

Step 1 Place the cursor over the active icon that represents the object class to be added. In this case, the Site icon is in the middle of the Class Palette.

Step 2 Press and hold the left mouse button.

Step 3 Drag the selected icon to the desired location on the map, and then release the mouse button. The selected icon appears on the map, and the Deployment Wizard is displayed.

Generic objects such as sites are non-technology-specific. The CDM allows the following generic objects to be deployed:

- Bay

- IP device

- Network, region

- SNMP agent

- SNMP MIB-2 agent

- SNMP proxied device

- Site

You can create the site by following these steps:

Step 1 Select the Deployment Profile for the site.

Step 2 Click Forward. You supply the details of this site.

NOTE   You can cancel the site-creation process before completing the process by clicking the Finish button.

Step 3 Enter the number of sites you want to create, and then click Forward. If you specify multiple sites, each will conform to the name you specify in the next step. You don't have to name each one individually.

Step 4 Enter the name of the site, and then click Forward. You should plan the naming standard carefully, because if you specified multiple sites in the preceding step, the other sites will use this name as a prefix by appending their ordinal value to this prefix. For example, if the prefix is SITE-1-, the objects are named SITE-1-1-, SITE-1-2-, and so on, up to SITE-1-10- for ten sites. This way, in a separate scenario, you can use automatic naming under the same parent object by specifying a different prefix. For example, if you specify SITE-2- as the prefix, another ten sites would be named SITE-2-1-, SITE-2-2-, and so on, up to SITE-2-10-.

Step 5   Click the Select button to bring up the Object Selector window. Select where the new objects will be placed in the Physical view by clicking the parent objects.

Step 6   Click Apply to move to the Deployment Wizard Summary window.

Step 7   Click Finish to deploy the new site (or other) object onto the map and to display the Deployment Wizard–Summary window. This window summarizes the deployment you have created and allows you to commit or reject the deployment. If you are satisfied with the deployment, click Finish.

To deploy another type of generic object, follow these steps:

Step 1   Place the cursor over a relevant object to determine the objects you can deploy from. If there are no additional menus, nothing can be deployed from this object.

Step 2   Click and hold down the right mouse button.

Step 3   Select Deploy, Generic Object from the pop-up menu.

You can manually deploy the following classes of objects:

- Generic classes (such as sites)

- Chassis

- NI-2 modules. (Deployment is usually needed only when you replace NI-2 cards, because deploying the chassis automatically deploys the NI-2 itself.)

- Line cards. (As with the NI-2, deployment of line cards is usually needed only after replacement, because deploying a chassis automatically deploys any installed line cards, especially if they have been preprovisioned.)

Chassis Deployment

From an existing site, the chassis deployment itself is a two-stage process:

- The first stage is chassis deployment. The Cisco 6000 series chassis can be manually deployed or autodiscovered.

- The second stage of the deployment process is to deploy the Cisco IP DSL Switch objects at the subchassis level. This involves autodiscovering the subchassis objects and/or deploying additional subchassis objects manually.

As with the site, you manually deploy a Cisco DSLAM chassis using the Deployment Wizard. One way to begin this process is from the Map Viewer window. To access the Map Viewer, click the Viewer icon (the spectacles) on the Launchpad. When you deploy a Cisco IP DSL Switch chassis, you configure the chassis and its SNMP parameters. Here are the steps:

Step 1   On the left side of the Map Viewer window, within the CDM Manager view, right-click cdmManager to access the object menu.

Step 2   Choose Deployment, Deploy Cisco DSLAM. The Deployment Wizard–Templates window opens.

Step 3   Click Create 6160 under auto named shelf or Create 6160 Chassis under user named shelf, and then click Forward. You can have CDM name the DSLAM chassis, or you can create a name for the chassis.

The first Deployment Wizard–Object Parameters window opens, shown as the uppermost window.

If you choose to deploy a chassis under a user-named shelf, the IP and SNMP fields are displayed in two separate Deployment Wizard–Object Parameters windows.

Step 4   Click Forward to proceed.

Step 5   Enter the number of IP DSL Switches to be deployed; Cisco recommends initiating one at a time.

Step 6   Click Forward to proceed. The next Deployment Wizard–Object Parameters window opens.

Step 7   In the Prefix for unit name field, accept the default prefix that CDM generates, or enter a unique prefix for the unit name.

The value you enter in the Prefix for unit name field carries over to the Chassis Name field to minimize duplicate data entry. You can use the default value, change the value, or delete the default value to exclude it from part of the Chassis Name field.

Step 8   Click Forward to continue. The Deployment Wizard Views window opens.

Step 9   Click Select next to the Physical field to select the physical site under which you want to deploy this chassis. The Object Selector dialog box opens.

Step 10 Click the + (plus sign) next to the Physical field to display the sites that are deployed.

Step 11 Click the site under which you want to deploy this new chassis.

The Deployment Wizard–Views window reopens and displays the site you selected in the Object Selector dialog box, next to the Physical and Component Managed fields.

Step 12 Click Forward to continue. The next Deployment Wizard–Object Parameters window opens.

Step 13 Enter the appropriate information in the fields in this window, as follows:

    (a) In the Chassis IP Address field, enter the valid IP address for the chassis you are deploying; the maximum alphanumeric limit is 15 characters.

    (b) In the SNMP V2c Read Community field, enter the name for the read-only relationship; the name you enter must match the SNMP read community string on the Cisco IP DSL Switch. Be sure to match the string you entered via the Cisco IOS Software CLI, as you learned in Chapter 6.

    (c) In the SNMP V2c Write Community field, enter the name for the read-write relationship; the name you enter must match the SNMP write community string on the Cisco IP DSL Switch. You must replace the default entry to match the privileges on the IP DSL Switch.

    (d) In the SNMP Version field, enter the version of SNMP used on this device. It will almost certainly be the commonly-used snmpv2c, although the following choices are available:

        • snmpv1

        • snmpv2c

        • snmpv3 (not supported at this time)

    (e) In the Chassis Name field, use the default chassis name generated by CDM from your entry in the Prefix for unit name field, or enter a unique name for the chassis you are deploying.

Step 14 Click Forward to complete the deployment process. The Deployment Wizard Summary window opens to inform you that CDM is ready to deploy the DSLAM chassis.

The Deployment Wizard Summary window prompts you to commit or reject the deployment. When you deploy a chassis, a shelf object is also created, thus deploying two objects.

Step 15 To commit the deployment, click Finish; to reject the deployment, click Cancel.

If the deployment is successful, the object appears in the chassis view. If the deployment is unsuccessful, the Deployment Wizard–Summary window informs you that the deployment failed.

Later in this chapter you'll learn how to commission the chassis, the last procedure in rendering the chassis operatively manageable. You should also be familiar with the procedures to deploy an NI-2 card and individual DSL line cards, although this is typically required only for replacement activity.

NI-2 and DSL Line Card Deployment

An NI-2 management card can be manually deployed under a Cisco 6000 series IP DSL Switch chassis from the Map Viewer application in the CDM Manager view.

The Deployment Summary window summarizes the deployment that has been created and gives you the option of committing or rejecting the deployment. When an NI-2 management card has been deployed, interfaces representing the ports on the NI-2 card are automatically created.

If an OC-3 NI-2 is being deployed, two OC-3 interfaces are deployed, representing the two OC-3 trunk ports on the NI-2 card. If a DS3 NI-2 is being deployed, three DS3 interfaces are deployed, representing the three DS3 ports on the NI-2 card. Similarly, if the IMA NI-2 card is deployed (eight T1/E1s and one DS3), a total of nine interfaces are deployed.

For both NI-2 card and DSL line card deployments, start the deployment procedures as explained previously for the chassis deployment. That is, from the left side of the Map Viewer window, within the CDM Manager view, right-click cdmManager to access the object menu. Choose Deployment for the appropriate object, and respond to the Deployment Wizard's prompts.

IP Autodiscovery of the Cisco 6*xxx* Chassis

CEMF autodiscovery examines the network for IP and SNMP devices and creates a managed object for each new device discovered.

Three mechanisms for autodiscovery are

- IP
- SNMP
- IP and SNMP

As you probably know, autodiscovery is efficient at reducing labor.

Suppose that a Cisco 6*xxx* detected during autodiscovery and an object representing the chassis have been created and placed under the site where autodiscovery was launched.

When autodiscovery is launched from a site object, the process automatically populates the Physical view. When autodiscovery is selected from any other object, you must select the physical containment required.

Chassis Commissioning

Commissioning (activating) a chassis is a part of configuration in CDM. All the configuration tasks are performed in the Physical view. After the chassis has been commissioned, alarm, performance, and status data can be collected for the chassis and the modules within the chassis. The initial status of a commissioned chassis is Normal. The initial status for a commissioned module is either Normal or Preprovisioned (if the physical module hardware is not detected in the chassis).

You can commission an IP DSL Switch chassis within the Map Viewer by right-clicking the chassis object to be commissioned and then clicking the Commission button.

When a chassis is commissioned, subrack discovery begins. This discovers all modules within the chassis and commissions them if possible. On a newly deployed system, subrack discovery is recommended, because it can deploy and commission many modules at a time. If only one module needs to be deployed and commissioned, manual deployment should be used instead.

CDM Configuration Management

After commissioning, there are five other components to CDM Configuration Management of the Cisco 6000 series of IP DSL Switches:

- Management information
- Configuration backup and restore
- Logs
- IOS image download
- SNMP management

Each of these is discussed in the following sections.

Management Information

The Management Information window lets you view generic management information for a specified chassis, such as the IP address, system name, contact, location, and password information. You can perform the following tasks:

- View and add generic management information:
    - IP address
    - System name
    - System location information

- Set the Cisco IOS Software username and password (of course, this username and password must be matched in the Cisco IOS Software itself!).

Here are the steps to enable management:

Step 1   In the Physical view, with the list box of objects on the left, click the chassis (shelf) object to display the Configuration tab of the Management Information window.

The Configuration tab displays the following parameters:

— IP address

— System name

— System contact

— System location

— Extra location information (for optional, freeform text information)

You can select any of these tabs to enter information about a selected chassis.

Step 2   The IOS/Command Line tab in the Management Information window opens a panel that can synchronize login information between CDM and Cisco IOS Software. On this panel, the User Name, Exec Password, and Login Password can be entered. You have two options for saving changed information on this panel:

— You can click Save Locally to save the passwords locally on the selected chassis.

— You can click Save to Device to reconfigure the passwords on the IP DSL Switch itself if previous passwords have been specified. In this case, be sure to configure the IP DSL Switch through Cisco IOS Software to match this data and to communicate the change(s) to other users.

Configuration Backup and Restore

The Configuration Backup and Restore configuration option allows you to perform the following tasks:

- Upload the current running configuration onto a TFTP (Trivial File Transfer Program) server

- Download a configuration file from a TFTP server to an NI-2 card

- Create regular backups to allow for recovery in the event of a hardware failure

Cisco Systems, Inc., warns users to not edit an uploaded configuration off the platform itself.

An important precondition to backing up and restoring operations is that the CLI password must be set in the Management Information window.

The Configuration Backup/Restore window allows you to upload the current Cisco 6000 series IP DSL Switch running configuration from the selected device and save it as a file to any TFTP server. The file can later be downloaded from the specified TFTP server to a user-specified Cisco 6000 series IP DSL Switch, either the original device or a different one for configuration cloning.

Regular configuration backups allow recovery in the incredibly unlikely event of a Cisco hardware failure. For example, if an NI-2 were to fail, a replacement NI-2 could be inserted into the chassis, and the configuration data would be restored. Changes in configuration data between the last backup and the time of the failure would be lost.

As with the other components of CDM configuration, you start from the Physical view and right-click the chassis whose configuration you want to upload or restore. Click the Save icon, a standardized filc button.

At the Configuration panel, enter the backup server's TFTP IP address. For general policy, click the drop-down arrow beside Backup After Every Action to select either Enable or Disable. If you select Enable, a backup is made after every configuration change. If you select Disable, no backups are made.

For immediate operation, make your choice from the Actions panel in the lower part of the window. You can click Backup, Restore, or Schedule Backup:

- **Backup**—Immediately backs up the running configuration of a Cisco 6000 series IP DSL Switch.

- **Restore**—Immediately restores the running configuration of a Cisco 6000 series IP DSL Switch.

- **Schedule Backup**—Schedules the backup for a later date and time. When you click Schedule Backup, the Schedule Dialog window appears.

The backup and restoration speed depends on the file's size, the TFTP server processor's power, and other variables.

Logs

This component of CDM configuration uses two types of logs:

- **System Log (SysLog)**—Keeps a record of everything that happens on the device (chassis) that is not user-initiated.

- **Command History Log**—Keeps a record of all configuration changes on the device (chassis) that are user-initiated.

System Log

An example of a System Log event is a loss of traffic. This event is device-specific and is not initiated by the user. You can filter SysLog events' display by severity, from highest to lowest.

To view the System Log, start in the Physical view. Right-click the desired chassis and select View, System Log. Then select the desired device from the IOS Host list on the left. The corresponding logs should appear in the table on the right. To specify the results, follow these steps:

Step 1   Click the Maximum Table Entries number in the SysLog Message Details panel. Enter the number of events to see at one time.

Step 2   Click the drop-down arrow next to Max. SysLog Severity. Select a level of severity from which to view events. Debug is the lowest severity level and is used primarily by engineers to view errors in the code. The highest severity level is Emergency.

Step 3   Click the drop-down arrow next to Notifications Enabled. Select False if alarm notification is turned off; select True if alarm notification is turned on.

Command History

The Command History window keeps a record, in table format, of all configuration changes on the device (chassis) that are user-initiated. An example of a stored event is the configuration of a chassis or module. The Command History maintains details of the time and source of specified changes.

To view the System Log, start in the Physical view. Right-click the desired chassis and select View, System Log. Select the desired device from the IOS Host list on the left. The corresponding log details appear in the scrollable list on the right.

IOS Image Download

This CDM configuration function allows you to download a current version of the IOS image software on your device. However, you must have SNMP configured.

As with the other CDM configuration functions, you start in the Physical view. Right-click the desired chassis and select Image Download.

To download a new IOS image, follow these steps:

Step 1   Select the device on which to perform an IOS download from the Generic Processor list on the left.

Step 2   Enter the TFTP Server IP Address—the source of the IOS image software to be downloaded.

Step 3   Enter the Destination File System name—either Bootflash or Flash.

Step 4   Enter the Source File Name, specifying the IOS image download filename.

Step 5   Enter the Destination File Name. Specify the file's name, making sure it matches the one stored in the CDM's file system.

Step 6   Select the Format the destination device option to erase a PCMCIA disk or NI-2 memory before the new software is downloaded. If the destination device is not formatted first, you might run out of space on that device.

Step 7   Select the Reset device using new image option to reset the device to start using the new software. The Status panel displays the date and time of the last download.

Step 8   Click the Download button to perform the download immediately. To schedule the download to be performed at a later date, click the Schedule Download button.

SNMP Management

This last and vital function of CDM configuration lets you do the following:

- Change the SNMP version (obviously, a unique event)

- Read or write community names for a selected device

- Enable or disable trap generation

As with the other CDM configuration functions, you start in the Physical view. Right-click the desired chassis and select SNMP Management.

To make modifications, follow these steps:

Step 1   Select the device (chassis) from the IOS Host list box on the left.

Step 2   SNMP version 2 is probably in use. If it is, enter the community names under V2 Read and V2 Write. If version 1 of SNMP is being used, enter the community names in the Community Names panel for V1 Read and V1 Write.

Step 3   Click the drop-down arrow next to SNMP Version and select the SNMP version (V1 or V2C). SNMP version 3 is not supported at this time.

Step 4   To enable or disable trap generation, click the appropriate button. When trap generation is enabled on a selected chassis, any SNMP traps generate alarms and send them to the specified chassis's IP address. This means that alarms are visible to the user in the appropriate view of CDM. This feature can also be disabled so that no traps are generated and no alarms are sent.

Subscriber Management for NI-2

This section describes how you add subscribers and apply profiles to a subscriber using the Cisco Digital Subscriber Line Manager software. CDM has the following types of subscriber management options, all of which can be applied to the subscriber configuration:

- Profile configuration, including ATM quality of service (QoS) profiles, DMT profiles, and Asymmetric DSL (ADSL) profiles

- PVC and SPVC configuration

- Virtual Channel Link (VCL) configuration

- Uploading profiles and connections

Following are the processes that apply to a subscriber connection:

- Creating an ATM QoS profile

- Creating an ADSL profile

- Creating a DMT profile

- Applying your DMT profile to a DMT port on a DMT line card

- Applying your ADSL profile to an ADSL line on a DMT line card

- Creating a PVC or SPVC object

- Applying your ATM QoS profile to the PVC

- Activating the cross-connection on the device through CDM

- Configuring the VCL

- (Optional) Starting performance polling on the connection, which gathers performance information for that connection

Creating an ATM Quality of Service Profile

ATM QoS profiles are different from the ADSL profiles you learned about in Chapter 6 when we discussed Cisco IOS Software configurations. These ATM profiles are also called *ATM traffic descriptors*. Like DSL profiles, traffic descriptors are applied to one or more PVCs. ATM QoS profiles are stored in the CDM.

To create an ATM QoS profile, do the following:

Step 1   Select Cisco DSL Manager, Logical, Connection, QoS Profile. The ATM QoS Profiles window appears. Optionally, you can create and apply profiles and connections in the Map Viewer application. When you are in the Map Viewer application, within the CDM Manager view, you can right-click a chassis object to display the relevant menus.

The ATM QoS Profile Parameters fields are as follows:

— **Profile Name**—Enter the name of the new profile. When you create a profile in CDM, use a single word or a continuous expression to name the profile. Do not use spaces in the name. Your profile name should be compatible with the Cisco IOS Software CLI, which recognizes a space as the end of a profile name. For example, instead of entering **new profile name**, you should use the string **newprofilename**.

— **Profile Type**—Enter the type of profile you are creating (in this instance, an ATM QoS profile).

— **Profile Description**—This optional, free-form text descriptor can be used to identify the marketed service level—something like Business-Class High-Speed.

Step 2   Click the RxTx Parameters tab to display two panels: Receive Parameters and Transmit Parameters. These panels contain identical fields:

— **QoS Category**—The selected profile's current QoS category, such as SCR (Sustained Cell Rate).

The type of CLP (cell loss priority) you choose causes certain fields in the Receive Parameters and Transmit Parameters areas to become dimmed. Only parameters that are valid for the type of CLP you choose can be edited.

Enter a value in the CLP field, which indicates the value in the ATM cell header that determines the probability of the network's dropping a cell when the network becomes congested.

Here are the valid choices and their editable parameters:

- **ABR**—pcr, mcr, cdvt
- **CBR**—pcr, cdvt
- **UBR-pcr**—mcr, cdvt
- **VBR-RT**—scr, pcr, mbs, cdvt
- **VBR-NRT**—scr, pcr, mbs, cdvt

Cells that have 0 in the CLP field have ensured priority and are unlikely to be dropped. Cells with 1 in the CLP field have best-effort priority. This means that they might be dropped during periods of congestion so that resources are free to handle ensured traffic.

— **PCR (Peak Cell Rate)**—The maximum transmission rate of cells before they are dropped. Do not select a PCR greater than 2050. Bear in mind that the profile must be coordinated with many other factors in the line, such as bandwidth capability. If you want more than one PVC, use a value much less than 2050.

— **SCR (Sustainable Cell Rate)**—The maximum ongoing traffic parameter that is allowed for connections in a traffic direction on an interface.

— **MCR (Minimum Cell Rate)**—The lowest acceptable transmission rate (specified in cells per second) for traffic received on the interface for this service category.

— **MBCS (Maximum Burst Cell Size)**—The maximum burst cell size permitted by cells of connections received on this interface before cells are dropped.

— **CDVT (Cell Delay Variation Tolerance)**—The cell delay variation estimated to be accommodated by cells of connections received on this interface.

You can also modify an existing ATM profile:

Step 1   Select the profile you want to use as a template from the profile list box on the left side of the window.

Step 2   Enter the type of the new profile in the Profile Type field.

Step 3   Enter a description of the new profile in the Profile Description field.

Step 4   Modify the parameters on the RxTx Parameters tab if necessary.

Step 5   Click Create Profile.

Step 6   Enter a name for the profile in the Prompt dialog box. When you create a profile in CDM, use a single word or a continuous expression to name the profile, and do not use spaces in the name. Your profile name should be compatible with the Cisco IOS Software CLI, which recognizes a space as the end of a profile name. For example, instead of entering **new profile name**, you should use the string **newprofilename**.

After finalizing your selections and creating as many ATM QoS profiles as you will have levels of service, you should save the ATM profile for later application.

ADSL Profiles

Bear in mind that DMT is merely the most common kind of ADSL (although there are other modulations of ADSL). ADSL profiles are created to apply to DMT interfaces. One ADSL profile can be applied to multiple DMT interfaces on a card, because all profiles are saved and stored in CDM.

After you create an ADSL profile, you can edit that profile only if it is not being used. If any connections are using that profile, you are not allowed to alter it. You can view and identify the connections that are using a certain profile by running a CEMF query against the profile name. Refer to the *Cisco Element Management Framework User Guide* for details about running a query. To view the ADSL Profiles window, select Cisco DSL Manager, Physical, Interface, ADSL, Open Profile. The ADSL Interface Profile window appears.

The ADSL Interface Profile window contains two areas—Profile Details and ADSL Parameters. If you are starting with an existing template, you can highlight the name of the profile you want to use as a template in the list box on the left side of the window.

Step 1 Click Create Profile whether you are starting with an existing template or not.

Step 2 Enter the name of the new profile in the Prompt dialog box, and then click OK. When you create a profile in CDM, use a single word or a continuous expression to name the profile, and do not use spaces in the name. Your profile name should be compatible with the Cisco IOS Software CLI, which recognizes a space as the end of a profile name. For example, instead of entering **new profile name**, you should use the string **newprofilename**.

Step 3 Enter the type of profile in the Profile Type field.

Step 4 Enter a description of the profile in the Description field.

Step 5 In the ADSL Parameters area, enter the appropriate information in the available Downstream and Upstream fields:

— In the Target Signal/Noise Margin (tenth dB) field, enter a value to set the noise margin that the modem must achieve with a BER of 10E–7 or better to successfully complete initialization.

If the noise margin is above this level, the modem should attempt to reduce its power output to optimize its operation. If the noise margin falls below this level, the modem attempts to increase its power output. If the increase is not possible, the modem attempts to reinitialize or shut down.

Configured allocation ratios of excess transmit bandwidth between fast and interleaved channels apply only when two-channel mode and RADSL are supported.

— In the Interleave Channel Delay (ms), enter the interleave delay setting for this channel.

Interleave delay applies only to the interleave channel. It defines the mapping, or relative spacing, between subsequent input bytes at the interleave input and the placement of the input bytes in the bit stream at the interleave output.

— In the Interleave Minimum Transmit Rate (bps) field, enter the value for the configured minimum transmit rate for interleave channels in bits per second.

— In the Interleave Maximum Transmit Rate (bps) field, enter the value for the configured maximum transmit rate for interleave channels in bits per second.

Step 6   When you have finalized your selections, save the ADSL profile. You can click the Save icon on the toolbar or select File, Save to save your changes.

Creating a DMT Profile

DMT profiles are applied to the DMT interfaces, which are individual ports on DMT line cards. DMT profiles are saved in CDM. After you create a DMT profile, you can edit it only if it is not being used. If any connections are using that profile, you are not allowed to alter it. You can view and identify the connections that are using a certain profile by running a CEMF query against the profile name. Refer to the *Cisco Element Management Framework User Guide* for details about running a query.

To create a DMT profile, follow these steps:

Step 1   Select Cisco DSL Manager, Physical, Interface, DMT, Profile. The DMT Interface Profile window appears. It contains only the Profile tab.

Step 2   Click Create Profile.

Step 3   Enter the name of the profile in the Prompt dialog box, and then click OK. When you create a profile in CDM, use a single word or a continuous expression to name the profile, and do not use spaces in the name. Your profile name should be compatible with the Cisco IOS Software CLI, which recognizes a space as the end of a profile name. For example, instead of entering **new profile name**, you should use the string **newprofilename**.

Step 4   In the Profile Type field, enter the type of profile you are creating (in this instance, a DMT interface profile).

Step 5   In the Profile Description field, enter a description for this profile. If you are copying a profile, use the horizontal and vertical scroll bars to view all the text in this field.

Step 6 Depending on the particular Cisco 6000 series platform and the version of CDM software, you may ignore the Bit Swap field. For instance, bit swapping is not applicable to the Cisco 6015 IP DSL Switch. You must consult your product's official documentation and the CDM version's release notes.

Step 7 In the Bit Swap Margin From (in dB) field, enter an appropriate value in the range of 1 to 9.

NOTE

The ATU-C marks a bin as a from bin if the bin margin falls below a specified target value and the difference between the margin and target exceeds a specified threshold value.

If you set this value too low, the ATU-C might frequently toggle the bit allocation on bins. If impulse noise is present, the frequent toggling of bit allocation can cause errors. If you set this value too high, the ATU-C might not identify an adequate number of bins from which it can swap bits. This situation decreases the ATU-C's ability to equalize the margin across all bins.

Step 8 In the Bit Swap Margin To (in dB) field, enter an appropriate value in the range of 1 to 9.

Step 9 In the Training Mode field, use the down arrow to select fast or standard training. This setting displays the mode that the downstream and upstream devices use when the devices are training against each other. One of two training modes can be used. The default training mode for ADSL modems is standard.

Step 10 In the Trellis Coding field, use the down arrow to select enable or disable to set whether trellis coding is used on the DMT line.

Step 11 In the Operating Mode field, use the down arrow to select which line-operating mode the ADSL line will use. An ADSL line uses of one of two operating modes—automatic or splitterless.

Step 12 In the Overhead Framing field, use the down arrow to set the negotiated overhead framing structure that the downstream and upstream devices use:

- 0 = Full Asynchronous. Full-overhead framing with asynchronous bit-to-modem timing (enabled synchronization control mechanism).

- 1 = Full Synchronous. Full-overhead framing that uses synchronous bit-to-modem timing, a disabled synchronization control mechanism.

- 2 = Reduced Separate Fast. Reduced-overhead framing that has separate fast and sync bytes. Bytes exist in fast and interleaved latency buffers (64 kbps framing overhead).

    — 3 = Reduced Merged Fast. Reduced overhead framing with merged fast and dsync byte, using either the fast or interleaved latency buffer (32 kbps framing overhead). This is the recommended setting. Additionally, G.992.2 (G.lite) line rates allow for only an overhead frame value of 3.

Step 13 In the Check Bytes (in bytes) field, use the down arrow to specify the initial number of FEC redundancy bytes that the downstream and upstream device frames transmit over the interleaved channel during the training sequence.

    The downstream device can fall back from this value, depending on the aggregate data rate achieved during training. The value of this object must be an integral multiple of the value displayed in the Codeword Size field. Valid choices include 0, 2, 4, 6, 8, 10, 12, 14, and 16.

Step 14 In the Codeword Size (in symbols) field, use the down arrow to select the number of symbols per codeword that the downstream and upstream messages use on an interleaved channel during the training sequence.

    The downstream can fall back from this value, based on the aggregate data rate achieved during training. Valid choices include 0, 1, 2, 4, 8, and 16.

Step 15 Click the Save icon or choose File, Save.

Applying a DMT Profile to a DMT Port

After creating a DMT profile, you can apply that profile to one or more DMT interfaces, the ports on the DMT line cards.

To view the DMT Interface Configuration window, follow these steps:

Step 1 Select Cisco DSL Manager, Physical, Interface, DMT, Config. The DMT Interface Configuration window appears.

Step 2 From the list boxes on the left, select the desired Chassis, Module, and DMT Interface to which you want to apply the DMT Profile. Any current profiles applied to the selected DMT interface appear in the tab on the right.

Step 3 Select Edit, Apply Profile. A list of DMT profiles appears. Click the named DMT profile to apply. After the profile has been applied, a status line appears briefly in the lower-left corner of the window. It contains information about whether the profile was applied successfully. The information for the selected profile appears in the tab on the right.

Applying an ADSL Profile to an ADSL Interface

After you have created an ADSL profile, you can apply it to one or more ADSL (DMT) interfaces.

When you deploy an 8xDMT line card, the software automatically creates eight DMT interfaces. To be precise, the DMT interfaces are actually ATM over ADSL over DMT interfaces. These three technologies are all supported in one interface.

Step 1   On the left side of the Map Viewer window, within the CDM Manager view, right-click a DMT line card to access the object menu.

Step 2   Choose Cisco DSL Manager, Physical, Interface, ADSL, Configuration from the object menu. The ADSL Interface Configuration window opens. The chassis, card, and ADSL (DMT) interface you selected are highlighted in the list boxes on the left side of the window. Any current ADSL profiles that are applied to the selected DMT interface appear on the right side of the window.

Step 3   Choose Edit, Apply Profile to display a list of ADSL profiles.

Step 4   Click the named ADSL profile you want to apply.

Step 5   Click the Save icon or choose File, Save.

PVC and SPVC Configuration

A *PVC* is a permanent logical connection that must be configured manually from source to destination. You can start in either direction, because PVCs are bidirectional, but the preferred method is to configure the PVC from the DSL line card port to the ATM trunk port. In the CDM context, you create the PVC and then apply an ATM traffic descriptor to the PVC.

Deploying a PVC creates a cross-connection within one device. Deploying an SPVC creates a connection between the incoming port on one device and the outgoing port on another device.

After you create a PVC or SPVC, you can view it only within the Component Managed view. It does not appear in the CDM Manager view.

To view the Deployment Wizard window, select Deployment, Generic Component Objects, Logical, ATM Connections, PVC. The Deployment Wizard appears. For this step, you can start from any object's pop-up menu, but be sure to right-click something other than a DMT port.

A subscriber connection is created through a PVC or soft-PVC (SPVC) on the network device. When a PVC is created, two VCLs are created automatically in CDM. One VCL represents the source or incoming port, and the other VCL represents the destination or outgoing port. You will see shortly how to manage VCLs.

Consider the following guidelines before you configure ATM virtual channels:

- You can provision more than one PVC for each subscriber.

- Each PVC contains both a network-side and a subscriber-side virtual channel connection (VCC).

- Each VCC has both a VPI and a VCI.

- For permanent virtual paths (PVPs, called virtual path channels [VPCs] in CDM software), you must read the release documentation for the CDM version. For instance, VPC switching is not supported in CDM version 3.3(3).

- If you enter VCI numbers, you must also enter VPI numbers. That is, you must specify complete information without assuming that the system will carry over the previous VPI.

The following steps create PVCs and SPVCs that have endpoints that are managed by CEMF. If you choose to deploy an SPVC with a CEMF endpoint, there is only one difference—an extra screen. Otherwise, all windows are the same for both PVCs and SPVCs. To create and deploy an SPVC that has a non-CEMF endpoint, see the appropriate CDM documentation on the topic of deploying an SPVC with a non-CEMF endpoint.

Step 1 On the left side of the Map Viewer window, within the CDM Manager view, right-click the line card for which you want to create a PVC or SPVC.

Step 2 Choose Deployment, Deploy ATM Connection, PVC (or SPVC) from the object menu. Regardless of the type of connection, the first of a series of Deployment Wizard–Object Parameters windows opens.

Step 3 Enter the number of PVCs or SPVCs you want to create, and then click Forward. The second Deployment Wizard–Object Parameters window opens.

If you chose to deploy an SPVC from the object menu in Step 2, the Deployment Wizard–Templates window opens. It has only two options. You can select Template for CiscoSPVC with CEMF end point or Template for CiscoSPVC with non-CEMF end point. Make the appropriate selection, and then click Forward.

Note that the remaining instructions apply to both creating PVCs and creating SPVCs with a CEMF endpoint.

Step 4 Enter the PVC or SPVC name, making sure that you have specified a unique name.

Step 5 In the second field in this window, you can enter your subscriber ID if you want to set one, or you can leave the value undefined. Click Forward. The Deployment Wizard–Views window opens.

Step 6 Click Forward.

Step 7 Click the first Select button to specify an incoming port for the PVC or SPVC. The Object Selector window opens.

Step 8 Select a DMT interface for the incoming port:

    (a) Click your selection to highlight it.

    (b) Click Apply. Your selection populates both fields. However, you must use a different selection for your outgoing port.

Step 9 Click the second Select button to specify an outgoing port.

Step 10 If you are creating a PVC, select a DS3 interface on the NI-2 management card for the outgoing port.

Step 11 If you are creating an SPVC, select the destination ATM endpoint for the connection. (It was at this point in the CLI Cisco IOS Software configuration that you identified and entered the end device's lengthy ATM address.)

Step 12 Click your selection to highlight it.

Step 13 Click Apply.

Step 14 Make sure that both your selections are appropriate. If you do not select the correct ports, your PVC or SPVC deployment will fail, leading to frustration and possible anguish.

Step 15 Click Forward. The Deployment Wizard–Summary window opens, requiring you to choose either Cancel or Finish. When you create a PVC or SPVC, the software also creates two VCLs that represent the two incoming and outgoing endpoints. If you are creating an SPVC with a non-CDM endpoint, the software creates only one VCL.

You can configure and view the status and performance of these VCLs, as explained in the section "VCL Management."

Step 16 Click Finish to complete the deployment. You can use the Map Viewer to see the designated connection.

Deploying a PVC or SPVC does not create the connection on the device. To create the actual connection, you must apply an ATM QoS profile (as discussed in the following section).

Applying an ATM QoS Profile

Now that you have created a PVC or SPVC, you can apply the ATM QoS profile to it and activate the connection.

Follow these steps:

Step 1 Select Cisco DSL Manager, Logical, Connection, QoS Management. The ATM Connection QoS Configuration window appears.

Step 2 Select the appropriate chassis, module, interface, and connection (PVC or SPVC) from the list box on the left. Any current ATM QoS profiles applied to the selected PVC or SPVC appear in the tabs on the right.

Step 3 Select Edit, Apply Profile. A list of ATM QoS profiles appears.

Step 4 Select the named ATM QoS profile to be applied. After you apply the profile, a status line appears briefly in the lower-left corner, specifying whether the profile was applied successfully. The information for the selected new profile appears in blue in the tabs on the right. (The blue changes to black after you save the changes.)

Activating the Cross-Connection in CDM

To start activating the PVC or SPVC, follow these steps:

Step 1 Select Cisco DSL Manager, Logical, Connection, Cross Connection Management. The ATM Connection Management window opens.

Step 2 On the left side of the window, select the related chassis, card, interface, and connection you want to create.

Step 3 On the Configuration tab, enter the desired information in these fields:

— **Subscriber ID**—Enter the subscriber ID.

— **Source VPI**—For Cisco CPEs, this value can be 1. For SPVCs and non-Cisco CPEs, this value can be 32 to 4000.

— **Source VCI**—For Cisco CPEs, this value can be 0 to 3. For SPVCs and non-Cisco CPEs, this can be 1 to 1000.

— **Auto Allocation**—The source VPI and source VCI values are provided automatically if you select the Auto Allocation button on each side (Source and Destination).

Clicking the Source Port button displays the ATM Configuration window for the selected PVC or SPVC.

Clicking the Source VCL button displays the VCL configuration window for the selected PVC or SPVC. These buttons allow you to view or perform more-detailed configuration on both VCLs.

— **Destination VPI**—Specifies the VPI and VCI values of the destination VCL. If you set the VPI value to 0 or 2 to 27, VCI can be 0 to 399. If you set the VPI value to 1, VCI can be 1 to 1599.

— **Destination VCI**—The source VPI and source VCI values are provided automatically if you select the Auto Allocation button on each side (Source and Destination).

— **NSAP Address**—The ATM address you must provide if you are configuring an SPVC. It is applicable only to SPVCs, not PVCs. When your configuration includes a subtended chassis, you must provide the NSAP address for the connection's destination ATM endpoint.

Clicking the Destination Port button displays the ATM Configuration window for the selected PVC or SPVC. Clicking the Destination VCL button displays the VCL Configuration window for the selected PVC or SPVC.

Together, these buttons allow you to view and perform more detailed configuration on both VCLs.

Step 4 Click the Connect button in the Action area.

You are prompted to confirm this action. The Connect button creates the subscriber connection on the device. The connection object changes to the Normal state.

This completes the minimum mandatory procedures to create and activate a cross-connecting PVC or SPVC on the Cisco 6000 series of IP DSL Switches. There might be subtle but important differences between the various platforms and between various versions of software. You should become aware of limitations and additional functionality by researching the appropriate release documentation.

For optimal management of the IP DSL Switches, you should know and use the following information about VCL management and reporting.

VCL Configuration and Management

When a PVC is created, two VCLs are created automatically. One represents the source or incoming port, and the other represents the destination or outgoing port. You can use the VCL Management windows to view and or modify the configuration, performance, and status of VCLs.

VCL Management

To open the VCL Management window, proceed as follows:

Step 1 In the Map Viewer window, within the Component Managed view, right-click the interface that has a PVC already created and for which you want to configure a VCL.

Step 2 Choose Cisco DSL Manager, Connection, VCL Management, Config from the object menu. The ATM VCL Configuration window opens.

Step 3 Select a VCL from the list box on the left side of the window. The Configuration tab contains four areas:

— VPI/VCI (Read Only) (in CDM version 3.4, this is called VCL parameters)

— Traffic Information

— Encapsulation Parameters

— OAM Information

Step 4 The VPI/VCI (Read Only) area contains values for either the source or destination VCL, depending on the type of VCL you select.

Step 5 In the Traffic Information area, enter the following information:

— In the UPC (Usage Parameter Control) Mode field, use the down arrow to select pass, tag, drop, or local shaping for the Usage Parameter Control Mode on the established connection.

— In the EPD (Early Packet Discard) Mode field, use the down arrow to select enable or disable to enable or disable early packet discard at this specific connection.

Step 6 In the Encapsulation Parameters area, determine whether to set the following fields:

— If the Encapsulation Flag is set to aal5Mux, use the down arrow in the Encapsulation Protocol field to specify the protocol for the terminating VC. If the Encapsulation Flag is not set to this value, you do not need to set this parameter.

Valid choices include every known networking protocol, such as IP, Novell NetWare IPX, AppleTalk, and so on.

— In the Encapsulation Flag field, use the down arrow to specify the encapsulation type for the terminating VC. Valid choices include the following parameters:

  • **aal5Snap**—AAL5 subnetwork access protocol

  • **aal5Nlpid**—AAL5 network layer protocol ID

  • **aal5FrNlpid**—AAL5 Frame Relay network layer protocol ID (not used)

- **aal5Mux**—AAL5 multiprotocol over ATM

- **aal34Smds**—AAL3/4 switched multimegabit data service

- **aalQsAal**—Signaling AAL

- **aal5Ilmi**—AAL5 integrated local management interface

- **aal5Lane**—AAL5 LAN emulation

- **aal5Pnni**—AAL5 Private Network-to-Network Interface

ATM Adaptation Layer 5 (AAL5) segments and reassembles data units up to 65,535 octets into ATM cell payloads. AAL5 is suited for variable bit rate traffic such as TCP/IP and signaling.

— If the Encapsulation flag field is set to aal5Lane, use the down arrow to set the AAL User Type parameter. If the Encapsulation Flag is not set to aal5Lane, you do not need to set this parameter. Valid options include the following parameters:

- **other**

- **boxConfigure**—Shared client/server end of the Configure VCC

- **busForward**—BUS end of the Data Forward VCC

- **busSend**—BUS end of the Data Send VCC

- **clientConfigure**—LE (LAN Emulation) client end of the Configure Direct VCC

- **clientData**—One end of the Data Direct VCC

- **clientDirect**—LE client end of the Control Direct VCC

- **clientDistribute**—LE client end of the Control Distribute VCC

- **clientForward**—LE client end of the Multicast Forward VCC

- **clientSend**—LE client end of the Multicast Send VCC

- **configure**—Config server end of any Configure VCC

- **serverConfigure**—LE server end of the Configure VCC

- **serverDirect**—LE server end of the Control Direct VCC

- **serverDistribute**—LE server end of the Control Distribute VCC

Step 7 In the OAM (operation, administration, and maintenance) Information area, enter the following information:

— In the AIS (Alarm Indication Signal) Mode field, use the down arrow to select enable or disable. This field enables or disables the Enable Alarm Indication Signal OAM cell generation if the interface fails when cross-connecting the virtual channel.

— In the RDI (Remote Defect Indication) Mode field, use the down arrow to select enable or disable. This field enables or disables the Enable Remote Defect Indication OAM cell generation. In ATM, if the physical layer detects loss of signal or cell synchronization, RDI cells report a VPC/VCC failure. RDI cells are sent upstream by a VPC/VCC end point to notify the source VPC/VCC end point of the downstream failure.

Step 8 Click Save on the toolbar to save your configuration settings. The configuration information for the selected VCL is displayed on the right side of the window. You can view or modify this information. The Layer 3 Configuration tab is not used in CDM version 3.4.

Viewing ATM VCL Performance

You can start performance logging for a selected connection to gather performance data for that connection in the VCL Performance window. You can view this performance data by using the Performance menu or in the Performance Manager window.

Complete the following steps to view ATM VCL performance:

Step 1 On the left side of the Map Viewer window, within the Component Managed view, right-click the chassis object whose VCL performance you want to monitor.

Step 2 Choose Cisco DSL Manager, Connection, VCL Management, Performance from the object menu. The ATM VCL Performance window opens to the Performance tab.

In the VCL Performance Window, you can start Performance Logging for a selected connection. Performance Logging gathers performance data for that connection. The performance data can be viewed using either the Performance menus or Performance Manager.

The Bandwidth Utilization panel in the Performance tab has the following parameters:

- **Receive**—Indicates the amount of bandwidth used on receiving information on the connection.

- **Transmit**—Indicates the amount of bandwidth used on transmitting information on the connection.

The VC Statistics panel in the Performance tab has the following parameters:

- **In Cells**—Indicates the total number of cells received on this VCL.

- **Out Cells**—Indicates the total number of cells transmitted on this VCL.

- **UPC Violations**—Indicates the total number of UPC violations on this VCL.

- **Packets In**—Indicates the total number of packets received on this VCL.

- **Cell Drops**—Indicates the total number of cell drops on this VCL.

- **Packet Drops**—Indicates the total number of packet drops on this VCL.

- **Performance Monitoring**—The Start button is the only one on this panel. You can click it to begin Performance Polling on the selected VCL. Performance Polling allows performance data to be collected on the object and viewed in the Performance windows or the Performance Manager.

Viewing VCL Status

To view VCL status, follow these steps:

Step 1 On the left side of the Map Viewer window, within the Component Managed view, right-click the line card interface whose VCL status you want to view.

Step 2 Choose Cisco DSL Manager, Connection, VCL Management, Status from the object menu. The ATM VCL Status window opens.

Step 3 The line card you selected is highlighted on the left. Or, from the list box on the left side of the window, select a VCL. The status information for the selected VCL is displayed on the right.

The Status tab has four areas:

- VCL Status

- Characteristics

- Soft PVC Details

- OAM Details

Following are descriptions of the fields in the VCL Status panel:

- **Operational State**—Displays the status of the VCL connection.

- **Last Change**—Displays the time elapsed since the last status change.

- **Install Time**—Displays the time elapsed since the last installation.

The Characteristics panel includes the following fields:

- **Span Type**—Displays the VCL span type.

- **Connection Type**—Displays the virtual connection configuration type.

- **Cast Type**—Displays the virtual connection cast type.

The fields in the Soft PVC Details panel are as follows:

- **Location**—Indicates the calling or called side of a SPVC.

- **Number of Attempts**—Indicates the number of attempts made to install this SPVC.

- **Last Release Cause**—Indicates the cause of the last connection release.

The OAM Details panel has these fields:

- **Segment Loopback**—Indicates whether the segment loopback is enabled or disabled on the virtual channel selected.

- **Loopback Interval**—Indicates the frequency with which the OAM loopback cells are generated.

This completes the descriptions of VCL configuration and management. Rather than configuring new sets of parameters such as profiles, another way of configuring subscribers is to apply already-defined parameters. This is described in the next section.

Uploading Profiles and Connections (Optional)

You can use Telnet to upload the following connections and profiles that are already configured on a device and that need to be brought into the CDM:

- ATM connections and ATM QoS profiles

- ADSL profiles and DMT profiles

Before you upload any connections or profiles, be sure that the Telnet passwords are configured in the CDM.

Verify Telnet passwords by right-clicking a chassis object and choosing Cisco DSL Manager, Physical, Chassis, Management Information. The Management Information window appears.

The next section describes how to upload ATM connections and profiles if you want to apply existing parameters to different subscribers.

Uploading ATM Connections and ATM QoS Profiles

When existing ATM connections and ATM QoS profiles are uploaded, any existing ATM connections are discovered and placed into the Normal state so that management of these connections begins automatically. When these connections/profiles are uploaded, they can be viewed and adjusted in CDM, as follows:

Step 1   Right-click a chassis object.

Step 2   Choose Cisco DSL Manager, Logical, Connection, Upload Management. The ATM Connection Upload window appears.

Uploaded ATM connections and ATM QoS profiles are named according to the following format:

- **ATM connections**—PVC–*index of incoming port.VPI value.VCI value.index of outgoing port.VPI value.VCI value*

- **ATM QoS profiles**—QoSProfile_*assigned number*

The next section discusses how to upload existing ADSL and DMT profiles to apply to new or changed subscribers.

Uploading ADSL and DMT Profiles

When existing ADSL and DMT profiles are uploaded, any nonexisting ADSL and DMT profiles are created in CDM. You can view and edit uploaded profiles in CDM by following these steps:

Step 1   Right-click a chassis object.

Step 2   Choose Cisco DSL Manager, Physical, Interface, ADSL (or DMT), Upload. The ADSL or DMT Profile Upload window appears.

Uploaded ADSL and DMT profiles are named according to the following format:

- **ADSL profiles**—ADSLManager_*assigned number*

- **DMT profiles**—DMTManager_*assigned number*

Fault Management

The Cisco 6*xxx* supports a number of alarm sources, including SNMP traps and SNMP alarm tables from Cisco 6*xxx* MIBs. Additionally, a number of event derivations can be made by the Cisco 6*xxx* CDM.

All alarm sources of the Cisco 6*xxx* CDM are displayed in windows, providing an integrated fault management solution. Fault management in CDM has two components, Viewing Alarms and Viewing Status. This section outlines the sources of Cisco 6*xxx* CDM alarm information and shows how these sources are represented within the Cisco 6*xxx* CDM and CEMF applications.

Following are the policies underlying CDM fault management of IP DSL Switches:

- Polling is the active interrogation of network equipment for connectivity.

- Traps are the unsolicited SNMP messages from the hardware. CDM processes two types of traps: Assert and Clear. All traps have a pair relationship, meaning that for each Assert alarm there is a corresponding Clear alarm. For reference, CEMF uses the Cisco-Entity-Alarm MIB.

  Events are raised in CDM by a polling failure or by a trap received, and a designated severity is assigned to the event. An event propagates up through the maps, allowing the monitoring of many network objects by viewing from a high-level map.

Alarms and Events

Event details are viewed through the Event Browser. When you have corrected the fault, or manually cleared it in CDM, the event clears automatically in CDM.

There are at least four ways to view CDM events. The most obvious is to click the Events icon in the CEMF Launchpad. This lets you view all alarms on all objects and filter using the Query Editor window, which opens automatically. The Query Editor window is a filter for selected display.

Here is how to use the Query Editor:

Step 1   Set your query criteria in the window. The Query Editor contains many tabs that you can use to define and refine your alarm search criteria. You can use the >> or << arrows to move the available values to the right side of the tab to select them.

Step 2   Click Activate after you specify the values for the alarms you want to view. The Event Browser displays all alarms that match your query criteria.

You can also view CDM events using either of the following methods:

- Right-click an object on the relevant chassis in the MapViewer window, and then select the Tools, Open Event Browser option.

- Right-click an object in an object list, and then select the Tools, Open Event Browser option.

The Event Browser window appears no matter which option you choose.

You can also view a specific alarm or event as follows:

Step 1   In the Map Viewer window, right-click the object (such as a DMT card) that generated the alarm.

Step 2   Choose Tools, Open Event Browser from the object menu.

Only the alarm for the object you selected appears. You can open the Query Editor from this window to modify your criteria.

You can get more-specific information about events that appear in the Event Browser window by opening the Full Event Description window. Follow these steps:

Step 1 In the Event Browser window, right-click the event whose details you want to view to open the object menu.

Step 2 Choose Event Information, Event Information dialog from the object menu.

The Full Event Description window fields are as follows:

— **Object name**—Displays the name of the CEMF managed object for the event.

— **Severity**—Displays the severity of the reported event.

— **Time and Date**—Displays the time and date that the system reports the event.

— **Event State**—Indicates whether the event is active or cleared. When the event is cleared, the Clearing Method, User Responsible for Clearing, and Clearing Time and Date fields become active. If the event is not cleared, the Event State field displays Active, and the other fields are dimmed. You cannot modify the displayed information.

— **Management Domain**—Indicates the management domain that is the source of the event.

— **Communication Domain**—Indicates the communications domain that is the source of the event.

— **Event Description**—Provides a summary description of the reported event.

— **Acknowledgement User**—An operator who acknowledges the alarm can use this field to enter his or her name. When other operators view that alarm, they can see that this alarm has been acknowledged and by whom.

— **Acknowledgement Time and Date**—An operator who acknowledges the alarm can use this field to enter the time and date of acknowledgement. When other users view that alarm, they can see when this alarm was acknowledged.

— **Acknowledgement Comment**—An operator who acknowledges the alarm can use this field to enter comments. Other users can then see any comments about this alarm.

— **Clearing Method**—Identifies when the network or user cleared the event.

— **User Responsible for Clearing**—Displays the name of the user responsible for clearing the event.

— **Clearing Time and Date**—Indicates the time and date the event was cleared.

— **Clearing Reason**—Identifies the information that was entered in the Events Clearing window, which is completed when the Clear indicator is selected.

Step 3   When the system has cleared an event, you can view the method used to clear it by clicking Clearing Event.

Step 4   Click Close to exit the Full Event Description window.

Step 5   Click Close to exit the Event Browser window.

You should refer to the Cisco documentation for detailed explanations of the many alarms that can be raised, because these are dependent on the precise platform (Cisco IP DSL Switch model) and version of CDM.

Another type of information is detailed in ATM interface faults, providing information about ATM trunks. To view ATM interface faults, do the following:

Step 1   In the Map Viewer window, in the Component Managed view, right-click the chassis object for which you want to view ATM interface faults to access the object menu.

Step 2   Choose Cisco DSL Manager, Interface, Faults, ATM. The ATM Interface Faults window opens. The Fault tab consists of three panels: General Errors, SONET Frame errors, and DS1/E1/DS-3/E3 errors. The latter two panels currently are inoperative for the Cisco 6000 series of IP DSL Switches. You should research your CDM version and specific platform documentation to determine if these are available.

The General Errors panel displays the following error information:

- Transmitted Message Errors displays the number of incorrect messages transmitted on the interface.

- The Incorrect Messages counter reflects any sort of incorrect information in a message.

- Detected Message Errors displays the number of incorrect messages detected on the interface.

- SSCOP Errored PDUs displays the sum of the following errors: Invalid PDUs are defined in SSCOP and consist of PDUs with incorrect length (MAA-ERROR code U), undefined PDU type code, or not 32-bit aligned. PDUs that result in MAA error codes are discarded.

Status

You can view status summaries for interfaces, the chassis itself, and any module on the chassis. These detailed status windows are as follows:

- **ADSL Interface Status**—ADSL line and channel status.

- **DS3 Interface Status**

- **ATM Interface Status**—ATM transmit, receive, physical layer, and port status.

- **DMT Interface Status**—DMT line and channel status.

- **SONET Interface Status**—SONET medium, section, line, path, and virtual tributary status information, all of which are equivalent to viewing the OC-3 interface information.

- **Chassis Status**—Generic status details such as availability, LED status, facility alarm status, power supply details, temperature details, and fan details for any selected chassis.

- **Module Status**—Module details, such as module availability for any selected module.

The instructions presented in this section are for a subset of all the possibilities—the most common status checks—but these are certainly not all that are available in CDM. You should investigate status reporting for the interfaces and types of data that serve you best, referring to the CDM documentation that came with your software, or going online.

There are two types of status icons—the black box and the traffic light:

- Black boxes with slashed circles indicate no values returned for that field.

- Traffic light icons can represent the following three values:

    - Green if the status is OK

    - Yellow if the status is warning

    - Red if the status is an error state

ATM Interface Status

The ATM Interface Status window displays status information for a selected ATM interface. To open the ATM Interface Status window, complete the following steps:

Step 1   On the left side of the Map Viewer window, within the CDM Manager view, right-click either an NI-2 card or a line card whose ATM status you want to view.

Step 2   Choose Cisco DSL Manager, Physical, Interface, ATM, Status. The ATM Interface Status window opens. (Note that this window has a slightly different appearance in CDM 3.4 than what is described here.)

The ATM Interface Status window has one tab, the Status tab. The Status tab has five panels:

- ATM Transmit Status
- ATM Receive Status
- Physical Layer Status
- ATM Port Status
- Action

Here are the details of the fields in the ATM Transmit Status window:

- **Bit Rate Type**—The service category to which the row applies. This can be one of the following values:

    - **cbr**—Constant bit rate

    - **vbrRt**—Real-time variable bit rate

    - **vbrNrt**—Nonreal-time variable bit rate

    - **abr**—Available bit rate

    - **ubr**—Unspecified bit rate

- **Available Cell Rate**—Indicates the available cell rate, specified in cells per second, for traffic that is sent out through the interface for this service category. This value is the bandwidth available for connections. For guaranteed service categories, this value decreases as a result of connection setup and increases as a result of connection release. For nonguaranteed service categories, this value does not change as a result of connection setup and connection release.

- **Allocated Cell Rate**—Indicates the allocated cell rate, specified in cells per second, for traffic that is sent out the interface for this service category. This value is the bandwidth that is allocated to connections. For guaranteed service categories, this value increases as a result of connection setup and decreases as a result of connection release. For nonguaranteed service categories, this value is always 0.

- **LED Status**—Indicates the transmit LED color for the selected port.

- **Maximum Cell Transfer Delay**—Indicates the maximum cell transfer delay estimated to be experienced by cells of connections transmitted out this interface or this service category. This estimate does not distinguish between cell loss priority (CLP) 0 and CLP1 cells. This object is valid for service categories cbr and vbr-nrt. For other service categories, this object is not defined.

- **Peak To Peak Cell Delay Variation**—Indicates the estimated peak-to-peak cell delay variation for cells of this service category that are transmitted out of this interface. This estimate does not distinguish between CLP0 and CLP1 cells. This object is valid for service categories cbr and vbr-nrt. For other service categories, the object is not defined.

- **Cell Loss Ratio**—Indicates the estimated cell loss ratio for cells of this service category that are transmitted out of this interface. This ratio value is an estimate for CLP0 cells. The units of this object are negative powers of 10 (so an object value of –8 means –10E8). This object is valid for service categories cbr, vbr-rt, and vbr-nrt. For other service categories, the object is not defined.

- **Available Cell Rate**—Indicates the available cell rate, specified in cells per second, for traffic that is received by the interface for this service category. This value is the bandwidth that is available for connections. For guaranteed service categories, this value decreases as a result of connection setup and increases as a result of connection release. For non-guaranteed service categories, this value does not change as a result of connection setup and connection release.

- **Allocated Cell Rate**—Indicates the allocated cell rate, specified in cells per second, for traffic that is received by the interface for this service category. This value is the bandwidth allocated to connections. For guaranteed service categories, this value increases as a result of connection setup and decreases as a result of connection release. For nonguaranteed service categories, this value is always 0.

- **LED Status**—Indicates the receive LED color for the selected port.

- **Physical Interface Status**—Indicates the status of the physical interface. The value of this object is valid only when the interface of Admin Status has the value up. Some of the enumerated values are specific to a particular physical layer. Values displayed are as follows:

  - **normal**
  - **los**—Loss of service
  - **lof**—Loss of frames
  - **loc**—Loss of cell delineation
  - **ais**—Alarm indication signal
  - **yellowLine**
  - **yellowPath**
  - **lop**—Loss of pointer
  - **idle**
  - **yellowAlarm**
  - **plcpLOF**—Physical layer convergence procedure loss of frame
  - **plcpYellow**—Physical layer convergence procedure warning
  - **maFERF**—Far-end receive failure

- — **pathAis**—Path alarm indication signal

- — **ocd**—Over current detector

- **Clock Source Status**—Indicates the network clock source status of this interface:

  - — **notSelected**—Indicates that this interface is not selected as the network clock source.

  - — **selected**—Indicates that this interface is selected as the network clock source.

- **Physical Port Type**—Indicates the physical layer medium on the port. The type is one of the following port types:

  - — other

  - — cpu

  - — Ethernet

  - — DS3

  - — E3

  - — OC-3

  - — OC-12

- **Number of VPCs**—The number of VPCs (PVCs and SVCs) that are configured for use at this ATM interface. At the ATM UNI, the configured number of VPCs (PVCs and SVCs) can range from 0 to 256 only.

- **Number of VCCs**—The number of VCCs (PVCs and SVCs) that are configured for the ATM interface.

- **Number of PVCs**—The number of PVCs at this interface.

- **Number of PVPs**—The number of permanent virtual paths at this interface.

- **Number of PCs**—The number of permanent connections (virtual channels or virtual paths) of this service category that are currently allocated to the interface.

- **Number of SCs**—The number of signaled connections (virtual channels or virtual paths) of this service category that are currently allocated to the interface.

- **Total Connections**—The number of existing connections at this interface.

- **Admin Address**—(This is not used in CDM 3.3.x.) The address that is assigned for administrative purposes, such as an address that is associated with the service provider side of a public network UNI. If the interface has no assigned administrative address, or if the address used for administrative purposes is the same as that used for ifPhysAddress, the Admin Address is an octet string of 0 length.

- **ATM Address Type**—The type of primary ATM address that is configured for use at the ATM interface.

- **NSAP Address**—Self-explanatory.

- **Configured VP Interface**—The number of configured VP interfaces at this physical interface.

- **SVC Minimum VCI**—The minimum value in the range of values from which VCIs are assigned to new SVCs. As this value increases, the number of VCIs that are available for PVCs increases. This value applies to each VPI of the physical interface and each logical port.

- **Active SVPs**—The number of active switched virtual paths at this interface.

- **Active SVCs**—The number of active switched virtual connections at this interface.

- **Show Connections button**—CDM issues a query to identify the connections that are currently configured for the selected interface. An action log opens that lists all connections that CDM found on the selected interface.

IMA Group Status

The IMA Group Status window displays the status data for IMA groups. The IMA Link Status window displays status information about the IMA links. These windows are described in the following sections.

Complete the following steps to open the IMA Group Status window and view the status of the IMA group settings:

Step 1 On the left side of the Map Viewer window, from within the IMA hierarchy view, right-click the IMA group whose status you want CDM to display.

Step 2 Choose Cisco DSL Manager, Physical, Interface, IMA Group, Status from the object menu. The IMA Group Status window opens.

This window contains the following areas:

- IMA ID

- IMA Links

- Operational Status

- Transmit/Receive Status

- IMA Group Details

- ICP—Intelligent Call Processing

The fields in the IMA Group Status window are as follows:

- **Group ifindex**—Displays the interface index for the IMA group.

- **Far-End IMA ID**—Specifies the far-end IMA group ID.

- **Least Delay Link Ifindex**—Specifies the interface index of the link that is configured in the IMA group and that has the smallest link propagation delay. The distinguished value of 0 may be used if no link has been configured in the IMA group or if the link with the smallest link propagation delay has not yet been determined.

- **Latest Max Differential Delay**—Displays the latest maximum differential delay (in milliseconds) that the network observes between the links that have the least and most link propagation delay among the receive links that are currently configured in the IMA group.

- **Near-End State**—Displays the current state of the near-end transmit link.

- **Far-End State**—Displays the current state of the far-end transmit link.

- **Last Change**—Displays the time of day that the IMA group last changed operational state (that is, the value of the imaNeGroupState variable changed).

- **Failure Status**—Displays the local failure status of a link belonging to an IMA group.

- **Far-End Clock Mode**—Displays the transmit clocking mode that the far-end IMA group is using.

- **Available Cell Rate in Active Links**—Displays in two columns—Transmit and Receive—the current cell rate (truncated value in cells per second) that this IMA group provides in the transmit or receive direction, considering all the transmit links in the Active state.

- **No. of Configured Links**—Displays in two columns—Transmit and Receive—the number of links that are configured to transmit or receive in this IMA group.

- **No. of Active Links**—Displays in two columns—Transmit and Receive—the number of links that are configured to transmit or receive and that are currently active in this IMA group.

- **Timing Reference Link Ifindex**—Displays in two columns—Transmit and Receive—the following values:

  — The interface index of the transmit timing reference link to be used by the near end for IMA data cell clock recovery from the ATM layer. The distinguished value of 0 may be used if no link has been configured in the IMA group or if the transmit timing reference link has not yet been selected.

  — The interface index of the receive timing reference link to be used by the near end for IMA data cell clock recovery toward the ATM layer. The distinguished value of 0 may be used if no link has been configured in the IMA group or if the receive timing reference link has not yet been detected.

- **Symmetry**—You can change this value only when the imaGroupRowStatus is active to allow the far end to recover from its Config-Aborted state without having to force the near-end Group State machine to go to the Not Configured state. Changing this value after group startup has completed causes a restart of the IMA group.

- **Transmit IMA ID**—You can establish or change this value only at IMA group startup. To change or modify this value, you must first set imaGroupRowStatus to notInService.

- **Alpha Value**—This value indicates the alpha value that CDM uses to specify the number of consecutive invalid ICP1 cells to be detected before moving to the IMA HUNT state from the IMA SYNC state.

- **Beta Value**—This value indicates the beta value that CDM uses to specify the number of consecutive errored ICP cells to be detected before moving to the IMA HUNT state from the IMA SYNC state.

- **Gamma Value**—This value indicates the gamma value that CDM uses to specify the number of consecutive valid ICP cells to be detected before moving to the IMA SYNC state from the IMA PRESYNC state.

IMA Link Status

Follow these steps to open the IMA Link Status window and view the status of the IMA group settings:

Step 1 On the left side of the Map Viewer window, from within the IMA hierarchy view, right-click the IMA link whose status you want CDM to display.

Step 2 Choose Cisco DSL Manager, Physical, Interface, IMA Link, Status from the object menu. The IMA Link Status window opens.

This window contains the following areas:

- IMA Group

- IMA Link—Transmit and Receive

    - The fields in the IMA Link Status window are as follows:

      - **IMA Group Index**—Specifies a unique value for the IMA group index.

      - **Transmit Link ID**—Specifies a unique ID for the transmit link.

      - **Receive Link ID**—Specifies a unique ID for the receive link.

      - **Near-End State**—Displays the current operational state of the near-end IMA group state machine.

- **Far-End State**—Displays the current operational state of the far-end IMA group state machine.

- **Near-End Failure Status**—Displays the current link failure status of the near-end receive link.

- **Far-End Failure Status**—Displays the current link failure status of the far-end receive link as reported via ICP cells.

SONET Interface Status Window

The SONET Interface Status window displays information for deployed SONET interfaces. This window has five tabs:

- Medium

- Section

- Line

- Path

- Virtual Tributary (not used at this time)

Follow these steps to view the SONET interface status:

Step 1   On the left side of the Map Viewer window, within the CDM Manager view, right-click the NI-2 card whose SONET status you want to view.

Step 2   Choose Cisco DSL Manager, Physical, Interface, SONET, Status. The SONET Interface Status window opens to the Medium tab.

The SONET Interface Status window contains the following tabs:

- Medium

- Section

- Line

- Path

- Virtual Tributary

These tabs are described in the following sections.

The chassis, card, and SONET interface you selected are highlighted in the list boxes on the left side of the window. The status information for the selected SONET interface appears on the right.

Medium Tab

The Medium tab provides information on the physical medium. The fields on this tab are as follows:

- **Type**—Indicates whether SONET is operating over the interface.

- **Line Coding**—This variable describes the line coding for this interface from one of the following parameters:

    — **sonet**

    — **sdh**—Synchronous Digital Hierarchy

    — **sonetMediumOther**

    — **sonetMediumB3ZS**—Bipolar with 3-Zero Substitution

    — **sonetMediumCMI**

    — **sonetMediumNRZ**—Nonreturn to Zero

    — **sonetMediumRZ**—Return to Zero

    The B3ZS and CMI parameters are used for electrical SONET/SDH signals (STS-1 and STS-3). The Nonreturn to Zero (NRZ) and Return to Zero (RZ) parameters are used for optical SONET/SDH signals.

- **Line Type**—Displays the interface's line type:

    — sonetOther

    — sonetShortSingleMode

    — sonetLongSingleMode

    — sonetMultiMode

    — sonetCoax

    — sonetUTP

    The line types are short- and long-range single-mode fiber or multimode fiber interfaces and coax and UTP for electrical interfaces. The value sonetOther should be used when the line type is not one of the listed values.

- **Valid Intervals**—Displays the number of previous intervals for which valid data has been stored.

- **Time Elapsed**—Displays the time elapsed (in seconds) since the beginning of the current error-measurement period.

- **Circuit ID**—Displays the vendor circuit identifier.

Section Tab

The SONET Interface Status window Section tab provides details of errors that the software encounters during framing, scrambling, error monitoring, and section maintenance.

The fields are as follows:

- **Loss of Frame**—Indicates the loss of framing failures since agent reset.

- **Loss of Signal**—Indicates the loss of signal failures since agent reset.

- **Defect or No Defect**—The transition from Failure to No Alarm state occurs when no defects (for example, LOF) are received for more than 10 seconds.

Line Tab

The SONET Interface Status window Line tab details errors encountered during multiplexing or synchronization.

The fields on this tab are as follows:

- **Alarm Indication Signal Errors**—A red light indicates that line signal errors are detected; a green light indicates that line signal errors are not detected.

- **Remote Defect Indication Errors**—A red light indicates that remote defect errors are detected; a green light indicates that remote defect errors are not detected.

- **Defect or No Defect**—The transition from Failure to No Alarm state occurs when no defects (for example, LOF) are received for more than 10 seconds.

Path Tab

The SONET Interface Status window Path tab displays errors encountered while mapping signals into the format required by the Line layer.

The fields on this tab are as follows:

- **Signal Label Mismatch**—Indicates a payload type signal label mismatch on a SONET line.

- **STS—Alarm Indication Signal**—Indicates whether the path alarm indication signal errors are enabled or disabled.

- **STS—Remote Defect Indication**—Indicates whether the path remote defect indication errors are enabled or disabled.

- **STS—Loss of Pointer**—Indicates whether the path loss of pointer errors are enabled or disabled.

- **Unequipped**—Indicates that the STS payload is unequipped—there is no path-originating equipment.

- **Defect or No Defect**—The transition from Failure to No Alarm state occurs when no defects (for example, LOF) are received for more than 10 seconds.

Virtual Tributary Tab

The SONET Interface Status window Virtual Tributary tab displays errors encountered while converting between STS and OC signals. It is not used in CDM 3.4.

The fields on this tab are as follows:

- **Remote Failure Indication**—A SONET port status indicator activates when a path remote defect indication (PRDI) occurs and does not clear throughout the alarm integration period, which is typically 2.5 seconds. A remote failure indication occurs when bit 5 of the G1 byte is set to 1 for ten consecutive frames.

  This occurrence begins the alarm integration period. If this period elapses without the detection of ten consecutive frames in which all G1 bit 5s are set to 0, the path remote failure indication (PRFI) indicator activates. The PRFI indicator clears when a PRDI does not occur for a time interval equal to the alarm deactivation period (typically 10 seconds).

- **Alarm Indication Signal**—Reveals whether the virtual tributary alarm indication signal errors are enabled or disabled.

- **Loss of Pointer**—Indicates whether the virtual tributary loss of pointer errors are enabled or disabled.

- **Remote Defect Indication**—Reveals whether the path remote defect indication errors are enabled or disabled.

- **Unequipped**—Indicates that the STS payload is unequipped—there is no virtual tributary originating equipment.

- **Signal Label Mismatch**—Incorrect payload type signal label mismatch on a SONET line.

- **Defect or No Defect**—The transition from Failure to No Alarm state occurs when no defects (for example, LOF) are received for more than 10 seconds.

Chassis Status

You can view chassis availability details in the Chassis Fault Management window. Follow these steps to open it:

Step 1   On the left side of the Map Viewer window, within the CDM Manager view, right-click a chassis whose fault management status you want to view.

Step 2   Choose Cisco DSL Manager, Physical, Chassis, Fault Management. The
Chassis Fault Management window opens.

The Chassis Fault Management window has four tabs: General, Power Supply, Temperature,
and Fan. Of these, only the General tab is used in CDM. It has three panels:

- **Chassis Availability**—Contains attributes that reflect the chassis's availability:

    — Up Time displays the up time since the last reset.

    — Last Changed Time displays the time the chassis was last modified.

    — Last Restart Reason displays the reason for the last restart.

    — Last Authentication Failure Address displays the last authorization failure IP
    address for the selected chassis.

    — Clock Source Status is not applicable for CDM.

- **LED Status**—This panel is not applicable for CDM.

- **Cisco Contact Details**—This free-form panel displays any provided Cisco contact
details, such as name(s), telephone number(s), and escalation path.

Module Status

You can view any card's (module's) fault management status, including NI-2 cards and line
cards, in the Module Fault Management window. Follow these steps to view module or card
status:

Step 1   On the left side of the Map Viewer window, within the CDM Manager view,
right-click an NI-2 card or line card whose fault management status you want
to view.

Step 2   Choose DSL Manager, Physical, Module, Fault Management from the
object menu. The Module Fault Management window opens.

The Fault Management tab has two panels: Module Availability and Cisco Contact Details. The
latter is a panel of free-form fields for noting Cisco support personnel information.

The Module Availability panel displays the following details:

- **Up Time**—Displays the up time since the last reset.

- **Free Memory**—Displays the memory space (in bytes) currently unused by the interface.

- **Last Restart Reason**—Provides the reason for the last restart.

- **Last Authentication Failure Address**—Provides the IP address of the NI-2 card that last
failed authentication.

- **Operational Status**—Displays the current operational status of the selected NI-2 card. Possible values are as follows:

    - **No Label**—The card is not specified.

    - **Up**—The card is recognized by the device and is operational.

    - **Down**—The card is not recognized by the device or is not enabled for operation.

    - **Standby**—The card is enabled and is acting as a standby.

CDM Performance Management

You can view performance data in CDM in two ways. You can use the Performance Manager, which displays historical data and current data in your choice of a line chart, bar chart, or table. You also can choose the Performance menu option, which displays only current data in raw, numerical format.

Both performance options are accessed through the Map Viewer application. The Performance Manager is opened in the Physical view; the Performance option is opened in the CDM Manager view.

You can open the Performance Manager on the following objects:

- OC-3 interfaces

- DS-3 interfaces

- ATM over ADSL over DMT interfaces

You can monitor statistics gathered from network elements, although performance monitoring is disabled by default. Performance monitoring is enabled from specific Element Manager screens. You can monitor particular attributes or parameters.

The CDM Performance menus allow current real-time performance information to be viewed at 10-second polled intervals on standard dialogs for interfaces and modules. Performance data can be viewed for the following CDM interfaces and modules:

- DS-3 interface

- ADSL interface

- ATM interface

- SONET (OC-3) interface

- Module performance, including NI-2 management cards and DMT line cards

- VCL connections

ATM Interface Performance

Four DMT interfaces are created automatically when you deploy a DMT line card. These DMT interfaces are actually ATM over ADSL over DMT interfaces, to be precise. In reality, all three interface types are referred to as a DMT interface. This means that performance data for an ATM interface of a line card is called DMT interface data.

Follow these steps to open the ATM Interface Performance Data window:

Step 1 In the Map Viewer window, within the CDM Manager view, right-click either a DMT line card or an NI-2 card to access the object menu.

Step 2 Choose Cisco DSL Manager, Physical, Interface, ATM, Performance. The ATM Interface Performance window opens.

The ATM Interface Performance window's single tab contains four panels:

- Transmitted

- Received

- Connection Established

- SSCOP

The fields in these four panels are as follows:

- **Restarts**—The number of Restart Activity errors that are transmitted from this interface. The Restart Activity counter provides a count of host, switch, or network restart activity. This counter is incremented when transmitting a Restart message.

- **Timer Expires**—The number of Timer Expiries transmitted from this interface. The Timer Expires counter provides a count of network timer expiries and, to some extent, host or switch timer expiries. The Timer Expiries counter is incremented whenever one of the following conditions occurs:

  — Expiration of any network timer

  — Receipt of a Release or Release Complete message

  — Recovery on timer expiration

- **Called Party Events**—The number of unsuccessful call messages transmitted from this interface for which the called party is responsible. This counter is incremented when a Release, Release Complete (only when it isn't preceded by a Release message for the same call), Add Party Reject, or Status message is transmitted that contains one of the following cause code values:

  — **17**—User busy

  — **18**—No user responding

  — **21**—All rejected

— **22**—Number changed

— **23**—User rejects all calls with calling line ID restriction (CLIR)

— **27**—Destination out of order

— **31**—Normal, unspecified

— **88**—Incompatible destination

A cause code value alerts you that something is wrong with your ISDN connection. A cause code value applies to both User Network Interface (UNI) version 3.0 and UNI version 3.1. A UNI is an interface point between ATM end users and a private ATM switch, or between a private ATM switch and the public carrier ATM network.

• **Calling Party Events**—The number of Calling Party Events messages transmitted from this interface. This counter monitors error events that occur when the originating user performs an incorrect action. This counter is incremented when a Release, Release Complete (only when it isn't preceded by a Release message for the same call), Add Party Reject, or Status message is transmitted that contains one of the following cause code values:

— **28**—Invalid number format (address incomplete)

— **43**—Access information discarded

— **57**—Bearer capability not authorized

— **65**—Bearer capability not implemented

— **73**—Unsupported combination of traffic parameters

— **78**—AAL parameters cannot be supported (UNI 3.1 only)

— **91**—Invalid transit network selection

— **93**—AAL parameters cannot be supported (UNI 3.0 only)

• **Unavailable Routes**—The number of Route Unavailability messages transmitted from this interface. This counter is incremented when a Release, Release Complete (only when it isn't preceded by a Release message for the same call), Add Party Reject, or Status message is transmitted that contains one of the following cause code values:

— **1**—Unallocated (unassigned) number

— **2**—No route to the specified transit network

— **3**—No route to the destination

For this counter, Release Complete messages that are a reply to a previous Release message and that contain the same cause code value are redundant (for counting purposes) and should not be counted.

- **Unavailable Resources**—The number of Resource Unavailability messages transmitted from this interface. This counter is incremented when a Release, Release Complete (only when it isn't preceded by a Release message for the same call), Add Party Reject, or Status message is received that contains one of the following cause code values:

  - **35**—Requested VPCI/VCI unavailable

  - **37**—User cell rate unavailable (UNI 3.1 only)

  - **38**—Network out of order

  - **41**—Temporary failure

  - **45**—No VPCI/VCI available

  - **47**—Resource unavailable or unspecified

  - **49**—Quality of service unavailable

  - **51**—User cell rate unavailable (UNI 3.0 only)

  - **58**—Bearer capability unavailable

  - **63**—Service or option unavailable or unspecified

  - **92**—Too many pending add party requests

- **Setup Attempts**—The number of call setup attempts (both successful and unsuccessful) transmitted on this interface.

- **Number of Cells**—The number of cells transmitted on this interface, including p2p and p2mp cells.

- **Bandwidth Utilization**—Displays the used bandwidth as a percentage of the maximum bandwidth supported by the port.

- The Connection Established area fields are as follows:

  - **Incoming**—The number of SVC VCCs established at the signaling entity for incoming connections.

  - **Outgoing**—The number of SVC VCCs established at the signaling entity for outgoing connections.

- The SSCOP Area fields are as follows:

  - The Service-Specific Connection-Oriented Protocol (SSCOP) area displays the Connection Event. This field displays the SSCOP Connection Events counter. It counts the sum of the errors, described as follows:

    - **SSCOP Connection Disconnect Counter**—The abnormal occurrence of the event is characterized by the expiration of Timer_NO_RESPONSE. (The event is communicated to the layer management with MAA-ERROR code P. Refer to ITU-T Q.2110.)

- **SSCOP Connection Initiation Failure**—This condition indicates the inability to establish an SSCOP connection. This event occurs whenever the connection control timer's (Timer_CC's) number of expires exceeds the MaxCC or upon receipt of the connection reject message Begin Reject (BGREJ) PDU. (The event is communicated to layer management with MAA-ERROR code O. Refer to ITU-T Q.2110.)

- **SSCOP Connection Re-establ/Resynch**—Occurs upon receipt of a Begin (BGN) PDU or RESYNC PDU.

Performance Polling

- Increasing the poll frequency places a heavier load on the CEMF server.

- Attributes must be fetched and stored more frequently for every object of the given CEMF class.

- Management network bandwidth can be a scarce resource.

- Consider the impact on the overall system responsiveness before enabling any polling.

If you need to enable polling, there are different steps for the three types of objects (chassis, module, and interface).

Follow these steps to enable performance monitoring on a chassis:

Step 1 In the Map Viewer window, within the Physical view, right-click the appropriate chassis.

Step 2 Select Configuration. The Chassis Configuration window opens.

Step 3 Click the Start button in the Global Performance Logging panel.

Follow these steps to enable performance monitoring on a module:

Step 1 In the Map Viewer window, within the Physical view, right-click the appropriate module.

Step 2 Select Performance.

Step 3 Click the Start button in the Performance Logging panel.

Follow these steps to enable performance monitoring on an interface:

Step 1 In the Map Viewer window, within the Physical view, right-click the appropriate interface.

Step 2 Select Generic.

Step 3 Select Performance.

Step 4 Click the Start button in the Performance Logging panel.

Adjusting Polling

You may choose to adjust polling intervals and other parameters to enhance CPU performance, especially for stable networks. The NI-2 is polled for the following parameters in the OLD-CISCO-CPU-MIB:

- **BusyPer**—The CPU busy percentage in the last 5-second period. This is not the last 5 seconds in real time, but the last 5-second period in the scheduler.

- **avgBusy1**—A 1-minute, exponentially decayed moving average of the CPU busy percentage.

- **avgBusy5**—A 5-minute, exponentially decayed moving average of the CPU busy percentage.

To change the default poll rate for a particular class of objects, you must examine the state machine configuration files:

```
CEMFROOT/config/*Con/StateMachines
```

The command syntax is as follows:

```
NAME = Task name
RUN_INTERVAL = Polling time in seconds
```

You must run the sysmgrClient command from a cemf shell to stop and restart the process.

Viewing Historical Data

A selected object or groups of objects have a number of attributes. Monitoring an area of the network, for example, provides the performance statistics of a particular attribute. The information obtained can then be used to evaluate the performance of the vendor's equipment and assess the requirements for upgrades or software downloads.

Performance statistics also provide a summary view of the performance of network elements. The statistics help determine the degree to which the network is meeting assigned service levels.

You define history storage criteria to determine which attributes are to be monitored on specified objects. Every criterion can be identified by a unique name.

When network objects are polled, the retrieved raw, current data is stored by CEMF and can be viewed using the Performance Manager. History storage criteria may also specify summary intervals, such as hourly or daily, and rules to be applied to the raw data. The resulting data is summarized.

For each attribute on each network element specified in the history storage criteria, CEMF stores and manages a historical record of the attribute's value.

Default history storage criteria files are loaded upon installation of element managers such as CDM. If no history storage criteria are specified, no attributes on any objects are monitored.

In some cases, an object might fail to be polled, such as if communication to the object is lost. Such a condition is called a missed poll. All missed polls are indicated on Performance Manager graphs and charts.

Performance Manager graphs and charts also indicate when an attribute started and stopped being polled due to history storage criteria being added, edited, or removed.

A Performance Manager GUI can be opened for each network element to be monitored. To view up-to-date information on the Performance Manager GUI, click Refresh.

Historical performance monitoring must be enabled manually. There are three ways to do this:

- Globally enables polling for all modules and interfaces.

- Individual module basis enables polling for a specific module.

- Individual interface basis enables polling for a specific interface.

Behind the scenes, monitoring attributes are specified in *CEMFROOT*/config/HistoryCriteria files.

You view historical data through the Performance Manager. It can be opened from pop-up menus on selected objects in Map Viewer, Event Browser, and Object Group Manager.

You can accomplish the following tasks from the Performance Manager screen:

- Identify all monitored attributes on a selected managed object.

- Identify all time periods configured for sampling each monitored attribute.

- Identify all summary methods configured for selected monitored attributes and selected summary periods.

- View historical performance data over a requested period of time, in tabular or graphical format.

- Print performance data to a printer or file.

Follow these steps to view performance statistics:

Step 1 From the Monitored Attributes list, select the attribute that will be monitored. Hold down the Shift key to select multiple attributes. The information for all selected attributes appears in the Table Display. Only the first selected attribute is shown in the Line Chart or Bar Chart.

Step 2 Set a start time and end time using 24-hour notation. The format must be mm/dd/yyyy.

To set the End Date, you have two options. In the End Date data entry boxes, enter the date on which the view of the performance statistics should stop. Or, select the Now checkbox to view the data from the selected start date to the current time. If you select the second option, the end date and time fields don't have to be updated.

Step 3   From the drop-down list, select the Summary Interval rule to be used. This varies according to the attribute selected. The summary interval is the period of time over which the rule is applied. This menu always contains the option to select Raw. This displays the data in raw format, which is performance data in its most detailed format (not summarized). When Raw is selected, the Bar Chart view is unavailable, and the Summary Rule option is grayed out.

Step 4   From the drop-down list, select the Summary Rule to be used. The rule provides the option to summarize data to a lower granularity.

Step 5   Click the Refresh button. By default, a line chart of the performance information to date is displayed. Line Chart, Bar Chart, and Table Display formats are available for viewing data.

The performance information displayed corresponds to the attributes' raw values. If a summary period is selected, the information is displayed according to the summary rule. No summary period is associated with raw data.

CEMF provides the option to view raw data as it is received without any summarization. History storage criteria define which attributes are to be monitored on specified objects. When these objects are polled, the retrieved data is stored by CEMF and can be viewed using the Performance Manager.

The Summary Rule option and the Bar Chart view are unavailable when the option to view raw data is chosen.

Saving Historical Data

No performance data is saved automatically. To save data, you must select Export to File to save the current data to a file.

Follow these steps to save performance data:

Step 1   Open the Performance Manager, and view the performance statistics you want to save.

Step 2   Select File, Export to File, or click the Save As icon on the toolbar.

Step 3   The File Chooser window appears. The left panel displays the directories, and the right panel displays the files. Use the scroll bars to locate the desired file. Click Filter to expand the list of options.

Step 4   Select the file. The full path name of the selected file is displayed in the File
Filter box, as well as the Choice box.

Step 5   Click Apply to save the file or Cancel to return to the Performance Manager
window.

CDM Inventory Summary

CDM provides inventory details for the Cisco 6000 series IP DSL Switch chassis and each
module within the chassis. You can retrieve inventory information within the Map Viewer
application by right-clicking either the chassis object or any module (an NI-2 management card
or a DMT line card) and then selecting Inventory.

The Chassis Inventory window lets you view inventory information for a selected chassis. It has
two tabs: General and Asset Tracking. The General tab provides general details about the
specific chassis, and the Asset Tracking tab provides various identification numbers relevant
to the specific chassis.

The General tab has five panels:

- Chassis Details

- System Details

- Version Details

- PCMCIA Slot Details (this is not applicable for CDM)

- Power Supply Details (applicability varies by CDM version; specifically, CDM version
  3.4 provides details of the Power Entry Module [PEM] for the Cisco 6260)

The Asset Tracking tab has a single panel.

The Module Inventory window is quite similar to the Chassis Inventory window.

The Module Inventory window also has two tabs: General and Asset Tracking. The General tab
provides general details about the specific module, and the Asset Tracking tab provides various
identification numbers relevant to the specific module.

The General tab has four panels:

- Module Details

- System Details

- Version Details

- Slot & Ports

The Asset Tracking tab has a single panel.

CDM Subtended Configuration and Subtended PVC Creation

You should remember what you learned in Chapters 4 and 6 about subtending:

- Subtending allows the IP DSL Switch to collect the bandwidths of a large number of subscribers in different IP DSL Switches into a single node before delivering them into an ATM network.

- Two NI-2 subtending topologies are supported—daisy chain and tree—depending on the number of subtended ports available, which in turn depends on the type of NI-2 card.

The CDM Subtend Manager is a set of subdomain management processes that provide inter-management capabilities for Cisco IP DSL Switch products. This Manager provides a dialog to allow you to update the topology and configuration of an IP DSL Switch or discover the subtend group to which an IP DSL Switch belongs. The CDM Subtend Manager also provides a dialog to allow you to set up or remove a subtend connection, including subtended PVC management.

Two views are unique to CDM subtending: Subtend and SubtendPVC. The top level of the Subtend view contains the entire list of head network elements and standalone network elements. Upon completion of a subrack discovery, the Subtend controller is called to update the subtend topology in the Subtend view.

It is from this window that you can add more subtended technology.

You can use the pop-up menu in the Cisco DSL Subtend Manager to launch the subtend dialogs.

You can configure a subtended connection between IP DSL Switches using the Subtend Configuration dialog.

You must do the following:

- Update the subtend topology.
- Discover and update the subtend topology for the entire subtend group.

To add a subtended PVC, follow these steps:

Step 1 Select the ADSL port to add the Subtend PVC to.

Step 2 Enter the subscriber VPI/VCI and head node trunk VPI/VCI.

Step 3 Apply an ATM QoS profile.

Step 4 Click the Add button.

Summary

In this chapter, you learned about the following:

- CDM's key features

- CDM navigation

- CDM IP DSL Switch deployment

- CDM configuration management

- Subscriber management for the NI-2

- How to set up CDM fault and performance management

- CDM subtend topology

Review Questions

1 Data viewed in the Performance Manager is which of the following? (Select all that apply.)

   A Summarized

   B Raw

   C Comma-delimited

   D None of the above

2 The CDM Element Manager contains which two distinct functionalities?

   A Launchpad

   B FCAPS

   C OAM

   D B and A

   E B and C

3 The ObjectStore database for CEMF is installed on which of the following?

   A Client only

   B Server only

   C Either the client or the server

   D Neither; it's a CDM database

4 True or false: SNMP version 3 is supported by CDM 3.3.

5 When a PVC is created in CDM, which of the following is also created?

   A Channels

   B Virtual channel links

   C Virtual channels

   D Linked channels

6 Which log in CDM keeps a record of everything that happens on a device that is not user-initiated?

   A Command History Log

   B Device Log

   C System Log

   D None of the above

7 When a DMT card is deployed in CDM, how many interfaces are created automatically?

   A 6

   B 4

   C None

   D 1

8 What does a black box with a slash through it represent when you view status in CDM?

   A No device is present.

   B The device is present but not provisioned.

   C No value has been returned.

   D You must right-click and select View Status to see information on this object.

Answers to Review Questions

This appendix contains the answers to the questions found in the "Review Questions" section at the end of each chapter. The questions are repeated here for your convenience. The answers and their explanations are in bold.

Chapter 1

1 Of the following, which xDSL types are most closely related?

 A CAP and SDSL

 B Lite and HDSL

 C ANSI T1.413 and G.992.1

 D HDSL and G.SHDSL

 Answer: C. They are both DMT standards. Although HDSL2 and SHDSL are both symmetric, only G.SHDSL is a standard.

2 How is analog voice traffic integrated with SDSL?

 A Signals are split by frequency

 B A microfilter is used

 C One wire of the pair carries voice, and the other one carries data

 D The analog voice traffic may not be integrated with SDSL

 Answer: D. SDSL, including SHDSL, uses all frequencies on the twisted wire pair, including the lower frequencies that would otherwise be used by POTS signals.

3 DSL is considered to exist in which OSI reference model layer?

 A Layer 2 or 3, depending on the modulation

 B DSL is not represented in the OSI reference model

 C Layer 1

 D Layer 2

 Answer: C. DSL is a physical layer technology that exists only along the twisted wire pair from the end user to the central office equipment.

4 Which of the following best describes the relationship of voice, video, and data applications?

   A Voice, video, and data require the same QoS.

   B Voice and video require the same QoS.

   C Data and video require the same QoS.

   D Data and voice require the same QoS.

   Answer: B. Voice is the most delay-sensitive type of traffic, followed closely by video in sensitivity to delay. Routine data has a lower QoS priority.

5 Which parameter is not part of the DSL QoS?

   A Maximum burst size

   B Bit rate

   C Coding gain

   D Framing mode

   Answer: A. This is an ATM parameter.

Chapter 2

1 Which of the following impairments always prevents ADSL implementation?

   A AM radio interference

   B Impedance mismatch

   C Load coils

   D Bridged taps

   Answer: C. Load coils were designed specifically to block frequencies above the standard voice range, 0 to 4 kHz, which includes the range of DSL traffic. AM radio interference, impedance mismatches, and bridged taps are hindrances to DSL service but do not automatically prevent ADSL service.

2 Which of the following is *not* one of the three primary methods of forward error correction in ADSL?

   A Trellis Coding

   B DMT

   C Interleaving

   D Reed-Solomon Encoding

Answer: B. Discrete multitone (DMT) is simply a type of modulation for DSL. Division into multiple tones does not correct any errors. Trellis Coding and Reed-Solomon Encoding are complex mathematical algorithms that correct bit errors by interpreting and reconstructing errors. The efficiency of these error-correction algorithms is enhanced with the use of bit interleaving, which spreads out the impact of bit errors. Together, bit interleaving and error-correction algorithms comprise forward error correction, meaning that errors are corrected as traffic moves forward through the network, rather than needing retransmission from end to end.

3 Reed-Solomon Encoding divides the data frame into several parts that are called what?

A Cells

B Code words

C Tins

D Codes

Answer: B. Code words are sections of the original transmission that include redundant check bytes to verify the accuracy of the Reed-Solomon Encoding.

4 What does Trellis Coding do with small data errors?

A It retransmits them to the sender.

B It adds correcting cells and retransmits to the sender.

C It fixes the errors without resending them.

D Trellis Coding cannot handle small data errors.

Answer: C. Trellis Coding works especially well on dribbling bit errors, mathematically reconstructing the missing or misplaced bit sequences. This eliminates the need for retransmission.

5 Which of the following describes the interleaving process?

A It reorders bits so that errors due to impulse noise are spread over time.

B It reorders frames so that errors due to impulse noise are spread over time.

C It reorders cells so that errors due to impulse noise are spread over time.

D It corrects burst errors through mathematical reconstruction.

Answer: A. Bit interleaving shuffles the stream of bits so that the inevitable errors due to impulse noise and other impairments are minimized. No one time period of the stream is unduly affected more than others, making it easier for sophisticated error-correction algorithms to re-create the original bit stream.

6 The SNR margin represents which of the following?

   A Error correction

   B Separation between the desired signal and the noise signal

   C Overcoming distance attenuation

   D The precedence of signal purity over signal bit rate

   Answer: B. The Signal-to-Noise Ratio (SNR) margin of separation measures the decibels separating the traffic signal and the impairing noise. This simple measurement corrects no errors and does not overcome any impairments, such as attenuation. It is one of several factors that are considered for rate adaptation, preserving signal purity over signal bit rate, but it is just a measurement of separation by itself.

7 True or false: Bridged taps prevent DSL operation.

   Answer: False. Bridged taps must be documented when guaranteeing minimum levels of DSL service because of their added distance and echo effect in signal transmission, but by themselves, bridged taps do not prevent DSL operation.

8 Reed-Solomon Encoding is most effective on what type of errors?

   A Large gaps in sequential bits

   B Bursty errors

   C T1 binder group interference

   D Impedance mismatches

   Answer: B. Reed-Solomon Encoding uses a complex mathematical procedure to reconstruct missing bits from the context of their accompanying bits. This means that a burst of bit errors can be reconstructed easily, as long as there were accurate preceding and ensuing bit sequences. Large gaps in sequential bits cause the processor(s) to work harder to perform the Reed-Solomon calculations and might not yield complete error correction. Binder group interference and impedance mismatches are physical impairments, which cannot be corrected by Reed-Solomon Encoding's logical reconstruction.

9 What makes it much easier for Trellis Coding and Reed-Solomon Encoding to correct errors?

   A FEC

   B SNR

   C Interleaving

   D Crosstalk

Answer: C. The complex, processor-intensive mathematical calculations of Trellis Coding and RS Encoding depend on minimized bit errors for maximum efficiency. Interleaving spreads out traffic hits over time so that the error-correction algorithms don't have as much missing data to reconstruct. Together, bit interleaving and the error-correction algorithms comprise forward error correction (FEC). Signal-to-Noise Ratio (SNR) is a simple measurement in decibels of desired signal strength to undesired noise strength. Crosstalk is a physical effect that is unaddressed by Trellis Coding and RS Encoding.

10 What is one way to compensate for the amount of attenuation in a signal path?

  A Add a repeater to the cable to boost signal strength.

  B Boost signal strength by adding loading coils.

  C Change the cable pair to unshielded twisted-pair to increase signal strength.

  D Nothing can reduce the amount of attenuation in a line.

  Answer: A. With the advent of DSL repeaters from such companies as AdTran, DSL traffic can be regenerated and transmitted over distances beyond the former limitation of the Carrier Serving Area.

11 What form of crosstalk occurs when a signal is affected by leaking digital signal energy moving in the opposite direction?

  A FEXT

  B NEXT

  C Front-end

  D FEXT and NEXT

  Answer: B. Near-end crosstalk causes spillover noise to move in the opposite direction it was transmitted. Far-end crosstalk causes noise seepage in the same direction as the original transmission.

12 Which of the following factors inhibits DSL service at the remote terminals?

  A Access

  B Environmental factors

  C Space

  D All of the above

  Answer: D. Access is limited by business and regulatory considerations, when an incumbent provider who owns the remote terminal is unable or unwilling to furnish access to a competitive DSL provider. Because these remote terminals are unmanned and are not usually hardened against extremes of temperature,

humidity, and so on, DSL equipment must be environmentally hardened for use in remote terminals. Remote terminals are almost always dedicated to T1/E1 connectivity for voice traffic, meaning that equipment space, including physical separation of the DSL equipment from the spectrally-poisonous T1/E1 equipment, is very limited. Remote terminals' expansion is limited by zoning and landscaping considerations as well.

13 What is the primary function of digital loop carriers?

  A To bundle multiple ISDN lines in a service area

  B To terminate subscribers' ISDN lines from the central office

  C To overcome the limitations of the central office coverage area

  D To add, move, and delete subscribers in a central office

  Answer: C. Remote terminals extend the voice service coverage area beyond the Revised Resistance Design rules, providing service to suburbs and areas more than 18,000 feet (5482 meters) from a central office. This voice service coverage was provided by T1/E1 multiplexing and increasingly is provided by fiber connectivity.

14 Why must load coils be removed?

  A They limit frequency response to below DSL frequency range.

  B They create crosstalk.

  C They add attenuation.

  D They need not be removed completely for DSL service at lower bit rates.

  Answer: A. Load coils were designed and installed to curtail noise leaking into the voice range (0 to 4 kHz) toward the end of longer voice loops.

15 Which of the following is *not* an objective of DSL cable qualification?

  A Locate faults that cause bad, poor, or no service so that they may be cleared.

  B Confirm the functionality of the physical line between the subscriber and the serving central office.

  C Determine which service levels can be offered to the customer.

  D Determine the number of devices required for service.

  Answer: D. The number of devices is immaterial to DSL service.

16 Which test works by injecting a pulse of energy into a line and timing the return of any reflections caused by cable abnormalities?

  A Service

  B TDR

  C 256-tone DMT loss test

  D Frequency response

Answer: B. Time domain reflectometry (TDR) depends on a precise time measurement of signal reflections, which determine the number, location, and severity of physical impairments.

17 Which test indicates the line's available bandwidth?

  A TDR

  B Load coil detection

  C Frequency response

  D Noise and impulse noise

Answer: C. If a physical cable has more available frequencies at the high end, more bandwidth is available for discrete multitone service, because more individual carrier frequencies can be used.

18 Initial qualification consists of a what?

  A Record check

  B TIMS test

  C 256-tone DMT loss test

  D TDR test

Answer: A. Before dedicating labor and equipment to testing a physical circuit, a simple and cheap review of the available local loop records is the best first step.

19 Which test's measurements let the service provider identify disturbances that could affect the transmission of data between the provider and the subscriber?

  A Noise and impulse noise

  B Load coil detection

  C Frequency response

  D Service tests

Answer: A. The test for noise on the line runs for hours or days, providing a good profile of any disturbances on the line.

Chapter 3

1 How is the number of required PPPoE servers determined?

A By determining the number of connections needed

B By determining how many DSLAMs are required

C Through the assignment of IP addresses

D By determining the number of subscribers supported

Answer: A. IP addressing does not determine the number of connections. Because PPPoE supports multiple online sessions per PPPoE connection, the precise number of subscribers cannot be known.

2 The characteristics of PPPoE most closely match the characteristics of what?

A Dial mode

B Server mode

C PPP mode

D None of the above

Answer: A. PPPoE's individual connection, with possible multiple end users sharing that connection, is most similar to the dial model.

3 Determining whether the service provider or the final service destination is providing the IP address to the subscriber's PC is an example of what?

A PPPoE advantage

B PPPoE implementation consideration

C PPPoE disadvantage

D PPPoE application

Answer: B. As soon as this decision is made, configuration and deployment can proceed.

4 Which of the following PPPoE processes is *not* the same as for PPPoA?

A Accounting

B Authorization

C Authentication

D Client configuration

Answer: D. Client configuration for PPPoE is quite different from that for PPPoA. No client software is required on the user PC for PPPoA.

5 What is an advantage of using PPPoE over IRB?

   A   It provides scalability.

   B   It provides security.

   C   It can use simple, already-deployed DSL modems.

   D   All of the above

   Answer: D. PPPoE's advantages can be implemented using the same bridging CPE as in present legacy networks.

6 PPPoE is based on which protocol?

   A   SSG

   B   AAL5

   C   OSPF

   D   None of the above

   Answer: D. PPPoE is its own protocol.

7 Which of the following is *not* part of PPP's LCP functions?

   A   Link establishment and configuration

   B   Link termination

   C   Transmission layer protocol negotiation and configuration

   D   Link layer quality consideration

   Answer: C. LCP lays the groundwork for the network layer configuration, which then enables the higher layers such as the transmission layer.

8 What is a disadvantage of using RFC 2684 bridged?

   A   When the CPE is in bridging mode, it is not concerned with which upper-layer protocol is being encapsulated.

   B   It has no user authentication.

   C   Minimal configuration of the CPE is required.

   D   It has multiprotocol support for the subscriber.

   Answer: B. RFC 2684 bridging, both IRB and RBE, does not provide for user authentication.

9 Where could the user PC using DHCP get its IP address with RFC 2684 bridged configurations? (Select all that apply.)

A Aggregator

B NSP DHCP server

C DSLAM

D ATU-R

E IP/DSL Switch

Answer: A, B, E. The aggregator must have Layer 3 functionality, including IP address pooling for DHCP. The Network Service Provider DHCP server could be the source of the addresses, either private or registered. The IP/DSL Switch has Layer 3 functionality as well. The DSLAM has only Layer 2 functionality in its limited function as a multiplexer. The ATU-R in bridging cannot be configured for the DHCP server.

10 With RBE configured on a Cisco 6400, the interface automatically _____ data traffic.

A Bridges

B Routes

Answer: B. RBE does not merely translate between bridging and routing networks, as does IRB with its BVIs. RBE also assumes that incoming traffic is to be routed unless it is explicitly designated otherwise.

11 With RFC 2684 bridged, the ATM cells carry what?

A IP packets only

B LLC/SNAP frames

C Ethernet frames

D IPX packets only

Answer: B. RFC 2684 bridging is defined specifically for LLC/SNAP frames. The contents of those frames may be bridged Ethernet, IP, or IPX. In the case of DSL bridged access, the contents are bridged Ethernet frames.

12 Which of the following is an advantage of using RBE?

A It provides QoS.

B It has less security vulnerability than IRB.

C Its CPE software provides traceability.

D It provides authentication.

Answer: B. QoS may be achieved with any architecture through the central office Layer 3 equipment. No CPE software is required for RBE connectivity, unlike PPPoE. There is no authentication in RBE.

13 Which of the following statements about RBE is not true?

A Spanning tree is enabled on all bridged interfaces to avoid loops.

B The ATU-R does not require an IP address. If management is desired, the CPE must be assigned an IP address.

C IP addresses can be provided by a DHCP server, which can be on the 6400 or any router or DHCP server in the service provider network.

D The number of supported interfaces is based on VC limits.

Answer: A. Spanning tree is not used in RBE, unlike IRB.

14 What is the function of the CPE DSL modem in the RFC 2684 bridged architecture?

A RIP v1

B RIP v2

C Static routing

D Transparent bridge

Answer: D. The DSL modem has limited functionality, just a Layer 2 bridge, in RFC 2684 bridging.

15 Using PPPoE, what is the default setting on a virtual circuit in the Cisco world to limit DoS attacks?

A 50 sessions per VC

B 100 sessions per VC

C 500 sessions per VC

D 250 sessions per VC

Answer: B. This number is adjustable and is usually decreased.

16 What is an advantage of using PPPoE?

A It provides QoS

B It provides security

C None of the above

D A and B

Answer: B. QoS may be achieved with any architecture through the central office Layer 3 equipment.

17 Attributes that are used to authenticate the tunnel user are kept at which location in the L2TP environment?

A The LAC

B The AAA server at the LAC

C The LNS

D The AAA server at the LNS

Answer: D. AAA at the LNS provides user information, whereas the LAC provides tunnel information and initiation.

18 What must be created on the LAC to allow it to accept an incoming tunnel request?

A Local authentication database

B VPDN group

C LNS AAA server address

D PPP login

Answer: A. Of the given choices, this is the only answer. Alternatively, the LAC's authentication prerequisite knowledge can be maintained in a RADIUS server.

19 Which of the following statements are true of L2TP?

A L2TP tunnel identifiers have network-wide significance.

B The LAC and LNS sides of the tunnel have different IDs.

C Tunnel IDs are selected and exchanged during tunnel setup.

D The session ID is set equal to the tunnel ID.

Answer: A, B, C. The session identification designations are not only different from the tunnel ID, they are different on each end of the same tunnel.

20 Which L2TP component usually initiates the L2TP tunnel?

A LNS

B AAA server

C CPE

D LAC

Answer: D. The LAC responds to the call from the LNS, on behalf of the DSL modem, and initiates the tunnel.

21 Which of the following statements is false?

A The LAC partially authenticates the end user with CHAP or PAP.

B The end user is authenticated on the LNS.

C The user's IP address is used to verify that the user is a VPDN client.

D End user traffic is carried in a tunnel session.

Answer: C. Authentication requires usernames and passwords.

22 Which PPP protocol contains information about higher-layer protocols, including IP and IPX and their control protocols (IPCP for IP)?

A NCP

B LLC

C PCP

D NLP

Answer: A. NCP specifies the routed protocol after LCP establishes the physical link satisfactorily.

23 Where are user PDUs encapsulated in PPP frames for PPPoA?

A At the central office

B At the DSLAM

C At the ATU-R device

D None of the above

Answer: C. No matter the format of user data, the ATU-R encapsulates those PDUs in the PPP format.

24 The Ethernet frame header and trailer are transmitted from the PC to the what?

A ATU-R

B DSLAM

C NSP's aggregator

D NSP's IP DSL Switch

E Central office

Answer: A. The user PC's IP packet is encapsulated by the ATU-R's PPP procedure and AAL SAR process.

25 What is the greatest advantage of using PPPoA?

A It has a single session per CPE on one VC.

B It makes optimal use of Layer 3 features.

C Using multiple VCs increases configuration complexity.

D Authentication overcomes the lack of security present in a bridging architecture.

Answer: B. Although authentication (answer D) is certainly an asset of PPPoA, it is just part of the overall L3 features.

26 The IP address of the subscriber's PC can be provided by what? (Select all that apply.)

A Static configuration

B DHCP server on the ATU-R

C DHCP server on the aggregation router

D DHCP server on the RADIUS device

Answer: A, B, and C.

27 Determining whether the service provider or the final service destination is providing the IP address to the subscriber's CPE is an example of what?

A PPPoA advantage

B PPPoA implementation consideration

C PPPoA disadvantage

D PPPoA application

Answer: B. Address allocation and source must be planned before deployment but then may be automated.

28 Which of the following is *not* one of PPP's LCP functions?

A Link establishment and configuration

B Link termination

C Transmission layer protocol negotiation and configuration

D Network layer quality consideration

Answer: C. LCP lays the groundwork for the network layer configuration, which then enables the higher layers such as the transmission layer.

29 Which of the following is a PPP NCP function?

A Verification of magic numbers

B Encapsulation into the PPP frame

C Authentication

D Identification of user data protocol

Answer: D. NCP enables the higher-layer protocols. Answers A, B, and C are handled by other protocols and procedures.

30 In MPLS, where is the analysis of the Layer 3 header performed?

A At each node

B At the CPE

C At the ingress edge LSR

D At the egress router

Answer: C. Although the label is examined at each node, it is thoroughly analyzed only once, at the edge LSR. This one-stop analysis is perhaps the greatest benefit of MPLS.

31 A label can be inserted where? (Select all that apply.)

A Between the Layer 2 and Layer 3 header

B In the AAL5 trailer

C In the VPI/VCI field

D In the SNAP header

Answer: A, C. ATM permits this insertion into the VPI/VCI field.

32 An IP/DSL Switch can be configured as what?

A CE

B LSR

C LDP

D PE

Answer: D. The IP/DSL Switch contains sufficient L3 functionality to operate as a PE router in MPLS.

Chapter 4

1 What is the NSP switch default ATM protocol?

   A LAPD

   B X.25

   C UNI 4.0

   D ISDN

   Answer: C. This is the only ATM protocol listed.

2 Which of the following best describes SONET APS on the 6400 system?

   A Redundant NLC cards supplying OC-3 traffic to the NSP

   B Redundant NRP2 ports supplying OC-C traffic to the NSP

   C The 6400 system does not support SONET APS

   D Redundant NSP configured for failover

   Answer: A. The NLC is the only 6400 module that supports SONET and its international equivalent, SDH.

3 When two NRP2s are configured in a redundant configuration, which of the following is true?

   A Both NRP2s provide redundant traffic to the NSP

   B Both NRP2s provide redundant traffic to the NLC

   C Both NSPs provide redundant traffic to the NPP

   D None of the above

   Answer: A. The NSP is the switch for the traffic coming through the NRP2s.

4 What is the maximum card load that the present Cisco 6260 chassis supports?

   A 28 DMT cards and four NI-2 cards

   B 30 DMT cards and one NI-2 card

   C 30 DMT cards and two NI-2 cards

   D 32 DMT cards and two NI-2 cards

   Answer: C. The Cisco 6260, 19 inches wide, has 30 slots for line cards and two slots for optionally redundant NI-2s.

5 Which function is *not* provided by the NI-2 card?

A Cisco IOS Software support

B SNMP Agent

C ATM switch fabric

D Four ATU-C modems

E Subtending

Answer: D. The line cards (the ATU-Cs) are separate modules. The NI-2 contains the software images for the IP DSL switch as a whole, as well as for the individual line cards. It can transmit and receive SNMP traps and other SNMP messages. It is the ATM switch for the 6000 series of switches. It also provides subtending support by linking to other IP DSL switches.

6 The present Cisco 6160 chassis can support which of the following maximum card loads?

A 28 DMT cards and four NI-2 cards

B 30 DMT cards and one NI-2 card

C 30 DMT cards and two NI-2 cards

D 32 DMT cards and two NI-2 cards

Answer: D. The Cisco 6160 is designed for the North American market, where telco racks are customarily 23 inches wide. This gives the 6160 space for 32 line card slots as well as two slots for the optionally redundant NI-2 cards.

7 The out-of-band alarm relay functions on the 6260 are provided by what?

A The NI-2 card

B The lead DMT card

C The power supply

D The wire wrap connector

Answer: D. Both the 6260 and 6160 can be hard-wired to third-party alarm platforms for yet another layer of redundancy. The wire-wrap connector on the IP DSL switch offers several levels and types of alarms, from minor to critical, and both visible and audible.

8 True or false: The 6260 fan tray must be installed before the PEMS.

Answer: False. Due to its compactly engineered design to fit in the 19-inch racks, the lip of the fan tray fits over the top of the PEM(s). Take care when replacing or inserting a PEM, because the fan stoppage generates an alarm after 3 minutes of no ventilation.

9 On the IP DSL switch, the DS-3 trunk is connected on which of the following?

A The DS-3 NI-2 card

B The DS-3 I/O module

C The network line card

Answer: B. This module is integrated smoothly into the back of the Cisco 6160 and is a floating plane on the front of the Cisco 6260. The NI-2 card itself is designed to control the coaxial connection, but the coaxial ports themselves are not on the NI-2, as are the fiber-optic connections for that version of the NI-2.

10 What is the function of the CO splitter?

A Equalize the circuit

B Generate ringing voltage

C Manage ADSL signaling

D Separate low and high frequencies

E None of the above

Answer: D. The passive splitter is an array of simple filter cards that separate the higher frequencies of DSL data from the lower frequencies of voice signals. From the splitter, DSL signals are directed to the IP DSL switch, and voice signals proceed to the Class 5 switch and then on to the POTS network.

11 In the NI-2-equipped IP DSL switch system, how is the splitter function performed?

A By the network interface module

B In the line module

C In the system controller card

D In the PSC

E None of the above

Answer: D. PSCs are made by such manufacturers as Corning and ADC and are usually designed to match specific IP DSL switch models with appropriate numbers of ports.

12 All subscribers in a subtended IP DSL switch report that their CPE trains up OK, but no one can access the Internet. Subscribers in the host switch are not experiencing a problem. Both DIP DSL switches are equipped with OC-3 NI cards. Which of the following could cause this error?

   A A defective OC-3 patch cord is connected to the transmit output of ATM port 0/1 on the host system.

   B ATM port 0/1 in the host system is out of service (shut down).

   C ATM port 0/1 in the subtended system is out of service (shut down).

   D A defective OC-3 patch cord is connected to the receive input of ATM port 0/2 on the subtended system.

   Answer: C. The uplink from the subtended IP DSL switch is designated 0/1. The other end of this same cable, the subtended link to the host system, is designated 0/2 on that system. If port 0/1 on the host system were inoperative for whatever reason, no subscribers would read Internet traffic.

13 A DSLAM is equipped with two PEMs, and –48 VDC is connected to each PEM. The circuit breaker on the right-side PEM is switched to the off position. What is the effect on customer service or system operation?

   A Subscribers served by ATU-C slots 12 to 17 and 27 to 32 are out of service.

   B Subscribers served by ATU-C slots 18 to 26 and 27 to 32 are out of service.

   C There is no effect on customer service.

   D Subscribers on systems subtended from this DSLAM are out of service.

   Answer: C. PEMs are redundant on all IP DSL switches.

Chapter 5

1 Which of the following typically controls end-user access through AAA to a specific network service?

   A Dial-in access number

   B PPP login

   C Network profile

   D Service profile

   Answer: B. The PPP login determines what service profile to invoke for the current user.

2 Which of the following statements about RADIUS are true?

A   RADIUS can collect accounting data for transfer to the ISP billing system.

B   RADIUS is a less-complex AAA protocol than TACACS+.

C   A single common RADIUS server can be accessed by many different NASs.

D   Each NAS authenticates with RADIUS using a secret authentication password.

E   All of the above.

Answer: E. These four features of RADIUS all apply.

3 Which parameter is contained in the Accounting-Request packet?

A   Username

B   IP address of the RADIUS client

C   Unique session number

D   Calling number

E   All of the above

Answer: E. The Accounting-Request packet is sent from the NAS to the RADIUS server.

4 In the DSL environment, what could be the RADIUS client?

A   ATU-R

B   DSLAM

C   NRP

D   Home hub

Answer: C. The Cisco 6400 UAC's NRP can serve as the RADIUS client.

5 Which attribute is *not* returned in an Access-Accept packet from the RADIUS server?

A   User authentication password

B   End user's IP address

C   Static route to the NAS

D   Service type

E   Access list

Answer: A. The Access-Accept packet depends on earlier authentication in defining the new connection.

6 RADIUS uses VSAs to do what? (Select all that apply.)

A   Add extra security features

B   Replace base dictionaries

C   Differentiate vendor products

D   Make RADIUS interoperable with older software

Answers: A, C. All vendors have the same default values with which to work, and the VSAs allow customization.

7 The Start Accounting-Request is sent from the NAS to the RADIUS server at what point?

A   When the access device is powered on

B   After the Access-Reject is received

C   After the Access-Accept is received

D   Upon logout of the session

Answer: C. Accounting is started immediately after the RADIUS server accepts the remote access.

8 Which function is performed by the RADIUS client?

A   Creates an Access-Request packet

B   Returns an Access-Reject packet

C   Initiates the service request

D   Returns an Access-Accept packet

Answer: A. The Access-Request packet is created by the RADIUS client in response to the service request initiated by the end user's login. This original request may come from the PPPoE client software in the user PC or from the L3-capable DSL modem itself in the case of PPPoA.

9 Which of the following is *not* a valid response from the RADIUS server to an Access-Request packet?

A   Access-Accept

B   Access-Reject

C   Challenge

D   Access Restricted

E   Change Password

Answer: D. Access restriction is a detail not performed by the RADIUS server, which makes more-basic "yes/no" decisions. Specific service restrictions are implemented in the SSG.

10 With Layer 3 SSG, if a dashboard (SSD) user requests a connection to the user's corporate network, which of the following profiles contains the IP address of the corporate gateway?

A User profile

B Service profile

C Client profile

D Dashboard profile

Answer: B. The service profile defines IP addresses for requested services.

11 Which attribute(s) is/are contained in the user profile?

A The username and password

B The attributes that describe a particular service

C The type of RADIUS client

D The IP address of the RADIUS server

Answer: A. The RADIUS server checks the Access-Request packet's username for a matching user profile. If the user profile exists, the RADIUS server attempts to match the packet's password in the user profile.

12 Which of the following is *not* part of the service profile?

A The IP address of the RADIUS server

B The IP address of the DNS server

C The IP address of the RADIUS client

D The labels for the service buttons

Answer: C. The service profile is not related to the RADIUS client address.

13 Which attribute is contained in the client profile?

A The IP address of the DNS server

B The username and password of the dashboard user

C The service network address

D The IP address of the RADIUS client

Answer: D. The client profile also contains the shared secret password.

14 Which profile contains a list of services to be displayed on the service selection screen?

A User profile

B Service profile

C Client profile

D Dashboard profile

Answer: A. The different services available for each user may be individualized.

15 Why can Layer 2 service selection connect to only one service at a time?

A It can store only one service profile.

B It is linked to the PPP username.

C It requires SSD support for multiple connections.

D It uses a web interface.

Answer: B. The structured username uniquely pairs the current user login with a single service at a time.

16 Why does Layer 3 service selection provide personalized services?

A It is based on the PPP login.

B It is preconfigured for each user.

C It is sold at a higher price.

D It is based on a unique SSG login.

Answer: D. This cause and effect is presented as such in this chapter, and is asked this way here, only because this is very similar to a question on the certification exam. However, you should be aware that this is not the complete nor even the best answer. Although it is true that the unique SSG login is related to L3 personalized services, it is also true that the more sophisticated routing tables available with L3 functionality permit multiple concurrent logins to various services.

17 Which service selection component authenticates the user login at the SSD?

A Web interface

B User profile

C Dashboard server

D RADIUS server

Answer: C. The dashboard server receives the username and password from the RADIUS server.

18   Which service selection component is responsible for sending the RADIUS Access-Request packet?

A   ATU-R

B   SSD

C   RADIUS client (NRP)

D   RADIUS server

Answer: C. The end user's CPE initiates the procedure by passing on the login, and the RADIUS client formalizes the request to the RADIUS server.

19   Which of the following initiates Layer 2 service selection?

A   DSL profile

B   RADIUS profile

C   Structured PPP username

D   The web selection screen

Answer: C. The username may clearly indicate the single domain available.

20   Layer 3 service selection offers which of the following benefits? (Select all that apply.)

A   Sell advertising space on the web selection screen

B   Dynamically select from a list of available services

C   Dynamically select service quality

D   Prevent unwanted telemarketer calls

Answers: A, B, C. Although not many DSL providers are truly taking advantage of the flexibility of dynamic selection by users, this bandwidth-determining enhanced service and revenue source is a compelling argument in favor of L3 service selection.

Chapter 6

1   What does the command **ip unnumbered gigabit ethernet 0/0/0** accomplish?

A   It enables IP on the interface without assigning a specific IP address.

B   It selects the authentication protocol and an optional secondary protocol.

C   It associates a virtual template with a virtual template interface.

D   It specifies a dynamic IP address assignment method, from either an IP address pool or a DHCP server.

Answer: A. Rather than use a valuable IP address on this virtual interface, it will be associated with the already-assigned Gigabit Ethernet IP address.

2   Which of the following apply to the NRP?

   A   Layer 3 services

   B   High-speed ATM switch

   C   Central control for the 6400

   D   Traffic shaping

   Answer: A, D. The NRP provides Layer 3 services such as encapsulation and routing and can be used for traffic shaping of ATM connections.

3   Which of the following apply to the NSP?

   A   Central control of the 6400

   B   Layer 3 packet services

   C   Terminates PPP

   D   End-to-end transport authentication

   Answer: A. The NSP is the controlling module of the 6400, although it only switches across the backplane and performs no L3 services.

4   Which of the following apply to the NLC?

   A   Optical interface

   B   Automatic protection switching

   C   Layer 3 services

   D   Terminates PPP

   Answer: A, B. The NLC comes in optical fiber versions such as OC-3/STM1 and can provide industry-standard APS.

5   True or false: The 6400 must be configured with redundant NSP cards.

   Answer: False. Redundancy is optional.

6   The IP address for the subscriber's PC can be provided by what? (Select all that apply.)

   A   Static configuration

   B   DHCP server on the ATU-R

   C   DHCP server on the aggregation router

   D   DHCP server on the RADIUS server

   Answer: A, B, C, D. The CPE device may be assigned a static address, or DHCP may be used from any of these Layer 3 devices when properly configured.

7 The interface designation **int atm 0/0/0** on the 6400 designates what?

   A ATM interface slot 0, subslot 0, card 0

   B Backplane connection, subslot 0, port 0

   C ATM interface port 0, subslot 0, slot 0

   D ATM interface slot 0, port 0, subslot 0

   Answer: B. The beginning 0 indicates a backplane connection, and the numbers of the slots begin with 1.

8 From the NSP, interface designation **atm 1/0/0** indicates what?

   A Interface to the card in port 1, subslot 0, slot 0

   B Interface to the card in slot 1, subslot 0, card 0

   C Interface to the card in slot 1, subslot 0, port 0

   D Interface to the card in slot 1, card 0, port 0

   Answer: C. The order of identification is full-height slot, subslot, port.

9 What is the NSP switch default ATM protocol?

   A LAPD

   B X.25

   C UNI 4.0

   D ISDN

   Answer: C. The UNI standard is used in ATM switching for larger networks.

10 Which of the following best describes a BVI?

   A It provides the interface between a bridge group and the routed network.

   B It assembles packets coming from the bridge group into FR frames.

   C It restricts broadcast messages within a bridge group.

   D None of the above

   Answer: A. A BVI essentially converts a Layer 3 interface into a Layer 2-Layer 3 translation interface.

11 Which of the following best describes SONET APS on the 6400 system?

   A Redundant NLC cards supplying OC-3 traffic to the NSP.

   B Redundant NLC ports supplying OC-3 traffic to the NRP.

   C The 6400 system does not support SONET APS.

   D Redundant NSP configured for failover.

Answer: A. Think of the precise path of traffic transmission: from the NLC to the NSP, which then immediately forwards the traffic across the backplane to the NRP.

12   **ilmi-pvc-discovery** refers to the process of what?

A   The automatic discovery of configured PVCs on the NRP card

B   The automatic discovery of configured PVCs on the NLC card by the NRP card

C   The automatic discovery of configured PVCs on the NSP card by the NRP card

D   None of the above

Answer: A. The Layer 3 NRP automatically discovers, routes, and manages configured PVCs according to their VPI.

13   When two NRP-1s are configured in a redundant configuration, which of the following occurs?

A   Both NRP-1s provide redundant traffic to the NSP.

B   Both NRP-1s provide redundant traffic to the NLC.

C   Both NRP-1s provide redundant traffic to the NPP.

D   None of the above

Answer: A. In the case of the NRP-1, EHSA signaling is used to manage the relationship between the active and backup NRPs, which both provide traffic to the NSP, although the NSP chooses to respond to only the active NRP-1.

14   True or false: The function of the **encapsulation aal5mux ppp dialer** command is to specify the encapsulation type for the PPPoA PVC on the 827.

Answer: True. This command configures the incoming PVC as a PPP type and then points back to the dialer interface.

15   Which protocol contains information about higher-layer protocols, including IP and IPX, and their control protocols (IPCP for IP)?

A   NCP

B   LLC

C   PCP

D   NLP

Answer: A. NCP is a higher-level protocol that can recognize the routed protocols, such as IP and IPX.

Chapter 7

1 Data viewed in the Performance Manager is which of the following? (Select all that apply.)

   A Summarized

   B Raw

   C Comma-delimited

   D None of the above

Answer: A, B. The Performance Manager offers both real-time raw data, and summarized historical data.

2 The CDM Element Manager contains which two distinct functionalities?

   A Launchpad

   B FCAPS

   C OAM

   D B and A

   E B and C

Answer: E. The industry-standard goals of FCAPS are fault, configuration, administration, provisioning, and security. OAM stands for operation and maintenance.

3 The ObjectStore database for CEMF is installed on which of the following?

   A Client only

   B Server only

   C Either the client or the server

   D Neither; it's a CDM database

Answer: B. CEMF databases reside on the server.

4 True or false: SNMP version 3 is supported by CDM 3.3.

Answer: False. SNMP version 3 is not yet supported.

5 When a PVC is created in CDM, which of the following is also created?

   A Channels

   B Virtual channel links

   C Virtual channels

   D Linked channels

Answer: B. VCLs are unique to PVC and SPVC configuration in CDM. A single VCL is created for SPVCs, representing the single, local endpoint.

6 Which log in CDM keeps a record of everything that happens on a device that is not user-initiated?

A Command History Log

B Device Log

C System Log

D None of the above

Answer: C. System Log is frequently abbreviated Syslog.

7 When a DMT card is deployed in CDM, how many interfaces are created automatically?

A 6

B 4

C None

D 1

Answer: B. The four ports on the current generation of line cards are created automatically when the card is deployed and commissioned.

8 What does a black box with a slash through it represent when you view status in CDM?

A No device is present.

B The device is present but not provisioned.

C No value has been returned.

D You must right-click and select View Status to see information on this object.

Answer: C. The system polling has not yet encountered a reportable value.

ATM Overview

How can you control and manage differences in rates due to impairments for both asymmetric and symmetric DSL? How can you allocate bandwidth among different classes of service? Finally, how can ATM satisfy different applications' traffic requirements?

High-bandwidth constant-rate data is not needed for all applications. A technology that can integrate data types (voice, data, and video) with varying traffic quality contracts is required to mix traffic, including delay-sensitive voice and video service.

ATM represents the current best solution to accommodate these needs. The main advantages that ATM cell-based service provides over a frame-based service, such as Frame Relay, are different classes of service, less latency, bandwidth efficiency, and scalability.

This appendix provides sufficient and necessary ATM explanation if you have no knowledge of ATM or if you need a review. This ensures a good starting point for Chapter 1, "DSL Primer," and should add to your appreciation of the different network architectures presented in Chapter 3, "TCP/IP Over ATM."

The ATM Network

An ATM network consists of a set of ATM switches interconnected by point-to-point ATM links. ATM switches support two kinds of interfaces: User-Network Interfaces (UNIs) and Network-Network Interfaces (NNIs). Slightly different ATM cell header formats are defined in UNI and NNI. The DSL world, being limited to the last mile between the customer premises and the central office, relates to the UNI environment. These UNI ATM cells comprise 53 bytes, with 48 bytes for the data payload plus 5 bytes of ATM header information. Generally, a UNI connects ATM end systems (such as hosts and routers) to an ATM switch. In the DSL world, the ATM end system is the user's DSL transceiver, and the ATM switch is the DSLAM/IP-DSL switch.

An NNI may be loosely defined as an interface connecting two ATM switches. More precisely, an NNI is any physical or logical link across which two ATM switches exchange the NNI protocol.

NOTE	The following sources provide more information on UNI and NNI standards:

  * www.atmforum.com

  * ftp://ftp.atmforum.com/pub/approved-specs/af-sig-0061.000.pdf

ATM Functionality

ATM is a cell-switching protocol that provides switched service with minimal switch overhead. Overall, ATM provides worldwide standardization for the transport of small, fixed-sized, 53-byte ATM cells. ATM cells behave with the predictability and trace capability of circuit switching and with the flexibility and dynamic rerouting of packet switching. ATM uses digital carrier systems and digital encoding to provide relatively error-free performance. Thus, ATM services do not include error correction overhead. They rely on the transmission path for end-to-end data integrity, resulting in higher throughput to the end user. The preferred digital path is optical fiber, either Synchronous Optical Network (SONET) for North America or Synchronous Digital Hierarchy (SDH) for Europe and most of the rest of the world.

ATM supports file transfer, interactive data, voice, and video. The selection of the appropriate ATM class of service (CoS) determines the latency and quality of a given circuit, as discussed in the next section. The CoS coupled with DSL's own quality of service (QoS) provide multiple traffic rates and traffic prioritization levels.

In a dedicated environment with leased lines, dedicated bandwidth allocation to meet the user's needs can be very costly and inefficient if the data is bursty. However, allocating less than the required bandwidth can lead to contention, which ultimately affects the overall application service being provided.

The key to efficiency is statistical multiplexing. However, traditional statistical multiplexing can result in discards during contention. Due to varying application requirements, these discards must be biased. For example, when there is congestion in the network, data from lower-priority applications should be discarded before data from higher-priority applications. Ultimately, statistical multiplexing with QoS yields an ideal environment.

ATM Classes of Service

ATM networks are designed to provide multiple levels of QoS circuits through a virtual network. The most common service class used for data traffic is unspecified bit rate (UBR). Variable bit rate (VBR) is becoming more important as providers increasingly begin fulfilling DSL's potential by integrating multiple types of traffic over the DSL network. VBR can support any requirement from synchronous protected service, with minimum cell loss, through asynchronous unprotected service, wherein cells can be discarded. These different types of traffic with their different service levels are easily defined and programmable by priority in terms of ATM CoS and DSL QoS.

Overall, ATM classes of service comprise the following:

- **Constant bit rate (CBR)**—Synchronous quality is guaranteed (highest level). This is used for constant bit rate voice, video, data, and telco circuit emulation.

- **Variable bit rate real-time (VBRrt)**—Synchronous with burst tolerance, this is known for predictably bursty traffic with strict end-to-end delay requirements. It is used for videoconferencing and compressed/packetized voice.

- **Variable bit rate nonreal-time (VBRnrt)**—Synchronous with burst tolerance, this is not guaranteed on delay bounds, and the network may buffer this traffic. It is used for time-sensitive bursty data.

- **Available bit rate (ABR)**—Asynchronous with a guaranteed minimum cell rate, this is used for data requiring committed but negotiable bandwidth.

- **Unspecified bit rate (UBR)**—Asynchronous quality is not guaranteed, and the rate is unknown. This is used for best-effort delivery of data applications such as TCP/IP traffic in normal file transfer.

  UBR+ is a special ATM service class developed by Cisco Systems. Neither an ATM-attached router nor an ATM switch provides traffic or QoS guarantees to a UBR virtual circuit (VC). As a result, UBR VCs can experience a large number of cell drops or a high cell-transfer delay as cells move from the source to the destination device.

  With UBR+, Cisco gives ATM interfaces the ability to communicate both the minimum and maximum cell rates to the ATM network, so the router can be assured of the necessary QoS for the traffic flow. On the router, the VC is created as a standard UBR VC from a traffic-shaping perspective.

By far the most common ATM class of service in the DSL environment is UBR. The least-used is CBR. This is because the majority of service providers around the world do not yet integrate packetized voice service over DSL. Two methods of providing packetized voice service over DSL include

- Voice over IP over ATM over DSL

- Voice over ATM over DSL

As the trend continues toward standardized integration of packetized voice and data services over DSL, VBR will become more widely used, because it is the most efficient compromise between CBR's rigidly protected bandwidth allocation and UBR's lower-priority vulnerability to cell discard. Another trend is to use a UBR virtual circuit for the data traffic and use a VBR virtual circuit for packetized voice services. Both of these virtual circuits travel on the same physical ATM-over-DSL connection.

ATM Adaptation Services: ATM Adaptation Layer

This section discusses the need to build ATM cell payloads based on application requirements instead of a general ATM cell payload format for all applications.

No matter what the original application and its type of protocol data unit (PDU), such as IP or IPX packets, ATM offers adaptation from the original PDUs to ATM cells and then back to the original format after transport across the ATM network. Small cells allow the interleaving of multiple application transmissions without any single application's experiencing a large delay. Hence, no one application takes an unusual delay penalty as it traverses the network. Small payloads fill faster, reducing delay during transmission preparation as ATM cells are constructed from the original packet units. Transmission preparation is performed slightly differently for different applications' needs, using one of several ATM adaptation services. ATM adaptation services provide the means of constructing a group of ATM cells from the original application's PDU, such as IP or IPX packets, and then back to the original format after transport across the ATM network. These ATM adaptation services are explained in the following sections.

To meet the various application needs, ATM uses the ATM adaptation layer (AAL) protocol. AAL provides a semilink data link layer service protocol over the ATM cell-switching network. Without such a protocol, the cell-switching service provided to ATM users would not be able to handle different upper-layer service demands.

Packets, such as TCP/IP packets, must pass through the AAL to be converted to small ATM cells. The step within the AAL of converting larger PDUs into ATM cells is called *segmentation and reassembly (SAR)*. Just as the PDUs are chopped into ATM cells at the sending end, the ATM cells must be reassembled into the original packet format at the receiving end using the same AAL.

Four AALs are defined with ATM, as shown in Figure B-1:

- **AAL1**—AAL1 was designed for delay-sensitive, high-priority traffic such as voice and streaming video. It is associated with a CBR. AAL1 requires timing synchronization between the source and the destination. For this reason, AAL1 depends on a medium such as SONET that supports clocking.

- **AAL2**—AAL2 was designed for VBR synchronous applications such as compressed voice, and will play an increasingly important role as VBR itself continues to be applied more often.

- **AAL3/4**—These two adaptation layers proved to be inefficient and are not used today, and are defined here only for completeness.

- **AAL5**—AAL5 with no error checking is preferred for TCP/IP-over-ATM operation, which is the majority of the traffic in DSL networks. The ATM Forum developed AAL5, which relies on the user's protocol services for end-to-end integrity (such as TCP), making it simpler and quicker to implement. AAL5 is associated with a UBR CoS. When first implemented several years ago, AAL5 was known as the simple and efficient adaptation layer (SEAL) because the SAR sublayer simply accepts the CS-PDU and segments it into 48-octet SAR-PDUs without adding any fields.

Figure B-1   *ATM Adaptation Layers*

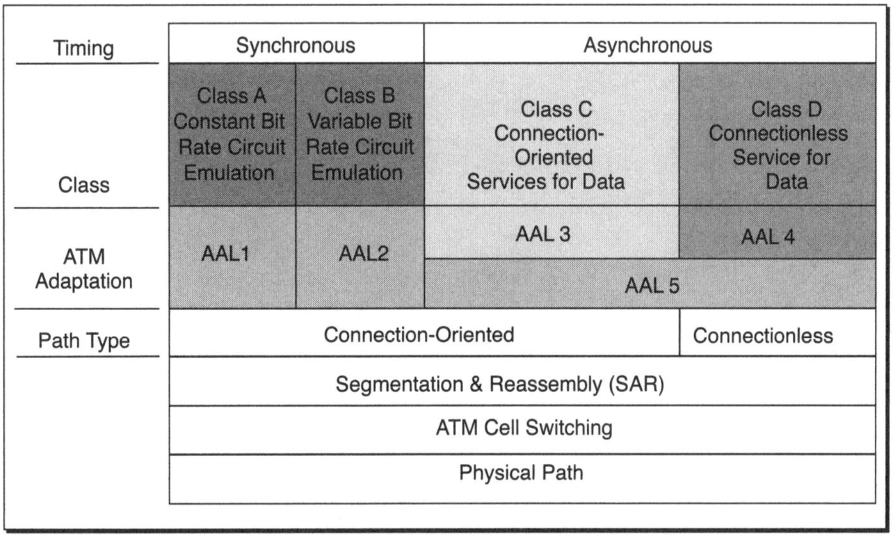

Timing	Synchronous		Asynchronous	
Class	Class A Constant Bit Rate Circuit Emulation	Class B Variable Bit Rate Circuit Emulation	Class C Connection-Oriented Services for Data	Class D Connectionless Service for Data
ATM Adaptation	AAL1	AAL2	AAL 3	AAL 4
			AAL 5	
Path Type	Connection-Oriented			Connectionless
	Segmentation & Reassembly (SAR)			
	ATM Cell Switching			
	Physical Path			

The most commonly used AAL in the DSL environment is AAL5, mainly because few service providers currently are delivering anything but data services over the DSL. As more providers can integrate packetized voice service with DSL , AAL2 will become more common, in conjunction with the VBR class of service.

AAL5 prepares a cell for transmission in three steps, as shown in Figure B-2.

First, the convergence sublayer (CS) appends a variable-length pad and an 8-byte trailer to a frame. The pad ensures that the resulting PDU falls on the 48-byte boundary of an ATM cell. Messages cannot be interleaved. The trailer includes the length of the frame and a 32-bit cyclic redundancy check (CRC) computed across the entire PDU. This allows the AAL5 receiving process to detect bit errors, lost cells, or cells that are out of sequence. Second, the SAR sublayer segments the CS-PDU into 48-byte blocks. Finally, the ATM layer places each block into the Payload field of an ATM cell. For all cells except the last, a bit in the Payload Type Identifier (PTI) field is set to 0 to indicate that the cell is not the last cell in a series that represents a single frame. For the last cell, the bit in the PTI field is set to 1. The PTI is a field within the 5-byte ATM header. The 5-byte ATM header is added to every 48-byte CS-PDU.

Figure B-2 *AAL5 Functionality*

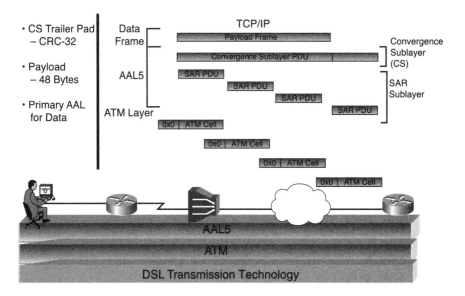

ATM Switching in the DSL World

Knowledge of ATM circuit types and virtual circuit mapping is absolutely critical to designing and maintaining a DSL network. The single most common cause of network connectivity issues in the DSL network is also the most easily understood: failure to design and adhere to a good virtual circuit-mapping plan.

Although the ATM Forum defines several connection types that are all theoretically applicable to DSL, the current world of DSL makes common use of only three:

- Permanent virtual circuit (PVC)
- Soft-PVC (SPVC)
- Permanent virtual path (PVP)

ATM virtual circuits are identified by the virtual path and virtual channel. A virtual path contains multiple virtual channels, like a large bundle of smaller pipes. Each individual traffic conduit is designated with a Virtual Path Identifier (VPI) and a Virtual Circuit Identifier (VCI), which together are written as VPI/VCI. These are shown in Figure B-3.

Figure B-3   *VPI/VCI*

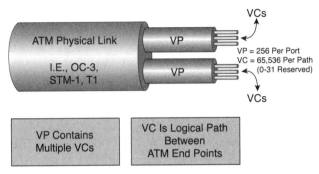

Connection Identifier = VPI/VCI
Must Be Unique Pair Per Physical ATM Interface!

The ATM Forum defined finite ranges of VPIs/VCIs for the UNI environment, the network access side of the ATM network in which DSL operates. A physical interface can have 256 virtual paths. Each virtual path can be divided into 65,536 virtual circuits. The virtual circuit is the data's transmission path.

Each logical connection (virtual circuit) must use a unique VPI/VCI pair. This uniqueness of identification allows thousands of logical connections to different sites using a single physical link. This concept is similar to Frame Relay. In Frame Relay, the virtual circuit is identified by a unique locally significant DLCI (Data Link Connection Identifier).

Traffic enters the ATM network as ATM cells. An ATM cell contains information that identifies its virtual path (VP) and its virtual circuit (VC). When an ATM switch receives the ATM cells, it examines the validity of the VPI/VCI in the ATM cell header to determine where the traffic should be forwarded.

The VPI and VCI can be changed at any time within the ATM network. They are almost always changed to ensure uniqueness. For instance, a service provider's inventory of CPE modems might be configured uniformly with a standard VPI/VCI pair and then be deployed to the field. Then those incoming DSL connections must be remapped to unique VPI/VCI numbers at the DSLAM/IP DSL switch. From the DSLAM/IP DSL switch into the ATM network, the VPI/VCI pair can also be changed at the intermediate ATM switches, as shown in Figure B-4.

For any user-side physical interface to the network side (UNI), the ATM Forum defines a maximum of 256 VP addresses (0 through 255) and 65536 VC addresses (0 through 65335) within a VP. In the NNI environment, the number of virtual paths is increased to 4096, with the same number of virtual channels.

Figure B-4 *VPI/VCI Renumbering*

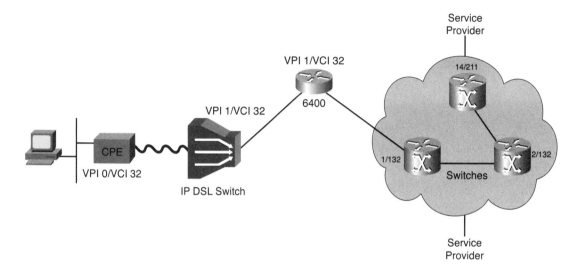

NOTE　As defined by the ATM Forum, certain VCIs are reserved and can't be used for user traffic. VCIs from 0 to 31 are reserved for signaling and management protocols. Additionally, some service providers reserve a particular VPI, such as VPI 0, for restricted management traffic, although these restrictions are not required by the ATM Forum.

In the DSL environment, no manufacturer (including Cisco) has developed the hardware and software memory to enable the full range of ATM Forum VP and VC possibilities at the DSL network edge.

The basic building block of ATM traffic is the PVC. Although it is the least-efficient way of mapping ATM traffic, you must understand it before implementing shortcuts. The following sections discuss the PVC and more-efficient ways of mapping ATM traffic—the soft-PVC and the PVP.

PVC: Basic ATM Mapping

PVC switching is the basic—and most configuration-intensive—option for ATM cell switching. A PVC is manually configured from ATM switch to ATM switch. The ATM switch is configured to take a specific VC in a VP and map it to another interface, optionally changing the VP and/ or VC addresses. This requires one proper PVC switching command configuration per VP/VC address pair on an ATM switch or router interface. PVCs are not scalable because their individual configuration at each node is so labor-intensive.

As soon as a PVC is established from the ADSL Transceiver Unit-Remote (ATU-R) at the source side through all the necessary switching nodes to the aggregation router at the destination, a fixed path exists between the subscriber and the routing subsystem.

Although the PVC can be easily traced, one disadvantage is the need for manual configuration at each ATM switch and/or router; this requires careful coordination among technicians configuring the ATM switches and/or router. Another important disadvantage of the PVC is evident when there is a link failure within the network, because there is no automatic rerouting of the PVC. Hence, the PVC must be manually rerouted around the network failure.

Although there are theoretically 256 paths, each containing 65,536 channels, in actuality, present industry-wide memory constraints limit the numbers of paths and channels.

Soft-PVC: Dynamic Switching in the ATM Core

A soft-PVC is a combination of permanent circuits, manually configured at each end of the connection, and an SVC through the middle of the connection. The ATM SVC depends on the ATM routing protocol to determine the best path through an ATM network. That is, in the core ATM network, the SVC path is dynamic and automatic, and the SVC finds its optimal path using the ATM routing protocol. Negotiating an alternative path around the link failure within the ATM core depends on the speed of the ATM routing protocol convergence time.

You must configure a PVC from the end device to the first switch, and another PVC from the last switch to the end device, but you do not manually configure each intermediate PVC. Along with the beginning and ending PVCs, the soft-PVC's CoS and QoS have to be defined at the start. Figure B-5 shows that the soft-PVC is pointed toward a specified ATM address.

Figure B-5   *Soft-PVC Mapping*

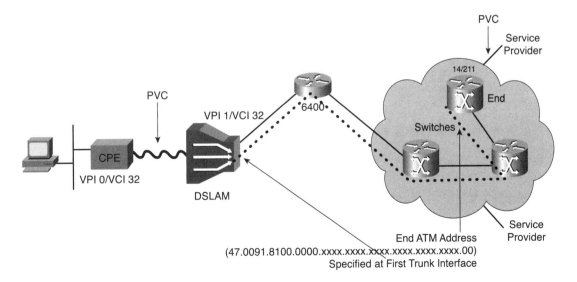

You need to specify only the ATM address of the end ATM switch, and the SPVC circuit automatically switches itself, like basic routing, through the intermediate ATM switches in the ATM cloud.

ATM addresses are known technically as ATM End Station Addresses (AESAs). Three address formats are used in private ATM networks:

- **Data Country Code (DCC)**—DCC numbers are administered by various authorities in each country. For example, ANSI has this responsibility in the U.S. All DCC address prefixes start with 39.

- **Encapsulated E.164 addresses**—E.164 addresses are essentially telephone numbers (ISDN) that are administered by telephone carriers. All E.164 address prefixes start with 45.

- **International Code Designator (ICD)**—ICD numbers are administered on an international basis by the British Standards Institute. All ICD address prefixes start with 47. This is the type of ATM address used by Cisco in DSL networks. All interfaces' ATM addresses therefore begin with 47.

Here is an example of an ATM address on a Cisco Universal Access Concentrator (UAC), where a soft-PVC would be pointed to from the DSLAM-IP/DSL switch:

```
47.0091.8100.0000.00b0.6495.6081.4000.0c84.8000.00
```

The second group, 0091, is Cisco's identification assigned by the British Standards Institute. The third and fourth groups, 8100.0000, are assigned by Cisco. The fifth and sixth groups, 00b0.6495.6081.4000.0c84.8000, are the interface MAC address. The last group, 00, is the Selector field. It is not used by the ATM network and simply passes through the network.

The soft-PVC has two disadvantages. First, extensive overhead traffic is required within the ATM network to support the ATM routing protocol and to maintain network convergence. Second, the SPVC dynamically negotiates its way through the network, changing VPI/VCI numbers as it goes, so it is harder to trace than a static and manually configured PVC.

However, the soft-PVC has three major advantages over the PVC. First, when a network failure occurs within the ATM core, the service is rerouted around the network failure. Second, SPVCs are much less labor-intensive to configure, because nobody has to configure each intermediate node. Third, this makes soft-PVCs more scalable than PVCs.

The limitation of how many SPVCs there can be per interface varies depending on the equipment vendor. This restriction is due to memory, CPU, and available switch fabric resources.

Permanent Virtual Path: Group Switching

The PVP is a manually configured connection that carries a bundle of virtual circuits. It is commonly implemented between ATM switches within an ATM network (node to node). The advantage of this type of connection is that a single VPI configured through several ATM switches carries thousands of VCs without the need to individually configure the VCs. This requires only one proper PVP switching configuration command on each ATM switch or router interface to support thousands of VC connections that share the common VPI number. The VPI number itself may be changed at any interface, but the VCI numbers can't be changed. PVPs can be used to produce a private backbone network. A PVP is mapped like a basic PVC, requiring a manual PVP switching configuration command at each intermediate ATM switch. The advantage is that all VCIs with a common VPI are mapped at one time. ITU standards indicate that PVPs can be point-to-point or multipoint.

ATM Cell Header

This section discusses the ATM cell header structure. The pertinent fields are shown in Figure B-6.

Figure B-6   *ATM Cell Header for UNI*

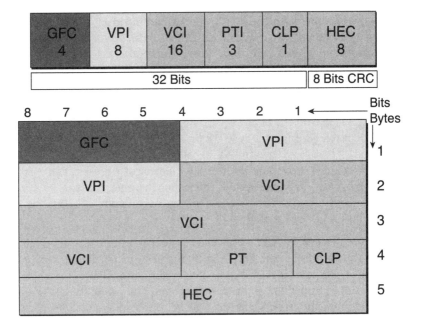

DSL transports ATM cells to the central office, and then the DSL traffic is switched as generic ATM in the ATM network. Understanding the ATM cell's header format and the usefulness of its individual fields is a requirement for understanding ATM's switching, error detection, congestion management, and CoS/QoS support.

The ATM cell is 53 bytes in length. When AAL5 is used for UBR traffic, the first 5 bytes are the ATM cell header, and the last 48 bytes are the cell payload. The ATM cell header consists of these fields:

- **Generic Flow Control (GFC)**—This field is used for flow control information across the UNI link. The ATM Forum reserved this field but did not define its contents. Cisco uses this field to identify linked (subtended) DSLAMs/IP-DSL switches in the central office so that they can share a single network uplink in fair queuing fashion, taking turns in network transmission up and down the shared network trunk.

- **Virtual Path Identifier (VPI)**—A virtual path is a bundle of virtual channels used to address virtual circuits. In the UNI environment of DSL, 8 bits are allocated in the ATM cell header for VPI numbering, meaning that 256 paths can be designated. In the ATM switch-switch environment of the NNI in the ATM cloud, the bits that were reserved for the GFC field in the UNI header are freed for VPI designation. This means that in the NNI cell header, a total of 12 bits are allocated for VPI designation, resulting in 4096 possible VPI numbers.

- **Virtual Channel Identifier (VCI)**—A VCI is used to address the virtual circuits inside a virtual path. 16 bits are available for VCI designation in both the UNI and NNI environments, meaning that 65,536 virtual channels may always be numbered within every virtual path, although no DSL equipment manufacturers presently enable this full ATM Forum capability.

- **Payload Type Identifier (PTI)**—The 3-bit payload type field is used to identify the type of payload that this ATM cell is carrying—user data or control data. If the first bit is a 0, the cell is carrying user traffic. If the first bit is a 1, the cell is carrying network traffic. The second bit indicates if this cell has encountered forward congestion. A 0 indicates that no congestion was encountered, whereas a 1 indicates that congestion was encountered. The third bit is used for virtual circuit connection management. This bit is called the service data unit (SDU) type. The SDU is currently only used by AAL5 to indicate which cell contains the end of the original PDU (SDU=1).

- **Cell Loss Priority (CLP)**—This bit is used to indicate if this cell should be considered a high- or low-priority cell. For UBR, all traffic is equally eligible for discard in the event of congestion, and CBR traffic takes precedence over UBR. This means that the CLP bit in UBR flips from 0 to 1 in the event of congestion before the CLP bit in CBR flips to indicate eligibility for discard.

  The CLP field is used to define a cell's priority relative to discardability in a congestive situation. This field is only 1 bit, so it has only two states: 0, for a high-priority cell that should not be discarded, and 1, for a low-priority cell that may be discarded in a congestive situation.

  In a congestive state, a switch discards all CLP=1 cells first. If this clears the congestive state, the CLP=0 cells remain untouched. However, if the congestive state remains, the CLP=0 cells are also subject to discard.

Either the CPE or the ingress switch can tag cells as low-priority cells. If the ingress switch tags the cells, this is done in response to their CoS contract. When the user exceeds a certain traffic threshold within the contract, subsequent cells are tagged as low-priority.

● **Header Error Control (HEC)**—This last field in the ATM cell header is used to perform error detection and correction over the cell header. Note that this is internal to the ATM cells themselves, without regard for the DSL forward error correction (FEC) techniques. HEC actually validates the first 4 bytes of an ATM cell header. If the HEC is valid, the cell is passed on. If the HEC is invalid, the ATM switch attempts forward error correction on the cell header using the HEC. If it is successful, the cell header is corrected and forwarded. This is successful only 89 percent of the time with a 1- or 2-bit error. ATM's initial definition used fiber options as the physical transmission medium. With fiber options, the possibility of a bit error is very small; hence, payload error detection was left to the final switch in the path using a higher-layer protocol, such as TCP.

Although these header fields are not absolutely required for DSL network implementation, you can interpret certain error messages more readily with these definitions. Similarly, the next section, which describes ATM routing protocols that are used in the reserved VCIs, is not critical to routine operation of a DSL network, but the knowledge helps you plan expansions, map traffic, and interpret errors.

ATM Reserved VCI Numbers

This section describes the VCI usage within an ATM cell. The reserved numbers of VCIs are shown in Figure B-7.

Figure B-7   *Reserved VCI Table*

VCI Channels Below 32
Are Reserved

Legend

A - Bit Is Available for Use by the ATM Layer
B - Bit to be Set to 0 by Originating Entity, but Network May Change Value
C - Congestion Experienced Indication Bit
L - Cell Loss Priority (CLP) Bit
U - ATM Layer User-to-ATM-Layer User Indication Bit
X - Any VPI Value: for VPI=0, the VCI Value Is Valid for Signaling With Local Exchange
Y - Any VPI Value
Z - Any VCI Value Other Than 0
Y - Any VCI Value Above 31
ILMI - Integrated Local Management Interface
PTI - Payload Type Identifier
PLOAM - Physical Layer OAM

Cell Type	VPI	VCI	PTI	CLP
Unassigned Cells	0	0		0
Metasignaling Cells	x	1	0A0	B
General Broadcast Cells	x	2	0AA	B
Point-to-Point Signaling Cells	x	5	0AA	B
Segment OAM Flow F4 Cells	y	3	0A0	A
End-to-End OAM Flow F4 Cells	y	4	0A0	A
Segment OAM Flow F5 Cells	y	z	100	A
End-to-End OAM Flow F5 Cells	y	z	101	A
Resource Management Cells	y	z	110	A
User Information Cells	y	y	0CU	L
ILMI	0	16	AAA	B
Physical Layer OAM	0	0	100	1
LAN Emulation	0	17	AAA	B
PNNI Routing Channel	0	18	AAA	B
VP Resource Management	y	6	110	A
VC Resource Management	y	z	110	A
Reserved for Physical Layer	y	0	PPP	1
Invalid	0	0		1
Reserved for VP Functions	y	7	0AA	A

In the 65,536 possible virtual channels in each of the 256 virtual paths on any given UNI interface, there are 32 reserved virtual channel numbers. Those are VCIs 0 to 31. Some of these channels are still undefined and are left for future use. Some of the reserved VCIs are critical to the ATM network.

Here are the key virtual channels that are used for various types of signaling across the UNI or NNI:

- **Call signaling (frequently called VPI 0/VCI 5)**—This is signaling information associated with the establishment, maintenance, and teardown of SVC connections. For example, when a user requests an SVC to be established across an ATM network, the initiating ATM device (such as the CPE) sends a Setup message to the ingress ATM switch. This setup message is transmitted on VCI=5. All corresponding responses that complete the setup of the SVC and its later removal from the intermediate nodes of the network also happen on VCI=5.

- **Integrated Link Management Interface (frequently called VPI 0/VCI 16)**—ILMI is used to transmit control information, configuration information, and link keepalives.

- **Private Network-to-Network Interface (PNNI) signaling (VCI 18)**—This connection allows for the exchange of ATM routing information between switches. PNNI is described as "the mother of all routing protocols" in the book *ATM Theory and Applications* by David McDysan and Darren Spohn (McGraw-Hill, ISBN 0-07-045346-2), because it combines features of IP distance-vector protocols and link-state protocols and even discovers and passes on configuration states such as whether network devices are UNI or NNI.

These and the other ATM protocols communicate much information that is almost always invisible to the user and that frequently is taken for granted even by the network administrator. Among the signaling and management data are references to ATM traffic units, which are described in the next section.

ATM Units

The ATM public network offers various traffic-measurement units to configure services. Of these units, only the peak cell rate is commonly used in today's DSL networks, but as DSL makes more use of the range of ATM definitions, the other units will become more applicable as well. The cell rates are as follows:

- **Peak cell rate (PCR)**—The upper limit of the cell rate from the source. A user may encounter the cell burst rate (see below) as integrated services use the network. Cells in excess of the PCR rate could be discarded if the carrier needs the bandwidth.

- **Sustainable cell rate (SCR)**—To prevent high cell loss, this rate identifies the maximum rate at which continuous cells can be issued without data loss. This value is lower than the PCR. SCR is also called average cell rate.

- **Minimum cell rate (MCR)**—The cell rate at which the source is always allowed to send.

- **Maximum burst size (MBS)**—The number of cells that the source can transmit back-to-back above SCR (but below PCR) without penalty.

- **Cell delay variation tolerance (CDVT)**—Specifies the delay variation that is introduced by the ATM network as a cell is transmitted through the network. This delay always differs from one cell to another and is unpredictable.

  Without CDVT, any two cells that would arrive with an intervening time gap longer than expected would be discarded. CDVT allows for some elasticity when bursting above contract, and thus accommodates for jitter that might be introduced by the edge devices or network equipment.

Not all ATM traffic parameters are used with all ATM service classes. The following are the parameters specified for the VBR and UBR service class:

- **VBRrt**—PCR, SCR, MBS, and CDV

- **VBRnrt**—PCR, SCR, and MBS

- **UBR**—None required; PCR is optional

- **UBR+**—PCR and MCR

As noted earlier, UBR+ is a Cisco invention; UBR and UBR+ account for the vast majority of ATM traffic definitions in DSL networks today. VBRrt and VBRnrt almost certainly will be the types of the near future. VBR is discussed in the next section.

DSL Usage of VBR Characteristics and Applications

VBR and its two subdivisions, real-time and nonreal-time, allow the best possible flexibility in a DSL network that combines latency-sensitive traffic such as voice and video and latency-tolerant traffic such as routine IP traffic. VBR has neither CBR's inefficient bandwidth reservations nor UBR's unreliability. VBR PVCs allow these three traffic parameters:

- SCR (mandatory)

- PCR (optional)

- MBS (optional)

As long as the user's traffic is less than or equal to SCR, all cells are passed as normal. If the rate exceeds SCR but is less than or equal to PCR and MBS, the cells are tagged as CLP and passed into the network.

Rates exceeding PCR are typically dropped as burst durations exceed MBS.

Typical VBR applications include interactive video (conferencing), interactive voice (telephone call), video/audio distribution and retrieval, and response-time-critical applications. For example, suppose a DSL provider currently supports only Internet data traffic but has received regulatory approval and has completed the network integration to begin offering voice service as well. The present UBR class of service will not sufficiently guarantee voice quality, but the bulk of the traffic will remain bursty data traffic, so a 24/7 bandwidth reservation scheme such as CBR does not work. In this case, VBR would be a good solution.

DSL Usage of UBR Characteristics and Applications

UBR is by far the most commonly used of the ATM classes of service in today's DSL networks, because most DSL providers are only now beginning to offer more than delay-tolerant Internet data traffic. The UBR traffic contract is designed for nonreal-time applications that are not constrained by delay or cell loss. No traffic parameters are used for UBR traffic contracts, although it is possible to specify the PCR parameter to provide the network with additional information. The PCR value would be information-only for network use. The network could use this to manage ATM connections more effectively. How this management would be done would be up to the vendor's implementation.

UBR does not provide for any guaranteed service. It is considered a best-effort service. UBR serves IP LAN-to-LAN traffic quite well, because TCP provides for retransmission and flow control. For example, a provider might decide to offer an inexpensive ADSL service to its customers, but it might not want to encounter provisioning problems associated with a guaranteed level of service. UBR would be the CoS of choice.

Summary

ATM is the *de facto* standard for DSL transport due to its small ATM cell size, scalability, multiprotocol capability, and standardization.

An ATM cell is 53 bytes long and consists of two parts: header and payload. The header is 5 bytes long and contains six fields: GFC, VPI, VCI, PTI, CLP, and HEC. The GFC field is used for flow control information across the UNI link. The VPI/VCI fields are used for destination addressing. The PTI identifies the cell as system or user data. The CLP identifies low/high discard priorities. The HEC provides header verification.

ATM provides for multiple CoSs, but only UBR and VBR are currently used in DSL networks. Within each CoS are additional traffic parameters to define the level of service (such as PCR).

DSL provides for numerous QoS parameters, which may be dictated by market differentiation and traffic types. DSL providers commonly use three ATM circuit types:

- PVCs

- Soft-PVCs

- PVPs

PVCs are manually configured by the service provider, meaning that they are easily traceable but require extensive configuration labor. Soft-PVCs are a combination of PVCs on the ends and a switched VC (SVC) in the ATM network core. PVPs are used between network nodes or between modules in a network node to bundle many VCs at one time, especially for transit.

Long-Reach Ethernet (LRE)

LRE significantly broadens the applications of Ethernet technology. It is an innovative networking solution that delivers highly affordable, high-performance broadband access to multiunit structures, such as dormitories, academic buildings, and administration buildings across the campus.

Ethernet is generally recognized as the most cost-effective networking technology available, with more than 750 million ports shipped over the past two decades. Not only is an Ethernet-based switching platform relatively inexpensive, particularly when compared to an ATM switching fabric, but LRE technology also lets Ethernet run over existing unconditioned telephone-grade wire that is already widely deployed. In addition, LRE transmissions can coexist with plain old telephone service (POTS), advanced Private Branch Exchange (PBX), or ISDN signaling services over the same pair of ordinary copper wires and can be provisioned in the same wire bundle as ADSL. Therefore, service providers can take advantage of their existing networking and telecommunications infrastructures in conjunction with LRE, providing broadband services for a very low overall cost.

Cisco LRE dramatically extends Ethernet over existing single-pair Category 1, 2, or 3 wiring, delivering speeds of 5 to 15 Mbps for distances of up to 5000 feet (1524 meters). It is a perfect broadband solution when high speeds are required but wiring is difficult to upgrade because of building age or cost.

The LRE market is expected to hit $3.4 billion by 2004, according to Cahners In-Stat Group. This market represents the last "low-hanging fruit" of broadband capabilities in the local loop environment. Specifically, LRE addresses needs for buildings with multitenant units (MTUs) and other types of multidwelling units (MDUs), such as apartment complexes, hotels, dormitories, and business campuses.

This appendix introduces Cisco LRE and its focus on the market of concentrated users, such as in business campuses, the hospitality industry, and apartment complexes. This appendix is both a bonus and a continuation of this book. Although LRE is not examined in either of the two Cisco DSL certification exams at this time, nor is it described in the Cisco course Building Cisco DSL Networks, LRE does make use of VDSL, and it occupies much of the same infrastructure space as xDSL in general.

Cisco LRE

Like ADSL, Cisco LRE facilitates the transport of symmetrical, bidirectional data over unshielded copper twisted-pair telephone wires originally intended for the frequency band between 300 Hz and 3.4 kHz. Cisco's development of LRE provides an extension to the IEEE 802.3ah standards. The IEEE calls the technology being defined by its task force "Ethernet in the First Mile" (EFM). The industry group promoting LRE is similarly called the Ethernet in the First Mile Alliance (EFMA). As of fall 2002, the IEEE 802.3ah EFM Task Force has reached consensus on a complete set of baseline technical proposals that will provide the foundation of the Ethernet in the First Mile standard. Adoption of the baseline proposals is the third major milestone in the IEEE standardization process and provides the basis on which the editors will write the first draft of the EFM standard.

In advance of industry EFM standardization, Cisco LRE technology provides a point-to-point link that can deliver half- or full-duplex Ethernet at up to a 15-Mbps data rate. LRE can coexist safely with voice traffic. Specifically, Cisco LRE technology supports transmission of POTS, PBX, or ISDN signaling simultaneously with data over the standard telephone-grade wire infrastructure and can be provisioned in the same wire bundle as ADSL.

Spectral compatibility with ADSL is made possible because LRE uses VDSL to encapsulate Ethernet packets to provide a high-speed connection between the LRE customer premises equipment (CPE) and the LRE switch over phone wires.

The VDSL modulation used for LRE employs Quadrature Amplitude Modulation (QAM). QAM uses both signal amplitude and phase to define each symbol. The system administrator may choose DSL profiles that go beyond simple user rates and Forward Error Correction provisions and use different modulations and frequency plans according to the line specification and rate definition. LRE is designed to support multiQAM in order to achieve performance as close to the physical limit as possible while maintaining low cost and low power.

The system employs Frequency Division Duplexing (FDD) to separate the downstream channel, the upstream channel, and POTS, ISDN, or PBX signaling services in the frequency domain. This lets service providers overlay LRE on existing POTS, ISDN, or PBX signaling services without disruption. Both LRE and POTS/ISDN/PBX services may be transmitted over the same line without interfering with each other.

When a PBX system is on-site, the Cisco LRE 48 POTS Splitter is sufficient for carrying POTS traffic and data traffic on the same line. If the POTS splitter is required to connect directly to the public network, it must be homologated, or certified for the requirements defined by that country. In addition, homologated splitters protect LRE equipment from power surge and lightning strike damage.

Cisco can refer customers for homologated POTS splitters to vendors who are certifying them in most countries in Asia Pacific/Japan, North and South America, and Europe/Middle East/ Africa. Because POTS splitters have different impedances and pass band frequencies, they are location-specific. In particular, homologated POTS splitters from Corning Cable Systems and Delta Electronics have been tested successfully for compatibility with Cisco's LRE products.

LRE technology encapsulates Ethernet packets for robust, high-frequency transmission over telephone wiring and extends the distance reach from 100 meters for traditional Ethernet over copper to up to 5000 feet (1524 meters). Ethernet is a standards-based highly regarded networking topology. With LRE, Ethernet is now expanding from being the predominant corporate LAN access technology to being a universal access technology. LRE enables the high-bandwidth services that users want over existing telephone wiring, which in turn saves significant service provider time and expense. LRE also introduces new service possibilities that were not possible using older xDSL technologies.

The Hospitality Industry

Hotels, hospitals, convention centers, and even airports offer a broad variety of business and entertainment services to their guests. In fact, many of these businesses generate substantial revenue from such value-added services.

For the most part, building owners have not provided broadband access because of the high cost and disruption of wiring existing buildings with Category 5 cabling. So, there is a great need for a cost-effective high-speed solution that does not require threading additional wire throughout a building.

Certainly, MTU owners are not alone in their quest for a solution that does not necessitate an expensive, burdensome rewiring of buildings. Hospitality and MDU buildings have an even greater need. Why? Because, unlike some newer office buildings, most hotels, apartments, and condominiums are not wired for Ethernet. In fact, many are older, historically significant buildings that could be wired only at tremendous cost and challenge. Others have significant accumulations of asbestos or are framed in concrete, making the deployment of Category 5 lines almost impossible.

With LRE, these challenges do not exist. LRE uses the existing telephone-grade wire infrastructure, typically Category 3 or lower-grade cabling. So there is no need to rewire a facility with Ethernet-grade (Category 5) cables, saving the cost of rewiring and the possible loss of revenue while areas are shut down for laying wires. In addition, significant fiber is being deployed in metropolitan areas, making it possible to bring true broadband connectivity to the basement of buildings. The end result: up to 15 Mbps per port can be delivered cost-effectively to locations that traditional Ethernet cannot reach.

Switching units simply need to be installed in the basement, along with the telephone equipment, using 100BASE-TX to uplink to the Internet router or local servers. Then it is a simple "plug-and-play" connection—a PC LAN connection is hooked up to the in-room CPE unit.

High-speed digital service should be able to connect trunk cables to the rings that circle cities. The market term for this technology in the last mile is metropolitan-area network (MAN) applications. Service providers can offer far more advanced services, especially those based on video. A particular beneficiary might be high-definition television (HDTV), a technology that has largely stalled due to unusable bandwidth. HDTV allows service providers to bring a broad portfolio of services directly to television sets. Thus, with LRE, service providers will be able to serve users from both their computers and their TVs.

Telecommuters, SOHO users, and road warriors all need secure access to the company LAN. With LRE coupled with virtual private network (VPN) technology, these users can link to the network securely. As a result, they can enjoy full access to their applications and data, enabling them to work from hotels, small offices, and home offices just as productively as from company headquarters.

Glossary

AAL (ATM Adaptation Layer)   A service-dependent sublayer of the data link layer. The AAL accepts data from different applications and presents it to the ATM layer in the form of 48-byte ATM payload segments. AALs consists of two sublayers: Convergence Sublayer (CS) and Segmentation And Reassembly (SAR). AALs differ on the basis of the source-destination timing used, whether they use Constant Bit Rate (CBR) or Variable Bit Rate (VBR), and whether they are used for connection-oriented or connectionless mode data transfer. Currently, the four types of AAL recommended by the International Telecommunication Union's ITU-T are AAL1, AAL2, AAL3/4, and AAL5:

- **AAL1**—Used for connection-oriented, delay-sensitive services requiring constant bit rates, such as uncompressed video and other isochronous traffic.

- **AAL2**—Used for connection-oriented services that support a variable bit rate, such as some packetized video and voice traffic.

- **AAL3/4**—One of the four AALs (merged from two initially distinct adaptation layers) recommended by the ITU-T. AAL3/4 supports both connectionless and connection-oriented links, but it is primarily used to transmit Switched Multimegabit Data Service (SMDS) packets over an Asynchronous Transfer Mode (ATM) network.

- **AAL5**—Supports connection-oriented VBR services and is used predominately for the transfer of classical IP over ATM and LANE traffic. AAL5, also known as SEAL (Simple and Efficient ATM Adaptation Layer), is the least-complex of the current AAL recommendations. It offers low-bandwidth overhead and simpler processing requirements in exchange for reduced bandwidth capacity and error-recovery capability.

ABR (Available Bit Rate)   A quality of service (QoS) class defined by the ATM Forum for ATM networks. ABR is used for connections that do not require timing relationships between source and destination. ABR provides no guarantees in terms of cell loss or delay, providing only best-effort service. Traffic sources adjust their transmission rate in response to information they receive describing the status of the network and its capability to successfully deliver data.

access network   The portion of a public switched network that connects access nodes to individual subscribers. The access network today is predominantly passive twisted-pair copper wiring.

access node   A point on the edge of the access network that concentrates individual access lines into a smaller number of feeder lines. Access nodes may also perform various forms of protocol conversion. Typical access nodes are Digital Loop Carrier systems concentrating individual voice lines to T1 lines, cellular antenna sites, Private Branch Exchanges (PBXs), and Optical Network Units (ONUs).

AMI (Alternate Mark Inversion)   A synchronous clock encoding technique that uses bipolar pulses to represent logical 1 values used with 64 Kbps channels. AMI requires the use of 8 Kbps of each channel's 64 Kbps to maintain synchronization. A T1 circuit has 24 channels, and an E1 circuit has 32 channels. For a T1, the loss due to AMI adds up to 192 Kbps, which means that, in reality, only 56 Kbps is available for data transmission. A logical 0 is represented by no symbol, and a logical 1 is represented by pulses of alternating polarity. The alternating coding prevents the buildup of a DC voltage level down the cable. This is considered an advantage, because the cable might be used to carry a small direct current to power-intermediate equipment such as line repeaters.

AMI coding was used extensively in first-generation Pulse Code Modulation (PCM) networks, but it suffers the drawback that a long run of 0s produces no transitions in the data stream. Therefore, successful transmission relies on the user's not wanting to send long runs of 0s. Therefore, this type of encoding is not transparent to the sequence of bits being sent.

ANSI (American National Standards Institute)   A U.S. standards-setting organization.

ATM25   An ATM Forum-defined 25.6Mbps cell-based user interface based on an IBM Token Ring network.

AWG (American Wire Gauge)   A measure of the thickness of copper, aluminum, and other wiring in the U.S. and elsewhere. Copper cabling typically varies from 18 to 26 AWG. The higher the number, the thinner the wire. The thicker the wire, the less susceptible it is to interference. In general, thin wire cannot carry the same amount of electrical current the same distance that thicker wire can.

B8ZS (Bipolar 8-Zero Substitution)   Also called Binary 8-Zero Substitution, clear channel, and clear 64. An encoding method used on T1 circuits that inserts two successive 1s of the same voltage (called a bipolar violation) into a signal whenever eight consecutive 0s are transmitted. The device receiving the signal interprets the bipolar violation as a timing mark, which keeps the transmitting and receiving devices synchronized. Ordinarily, when successive 1s are transmitted, one has a positive voltage and the other has a negative voltage.

baseband   Uses a medium's entire bandwidth to carry a single signal. Ethernet (CSMA/CD), for example, uses baseband transmission.

BERT (Bit Error Rate Test)   A test that reflects the ratio of errored bits to the total number transmitted. Usually shown in exponential form (10^{-6}) to indicate that one bit out of a certain number of bits is in error.

B-ISDN (Broadband Integrated Services Digital Network)   A digital network with ATM switching operating at data rates greater than 1.544 or 2.048 Mbps. ATM enables the transport and switching of voice, data, image, and video over the same infrastructure.

BRI (Basic Rate Interface)   An Integrated Services Digital Network (ISDN) interface typically used by smaller sites and customers. This interface consists of a single 16 Kbps data (D) channel plus two 64 Kbps bearer (B) channels for voice and/or data. BRI is also called Basic Rate Access (BRA).

bridge tap   An accidental connection of another local loop to the primary local loop. Generally it behaves as an open circuit at DC but becomes a transmission line stub with adverse effects at high frequency. It is generally harmful to DSL connections and should be removed. Extra phone wiring within your house is a combination of short bridge taps. A Plain Old Telephone Service (POTS) splitter isolates the house wiring and provides a direct path for the DSL signal to pass unimpaired to the modem.

broadband   Sharing a medium's bandwidth to carry more than one site. Typically data rates above 1.5/2.0 Mbps.

CA (Certification [or Certificate] Authority)   This feature of IPSec is a network authority, either software or a dedicated hardware device, that issues and manages security credentials for message encryption. As part of a Public Key Infrastructure (PKI), a CA checks with a Registration Authority (RA) to verify information provided by the requestor of a digital certificate. If the RA verifies the requestor's information, the CA can then issue a certificate.

Depending on the PKI implementation, the certificate includes the owner's public key, the certificate's expiration date, the owner's name, and other information about the public key owner.

IPSec can be implemented without CA, although the CA functionality is very much required for online commerce.

CAC (Connection Admission Control)   Algorithms that determine whether the network can support a new connection with a particular service request.

CAP (Carrierless Amplitude and Phase modulation)   Derived from Quadrature Amplitude Modulation (QAM). This technique uses a single high-band carrier and adjusts to noise.

CATV   Cable TV.

cbitadm   A framing mode of C-Bit ATM Direct Mapping.

CBOS (Cisco Broadband Operating System)   The operating system found on the obsolete 600 series of Cisco DSL Customer Premises Equipment (CPE).

CBR (Constant Bit Rate)   A class of quality of service (QoS) defined by the ATM Forum for ATM networks. CBR is used for connections that depend on precise clocking to ensure undistorted delivery.

CHAP (Challenge Handshake Authentication Protocol)   A security feature supported on lines using PPP encapsulation that prevents unauthorized access. CHAP does not itself prevent unauthorized access; it merely identifies the remote end. The router or access server then determines whether that user is given access.

CLEC (Competitive Local Exchange Carrier)   A type of telephone service provider. This term was coined in the U.S. after industry deregulation. A CLEC competes for local telephony business with the area's Incumbent Local Exchange Carrier (ILEC).

codec (coder/decoder)   An assembly comprising an encoder and a decoder in the same unit. A device that produces coded output from analog input and vice versa. In video, codec refers to compression and decompression. Specifically, it converts a voice-grade analog signal to u-law or A-law encoded samples at an 8 kHz sampling rate. DSL bypasses the codecs at the central office by separating the frequencies in a POTS splitter and passing the DSL signal to a DSLAM, the DSL equivalent of a codec.

core network   A combination of switching offices and transmission plant connecting switching offices. In the U.S., local exchange core networks are linked by several competing interexchange networks. In the rest of the world, the core network extends to national boundaries.

CPE (Customer Premises Equipment)   Encompasses the entire suite of user telephony equipment. May include the computer or workstation itself if it is adapted with hardware or software to serve as a transceiver. CPE includes all modems, telephone sets, and even wiring at the customer premises.

CSA (Carrier Serving Area)   An area served by a Local Exchange Carrier (LEC), Regional Bell Operating Company (RBOC), or telco, often using Digital Loop Carrier (DLC) technology.

CSU (Channel Service Unit)   See *DSU*.

DCE (Data Circuit- [or Communication-] Terminating Equipment)   Services provider equipment at the central office (CO) or exchange (which can also be found at remote, unmanned company sites) that terminates the user circuit and switches that signal elsewhere in the network cloud.

demodulation   Converting an analog carrier signal to digital information.

dialer interface   A WAN interface on the router that is not connected to a remote device all the time but that dials the remote device whenever a connection is required. Configuring an interface on a Cisco router to dial a specific remote device at specific times requires configuring dialer profiles.

A dialer interface configuration is a group of settings the router uses to connect to a remote network. One dialer interface can use multiple dial strings (telephone numbers). Each dial string is associated with its own dialer map class. The dialer map class defines all the characteristics of any call to the specified dial string. For example, the dialer map class for one destination might specify the amount of idle time as 3 seconds before calls are disconnected, and the map class for a different destination might specify 10 seconds.

dialer pool   Each dialer interface uses one group of physical interfaces called a dialer pool. One physical interface can belong to multiple dialer pools. When you use dialer profiles to configure dial-on-demand routing (DDR), the physical interface is configured only for encapsulation and the dialer pools to which the interface belongs. All other characteristics used to make calls are defined in the dialer map.

dialer profile   Used to configure the router's physical (serial) interface separately from the logical configuration required for a call. You can also configure the router to allow the logical and physical configurations to be dynamically bound on a per-call basis. All calls going to or from a destination subnetwork use the same dialer profile. A dialer profile consists of the following elements:

- A dialer interface (a logical entity) configuration with one or more dial strings, each used to reach a specific destination subnetwork.

- A dialer map class defining all the characteristics for any call to the specified dial string (telephone number).

- A dialer pool of physical interfaces to be used by the dialer interface. The physical interfaces in a dialer pool are ordered according to priority.

DLEC (Digital Local Exchange Carrier)   A carrier that provides digital telephony services in a particular user area.

DMT Issue 2 (Discrete Multitone Issue 2, ANSI T1.412.3.)   A technique that uses multiple transmission carriers (spread spectrum) to transmit its signal. Noise adjustments are made incrementally as multiple carriers. DMT is a form of Frequency Division Multiplexing.

DS0 (Digital Signal 0)   A 64 kbps digital representation of voice.

DS1 (Digital Signal 1)   Twenty-four voice channels packed into a 193-bit frame and transmitted at 1.544 Mbps. The unframed version, or payload, is 192 bits at a rate of 1.536 Mbps. (The extra bit is for synchronization and timing.)

DSU (Data Service Unit)   A digital interface device that connects end user data communications equipment to digital access lines. Also provides framing of sub-64 Kbps customer access channels onto higher-rate data circuits. A DSU may be combined with a Channel Service Unit (CSU) into a single device called a CSU/DSU.

DTE (Data Terminal [or Termination] Equipment)   Typically a device that transmits data, such as a personal computer or data terminal.

E&M   A receive and transmit interface that allows connection for PBX trunk lines (tie lines). E&M is a signaling technique for two-wire and four-wire telephone and trunk interfaces.

E1   A European basic multiplex rate that packs 30 voice 64 Kbps channels into a 256-bit frame and transmits at 2.048 Mbps.

echo suppressor/echo canceller   Active devices used by the phone company to suppress positive feedback (singing) on the phone network. They work by predicting and subtracting a locally generated replica of the echo based on the signal propagating in the forward direction. Modems deactivate these devices by sending the 2100 Hz answer tone with 180 phase reversals every 450 msec at the beginning of the connection.

Edge Label Switch Router (Edge LSR)   The edge device that performs initial packet processing and classification and applies the first label to the signal packets. This device can be either a router, such as the Cisco 7500, or a switch with built-in routing, such as the Cisco MGX 8800.

EHSA (Enhanced High Signal Availability)   A method of synchronizing and maintaining the precedence of primary and secondary (active and backup) modules, such as the NRPs on the Cisco 6400 Universal Access Concentrator (UAC).

ESF (Extended Superframe) format framing   In digital signaling, ESF is a method of framing a DS1 channel. (Framing is identifying the individual channels in the DS1 channel.) ESF framing groups 24 (193-bit) frames into an ESF superframe so that each DS1 channel consists of one ESF superframe. In each ESF superframe, the values in every 193rd bit (in bits 193, 386, and so on) are used for any of three purposes:

- Framing, as originally intended (frames 4, 8, 12, ..., 24)

- A 4 kbps link between endpoints (frames 1, 3, 5, ..., 23)

- A 6-bit cyclic redundancy check (CRC) value (frames 2, 6, 10, ..., 22)

ETSI (European Telecommunications Standards Institute)   A European telecom standards-setting organization.

FCAPS (Fault, Configuration, Accounting, Performance, and Security)   Describes program functionality in general.

FDM (Frequency Division Multiplexing)   A technique of multiplexing multiple signals on the same carrier medium by adjusting the individual signals' frequencies to prevent overlapping.

feeder network   The part of a public switched network that connects access nodes to the core network.

FEXT (Far-End crosstalk)   The interference that occurs between two signals at the end of the lines remote from the telephone switch.

FireWire   The standard high-speed serial bus. Supports up to 400 Mbps today, going to 3200 Mbps, and plug-and-play.

FTTC (Fiber To The Curb)   A network architecture in which an optical fiber runs from the telephone switch to a curbside distribution point close to the subscriber, where it is converted to a copper pair.

FTTCab (Fiber To The Cabinet)   A network architecture in which an optical fiber connects the telephone switch to a street-side cabinet, where the signal is converted to feed the subscriber over a twisted copper pair.

FTTH (Fiber To The Home)   A network architecture in which an optical fiber runs from the telephone switch to the subscriber's premises or home.

FXO (Foreign Exchange Office)   The FXO interface allows a connection to be directed to the PSTN's central office. The FXO interface also allows a connection to be directed to a standard PBX interface if the local telecommunications authority permits. The FXO interface can also be connected to analog PBX station lines. This interface is of value for Off-Premises eXtension (OPX) applications.

FXS (Foreign Exchange Station)   The FXS interface allows connection for basic telephone equipment and keysets. It supplies ring, voltage, and dial tone. The FXS interface can be connected to standard analog PBX central office/network trunk ports.

GRE (Generic Routing Encapsulation)   Originally defined in RFC 1701, GRE is a technique to encapsulate any protocol in any other protocol, thereby eliminating the need to reformat transmitted data into a intermediate, less-secure format on its way across multiple networks.

HDB3 (High-Density Bipolar order 3 encoding)   A European digital network transmission protocol that allows information and control data to be embedded in the transmission bit stream. The HDB3 code is a bipolar signaling technique (in other words, it relies on the transmission of both positive and negative pulses). It is based on Alternate Mark Inversion (AMI) but extends this by inserting violation codes whenever there is a run of four or more 0s. This and similar (more-complex) codes have replaced AMI in modern distribution networks.

HDSL (High data rate Digital Subscriber Line)   Modems on either end of one or more twisted-pair wires that deliver T1 or E1 speeds. Currently, T1 requires two lines, and E1 requires three.

HFC (Hybrid Fiber Coaxial)   A system (usually CATV) in which fiber is run to a distribution point close to the subscriber, and then the signal is converted to run to the subscriber's premises over coaxial cable.

hookflash   A U.S. term. The phrase Timed Break Recall is used in other countries. A hookflash indication is a brief on-hook condition that occurs during a call. On an analog phone, hookflash means pressing the switchhook for a moment (about one-half second) to produce a special stutter dial tone. It is not long enough in duration to be interpreted as a signal to disconnect the call. This stutter tone allows a user to invoke supplemental services, such as call waiting.

In the traditional telephone network, a hookflash results in a voltage change on the telephone line. Because this voltage change has no equivalent in an IP network, the ITU H.245 standard defines a message representing a hookflash. To send a hookflash indication using this message, an H.323 endpoint sends an H.245 User Input Indication message containing a signal structure with a value of !. This value is a hookflash indication.

Cisco H.323 version 2 includes limited support for relaying hookflash indications. H.245 User Input Indication messages containing hookflash indications received on the IP call leg are forwarded to the POTS call leg if the POTS interface is FXO. If the interface is not FXO, H.245 hookflash indications are ignored. This support allows IP telephony applications to send hookflash indications to a PBX through the Cisco gateway, thereby invoking the PBX's supplementary services if available.

The acceptable duration of a hookflash indication varies by equipment vendor and country. Although one PBX might consider a 250 ms on-hook condition to be a hookflash, another PBX might consider this condition to be a disconnect.

IDSL (ISDN over Digital Subscriber Line)   Uses ISDN transmission technology to deliver data at 128 kbps in an IDSL modem bank connected to a router.

IEC (Interexchange Carrier)   See *IXC*.

IKE (Internet Key Exchange)   A security protocol implemented in conjunction with the IPSec standard, providing negotiation services and key derivation services for IPSec. IPSec can be configured without IKE, but IKE enhances IPSec. IKE uses User Datagram Protocol (UDP) port 500. The IPSec Encapsulating Security Payload (ESP) and Authentication Header (AH) protocols use protocol numbers 50 and 51. Therefore, when IKE is in place, access lists must be configured so that protocols 50 and 51 and UDP port 500 traffic is not blocked at interfaces used by IPSec. In some cases, an explicit statement must be added to access lists to permit this traffic.

ILEC (Incumbent Local Exchange Carrier)   A term coined after the U.S. telephone industry deregulation to refer to the original company providing telephony services in a particular area. Deregulation requires the incumbent to compete fairly and openly with other companies for user business in that area.

ISDN (Integrated Services Digital Network)   Gives a user up to 56 kbps of data bandwidth on a phone line that is also used for voice (U.S.) or up to 128 kbps if the line is used only for data.

ISP (Internet service provider)   An entity that provides commercial access to the Internet. It can range in size from someone operating dialup access with a 56 Kb line and several dozens of customers to providers with multiple points of presence (POPs), or telephone network access points, in multiple cities and substantial backbones and thousands or even tens of thousands of customers.

ITU (International Telecommunication Union)   Sets international telecommunications standards. ITU-T is the ITU's standardization body.

IXC (Interexchange Carrier)   The post-1984 name for long distance phone companies in the U.S. AT&T is the largest, followed by WorldCom and Sprint, but several small IXCs exist, and more are being created.

L2TP Access Concentrator (LAC)   A LAC can be a Cisco network access server connected to the public switched telephone network (PSTN). This is the device to which the client directly connects, and whereby PPP frames are tunneled to the L2TP network server (LNS). The LAC need only implement media for operation over L2TP to pass traffic to one or more LNSs. A LAC can connect to the LNS using a LAN or WAN, such as public or private Frame Relay. The LAC initiates incoming calls and receives outgoing calls. It may tunnel any protocol carried within PPP.

label   A header used by an LSR to forward packets. The header format depends on network characteristics. In router networks, the label is a separate 32-bit header. In ATM networks, the label is placed to the Virtual Path Identifier/Virtual Channel Identifier (VPI/VCI) cell header. In the core, LSRs read only the label, not the network layer packet header. One key to MPLS's scalability is that labels have only local significance between two devices that are communicating.

Label Switch Router (LSR)   The core device that switches labeled packets according to precomputed switching tables. This device can also be a switch or a router.

Label Switched Path (LSP)   A path defined by all labels assigned between endpoints. An LSP can be dynamic or static. Dynamic LSPs are provisioned automatically using routing information. Static LSPs are explicitly provisioned.

Label Virtual Circuit (LVC)   A hop-by-hop connection established at the ATM transport layer to implement an LSP. Unlike ATM VCs, LVCs are not implemented end-to-end and do not result in wasted bandwidth.

LATA (Local Access and Transport Area)   Created by the 1984 divestiture. Defines the geographic area over which the LEC (Local Exchange Carrier) may provide toll calls. The area is often smaller than that covered by a long distance area code. Even though ten or 20 LATAs are normally found within the territory of a LEC, the LEC may not provide calls that cross LATA boundaries. Such inter-LATA traffic is the exclusive domain of the IXC.

LEC (Local Exchange Carrier)   One of the U.S. telephone access and service providers that appeared after the deregulation of telecommunications.

LFI (Link Fragmentation and Interleaving)   Reduces the delay and jitter of voice packets. When there is a mix of traffic, such as large datagrams and small delay-sensitive packets (such as IP voice packets), LFI fragments the large datagrams to packets small enough to satisfy the delay requirements of the delay-sensitive traffic. The delay-sensitive packets are interleaved between the fragments of the large datagrams. Note that the data fragment size must be greater than the voice packet size. Otherwise, the voice packets will get fragmented, and voice quality will worsen.

LH (Long Haul)   Refers to optical fiber.

LLQ (Low-Latency Queuing)   Provides a low-latency strict priority transmit queue for real-time traffic, such as VoIP traffic. Strict priority queuing allows delay-sensitive data such as voice to be dequeued and sent first (before packets in other queues are dequeued), giving delay-sensitive data preferential treatment over other traffic. This reduces jitter in voice conversations.

LNS (L2TP Network Server)   Almost any Cisco router connected to a LAN or WAN, such as public or private Frame Relay, can act as an LNS. It is the server side of the L2TP protocol and can operate on any platform that terminates PPP sessions. The LNS initiates outgoing calls and receives incoming calls. PPP frames are processed and passed to higher-layer protocols.

loading coil   A device used to extend the range of a local loop for voice-grade communications. It is an inductor added in series with the phone line that compensates for the line's parallel capacitance. Loading coils benefit the frequencies in the high end of the voice spectrum at the expense of the frequencies above 3.6 kHz. Thus, loading coils prevent DSL connections.

loop, local loop   A twisted-pair copper telephone line, moderately twisted for the entire length between the telephone company's end office and the user premises (the common telephone set), forms a loop, so it is called the local loop. This loop gives a user access to the global telecommunications infrastructure that is installed all over the world. Historically, the local loop was designed to provide voice-grade audio service. The circuit is powered from the central office with 48V (open-circuit voltage), limited in current to a value somewhat higher than 20 milli-Ampheres (mA). This current is used to signal phone access, burn off moisture, break through metallic oxides caused by corrosion, and power a carbon microphone. The original telephone equipment contained no active electronics. The actual wiring of the local loop may be considered a lossy transmission line. T1 modulation (Alternate Mark Inversion [AMI]) has been doing this for years.

loop qualification   The process of determining if a line (or loop) will support a specific type of DSL transmission at a given rate.

LX   Referring to Gigabit Ethernet fiber, the L in LX indicates a relatively long wavelength of 1310 nm. See also *SX*.

M23   A multiplexer from DS2 to DS3 level. The M23 multiplex scheme provides for transmission of seven DS-2 channels. Because each DS-2 channel can contain four DS-1 signals, a total of 28 DS-1 signals (670 DS-0 signals) are transported in a DS-3 facility. The existing DS-3 signal format is a result of a multistep, partially synchronous, partially asynchronous multiplexing sequence.

Working from the top down, a DS3 frame (44.736 Mbps) is made up of 7-bit interleaved DS2 frames (6.176 Mbps). The DS2 frames are constructed of 4-bit interleaved DS1 frames. The DS1 frame is a 1.544 Mbps (T1) digital interface consisting of 24-byte interleaved time slots called DS0s. Each DS0 is an 8-bit 64-Kbps channel used for voice or data.

MAC (Media Access Control)   The logic that controls access to the physical transmission medium (PHY) on a LAN. Common MAC layer standards are the CSMA/CD architecture used in Ethernet and the token-passing methods used in Token Ring, FDDI (Fiber Distributed Data Interface), and MAP (Manufacturing Automation Protocol).

MDU (Multidwelling Unit)   A building with multiple residences, such as an apartment building or dormitory, for which DSL service may be provided from an access multiplexer or IP-DSL switch located in a central location, such as the basement or ground floor.

modulation   A prescribed method of encoding digital (or analog) signals on a different waveform (the carrier signal). After it is encoded, the original signal may be recovered by an inverse process, demodulation. Modulation is performed to adapt the signal to a different frequency range (and medium) than that of the original signal.

MPLS terminology   An MPLS network consists of edge label switch routers (edge LSRs) around a core of LSRs. Customer sites are connected to the provider MPLS network. Here are the node designations:

- **Edge LSR**—Edge LSRs are located along with many peers at a network's boundaries, performing value-added network layer services and applying and removing labels to and from packets. These devices can be either general routers such as the Cisco 10000 or multilayer LAN switches such as the Cisco Catalyst 5000. An Edge LSR can also be the Cisco 6100/6200 series of IP DSL Switches or the Cisco 6400 Universal Access Concentrator (UAC). An edge LSR typically has several hundred customer sites. The Customer Premises Equipment (CPE) runs ordinary IP forwarding but usually does not run MPLS. If the CPE does run MPLS, it uses it independently of the provider.

- **LSR**—LSRs are high-speed routing devices in the network's core. These devices switch labeled packets or cells based on the labels. Label switches may also support full Layer 3 routing or Layer 2 switching in addition to label switching. Examples of label switches include the Cisco 6400, the Cisco 8540 Multiservice Switch Router, the Cisco BPX 8650, and the Cisco 7500. All LSRs exchange Layer 3 routing information and labels and forward packets or cells.

Here are some other MPLS network component terms:

- **Provider (P) router**—Any router in the provider's network that does not attach to customer edge (CE) devices. P routers function as MPLS transit LSRs when forwarding VPN data traffic between provider edge (PE) routers. P routers are required only to maintain routes to the provider's PE routers. They are not required to maintain a specific VPN routing information for each customer site.

- **Customer Edge (CE) router**—The CE router connects to the PE router. The CE router does not need to understand MPLS. The PE router looks like a standard backbone router to the CE router.

MTU (Multitenant Unit)   A building with multiple offices or businesses, such as a shopping center or office tower, for which DSL service may be provided from an access multiplexer or IP-DSL switch located in a central location, such as the basement or ground floor.

MXU (Multidwelling/Multitenant Unit)   A building with multiple DSL users, whether residential or commercial. This term refers to both MTU and MDU market segments.

NAP (Network Access Point) Another name for a provider of networked telephone and associated services, usually in the U.S.

NEBS (Network Equipment Building Standards) A U.S. standards body that specifies such construction characteristics as safety, environment, and performance that must be considered for telephony and electrical equipment.

NEXT (Near-End crosstalk) The interference between pairs of lines at the telephone switch end.

NID (Network Interface Device) A device that terminates copper pair from the serving central office at the user's destination and that is typically located outside that location.

NSP (Network Service Provider) This is not the 6400 UAC Node Switch Processor. It is an organization that provides value-added network services on a telecommunications network.

NTE (Network Termination Equipment) The equipment at the ends of the line.

OC-3 (Optical Carrier 3) An optical fiber line carrying 155 Mbps. A U.S. designation for the SONET standard generally recognized throughout the telecommunications community worldwide.

ONU (Optical Network Unit) A form of access node that converts optical signals transmitted via fiber to electrical signals that can be transmitted via coaxial cable or twisted-pair copper wiring to individual subscribers.

PAP (Password Authentication Protocol) An authentication protocol that allows PPP peers to authenticate one another. The remote router attempting to connect to the local router is required to send an authentication request. Unlike CHAP, PAP passes the password and host name or username in the clear (unencrypted). PAP does not itself prevent unauthorized access; it merely identifies the remote end. The router or access server then determines if that user is allowed access. PAP is supported only on PPP lines.

PCM30 (Pulse Code Modulation/30 channels) The specification for a physical network link with a 2.048 Mbps bandwidth that supports 30 data channels (E1). Because PCM30 links are well-established in Europe and elsewhere around the world, it was chosen as the physical layer for international ISDN networks.

PHY (Physical Layer interface) A direct interface to the transmission medium.

PNA (Phone Networking Alliance) A home networking standard for 1 to 10 Mbps over phone wire.

POP (Point of Presence) A node of an ISP containing a CSU/DSU, terminal server, router, and sometimes one or more hosts, but no network information center or network operations center.

POTS (Plain Old Telephone Service) Analog phone service. Takes the lowest 4 kHz of bandwidth on the loop.

PRI (Primary Rate Interface)   An Integrated Services Digital Network (ISDN) interface typically used by larger customers. This interface consists of a single 64 Kbps data (D) channel plus 23 or 30 bearer (B) channels for voice and/or data.

PTT (Post, Telephone, and Telegraph)   The generic name (originally and still predominantly European) usually used to refer to state-owned telephone companies.

QAM (Quadrature Amplitude Modulation)   A method of encoding digital data in an analog signal in which each combination of phase and amplitude represents one of 16 4-bit patterns.

RADIUS (Remote Authentication Dial-In User Service)   A widely deployed protocol enabling centralized authentication, authorization, and accounting (AAA) for network access. Originally developed for dialup remote access, RADIUS is now supported by virtual private network (VPN) servers, wireless access points, authenticating Ethernet switches, DDSL access, and other network access types. RADIUS is described in RFC 2865, "Remote Authentication Dial-in User Service (RADIUS)," (IETF Draft Standard) and RFC 2866, "RADIUS Accounting" (Informational).

RADSL (Rate-Adaptive DSL)   A DSL version in which modems test lines at startup and adapt to the fastest possible speed. All DSL modems based on DMT are inherently rate-adaptive.

RBOC (Regional Bell Operating Company)   One of the seven U.S. telephone companies that resulted from the breakup of AT&T.

SDH (Synchronous Digital Hierarchy)   A European standard that defines a set of rate and format standards over fiber-optic connections. Compare with *SONET.*

service contract   A contract negotiated between the user's end station and switch, defining bandwidth, burstiness, and other traffic characteristics. The network may opt to discard traffic that exceeds the service contract.

SONET (Synchronous Optical Network)   The specification for high-speed (up to 2.5 Gbps) fiber-optic connectivity. Approved as an international standard in 1988.

SSH (Secure Shell)   Considered the de facto standard for securing remote-access connections over Internet Protocol (IP) networks.

SSH provides a level of security on the network that client-side system security measures and firewalls cannot provide on client-side private networks. SSH secures connections over the Internet by encrypting all transmitted confidential data, including passwords, binary files, and administrative commands. The SSH software lets you remotely manage network hosts over the Internet. SSH was designed and developed by SSH Communications Security. After a security weakness in SSH1 was identified in 1998, SSH version 2.x was developed based on the SSH2 protocol. SSH2 is designed to be a complete replacement for the commonly used FTP and Telnet programs and for the **rlogin**, **rsh**, and **rcp** commands.

stateful inspection firewall   Also called a dynamic firewall. Provides a greater level of security intelligence by allowing or preventing network access based on a session's state. The firewall allows traffic to pass when requested by a user behind the firewall but prevents unauthorized network access.

STM-1   SDH basic transmission rate of 155.52 Mbps.

STS-1   SONET basic transmission rate of 51.84 Mbps.

SVC (Switched Virtual Circuit)   Found in Frame Relay and ATM networking. A virtual connection, with variable endpoints, is established through an ATM network when the call is initiated. The SVC is de-established at the conclusion of the call.

SX   Referring to Gigabit Ethernet fiber, the S in SX indicates a short wavelength of about 850 nm. See also *LX*.

symbol rate   The proper term for what is mistakenly called baud rate. A symbol is a waveform transmitted by the modem that contains a certain number of encoded bits of data to be moved across the link. In simple terms, the symbol can be viewed as an analog representation of a digital number.

T1   Designates the physical attributes of the transmission medium for DS1.

TDM (Time-Division Multiplexing)   A technique for combining multiple signals on the same transmission medium by allocating a slice of time for each signal in turn.

telco   The generic name for telephone companies throughout the world. It encompasses RBOCs, LECs, and Post, Telephone, and Telegraph (PTT) organizations.

traffic policing   Mechanisms that help networks determine whether the connection user has violated the service contract.

traffic shaping   Mechanisms used to modify traffic characteristics for contract conformance enforcement. Queues are used to limit surges that can congest a network. Data is buffered and then sent into the network in regulated amounts to ensure that the traffic fits in the promised traffic envelope for the particular connection. Traffic shaping is used in ATM, Frame Relay, and other types of networks. Also known as metering, shaping, and smoothing.

UBR (Unspecified Bit Rate)   A QoS class defined by the ATM Forum for ATM networks. UBR allows any amount of data up to a specified maximum to be sent across the network, but there are no guarantees in terms of cell loss rate and delay.

UTOPIA (Universal Test and Operations Interface for ATM)   An electrical interface between the sublayers of the PHY layer.

UTP (Unshielded Twisted Pair)   A cable with one or more twisted copper wires bound in a plastic sheath. Unshielded wire is preferred for transporting high-speed data to business workstations and telephones, because at higher speeds, radiation is created. If shielded cabling is not earthed correctly, the radiation is not released and creates interference.

VBR (Variable Bit Rate)   A QoS class defined by the ATM Forum for ATM networks. VBR is subdivided into a real-time (RT) class and a nonreal-time (NRT) class. VBR RT is used for connections that have a fixed timing relationship between samples. VBR NRT is used for connections that have no fixed timing relationship between samples but that still need a guaranteed QoS.

VDSL (Very high data rate Digital Subscriber Line)   A modem for twisted-pair access operating at data rates from 12.9 to 52.8 Mbps with a corresponding maximum reach ranging from 4500 feet to 1000 feet of 24-gauge twisted pair.

VPDN (Virtual Private Dialup Network)   A system that permits dial-in networks to exist remotely to home networks while giving the appearance of being directly connected. VPDNs use L2TP and L2F to terminate the Layer 2 and higher parts of the network connection at the LNS (L2TP Network Server) instead of at the LAC (L2TP Access Concentrator).

VPN (Virtual Private Network)   Lets IP traffic travel securely over a public TCP/IP network by encrypting all traffic from one network to another. A VPN uses tunneling to encrypt all information at the IP level.

ZX   An extended-wavelength single-mode optical fiber for up to 100 kilometers.

INDEX

Symbols

!, 200

Numerics

4DMT line card, 127–128
911 calling, 11

A

AAA, 59–60, 88, 154
  accounting, 155
  authentication, 154
  authorization, 154
  RADIUS, 157
    accounting phase, 160–161
    client profiles, 162
    client/server model, 157
    profiles, 161
    service profiles, 162
    transmission flow, 158–160
    user profiles, 162–163
  related RFCs, 154
AAL (ATM Adaptation Layer), 366–367
  AAL5, 62
access protocols, 153
access VPN services, LT2P, 168
accounting, 59–60, 155
accounting phase (RADIUS), 160–161
ACLs (access control lists), 152
activating PVCs, 297–298
adjusting polling intervals, 325
ADPCM (adaptive differential pulse code
  modulation), 113
ADSL (Asynchronous DSL), 13
  consumer-grade, 13
  DMT, 16–17
    DMT2, 17–19
    G.Lite, 20
  latency paths, 23
  PPoA, 82
    implementations, 86
    IP addressing, 84–85

    LCP, 83
    NCP, 83
  profiles
    applying to interfaces, 293
    creating, 289, 291
  protocol stack, 83
  VDSL, 13
ADSL2, 20
ADSL2+, 21
aggregators, 10
  Cisco 6400 UAC, 240
    ATM switching configuration, 249–250
    Layer 3 terminations, 250–261
    redundancy, 241–248
    VPN configurations, 262–264
alarms, viewing, 305–307
allocating IP addresses, 66
AM (amplitude modulation), 15
analog modems versus DSL, 6
applying
  ADSL profiles, 293
  ATM QoS profiles to PVCs, 297
  DMT profiles to DMT ports, 293
APS (Automatic Protection Switching), 125.
  See also SONET APS
  BER thresholds, configuring, 248
  configuration commands, 210–211, 213–214
  priority requests, 247–248
architectures
  data flow, 62–63
  IP addressing, 63
    address allocation, 66
    dynamic, 64
    NAT, 65
    PAT, 65
    PPP/IPCP, 65
    virtual templates, 63
  IRB, 67
    connectivity, 68
    IP addressing, 68–69
    protocol stack, 67–68
  of CEMF/CDM, 272
  point-to-point architecture, 9–11, 18–19, 59–96,
    155–166
  PPoA, 82
    implementations, 86
    IP addressing, 84–85
    LCP, 83

B

C

L

W

X